D1617325

For the Love of God
and People

The publication of this book was made possible by a gift from Mardi and Robert Rendell

For the Love of God and People

A Philosophy of Jewish Law

Elliot N. Dorff

2007 • 5768
The Jewish Publication Society
Philadelphia

JPS is a nonprofit educational association and the oldest and foremost publisher of Judaica in English in North America. The mission of JPS is to enhance Jewish culture by promoting the dissemination of religious and secular works, in the United States and abroad, to all individuals and institutions interested in past and contemporary Jewish life.

The Jewish Publication Society
2100 Arch Street, 2nd floor
Philadelphia, PA 19103

Design and Composition by Pageworks

Manufactured in the United States of America

07 08 09 10 11 12   10 9 8 7 6 5 4 3 2 1

Library of Congress Cataloging-in-Publication Data:

Dorff, Elliot N.
   For the love of God and people : a philosophy of Jewish law / Elliot N. Dorff.
      p. cm.
   Includes bibliographical references and index.
   ISBN-13: 978-0-8276-0840-5 (alk. paper) 1. Jewish law—Philosophy. I. Title.
   BM520.6.D67 2007
   296.1'801—dc22
   2007027044

JPS books are available at discounts for bulk purchases for reading groups, special sales, and fundraising purchases. Custom editions, including personalized covers, can be created in larger quantities for special needs. For more information, please contact us at marketing@jewishpub.org or at this address: 2100 Arch Street, Philadelphia, PA 19103.

In honor of

Rabbi Uzi Weingarten

Good friend and teacher, who has immensely helped me

to hone my philosophy of Jewish law by asking me to

defend every sentence in this book and by using his

extensive knowledge of Jewish tradition to make wonderful

suggestions, all with immense dignity, respect, grace, and love.

For Love of God:

You shall love the Lord your God with all your heart, with all your soul, and with all your might (Deut. 6:5).

———————

Love, therefore, the Lord your God, and always keep His charge, His laws, His rules, and His commandments (Deut. 11:1).

———————

The Lord commanded us to observe all these laws, to revere the Lord our God, for our lasting good and for our survival (Deut. 6:24).

———————

With everlasting love You have loved Your people Israel, teaching us Torah and commandments, statutes and laws. Therefore, Lord our God, when we lie down to sleep and when we rise, we shall think of Your laws and speak of them, rejoicing in Your Torah and commandments always. For they are our life and the length of our days; we will meditate on them day and night. Never take away Your love from us. Blessed are You, Lord, who loves His people Israel (Jewish liturgy for each evening).

For Love of People:

Rabbi Akiba said: ". . . Israel is beloved, for a precious instrument [the Torah] was given to them. As an extra measure of love, it was made known to them that they were given a precious instrument with which the world was created, as it is written, 'For I give you good doctrine, forsake not My Torah'" (Proverbs 4:2) (Mishnah Avot [Ethics of the Fathers] 3:18).

Rabbi Akiba said: "'Love your neighbor as yourself' (Leviticus 19:18): This is a fundamental principle of the Torah." Ben Azzai said: "'This is the record of Adam's line. When God created man, He made him in the likeness of God, male and female He created them' (Genesis 5:1). This is a fundamental principle greater than that, so that you do not say, 'Since I am despised, let my friend be despised with me, since I have become corrupt, let my neighbor become corrupt.'" Rabbi Tanhuma said: "If you do that, know Who it is whom you despise, for 'He made him in the likeness of God'" (Sifra Kedoshim, 4:12; Genesis Rabbah 24:7).

———————

Hillel said: "What is hateful to you, do not do to your neighbor. That is the whole Torah; the rest is commentary. Go and learn it" (B. Talmud Shabbat 31a).

———————

When a stranger resides among you, with you in your land, you shall not wrong him. The stranger who resides with you shall be to you as one of your citizens; you shall love him as yourself, for you were strangers in the land of Egypt; I the Lord am your God (Lev. 19:33–34).

Contents

CONTENTS

Preface

It may seem odd to think seriously about theory of law at all, let alone Jewish legal theory. After all, there are more than enough problems to concern us in the world, both practical and intellectual, so why bother with this, let alone write a whole book about it? Beyond that, what is a theory of law anyway, and why does it matter?

It is precisely because of such concerns that I wrote the first chapter of this book. In it, I do my best to explain what a theory of law entails and why anyone should care. I show that the kinds of questions addressed by a theory of law have major implications for how we think about ourselves as individuals and communities, the role and goals of law in our lives, the kind of people we want to become and the kind of society we want to create. Beyond this, a theory of law also has major implications for how one decides important practical matters, because how and why one makes such concrete decisions are ultimately rooted in the larger issues just mentioned.

I also discuss in Chapter One two important issues that set the context of my theory. First, I point out that, although models can be used to justify claims, I intend the model of Jewish law developed in this book instead to clarify, through analogy, claims that I make about Jewish law that I justify on other grounds. Second, I affirm that I believe in the historical development of Jewish sources, including the documentary hypothesis asserting that the Torah itself consists of four documents that were recorded at different times. Nevertheless, I believe the Torah is both divine and significant, and so I briefly describe my theory of revelation—that is, my theory of the authorship of Jewish law, a theory that also affects its authority and operation.

In Chapters Two and Three, I describe the core concepts of my theory of Jewish law—namely, that Jewish law should be seen as expressions of *love* between the People Israel and God, among the People Israel as a community, and between the People Israel and the rest of humanity. The most intense human experiences of love involve both our body and soul; because Jewish law too has both a body and a soul, it can serve as a vibrant expression of our love for both God and people.

As with human beings, the body and soul of Jewish law are intimately connected with one another, affecting each other at every turn. At the same time, it is helpful to understand certain features of Jewish law as those that come from its bodily nature—literally, its *corpus juris,* the body of the law. In Chapter Two, I spell out seven such elements of Jewish law whose functioning can be better understood if one thinks of Jewish law as, in part, a body.

Chapter Three portrays the other side of this integrated whole: the soul of Jewish law, which is the covenant between God and the People Israel, which, in turn, serves as the basis for our covenantal relationships with other Jews and with non-Jews. I discuss ten different aspects of Jewish law that can best be understood in terms of Jews' covenantal relationship with God. Like any analogy, this one, even though rooted in the Torah itself, has some problems, and I raise and respond to four of them. I then discuss some aspects of Jewish law that express our love for other people.

After describing the core convictions of my theory, I turn next to describing how they affect key aspects of Jewish law—namely, motivations to adhere to Jewish law (Chapter Four), continuity and change (Chapter Five), the many relationships among morality, theology, and Jewish law (Chapter Six), and the interactions of custom with Jewish law (Chapter Seven). I link my discussion of each of these topics to my fundamental theory that Jewish law has both body and soul and that Judaism uses both these components to help us to express our love for God and people, for I believe that these second-level, theoretical questions are very much influenced by the overarching perception that one has of the nature of Jewish law in the first place.

Many people think the only reason people observe the law—whether civil law or religious law—is that they believe they will be rewarded if they do and punished if they do not. In Chapter Four, I demonstrate that that is not at all the case, that enforcement surely does play a role in most legal systems' ability to garner compliance, but enforcement alone never works. Prohibition is the obvious example: Even with a constitutional amendment and the full force of the U.S. government behind it, the law could not survive because a small minority of Americans did not abide by it for other reasons. It is not surprising that Jewish tradition from its earliest sources has been aware of this. After all, the Torah portrays God announcing the Decalogue to the Israelites amid thunder, lightning, and earthquakes; if any group of people should be impressed by the intention and ability of the Lawgiver to enforce the law, they should have been. Yet, a bare 40 days later, they were worshiping the Golden Calf. In this chapter, then, I explore the multiple motives that the Torah itself provides for adhering to the law and then those that the Rabbis added. Individual modern Jews may be impressed and moved by some of these classical motives more than others; indeed, they may find that different motives from the ones that moved them yesterday are primary in their consciousness today. Still, many of these classical motivations are as powerful for us now as they were for our ancestors.

Chapter Five addresses the issue of continuity and change. Every legal system needs to balance them, for if law never changes, it becomes irrelevant or unworkable. On the other hand, if the law changes too much, it cannot fulfill its function of giving people a clear indication of what others can expect of them and what they, in turn, can expect of others. For Jewish law, striking this balance is all the more imperative, for Jews live all over the world and must therefore find a way to make Jewish law a vibrant part of their lives in vastly different circumstances. Moreover, Jewish law has an added problem that civil law does not face—namely, on what grounds and in what circumstances do human beings have the authority to interpret, let alone change, God's law? Both the Torah and the Rabbis were keenly aware of these practical and theological issues, and I discuss how they addressed them in what is a remarkably sophisticated understanding of how texts gain their meaning, an understanding that modern literary critics articulated only in the 1960s. The Rabbis further had an equally remarkable appreciation of how to integrate the divine and human in applying ancient texts to contemporary circumstances.

Two of the most important, ongoing factors that have influenced how rabbis over the generations have applied the tradition are morality and theology. There is clearly no one-to-one relationship between law and morality or even between religion and morality. That is, one can abide by the letter of the law and act immorally, and, conversely, one can in the name of morality defy the law ("civil disobedience"). Similarly, unless one claims that by definition a person can be religious only if moral, we all know people who are pious in their attitudes to God and who scrupulously abide by ritual practices but act immorally toward other people, and, conversely, we know very moral people who are not religious in either belief or action. Still, religion and law can and do contribute to morality. In Chapter One and the appendix of my book *Love Your Neighbor and Yourself* (2003), I describe the many ways in which *religion* is a detriment to morality as well as the ways in which it is an aid to moral consciousness and behavior. In Chapter Six of the present book, I describe 10 ways in which *law* contributes to morality. I also discuss how both morality and theology have affected Jewish law in the past and should do so today. If the law is, after all, like a living person and if we are in a continuing covenant with God and with other people, we should surely expect that our ongoing interactions with God and with humans, our new understandings of moral norms, and our applications of moral norms and theology to new circumstances should all affect how we rule on specific issues. I close this chapter with a recent, difficult, and controversial example within the Conservative movement—namely, homosexual relations and the eligibility of homosexuals for ordination as rabbis—showing that I am making a choice to use morality to shape the law, a choice that is well rooted in Jewish sources from Abraham to our own day but that is not obvious because another, competing strand within Jewish tradition urges passive obedience.

Chapter Seven addresses custom. Especially because Jews have been scattered all over the world for so much of Jewish history, it should not be surprising that local custom plays a major role in determining both the content of the law and the way it is practiced in any given community. In this chapter I distinguish two types of custom, one that permits actions and one that mandates them, and then I describe how customs and laws interact in all four logically possible ways—that is, law establishing customs or undermining them, and custom functioning as the source of laws or undermining them. The many aspects of women's roles in Jewish life then serve as my extended example of how custom affects Jewish law, both in the past and in our time.

Theories become clear not only by stating what they assert but by comparing them to others and by indicating the results of using them in practice. In the last two chapters, I address both of those tasks. In Chapter Eight, I explore the differences between my theory and those of two thinkers who have articulated philosophies that resemble mine in significant respects—specifically, David Hartman to my right and Eugene Borowitz to my left. This is a very brief chapter, but I hope it makes two points: that what I assert is not obvious because other serious Jewish philosophers have taken other stances and that two theories with some important similarities to mine are nevertheless distinct in focus and emphasis as well as in audience.

Finally, in Chapter Nine, I illustrate how my theory of Jewish law has affected my rabbinic rulings (*teshuvot*) on specific issues. I divide the rulings I discuss into three categories: those addressing changing realities and relationships, those embodying changing moral sensitivities, and those applying Jewish law to largely or totally new circumstances. I use these examples to demonstrate that one's view of Jewish law is not just a matter of intellectual preference but rather has significant ramifications for how one applies Jewish law to specific issues in people's lives.

A number of people have helped me in the process of writing this book, and I want to acknowledge that aid and thank them for it. First and foremost, my wife, Marlynn, has again gracefully tolerated the large amounts of time that I devoted to this project. I daily appreciate her patience and her love. My family—Tammy and her son, Zachary; Michael, Tanya, and their daughter, Zoe; Havi, Adam, and their daughters, Noa and Ayden; and Jonathan, Mara, and their son, Amiel—continue to be a source of sheer joy for me. I deeply treasure their love.

Several people read portions of this book and gave me good advice for revising them. I would like to thank Professor Neil Cogan of Whittier Law School for his comments on Chapter One; Professor Mark Greenberg of UCLA School of Law and Dr. Ronald Andiman for their comments on Chapter Two; and Professor Bernard Jackson of Liverpool University for his comments on Chapter Three.

Professor Arthur Rosett of UCLA School of Law, with whom I have team-taught a course on Jewish law for 30 years, has been a contin-

PREFACE

ual source of knowledge, questions, and inspiration for me in all kinds of ways but especially in my exploration of Jewish law as a legal system. I particularly want to thank him for his input to Chapter Seven on custom, an area of the law on which we have had numerous conversations in recent years.

Finally, I would especially like to thank Rabbi Uziel (Uzi) Weingarten, to whom this book is dedicated. Uzi took the manuscript that I thought was virtually finished and helped me stop to reconsider and revise a number of points—indeed, the entire thrust of the book. His knowledge, acute thinking, patience, good humor, and linguistic skills have all contributed immeasurably to my thinking and writing in this book. He is truly the kind of friend who is my teacher as well. None of what I say here can be attributed to him—as he often said, "I would write a different book!"—but every single sentence that I have written has benefited from his knowledge, line editing, and, most important, from his deep questions. It is both a privilege and a joy to know him.

ELLIOT N. DORFF

The American Jewish University
(formerly the University of Judaism)
May 2007

Acknowledgments

Creating my own theory of Jewish law has been a long process. It should not be surprising, then, that the basic thoughts of some of the chapters of this book appeared earlier in print. The sections of Chapter One describing the nature of a legal theory and why I am not a positivist are almost the same as what I wrote in my *The Unfolding Tradition* (2005). For the other chapters, my thinking began in the journals and volumes referenced in the following paragraphs, but what I write here differs substantially from what I said earlier and how I said it. I would like to thank the publishers of my earlier works, which serve as the basis for material in this book, for their critiques of my thinking through the publishing process and for enabling me to learn from the reactions of my readers.

Parts of Chapter One appeared in a slightly different form in my *The Unfolding Tradition: Jewish Law after Sinai* (New York: Aviv Press, 2005), pp. 13–24, 212–221. I would like to thank the Rabbinical Assembly for permission to reprint that material.

Chapter Three was first published in a substantially different form in the *Jewish Law Annual,* 7 (1988), pp. 68–96, and was reprinted in *Contemporary Jewish Ethics and Morality: A Reader,* ed. Elliot N. Dorff and Louis E. Newman (New York: Oxford, 1995), pp. 59–78.

I first addressed the topic of Chapter Four—the motivations to observe Jewish law—with Arthur Rosett in our book *A Living Tree: The Roots and Growth of Jewish Law* (Albany: State University of New York Press, 1988), pp. 93–109, 246–249. I then expanded that discussion into *Mitzvah Means Commandment* (New York: United Synagogue, 1989). The current chapter is a new articulation of that material.

Chapter Five, on continuity and change in Jewish law, is a briefer version of what I wrote in *Conservative Judaism: Our Ancestors to Our Descendants* (New York: United Synagogue, 1977, 1996), chap. 3, sec. B. Another version of that material appeared in *The Unfolding Tradition,* chap. 2.

I have addressed the topic of morality and Jewish law, covered in Chapter Six, in other ways in numerous places. Perhaps the most relevant for my work here are *To Do the Right and the Good: A Jewish Approach to Modern Social Ethics* (Philadelphia: Jewish Publication Society, 2002), append. A and B; *Love Your Neighbor and Yourself: A Jewish Approach to Modern Personal Ethics* (Philadelphia: Jewish Publication Society, 2003), append.; and *The Way into Tikkun Olam (Fixing the World)* (Woodstock, VT: Jewish Lights, 2005), chap. 3. The current discussion, however, is a new rendition of that thinking.

The material in Chapter Seven, on custom and Jewish law, is based in part on the chapter on custom in *A Living Tree* but more on my article "Custom Drives Jewish Law on Women," *Conservative Judaism* 49, no. 3 (spring 1997), pp. 3–21, and my response to critics in *Conservative Judaism* 51, no. 1 (fall 1998), pp. 66–73.

My analysis of David Hartman's theory of Jewish law first appeared in *The Unfolding Tradition,* pp. 437–444, and subsequently, in a different form, in the *Jewish Law Association Studies, Boston, 2004.* My interchange with Eugene Borowitz first appeared in *Conservative Judaism* 48, no. 2 (winter 1996), pp. 64–68 and 50, no. 1 (fall 1997), pp. 61–71; it was reprinted in *The Unfolding Tradition,* pp. 464–480. In the current volume, however, I restate those materials for purposes of comparison to my own philosophy of Jewish law.

Finally, the specific responsa that I discuss in Chapter Nine can all be found on the Rabbinical Assembly's website (www.rabbinicalassembly.org) under the link "Contemporary Halakhah." My responsa on artificial insemination, egg donation, and adoption; on end-of-life issues; and on assisted suicide were reprinted in my *Matters of Life and Death: A Jewish Approach to Modern Medical Ethics* (Philadelphia: Jewish Publication Society, 1998), chaps. 3, 4, and 8. My responsum on family violence can also be found in my book *Love Your Neighbor and Yourself,* chap. 5. My discussion of all these materials in this book, however, is new.

PART I

Foundations

CHAPTER ONE

Bringing the Topic Down to Earth

The very topic of this book, a philosophy of Jewish law, probably makes some people's eyes gloss over. They rightfully ask: What is a philosophy of law? Why should I care? The purpose of this chapter is to answer those questions and to make the topic understandable, interesting, and even important.

WHAT IS A PHILOSOPHY—OR A THEORY—OF LAW?

A comprehensive philosophy of law will address all of the topics listed in the Preface and described briefly in the following paragraphs. Not all treatments of Jewish law will explicitly discuss all these issues, and then it will be the task of the reader to unearth the assumptions that the author is making in the areas that he or she does not articulate, for often those very assumptions indicate the strengths and weaknesses as well as the range and limitations of the theory. So here is what you should look for in understanding and evaluating any philosophy of law, including any theory of Jewish law:

1. What is the broad picture of reality that the theory presents or assumes? Specifically, how does it understand the nature and status

of individual human beings and human communities? Are, for example, individuals solely self-interested and aggressive besides so that, as Hobbes suggested, life in a state of nature outside a social contract is "nasty, brutish, and short"; or, on the other end of the spectrum, are individuals reasonable and social by nature, as Locke depicted them, so that they enter a social contract not only (or even primarily) to protect each other but rather to cooperate in projects that will improve life, like roads and bridges and culture? Or is the truth about human beings somewhere in between?

2. Once a given theory describes its picture of the nature of the human being, the very next question is how it understands the goals, process, and functioning of human communities. Indeed, more broadly, how does it conceive of the connections between and among individuals, their families, their communities, the larger human community, the environment, and the transcendent element of human experience (imaged as God in Western faiths and in other ways in Asian faiths)? That, of course, also involves the way any given theory conceives of the nature not only of human beings and nature but also of God (or the transcendent element of human experience imaged in some other way).

3. In addition to these questions about its view of individuals, society, and God as they *are* now (the "is" questions), what is the given theory's understanding of what human beings and human societies *ought* to strive to be (the "ought" questions)? That is, what does the ideal human individual look like, and what does the ideal human society look like?

4. What is the role of law in society as it is now and in creating the ideal society? Or, why have law at all? This may sound like not much of a question, for it seems obvious that every society needs law. Paul, in the New Testament's Letter to the Romans, however, suggests that law is actually a bad thing because by defining what sin is, the law tempts one to sin. "Except through law I would never have become acquainted with sin. For example, I would never have known what it was to covet if the law had not said, 'Do not covet.' Through that commandment sin found its opportunity and produced in me all kinds of wrong desires. In the absence of law, sin is a dead thing" (Rom. 7:7–8). He therefore suggests that we should live not by the law but by spirit. We might "Pay Caesar what is due Caesar" (Luke 20:25) to maintain a basic minimum of an ordered society, but the ideal is to live by the spirit. Others would attack law as being too

restrictive on the ruling power. Nietzsche, for example, says that society should be ruled by the Master, who sets the law for others but does not have to live by it himself—and many dictators have in fact followed that course. So it is not by any means obvious that societies should have law. Instead, one has to argue for a society based on law, either through an appeal to its innate authority, which it gets from some source that must be defined and defended as authoritative or as a pragmatic measure for attaining some specific short-term and long-term goals.

5. What is the scope of the law—that is, what topics does it address and which topics, if any, are beyond its jurisdiction? How does its scope follow from its purposes in any given society?

6. What gives the law authority? There are usually multiple bases for a law's authority; enforcement alone will not suffice, as the fate of the U.S. constitutional amendment of prohibition graphically illustrates.

7. How shall the law be determined, and why should it be determined that way? For example, should it be determined by majority vote? Representatives of the majority? A group of people who qualify in some way other than by vote, such as wealth or education or lineage? A dictator's decree? A judge's ruling?

8. How does the law maintain continuity, coherence, and authority while at the same time allowing for change?

9. What is the relationship between law and morality? Law and religion? Law and economics and art and custom (the "relationship" questions)? How does the legal system handle conflicts of jurisdiction with another legal system?

COMPARING AMERICAN AND JEWISH LEGAL THEORIES

To make these theoretical questions clearer, I shall briefly compare some of the major features of two systems of law that the reader may know something about—namely, American law and Jewish law.[1]

The Broad View of Individuals and Community

American law is strongly rooted in Enlightenment assumptions, as articulated in the U.S. Declaration of Independence: "We hold these truths to be self-evident, that all men are created equal, that they are endowed by their Creator with certain unalienable rights, that among these are life, liberty, and the pursuit of happiness." The broad view on which American law is based, then, is that all people are individuals with rights. Whether we get these rights from our Creator, as Jefferson asserts, or from being recognized by legislators and courts, as the long history of "the rights of the Englishman" and the common law would suggest, much of American law and indeed the American psyche is based on claims of rights.

Like American law, Jewish law demands that each person be treated with respect, but for a different reason. In American law that is because "all men are endowed by their Creator with certain unalienable rights." For Judaism, the reason is instead that all human beings have been created in the image of God. In neither system, though, does this respect for individuals mean that everything that a person does is to be applauded or even condoned. Hence there are laws defining what people must and must not do, and penalties are prescribed for violating those laws. Still, even those condemned to death for committing a capital offense must, according to the Torah, be removed before nightfall from the post on which they were hanged, for, as the Torah says, "an impaled body is an affront to [literally, "a curse of"] God" (Deut. 21:23). That is, the image of God in each of us must be respected even with regard to someone who has committed the most egregious of crimes and even in the process of being punished for those crimes.

In American theory, every community is voluntary. I may join or leave any group at any time, including my religious community. This applies even to the United States itself. Gaining American citizenship is hard, but if I am already an American citizen and have not committed a felony, I may leave the country and renounce my citizenship at any time.[2]

The point should not be overstated. For all their individualism, a more pronounced individualism than exists even in other Western democracies, Americans nevertheless put great stock in their multiple forms of association with others. Former University of Chicago Law Professor and now Senator Barack Obama has stated this well:

> If we Americans are individualistic at heart, if we instinctively chafe against a past of tribal allegiances, traditions, customs, and cases, it would be a mistake to assume that this is all we are. Our

individualism has always been bound by a set of communal values, the glue upon which every healthy society depends. We value the imperatives of family and the cross-generational obligations that family implies. We value community, the neighborliness that expresses itself through raising the bar or coaching the soccer team. We value patriotism and the obligations of citizenship, a sense of duty and sacrifice on behalf of our nation. We value a faith in something bigger than ourselves, whether that something express-es itself in formal religion or ethical precepts. And we value the constellation of behaviors that express our mutual regard for another: honesty, fairness, humility, kindness, courtesy, and com-passion.

In every society (and in every individual), these twin strands— the individualistic and the communal, autonomy and solidarity— are in tension, and it has been one of the blessings of America that the circumstances of our nation's birth allowed us to negotiate these tensions better than most.[3]

Still, the individualism at the heart of American culture makes communities in America and American citizenship itself voluntary. In contrast, the Jewish community is organic. Classical Jewish law defines a Jew as someone who is born to a Jewish woman or reborn, as it were, into the Jewish community through the rites of conver-sion. Once a Jew, a person cannot relinquish that status. A Jew who converts to another religion becomes an apostate, a *meshumad* (one whose faith has been spiritually destroyed), or a *poshe'a Yisrael* (a rebellious Jew).[4] Apostasy subjects a Jew to some penalties in Jewish law: his testimony is inadmissible in court[5] (except to free a woman legally chained to her first husband[6]); he cannot marry, even retroac-tively through sexual intercourse, because he is assumed to be licen-tious;[7] the court may exclude him from his father's inheritance and pass it on to other members of the family who have not apostatized;[8] the Jewish community has no duty to redeem him from captivity and is actually forbidden to do so;[9] and Jews should not observe mourning rites for such a person.[10] In modern Israel, the Supreme Court has ruled that an apostate cannot claim Jewish status under the Law of Return (the Brother Daniel case).[11] Still, the Talmud asserts that "a Jew, even though he has sinned, remains a Jew,"[12] and so if he marries a Jew or even another apostate, the marriage is valid in Jewish law, and a man would need to give his wife a formal writ of Jewish divorce (a *get*) if they wanted to dissolve their marriage.[13]

That is also true for a convert to Judaism who subsequently returned to his or her original faith or became part of yet another faith community: once the person has become Jewish, even for an ulterior motive, the conversion makes the person part of the Jewish people, and his betrothal of a Jew or another apostate is valid, requiring a Jewish writ of divorce to dissolve.[14] Furthermore, as a Jew, an apostate woman passes Jewish identity on to her offspring.[15] Jewish identity, then, is construed as being part of the Jewish body politic; and just as a part of your body cannot on its own decide to leave the rest of it, so too no Jew can sever himself or herself from the Jewish community.

This thick sense of community has widespread legal implications in regard not only to membership and apostasy but also to a host of other areas, for it makes all Jews liable for each other's welfare: as the Talmud says, "All Israelites are responsible for one another" (*kol yisrael areivin zeh ba'zeh*).[16] So, for example, if I see someone drowning or accosted by robbers, I must, according to Jewish law, take steps to save the person while still protecting my own life.[17] In American law, if I tried to help someone in need and unintentionally hurt the person in the process, until recently, when most states passed "Good Samaritan laws," I could actually be sued for any harm done. Conversely, only three states—Vermont, Rhode Island, and Minnesota—have enacted statutory duties that require individuals to perform nonrisky rescues; and Wisconsin has a statute that requires persons present at the scene of a crime either to report the crime to the police or personally to assist the crime victim. All other American states accept the Common Law, which imposes no duty to rescue.[18]

The Role and Goals of Law

American law is dedicated to noble goals. In the words of the Preamble to the Constitution, it is intended "to form a more perfect Union, establish Justice, insure domestic Tranquility, provide for the common defence, promote the general Welfare, and secure the Blessings of Liberty to ourselves and our Posterity." These include the important, pragmatic goals of a nation constituted of individuals with rights who must give up some of those rights to achieve common purposes. This is enlightened egoism at its best.

In the central Jewish story, the Exodus from Egypt and the trek to Sinai and to the Promised Land, the people leave Egypt not as individuals but as a group, and it is as a community that they stand at Sinai. While there they receive and accept God's commandments, with rights phrased only as duties of others. So, for example, agricultural workers may eat their fill as they harvest the crop but may not take any fruit home with them, for the owner's duty includes feeding workers only during the process of work (Deut. 23:25–26).[19] Similarly, it is the owner's responsibility to give workers rest on the Sabbath, and it is phrased as such in the Decalogue (Exod. 20:10; Deut. 5:14). What is articulated as a right to privacy in American law is stated instead as a demand that lenders stand outside the home of borrowers when collecting their pledge (Deut. 24:10–11). The goal of the law, then, is not to secure rights, as it is in American law, but rather to follow God's will and gain the physical and spiritual rewards for doing so. As Maimonides later states this, the aim of God's law is to create a good society, one that contributes to the welfare of the body and mind of all its inhabitants through the duties it imposes.[20]

That theologically centered goal embodies in it the ultimate Messianic mission of Jewish law—to create a world in which swords are beaten into plowshares and in which there is no poverty, a world in which "God will instruct us in His ways and we will walk in His paths" (Isa. 2:2–4). What are God's paths? In arguing with God about Sodom and Gomorrah, Abraham already appeals to God's justice and faithfulness (Gen. 18:19), and God later describes Himself as merciful and loyal (Exod. 34:5–7). Moses similarly proclaims that God is pure, that "all His ways are just, a faithful God, never false [without evil], true and upright [righteous and honest] is He" (Deut. 32:4). Later, Maimonides, following the lead of Genesis 18:19, summarizes all of the divine characteristics as justice and righteousness and maintains that those who emulate God in acting in accordance with those divine characteristics "bring goodness and blessing to themselves."[21]

It is interesting that the ideal world of righteousness and justice that Jewish texts envision even provides for the possibility that although everyone will follow God's ways, each person will continue to worship his or her own god (Mic. 4:1–5). Along these lines, the Rabbis proclaim that God created a covenant with all human beings, the covenant of the children of Noah, and non-Jews fulfill God's will if they obey the seven requirements of that covenant.[22] Jewish sources require that Jews should follow God's more demanding covenant with the People Israel, but they contemplate a degree of tolerance and even pluralism that were truly unique in their day and are still rare in ours.[23]

Even if we construe the "general welfare" clause of the Preamble expansively, American law does not aspire to changing the whole world to be free of violence or want and certainly not to create one universal covenant with God; the goal is rather "the general welfare" solely "for ourselves and our posterity." After World War II, Americans provided much of the funding to rebuild Europe, and Americans have donated some small percentage of the yearly national budget to help other countries with their medical and other needs; but most would maintain that this generosity is motivated much more by the United States's own interests than by altruism or some vision of the messianic future. Thus even the most idealistic construction of American law focuses on the United States alone, in contrast to the universalistic goals embedded in Jewish literature, in which the People Israel are the primary partner in the covenant with God, but they are to serve as "a light to the nations" (Isa. 49:6, 51:4) of how everyone should live.

This has two important ramifications. First, Jewish law presumes that Jews can never be held to a lesser standard than that to which non-Jews are held. Therefore, sometimes when internal reasoning seems to suggest that Jews are subject to a more permissive stance than non-Jews, that result alone requires a rethinking of the reasoning that brought us to that conclusion; it requires going back to the drawing board, for that result contradicts the talmudic principle that "there is nothing permitted to an Israelite that is forbidden to a non-Jew."[24] So, for example, in the Talmud Rabbi Ishmael understands Genesis 9:6 to say that for non-Jews feticide is the equivalent of murder;[25] Jews, however, are actually required to abort a fetus to save the life of its mother because the fetus has a lesser legal status than its mother, as Exodus 21:22–25 declares.[26] That immediately raises the question, though, of how can it be that Jews are permitted to do what non-Jews are not? Jewish authorities resolve this by various methods. Most find reasons to permit non-Jews to abort for therapeutic reasons as well, despite their theoretical capital culpability for doing so. Some use that culpability for non-Jews to demonstrate how serious the decision to abort is for Jews as well, even when it is necessary and legally required to save the life of the mother and all the more so for other reasons.[27]

Second, the messianic goals of Judaism in general and Jewish law in particular can and do act as a source for critiquing any particular expression of it. When Jewish law is less just or compassionate than it can be, it fails in its function of being "a light to the nations." That requires Jewish authorities to reevaluate the law as it has come down to us and, if necessary, change it. I will discuss this at greater length in the chapter that discusses the relationship between Jewish law and morality. For now suffice it to say that because Jewish law aspires to create an ideal world, it can and should be assessed in any generation and on any issue as to the extent to which it is accomplishing that purpose.

The Scope of the Law

The First Amendment to the Constitution specifically bans Congress from making laws "respecting an establishment of religion, or prohibiting the free exercise thereof; or abridging the freedom of speech or of the press; or the right of the people peaceably to assemble, and to petition the Government for a redress of grievances." The remaining nine of the first ten amendments (the Bill of Rights) further restrict the government from interfering in other rights held by the people, including the Ninth Amendment's sweeping declaration that "The enumeration in the Constitution of certain rights shall not be construed to deny or disparage others retained by the people." While the Ninth Amendment is so expansive that the courts have hesitated to use it, they have used the First, Fourth, and Fourteenth Amendments in recent decades to establish a constitutional right to privacy which, among other things, prevents states from prohibiting abortion or from punishing consensual sex in private by adults, whether they be heterosexual or homosexual. In the last of those examples, Justice Kennedy stated at the very beginning of the majority opinion in the *Lawrence v. Texas* decision of 2003:

> Liberty protects the person from unwarranted government intrusions into a dwelling or other private places. In our tradition, the

State is not omnipresent in the home. And there are other spheres of our lives and existence, outside the home, where the State should not be a dominant presence. Freedom extends beyond spatial bounds. Liberty presumes autonomy of self that includes freedom of thought, belief, expression, and certain intimate conduct.[28]

Both federal and state law do prohibit some behaviors even when done in private, such as snorting cocaine or making one's own liquor, but the scope of American law is primarily restricted to areas of social interaction. Furthermore, the social nature of American law is clearly articulated in the purposes of the law enumerated in the Preamble of the Constitution.

Because Jewish law seeks not only to create a civil society but also to foster good character and spiritual growth—theologically put, to make people godly—it has a much broader scope. It does indeed intend to govern people's social interactions, and hence the Torah contains laws requiring, for example, just weights and measures (Lev. 19:35–36.). It also seeks to create an ideal society. So, for example, American law prohibits libel, slander, and defamation of character, but Jewish law goes much further in delineating how we should speak to and about each other.[29]

In addition, though, Jewish law governs private behavior, trying to elevate the moral and personal quality of our lives in private as well as in public. Thus Jewish law not only provides for marriage for those who wish to marry but establishes marriage as an ideal. It then spells out much more carefully than American law does the duties that spouses have toward each other. Jewish law also very much values procreation. The stories of the infertility problems that affected the Patriarchs and Matriarchs make it clear that the Torah recognizes that not everyone can procreate and that we must not exacerbate the frustration and pain of those who cannot. For those who can produce children, however, Jewish law requires that couples produce at least two children and preferably more.[30] Americans see marriage and procreation as private matters in which the state should not interfere.

Furthermore, Jewish law imposes a duty on both parents and grandparents to educate the family's children in the Jewish tradition and in a trade, and the Mishnah delineates exactly what the curriculum for Jewish studies should include.[31] Although all American states require parents to provide schooling for their children to a particular age and mandate that certain subjects be taught, parents retain the right to home school their children or to choose private or parochial education rather than public schools, and they are given considerable leeway in determining what their children are taught. For America, education is required to produce good citizens and productive contributors to society, but it is up to parents to decide how their child is to be formed morally and religiously. Thus even public schools must get specific permission from parents to teach sex education and other sensitive subjects, including evolution as opposed to "intelligent design."

Jewish legal requirements to visit the sick and aid the poor are yet further examples of how Jewish law asserts authority over a much broader scope of people's lives. This insistence on jurisdiction over our private as well as our public activities stems from the goals of Jewish law to enable us to lead not only productive and minimally decent lives but also morally ideal, spiritually fulfilling, and communally responsible ones.

On the other hand, because Jews have ruled themselves only in limited ways throughout most of their history, some areas of the law of most nations are either totally absent, sparse, or unused in Jewish law. So, for example, although there is some law about military campaigns in both the Torah and Jewish law thereafter, Jews have not had armies of their own to which to apply those laws since the Bar Kokhba revolt (132–135 C.E.); it is only with the establishment of the modern State of Israel that some writers are trying to resurrect these laws and apply them to contexts radically different from wars in the past, shaped by significantly new military technology.[32] To a somewhat lesser extent, this is also true for commercial law. Although Jewish law governed business dealings of Jews with other Jews until the modern period, the law itself was often influenced and sometimes totally shaped by the law of the land. Still, in most jurisdictions until the modern period, rabbinic rulings concerning contracts, torts, property, and sometimes even criminal matters governed Jewish communities. With regard to non-Jews, however, the situation was different. The third-century sage Samuel already taught that in commercial matters "the law of the land is the law,"[33] for Jews had no choice but to do business according to the state's law when dealing with non-Jews. In modern times, Jews living in Enlightenment countries gained freedom both of and from religion, and so many Jews no longer observe significant portions of Jewish ritual or marital laws.

Moreover, Jews living in nations governed by Enlightenment princi-ples commonly take their disputes to the civil courts, and they depend on the government to provide police, fire, and military pro-tection as well as public education, all of which the state governs. Thus in some ways the scope of Jewish law is much broader than that of American law and in other ways, much narrower.

The Origins and Functioning of the Law

In classical Judaism, God is construed as the author of the laws. This, of course, is very different from a government created by "We, the People of the United States." In the actual functioning of the law, though, American and Jewish law are not nearly as different from each other as their disparate origins might suggest. That is because in Deuteronomy 17 God authorizes the judges of each generation—later called "rabbis"—to interpret and apply those laws. Some Americans (strict constructionists) think that judge-made law is a violation of the American system because it is Congress that is sup-posed to make the laws; judges have authority exclusively to inter-pret and apply them. Others (loose constructionists) interpret judi-cial power more broadly to mean that judges test the constitutional-ity of laws and overturn some of them on that basis, as in the Supreme Court's decisions about segregation and abortion. In most state courts, judges create judge-made law quite regularly.

The latter practice is parallel to Jewish law, where there is no leg-islative body. As modern scholars have demonstrated beyond rea-sonable doubt, the Torah itself is composed of at least four docu-ments that were later edited together.[34] Coming from different peri-ods, these documents record laws that often supplement each other and sometimes are even at odds with each other. Furthermore, as Professor Michael Fishbane has demonstrated, even during biblical times new laws and interpretations emerged.[35] Once the Torah's canon was sealed in the time of Ezra (fifth century B.C.E.), there was no room for another author to add to or subtract from the scriptures declared sacred; but until that time, authors did in fact reinterpret the received tradition or, indeed, write whole new books that even-tually found their way into the Torah (for example, Deuteronomy). Deuteronomy 4:1 and 13:2 prohibit adding to, or subtracting from, the law given by Moses in regard to idolatry; and once the Torah was completed and recognized as sacred, the Rabbis understood these verses to apply much more broadly to all of the Torah's laws. Therefore, judge-made law has become the standard operating principle as rabbis throughout the ages have used their authority to stretch the law to apply to new circumstances. Thus, even though in theory Jewish law is based on the Torah's commandments, believed by most Jews through the ages to be an articulation of God's will in some way, in practice human beings acting as judges have had an immense role in determining the contents and shape of that law. American law gives authority to legislators to initiate, revise, and abrogate laws, and in this it differs from Jewish law; but in both systems human beings exert substantial legal authority.

In Jewish law, those human beings have not been chosen by majority vote, as legislators and even many police chiefs and judges are in American law. Rabbis instead gain their authority through a combination of two factors: (1) ordination, attesting extensive education in the Jewish tradition and personal commitment to it, and (2) appointment by a community as its rabbi. As a result, the authority of rabbis depends on their education and their willingness to model a Jewish life and just as critically on the agreement of Jews to accept their particular rabbi's interpretations and applications of the Jewish tradition, something not all that far from Jefferson's "consent of the governed."

Furthermore, in both systems—and, truthfully, in any legal system—*the operative law is determined by the interaction between what authorities say and what people who are governed by the law do.* No book of statutes or judicial rulings in and of itself defines the law. Even in America, where there are legislatures and police, the practice of the people is critical in deciding what is, and what is not, law. Conversely, the practices of the people do not completely define the law either: Sometimes legal authorities uproot accepted practices or institute new ones. I will discuss this interaction between law and custom in much greater detail in Chapter Seven.

Motivations to Adhere to the Law

Jewish and American legal systems differ significantly in tone and motivation as a result of their differing origins. American law, created, as it was, by the representatives of the people, must represent the

15

will of the people to remain authoritative. One obeys the law, then, primarily because one has committed oneself to abide by the will of the majority; that is the bargain into which one enters when one lives in a representative democracy. Americans also obey the law for other reasons, including the fact that they usually agree with it; they want an ordered society; they do not want to be punished by the police; and, in some cases, such as submitting to the military draft, because they see obedience as something they are called to do as patriotic Americans (love of country).

As a religious legal system, the motivations to adhere to Jewish law share in those practical concerns but go beyond them. The Torah itself and the later books of the Bible suggest a number of reasons why we should follow God's commandments, and the Rabbis and medieval and modern Jewish philosophers add to that list.[36] I shall discuss those at some length in Chapter Four. Suffice it to say here that there have always been multiple reasons individuals conform to Jewish law: For many the overriding motivations have been love for God; maintaining the ongoing, covenantal relationship between the People Israel and God; and the sense that Jewish law uplifts and edifies us, that it is—as both Jewish liturgy and rabbinic literature describe it—God's gift of love to us for our benefit. Thus twice each day, in the paragraph before the *Shema,* Jews proclaim that the Torah and its commandments are the product of God's "great love"(*ahavah rabbah*) and "everlasting love" (*ahavat olam*) for us, and at the end of *Musaf* on Rosh Hashanah, the liturgy describes Jewish law as benefiting us all our days (*l'tov lanu kol ha-yamim*).

One other motive deserves special attention—namely, the morality of the law. Jewish law includes many more ritual provisions than American law does. Rituals designate our life together as a community and give us ways to mark the seasons of life and of the year; in these respects, Jewish and American ritual laws have common goals. Jewish law, though, intends to shape our relationship with God as well as with each other; and thus Jewish law devotes more attention to ritual matters than American law does.

A significant percentage of the laws of both systems, though, deal with moral issues. Americans expect that the law will conform to moral norms; thus there can be a moral critique of the law, including even ritual laws. So, for example, it was moral concerns for racial equality that led Americans to change the laws of some cities and states requiring blacks to sit at the back of the bus or at different places at lunch counters. The same concern for racial equality led to changes in moral matters as well, as, for example, the Supreme Court's determination in *Brown v. Board of Education* (1954) that schools separated by race were inherently unequal. This ultimately led to the Civil Rights Act of 1964, which prohibited discrimination based on factors like gender and age as well as race. Another, more recent example is the *Lawrence* decision cited earlier, which over- turned the 1986 *Bowers v. Hardwick* decision that refused to give con- stitutional protection to homosexual sex by consenting adults in pri- vate. As Justice Kennedy said in writing the majority opinion to over- turn it, "It was not correct when it was decided, and it is not correct today."[37] The trickier part of using moral concerns to shape the law occurs when Americans disagree about what is moral; then, in my view and that of Thomas Jefferson, the government needs to stay out of the matter.[38] In contentious areas like that of abortion, we have seen how difficult that is to accept for significant portions of the American population. Despite their differences on some moral mat- ters, Americans expect their law to be moral because they them- selves want it to be, even if they, their legislators, and their judges sometimes badly misconstrue what that means—as in the *Dred Scott* decision of the Supreme Court.

In Jewish tradition, the morality of the law is rooted not in a given community's desire that the law be moral, but in God, who is Himself understood to be moral and to demand morality of us. There are, of course, problems with that assumption, not only as a result of the Holocaust but because of Job and the many like him who have suffered without apparent justification. Indeed, the Bible itself raises questions about God's morality, beginning with Abraham's ringing question, "Shall the Judge of all the earth not do justice?" (Gen. 18:25). That challenge, though, makes sense only if Abraham could presume that God is, in fact, just, and, despite some evidence to the contrary, that is the prevailing view in the Bible and in rabbinic lit- erature. Moses declares: "The Rock!—His deeds are without blemish, for all His ways are just; a faithful God, with no injustice, righteous and upright is He" (Deut. 32:4).[39] Therefore, a sense of morality per- vades the Jewish legal system to a greater degree than one expects in a set of laws instituted by human beings.

This tie to morality manifests itself in at least two ways: (1) Because Jewish law is supposed to be an expression of moral guide- lines and spiritual truths revealed to us by a morally good God, moral critiques of the law or of judgments rendered under it are clearly admissible and persuasive, much more so than in the American system, in which the will of the majority, whether moral or not, governs. (2) Despite moral critiques of traditional laws (even some in the Torah itself) that have lead Jewish legal authorities through the ages to narrow the scope of some laws or change them outright (for example, laws mandating the death penalty and penalizing the offspring of adulterous or incestuous unions [Deut. 23:3]), one of the important reasons Jews adhere to Jewish law is that they understand it generally to be moral—indeed, often the very definition of what it means to be moral, for it calls on us not only to fulfill the minimal requirements of how we should treat each other but also to aspire to imitate God, to elevate ourselves as much as we can to incorporate divine characteristics in our relationships with others. In Chapter Six, I shall explore this important tie between Jewish law and morality in greater depth.

This sketch illustrates some of the ways in which Jewish and American law differ in their fundamental assumptions—their views of the individual, the community, the scope and goals of the law, the way in which it should function, and the motivations to obey the law. Thus legal theories—even two with which American Jews identify—can differ significantly in how they construe everything about law and the individuals and communities it serves. I have not described the ways in which these two legal systems agree in their foundational principles, but any such list would clearly include their shared commitment to law as governing even kings and presidents and their shared concern to protect individuals against the majority (although for different reasons). American Jews warm to the ways in which the two legal systems to which they are committed overlap and reinforce each other and wrestle with how to balance or choose between the two legal theories where they differ.

WHY CARE ABOUT LEGAL THEORIES?

All of this may still seem abstract—interesting, perhaps, but not practically relevant. However, these abstract concepts have significant practical import.

First, the particular legal theory that you embrace says a lot about you. It bespeaks how you think of yourself, others in your community, humanity as a whole, God, the role of law in life, and even what you ultimately hope for. So pick carefully!

Second, legal theories often have a direct effect on the content of the law. For example, communists, in places like China and the former Soviet Union, who distrust individual autonomy and thus seek to exert communal control to squelch dissent, have historically established governments with strict surveillance of citizens and tight laws governing their activity. Socialists in countries like Sweden and on Israeli kibbutzim, who believe that group welfare must take precedence over individual well-being, have permitted considerable freedom of speech and creativity but have determined as a group how the bulk of the group's collective resources should be spent. In contrast to both of these forms of privileging the community over the individual, Americans believe that each individual is born with inalienable rights, and so they want only as much government as is necessary for security and other social services, with Republicans and Democrats often disagreeing as to how much that is. That does not preclude family and communal ties, as Senator Obama eloquently expressed in the passage cited earlier, but it certainly puts individual freedoms at the center of Americans' consciousness. Jews *qua* Jews will take a stand somewhere in between those extremes, with a tradition of a rich, organic sense of community as well as the divine image inherent in each human being. Such broad theories will produce very different laws governing privacy, legal protections from prosecution, government-mandated education for children, health-care decisions, the place and privileges of private business and social services, the role of government, and even the breadth of creative license in the arts.

Third, whatever legal theory you embrace will significantly affect what you identify as authoritative law and what not, both for yourself and for others. Legal theories speak about questions of authority—why pay attention to the law, why obey it, which laws are binding, which are not, why that is the case, and how those laws that are binding exert their authority. Thus legal theories will do nothing less than tell you what you must do or refrain from doing, even as conditions and practices change, and why.

Fourth, legal theories speak about tradition and change—which laws of the past still have authority, which do not, which new ones are now binding, and the proper procedures by which such decisions should be made. When most *people* in a society change the way they have been doing things, when and how does that get reflected in the *law*—or should those in charge of the law seek to resist the change and return the people to their former way of doing things? For example, if a substantial majority of Jews do not observe Jewish dietary laws (kashrut), does that mean they are no longer binding and the law should catch up with current practice, or does that mean that Jewish leaders need to reinforce their efforts to persuade Jews to keep kosher? Furthermore, by what authority and in what ways may *legal officials* change the law? For example, on what grounds and in what way, if any, may the law in the Torah forbidding a child born out of incest or adultery (a *mamzer*) from marrying a Jew for ten generations (Deut. 23:3) be nullified, at least in practice if not in theory? What about the Rabbis' ruling—even if it is not clear in the Torah—forbidding women from serving as witnesses?[40] What about laws that the Rabbis themselves instituted? How one deals with all of these aspects of law and change depends on how one understands the nature and authority of the law in the first place as well as the processes by which it can and cannot change—in other words, on one's theory of law.

In a course on jurisprudence I took at Columbia Law School, the instructor, Harry W. Jones, had a memorable way of describing the three major theories for how American judges should understand their role in interpreting the law. Using baseball slang for how umpires see their job, Jones said, "Some judges would say, 'I calls them as they are.' Others would say, 'I calls them as I sees them.' Still others would say, 'They aint nothin' till I calls them!' " Given that Jewish law does not have a legislature, it depends even more heavily on judicial opinions than American law does, and so these varying theories of the role of judges will become all the more important in defining how and when *Jewish* law should change.

In that same course, Jones told us that Benjamin Cardozo, later appointed by President Hoover as a justice of the U.S. Supreme Court (1932–1938), took a year off in the middle of his judicial career, which began in 1913, to study theory of law and to write a book about it, *Nature of the Judicial Process* (1921). Cardozo's decisions after he wrote that book, Jones told us, are markedly better than his earlier ones because they reflect a clearer perception of how any given decision fits into a larger understanding of the role of law and the functioning of judges. Indeed, it was Cardozo who, in his decisions and subsequent books, argued for a broad view of the law, including in

legal discussions and rulings matters of economics, social welfare, and even the relationship between law and literature, the subject of one of his books.

Finally, legal theories can motivate people to live by the law. That is because legal theories speak also of motivations, of why one should follow the law in the first place. Even in legal systems with full enforcement capabilities, such as American law, adherence to the law on the part of the populace can never be a matter of enforcement alone, for then, assuming an eight-hour work day, one would need three police officers for every citizen and then police officers to police the other police officers. The only way a legal system can operate effectively is if the vast majority of people obey the law for other reasons; then the police can enforce it on the few who do not (the real criminals) or the rest of us who sometimes stray in, say, driving too fast.

Like all other perspectives on Jewish law, my theory will be looking at the beating heart of Jewish law, how it courses through the body of the Jewish people, changing direction from time to time, but always delivering critical nutrients and life itself to the Jewish body and soul. It will seek to explain where the law comes from, why it is important and even authoritative, when and how it should change, and what its goals are. It will also describe how Jewish law is related to other parts of the Jewish experience—morality, theology, and custom, in particular, but also modern legal, social, economic, cultural, and political developments in North America and Israel. It will address the core convictions of how Judaism has understood and should now understand God; the world; Jews and non-Jews; the past, present, and future; belief; and practice. I hope that, as with Cardozo, studying my theory will enable readers to understand their Jewish commitments better so that my Jewish readers can incorporate Judaism into their decisions and actions in a more informed, reasoned, and sensitive way and that my non-Jewish readers will understand better how Jews do that and perhaps apply some of the Jewish experience with law to their own thought and practice. Ultimately, I hope that studying my theory will guide readers' actions so that they can live their lives more consciously and authentically according to the Torah's perceptions and values as clarified, modified, and applied by rabbis and other Jews throughout the centuries to our own day, for I am convinced that Judaism's views and values can enrich and ennoble our lives as we strive to imitate God. In the language of Jewish morning liturgy, may this study motivate us "to understand, to discern, to heed, to learn, and to teach, to observe and to fulfill all the words of the teachings of Your Torah (Instruction) with love."

I am now going to devote some space to two issues that are important theoretical foundations for my philosophy of Jewish law but not necessary for those who want to focus exclusively on the theory itself. The first issue is the epistemological status of two different kinds of models—that is, the claims to knowledge that they make— together with an explanation of the type that I am using in this book and how to evaluate proposed models such as the one I am suggesting. The second issue is how to integrate an historical approach to the Torah and later Jewish texts with a claim that God is somehow involved in their formation and application to this day. Although these issues are directly relevant to my legal theory, they deal with epistemology and theology rather than law. Therefore, *those who want to focus on the legal discussion of this book may find it best at this point to skip to Chapter Two,* and they need feel no shame for doing so.

THEORETICAL DISCUSSION 1: MODELS USED IN LEGAL THEORIES

Legal theorists, including those dealing with law in general and Jewish law in particular, sometimes use models as part of their thought. They do this in two very different ways. Because I will be suggesting a model to describe my own understanding of the nature of Jewish law, it is important to clarify the two kinds of claims being made by those suggesting that we use models and what I aim to do by using the one I am proposing.

Sometimes thinkers intend their theories to function as a means to *justify* claims that they are making about the phenomena they are investigating, to *establish some conclusion* that they are arguing for. When using models in this way, they are asserting a very strong link between the model and the phenomena, claiming that *because* something is true of the model, it is also true of the phenomena. For that to be true, the phenomena being investigated must be *just like* the model in all respects and possibly even integrally connected to the model in a chain of causation. For example, Freud seems to have intended his model of ego, superego, and subconscious to be an actual description of psychiatric phenomena, and he used the model to justify treatment modes while simultaneously using empirical results he discovered in his practice to create and adjust the model. Physicists use atomic theory and, more recently, string theory in much the same way. When models are used in this strong sense, they not only describe what is the case but suggest what to expect if the phenomena change, either of their own accord or through human manipulation. Such models, therefore, can be tested against further observations and conclusively verified or falsified by them.

Sometimes, though, models are used as an educational tool, and that is how I will be using the two models I employ to understand Jewish law. When education is the goal, the one proposing the model is not saying that the model is exactly like the phenomena being investigated and even less that features of the model cause things to happen, such that claims about the model can justify claims about the phenomena and vice versa. The one who proposes the model is instead saying that the phenomena being investigated are similar to the model and that, therefore, it is easier to understand the phenomena, to analyze them, and even to imagine what might happen in the future or how humans might interact with the phenomena in question to enhance, repair, or control them if one thinks about them in comparison to the model. It is an analogy to something more familiar.

Models accomplish this explanatory task in several ways. By comparing the phenomena being investigated to something known, they help people comprehend how the new phenomena work. Just as x maintains continuity through change via these mechanisms, for example, so too does y. Models also make it plausible that y functions as it does by pointing out that x, which is similar in important ways to y, operates in the same way. Models sometimes can also suggest what to look for in investigating other aspects of y by checking to see how x accomplishes the same or a similar task. Further, if x changes on its own over time in certain ways, maybe we should expect y to do likewise. In addition, if we humans can cause desirable changes in x through certain means, maybe we can change y in analogous ways.

Because those who suggest this type of model are not claiming that the model is exactly equivalent to the phenomena in question but only analogous to them, it is not fatal for the model if some aspects of the model are unlike the phenomena. Indeed, the very nature of analogy presumes that such dissimilarities exist; that is the fundamental distinction between analogy and equivalence. Moreover, people who propose this type of model are not claiming to establish their assertions about the phenomena being investigated on the basis of their analogies; they must do that on independent grounds. For example, if I say, as I do in the next chapter, that Jewish law is like an organism in that it has mechanisms to preserve continuity through change (a descriptive claim), I cannot do that by simply pointing out that organisms have such mechanisms; rather I must do that by pointing to features of Jewish law that have that effect and, if possible, even those that were specifically intended to have that effect. Those who disagree might claim that the aspects of Jewish law I am singling out either do not have that effect at all or that it is a sheer accident that they do and not an integral feature of Jewish law.

The need for arguments independent of the model is even more acute in regard to any prescriptive claims that the theorist makes. I say, for example, that Jewish law should be interpreted and applied in historical context rather than just citing chapter and verse of the received tradition. That organisms react to their environments, are very much shaped by them, protect their lives by taking environmental threats into account, and benefit themselves by taking advantage of what their environments have to offer (for example, by extracting nutrients from their environs) may be helpful in making a similar claim about Jewish law plausible. To justify that claim, however, I must demonstrate that my historically contextual approach to understanding past Jewish law and applying it to the present and future will have similar beneficial effects on the law and the community it is intended to govern.

In this book, I propose models of this second, educational type. In the next chapter, I claim that Jewish law is very much like a living organism, especially a human being, in its nature and operation. Thus I say things like, "Jewish law does this in ways very similar to the way that human beings do in their functioning as organisms." That should make certain aspects of Jewish law easier to understand. Moreover, conversely, if you see organisms changing in certain ways or gaining identity in certain ways, we should check to see if Jewish law does so likewise, for doing things that way is the nature of an organism and so it may also be the nature of the living, dynamic legal system known as Jewish law. I thus want my model to help explain Jewish law, not in the sense of the word "explain" meaning to justify my claims about it but rather in the sense that the model will, I hope, *make plain* and understandable various important features of Jewish law as it has functioned in the past (my descriptive claims) and to make plausible, although not to justify, the way I think Jewish law should be understood and applied in our own day and in the future (my prescriptive claims).

Precisely because a model is an analogy and not an equivalence, sometimes more than one model is helpful in explaining a given phenomenon. Thus physicists use *both* packets and waves to explain light because light behaves like packets in some respects and like waves in others. In the same way, I will be suggesting two different models for Jewish law, one as a physical organism and the other as a covenant, for some aspects of Jewish law are best analogized to the one and some to the other. I will be claiming, though, that the two models are actually integrated, and that Jewish law is best understood when one realizes that its organic aspects influence its covenantal elements, and vice versa. This is like saying that dogs are like people in some ways (they have moods, they can show loyalty, they like to play games, and so on), but they are like other, less personable animals in other respects (they walk on all fours, most have a shorter life span than humans, they cannot think abstractly, and so on), and the personality traits of a dog are very much affected by the physical traits they share with other animals, just as their physical expressions are affected by their personalities.

Sometimes, writers about Jewish law have invoked models from non-Jewish legal theories. For example, David Novak suggests that Jewish law is founded on natural law—that is, moral laws built into nature very much like the laws of physics.[41] Aristotle and Thomas Aquinas are other "natural law" theorists who make a similar claim in other traditions. There are philosophical and educational reasons for trying to apply a theory used in other cultural contexts to Jewish law. Because Jewish law functions in large measure as other legal systems do, one would expect that a legal theory worth its salt would be applicable to Jewish law as well. If the theory is philosophically correct, the areas where it fails to fit Jewish law should be directly attributable to the special religious character of Jewish law or to some other factor that distinguishes it from all other legal systems. Such comparisons to secular legal theories are thus potentially enlightening about both the particular legal theory and Jewish law: The application should test the validity of the legal theory on a somewhat unusual legal system, and it should reveal the extent to which Jewish law is both like and unlike secular legal systems and, perhaps, why. This philosophical goal coalesces with an educational one: A common educational technique is to compare an unknown quantity with something known, and so explication of Jewish law through the use of a theory intended to describe secular legal systems can be an effective method to gain better understanding of the nature and functioning of Jewish law.

How does one evaluate such models, whether taken from theories of other legal systems or not? The same way one would evaluate any analogy. That is, an analogy of Jewish law to something else is as strong as the number and importance of similarities between Jewish law and the object of comparison in the element(s) being compared. For example, I argue that Jewish law is like a living organism in the way it operates and deals with continuity and change. To the extent that there are many such similarities, and to the extent that such similarities are significant features of the functioning of Jewish law, the analogy is both strong and helpful in suggesting why Jewish law functions as it does.

On the other hand, my analogy of Jewish law to a living organism is weak and unhelpful if Jewish law and living organisms act very differently in the aspects I am comparing. Worse, it may even be misleading if it prompts people to conclude things about Jewish law that are not true. To judge whether it is deceptive, one must consider whether the model would lead most people to think that Jewish law has a particular characteristic that it does not have. For example, the fact that living organisms eat, sleep, and reproduce and Jewish law does none of those (except in a metaphoric sense that I shall develop) should not dupe people at all because nobody expects law to act in those very physical ways. These clear differences between a living organism and a legal system thus should not deceive anyone.

Theorists, of course, do not depend on analogies alone to explain what they want to say. Another common way to accomplish that task is to put the phenomena being investigated into a larger framework. One good way to do that for Jewish law is to compare it to other secular and religious legal systems. To spell out, for example, how Jewish law is like American law in certain respects and unlike it in others enables anyone familiar with either or both legal systems to better understand the similar and different tasks they seek to accomplish, the similar and different ways they fulfill those roles, and the ways in which the various elements in each of them ultimately work together to constitute a coherent whole. One can then understand the social (and religious) aims that produce legal systems in the first place, the obstacles that legal systems have to overcome to accomplish those goals, the choices varying legal systems make in addressing their problems and in trying to maximize their effectiveness, and the underlying values and perceptions of human beings and human societies that prompt legal systems to function in the various ways they do. Throughout this book, I will make such comparisons to shed light on Jewish law in this way as well.

Finally, it is important to distinguish between claims that *x* is like *y* (the analogies and comparisons I have been discussing) from claims that *x* is *y* or *x* is an instance of *y*. In the next chapter, I will be claiming that Jewish law is *like* an organism in many critical ways. In Chapter Three, however, I will be dealing with the Torah's claim that Jewish law *is* an agreement between God and the Jewish People, an agreement that stems from and whose terms are subject to the ongoing covenantal relationship between them.

Even though the Torah itself speaks of the relationship between God and the People Israel in covenantal terms, ancient Israelites clearly did not think that it was literally a covenant in the same way that human beings create covenants among themselves. Indeed, the model they were invoking was not what moderns usually mean by a "covenant" in the first place. A modern covenant of marriage, for example, is an agreement between equals establishing a long-term relationship and at least some of its terms. The Bible does invoke the covenant of marriage to describe the relationship between God and the People Israel, but it also uses the suzerainty treaties that many nations had with their sovereigns in the ancient world. That model suggested itself because there were some obvious similarities: it was, fundamentally, an agreement with a sovereign whom the people could not control (that is, the parties were unequal in power and status) but who voluntarily took upon himself certain promises to establish a richer relationship between himself and the people he was governing than he would have if he were simply ruling by dint of power.

Ancient Jews believed, though, that God was different from any human king, that he was, in fact, "King of kings" and had no physical shape. So even the ancients used this covenant model *as a metaphor* to describe their relationship with God; they could not be plausibly understood to be asserting that their covenant with God was *exactly the same,* let alone *an instance of,* the covenantal treaties that human sovereigns had with their subjects. Thus in Chapter Three I will be exploring both the strengths and the weaknesses of the covenantal model in both its marital and suzerainty forms as an explanatory tool to describe aspects of Jewish law.

In modern times, those Jews who believe that such an agreement and such a relationship existed in the past and continues to exist today may conclude that the covenant and the Jewish law embedded in it are authoritative for them. On the other hand, they may, like Eugene Borowitz, believe that the covenant was real for Jews of the past and is for Jews today, but its content is no longer articulated by Jewish law but rather emerges from the ongoing relationship between individual Jews with their tradition, community, and God.[42] Christians believe that Jewish law is not binding (except, perhaps, for the Decalogue) and that Jesus instituted a New Covenant with God, and they determine their obligations under it through their interpretation of the Bible, their own conscience, the pope or some other authority figure, or some combination thereof. Those Jews and non-Jews who believe that God's covenant with Israel at Mount Sinai never existed or no longer exists (say, after the Holocaust) may for that reason discount the authority of Jewish law altogether, but they may also think that Jewish law is authoritative for some other reason—family or communal ties, moral demands, or something else. Thus the use of the covenantal model is neither a necessary nor a sufficient condition for believing that Jewish law is authoritative in our time. Still, precisely because the Torah itself thinks of Jewish law as a covenant, it remains an authoritative and powerful metaphor for thinking about Jewish law; hence my interest in using it to complement my use of an organism to explain Jewish law.

In sum, then, I will be employing the analogies of organism and covenant to enhance our understanding of the nature and functioning of Jewish law. I also claim that to understand Jewish law properly, one must use the two models in tandem, such that the elements of Jewish law best analogized to a living organism influence those best analogized to a covenant in an ongoing way, and vice versa. I then make the prescriptive claim that for Jewish law to function well in the present and future, it must continue to be the product of the interaction between its body and its spirit (soul), its organic features and its covenantal features. The strength of my analysis will depend on the extent to which what I suggest accurately reflects the realities of Jewish law in the past and present.

THEORETICAL DISCUSSION 2: BIBLICAL CRITICISM AND REVELATION

Modern biblical scholarship has convinced me that the Torah originally consisted of oral traditions that were only later written down at different time periods.[43] The text of the Torah is thus for me a human document. What, then, gives it any connection to God at all, let alone divine authority? Put another way, in what sense, if any, is the Torah the revelation of God?

Some Jews, of course, including important modern thinkers like Mordecai Kaplan, think that the Torah is merely a human document. I, however, believe that the Torah is a divine document as well as a human one. The point of this section is to describe briefly how I see it as divine revelation and, therefore, the basis of a distinctly religious legal system. I intend to be intellectually honest and at the same time take the Torah seriously as a religious document, indeed, as the revelation of God.

In my view, revelation can occur in any event from the most common to the most unusual: what marks an event as a revelation of God is not that the event itself is of a special character but that it is interpreted as such by a human community. So, for example, the Holocaust may be just another ugly war for most of the world, but it may be a revelation by God of a 614th commandment for the Jewish People as Emil Fackenheim would claim—a commandment not to give Hitler a posthumous victory.[44] Whether it is a revelation of God or not depends on whether the Jewish community accepts it as such. Similarly, the decision of a particular rabbi about a matter of Jewish law may be just his or her opinion (and perhaps one that should be quickly forgotten!), or it may be nothing less than a revelation from God: which it is depends on how the Jewish community responds to it. Moreover, the Jewish community determines not only what events shall count as revelations but also how those revelations are to be interpreted and applied.

Jewish law, then, is of human authorship, a human, communal response to events that the Jewish community accepts as revealing God or God's will for us. The law is divine because of its internal wisdom (its soundness as a way of living, as demonstrated by experience), its moral goodness, and its durability (strength). Here, as usual, wisdom, morality, and power are characteristics that we call divine.[45] The authority of Jewish law for the Jew is then a function of both its communal acceptance and its divinity.

Some, like my teacher, friend, and colleague, Rabbi Neil Gillman, maintain that "My faith is that these experiences [of revelation] are true, not in any objective sense of that term but subjectively, existentially."[46] I, however, maintain that religious claims are indeed objectively true—at least as objectively as any human claims to truth can be.

In practical science we can use the scientific method to prove or disprove something, but as soon as we go beyond the particular to the level of theory (including scientific theory), that method will not work. Instead, we judge among competing theories in terms of their *clarity*, their *adequacy* to the facts of the case, their *consistency*, their *coherence*, and their *moral import*. That method for determining which theory is "true"—or at least as true as we can tell—is used in virtually every area of inquiry. So, for example, we would use those criteria to decide the historical question of whether the American Revolution was caused primarily by economic factors or by ideological ones, or the economic question of whether a nation's economy is best evaluated and stimulated through concern with the amount of money in circulation or the amount of goods, or the literary question of whether Shakespeare's *The Merchant of Venice* is an anti-Jewish polemic or a satire of the Anglican Church in disguised form, or the legal question of whether a given person is innocent or guilty, or the scientific question of whether light is best conceived as a series of waves or packets.

For me, then, we can and should evaluate religious claims in the same way we assess other theories about our experience. When one does that, I maintain that varying religious descriptions of reality are *not* equally true, or true for different people existentially in differing, individual ways. We can and should have respect for other religions, for people can be intelligent and moral and yet evaluate the evidence and respond to it differently from the way in which Jews do. Indeed, we can often learn from the strengths and weaknesses of other religions. Ultimately, though, being a Jew means that we believe that the Jewish description of reality and the Jewish response to our perceptions in feeling and in action are true and morally appropriate, at least as much as we, the Jewish community, can discern.

My view of revelation, then, consists of the following assertions.

1. Human moral, intellectual, and aesthetic faculties distinguish human beings from the animals, in degree if not in kind. As such, these capabilities are a touch of the divine within humanity in the root sense of "divine" as power, for they enable human beings to know, feel, and do things that other animals cannot.

2. The structure of the world is an objective base that serves as a criterion for the evaluation of any philosophic theory or moral code; and because I hold that the world was divinely created at least in the sense that its creation involves powers beyond our control, I think that God informed us about divinity and the world and gave us Jewish law in an *indirect* way—specifically, by creating the world in such a way that certain formulations of thought and practice fit the pattern of creation better than others. They are, in that sense, wiser than any alternative ways of thinking and acting.

3. I maintain, however, that the specific *content* of human theological ideas and codes of practice is created by human beings and hence is subject to error and change. Revelation occurs *in events that human beings interpret to be revelatory* of truths or norms of conduct; therefore, any event could be a source of revelation, although some may be more impressively so than others. I would also want to stress that, within Judaism, it is the Jewish community of the past and present that decides which events are revelatory and what the content of that revelation is, and that this communal check prevents revelation from being simply the figment of someone's imagination.

4. This approach helps me integrate the Documentary Hypothesis (that is, the claim that the Torah is made up of four separate documents written at different times and later edited together) and other claims of modern biblical and rabbinic scholarship with a serious, but intellectually honest claim that the Torah is nevertheless divine. What exactly was revealed at Mount Sinai (or Horeb)? The Torah's reference three times to *aseret ha-devarim*, "the 10 words" or "the 10

things (matters, topics)" (Exod. 34:28; Deut. 4:13, 10:4), indicates that at least one biblical strand saw the Revelation at Mount Sinai as being limited to the Decalogue. The rest of the Torah's laws God communicated to Moses and Moses, in turn, told the people. One rabbinic source, identified in one place as the school of Rabbi Ishmael, maintains that the Israelites heard only the first two clauses of the Decalogue.[47] This is in line with the talmudic tradition that the school of Rabbi Akiva asserted that every word of the Torah was revealed to Moses at Mount Sinai, but the school of Rabbi Ishmael taught that God revealed only the general principles of the law there, a tradition thoroughly discussed by Abraham Joshua Heschel and expanded by Gordon Tucker in his masterful commentary on that book.[48]

In the Middle Ages, Maimonides claimed that the Revelation was entirely nonverbal because the people heard only a voice but not distinct words.[49] Along the same lines, one Hasidic strand maintains that the Israelites heard only the first letter of the first word of the Decalogue, anokhi ("I"), the silent aleph.[50] In other words, for both these theories, the Revelation lacked all content.

This set the stage for Franz Rosenzweig in the early 20th century to assert that God gives only one command with specific content—namely, "Love Me!" The rest of the Torah's laws "turns into execution of the one initial commandment to love him" as modes of doing so.[51] That is, what was revealed at Mount Sinai was only God's presence in intimate relationship with Israel, a presence that Israel immediately recognized as commanding even though there were no specific laws announced there. We can understand this best, perhaps, if we think of similar, human interactions. As soon as a parent or teacher steps into the room, children sense that there is a commanding presence there, just as adults do when a president or other ruler does. This happens even when the parties are equal: One senses in the first days of marriage that one has duties to one's spouse that were never explicitly promised, orally or in writing, ranging from serious burdens like taking care of each other in times of serious illness to mundane duties like taking out the garbage.[52]

Later the French Jewish philosopher Emanuel Levinas generalized this sense of duty to all humanity, claiming that the very presence of another human being, even one unrelated to me and not Jewish, imposes infinite obligations on me to care for that person. He invokes the talmudic comment by Rav Abdimi bar Hama bar Hasa, who said that at Mount Sinai God "inclined the mountain over them [the Israelites] like an overturned tub and said, 'If you accept the Torah, all is well; if not, here will be your grave.'"[53] From this Levinas deduces that revelation is very different from most of our sources of knowledge. When we reason or experiment, we have time to seek evidence and decide both how to interpret it and how to respond to it. This story instead depicts revelation as a kind of knowledge that forces itself on us; it leaves no time for weighing arguments. This articulates, for Levinas, an important truth about Torah—namely, that the commitment to Torah precedes reasoning and excludes a choice made in freedom. Instead, as soon as we encounter people it is immediately evident that we have duties to them—and Levinas makes it clear that he means non-Jews as well as Jews.[54]

My own theory of revelation is essentially a combination of Rosenzweig and Levinas, one that leads me to see Jewish law as expressions of our love for God and people. I think that Rosenzweig and Levinas both, however, have taken the commanding nature of presence too far in that they do not acknowledge the times when people—and presumably God and Israel—simply enjoy each other's company without heavy tones of duty intervening. Love is like that: It certainly does entail duties, articulated in the case of the People Israel in Jewish law, but, at least as important, love also and often involves mutual growth and sheer joy. Thus God tolerates the arguments that Abraham, Moses, Jeremiah, Ezekiel, and others pose to Him throughout the generations, even changing His mind sometimes, as God did after the Golden Calf and spy incidents (Exod. 33–34 [esp. 33:17]; Num. 14 [esp. 14:20]); one gets the sense that God is enjoying the argument just as many parents do. Indeed, the Rabbis maintain that God even laughed when the Rabbis bested Him in an argument.[55]

An alternative theory that proposes that the Revelation at Mount Sinai lacked all content is that of Abraham Joshua Heschel. Heschel maintains that God revealed His will at Mount Sinai, but we do not have it in hand. All we have is our ancestors' and our own understanding of its contents. In his now-famous sentence, "As a report about revelation, the Bible itself is a *Midrash*."[56] For me too, human beings created the contents of Jewish sacred texts, including the Torah, and, like Heschel, I maintain that our ancestors wrote what they did in effort to communicate both their experiences with God and with each other, as well as the implications of those experi-

33

ences for action. I would emphasize, though, that they did this with a strong sense of love for God, for fellow Jews, and for humans generally, and that we in our day should carry on this task with those loving commitments as well.

5. I observe Jewish law (that is, Jewish Law has authority for me) both because it is the way *my people* have understood *the demands of God* in the past and do so now and because of its own intrinsic wisdom as a program for satisfying human needs, acting morally, and maximizing human potential in the world as we know it. Similarly, Jewish philosophic views from the Bible to modern times have special relevance to me because they represent the way my people have understood God, human beings, and the world. Both Jewish law and Jewish thought thus require attention to God, the Jewish people, and the interactions among them.

Because I identify conscientiously as a Conservative Jew, the "community" whose ideas and practices define God's word for me in our time is the body of Conservative rabbis and laypeople who actively live Conservative Judaism in what they think, say, and do. On legal issues, this is defined by the decisions of the Conservative movement's Committee on Jewish Law and Standards and on philosophical issues whose parameters were defined by the Commission on the Philosophy of the Conservative Movement in its document *Emet Ve-Emunah: Statement of Principles of Conservative Judaism.* Deciding matters of Jewish law and thought within the context of a Jewish community narrower than all Jews may not be ideal, but it is the way Jewish law has been applied and practiced for most of its history, albeit with greater coherence, and it is inevitable in the pluralistic societies in which we live today.

6. When a particular law is not moral or wise, I must be prepared to change it in consort with the rest of the Conservative community, taking due regard of the weight of tradition in the process. The same is true for specific Jewish beliefs. Evaluating traditional laws and concepts must be done deliberately, and commitment to the tradition requires that the burden of proof rests with the one who wants to change it. Moreover, the need for communal concurrence should help guard against precipitous changes. No mechanism can guarantee wisdom in such evaluations, however, and no simple rules can be applied to determine when to change an element in the tradition and when not to do so. That is why we must entrust such decisions to a

committee that is called on to use their collective *judgment*. We clearly use our own individual experience and reason when responding to the tradition; but for Judaism to retain continuity and coherence, we must discuss our evaluations with the other members of our community and make decisions as a group. This does not guarantee wisdom; but since human beings are not omniscient, this method is the one that holds the most promise for us in knowing the true, the good, and the holy.

7. Even though for lack of knowledge I must suspend judgment as to what actually happened at Sinai, there are elements of the texts attributed to that event that induce me to attach a divine quality to them. These include their scope, their inherent wisdom, and especially the demonstrated viability of the tradition that they fostered over the centuries and throughout many regions of the world. This clearly does not mean that Judaism's understanding of life is the only possible one. There are obviously other traditions that claim similar authority for their philosophies of life that have undergone a long period of intersubjective testing, too. Judaism itself recognizes the existence of prophets and saints among non-Jews and does not require Jewish belief or practice of non-Jews, even in judging who has the merit of attaining a place in the world to come.[57] In the end, all descriptions of the world and how we should live in it must be subjected to the same criteria of truth we use to test theories in history, economics, science, literature, and any other academic discipline—namely, their clarity, their adequacy to the facts, their consistency, their coherence, and their moral import. To assert the authority of Jewish beliefs and norms of conduct, in other words, we must be prepared to subject them to the same standards of truth and goodness that we would use in evaluating any other civilization's view of the world and its pattern of action.

When I do that, the amazing adaptability and endurance of Jewish law and ideology over the ages in a wide variety of places indicate to me that Jews have apparently hit on a pattern of life and thought that fits the structure of human beings and nature well, and so I ascribe truth to Judaism's claims. In fact, it appears to me that Judaism fits the structure of reality so well that I doubt that it could simply be the product of human minds. Consequently, although I cannot unequivocally affirm or deny belief in a verbal communication at Sinai, I do want to claim that the Jewish tradition embodies a degree of foresight, insight, and sheer wisdom that is abnormal for human beings, even especially sensitive ones, and that in this sense at least it is a revelation of divine (super-human) truth and will.[58]

8. Revelation, though, is ongoing. The Written Torah is our constitution, and as such has special significance and authority for us. Jewish law, however, is not equivalent to that in the Torah, even though much of it is based on the Torah. The Jewish tradition believes in an Oral Torah that accompanied the written one, and if we take an historical view of the Torah itself, revelation began well before the Mount Sinai event in laws that clearly bound the Patriarchs and Matriarchs, for otherwise the stories about them would make no sense. Revelation happens each time any of us reads the Torah again and sees new meanings in it. Hence the traditional blessings one recites when called to the Torah speak not only of God having given us the Torah (with verbs in the completed, or past, tense), but of giving it to us now (*noten ha-Torah* as either the current Giver of the Torah, the gerund, or, as the incomplete [present] tense of the verb, as giving it to us as we read it and interpret it anew).[59] As the Rabbis say, "there are seventy faces to the Torah,"[60] so that at any time we can discover new meanings in it. For that reason, Ben Bag Bag says in the Mishnah, "turn it over, and turn it over again, for everything is in it."[61] That is an exaggeration, but it surely alerts us to the Rabbis' recognition that revelation is ongoing as we discover new meanings in the Torah, in the tradition, and in the world that God created.

In my book *Conservative Judaism* I call my theory about revelation "objectivist" in contrast to more existentialist theories like those of Rabbis Louis Jacobs and Abraham Heschel.[62] That definitely does *not* mean that I am blind to the personal aspects of religious commitment. On the contrary, in my book *Knowing God* I have described how the personal and objective factors of my religious faith intertwine, including a much fuller treatment of my understanding of revelation.[63] I am an objectivist, then, only in that I emphasize publicly observable facts rather than private, personal experiences in arguing for Jewish belief and observance.

Despite the brevity of this section, I hope it gives readers at least some sense of how I integrate fully open and intellectually honest analysis of the texts of our tradition, including the Torah, with a strong faith that they really matter. Indeed, this should explain how I understand the role of God and revelation in the formation and the ongoing development of Jewish law, so that the texts matter not just in the way that other important things in life do, but in a special, transcendent sense. I turn now, then, to my core convictions about the nature and functioning of Jewish law, the legal system that is infused with both divinity and humanity and that expresses our love for both God and people.

ENDNOTES

1. For more on this, see Dorff, *To Do the Right and the Good*, chap. 1, append. B.

2. See travel.state.gov/law/citizenship/citizenship_776.html, which is the State Department website that describes the right to renounce one's U.S. citizenship as provided for in §349(a)(5) of the Immigration and Naturalization Act and the ways in which it must be done—specifically, by (1) appearing in person before a U.S. consular or diplomatic officer, (2) apply in a foreign country (normally at a U.S. embassy or consulate), and (3) signing an oath of renunciation.

3. Obama, *The Audacity of Hope,* p. 55.

4. Other terms are *mumar* (one who changes [faiths]), *apikoros* (heretic), and *kofer b'ikar* (one who denies a fundamental principle of Jewish faith).

5. M.T. Laws of Testimony 10:1–3; S.A. Hoshen Mishpat 34:1–3.

6. S.A. Even ha-Ezer 17:3.

7. Israel b. Pethahiah Isserlein, Terumat ha-Deshen, 1, 64–65, 83–84; Isaac b. Sheshet, responsa no. 11; Piskei Din Shel Battai Din ha-Rabbaniim b'Yisrael 7:35, 39–44; but cf. 54–56.

8. A son is heir to his father by the mere fact of kinship (Num. 27:8; B. Bava Batra 108a, 111a; and M.T. and S.A. on that passage). Nevertheless, the Mordecai (Kiddushin1) ruled that an apostate does not inherit from his father. Most authorities maintain that by strict law he does still have the right of inheritance, but to discourage apostasy, the court is authorized to pass his inheritance to family members who have not apostatized on the strength of the rule *hefker bet din hefker*—that is, the court has the right of expropriation. For that principle, see B. Yevamot 89b and B. Gittin 36b. For its use to deny apostates their inheritance, see Asher ben Yehiel, Piskei ha-Rosh to B. Kiddushin 22; responsa of Rabbi Solomon Cohen 3:37; M.T. Laws of Inheritance (*nahalot*) 6:12; S.A. Hoshen Mishpat 283:2.

9. M.T. Laws of Gifts to the Poor 8:14.

10. M. Sanhedrin 6:6; S.A. Yoreh De'ah 345:5 (unless the apostate met a sudden death, in which case it is assumed that he or she repented just before death: S.A. Yoreh De'ah 340:5, gloss; cf. 157 and Hoshen Mishpat 266:2).

11. Israel's High Court Case of *Rufeisen* (Brother Daniel) 72/62, PD 16:2428–2455.

12. B. Sanhedrin 44a; see Nahmanides on Deuteronomy 29:14.

13. B. Yevamot 30b; M.T. Laws of Marriage 4:15; S.A. Even ha-Ezer 44:9.

14. M.T. Laws of Forbidden Intercourse 13:17.

15. M.T. Laws of Marriage 4:15.

16. B. Shevu'ot 39a.

17. B. Sanhedrin 73a. For an extended treatment of this duty in Jewish law, see Kirschenbaum, "The 'Good Samaritan' in Jewish Law."

18. Hyman, "Rescue without Law," p. 683.

The Vermont statute is Vt. Stat. Ann. tit. 12, par. 519 (2002), which provides that "A person who knows that another is exposed to grave physical harm shall, to the extent that the same can be rendered without danger or peril to himself or without interference with important duties owed to others, give reasonable assistance to the exposed person unless that assistance or care is being provided by others." Violation carries a fine of no more than $100.

The Rhode Island statute is R.I. Gen. Laws par. 11-56-1 (2002), which provides that "Any person at the scene of an emergency who knows that another person is exposed to, or has suffered, grave physical harm shall, to the extent that he or she can do so without danger or peril to himself or herself or to others, give reasonable assistance to the exposed person." Violation is a petty misdemeanor, punishable by no more than six months imprisonment or a $500 fine, or both. Par. 11-1-5.1 also criminalizes the failure of a bystander to report a sexual assault, murder, manslaughter, or armed robbery "as soon as reasonably practical."

The Minnesota statute is Minn. Stat. Ann. par. 604A.01 (West 2000), which states that "A person at the scene of an emergency who knows that another person is exposed to or has suffered grave physical harm shall, to the extent that the person can do so without danger or peril to self or others, give reasonable assistance to the exposed person. Reasonable assistance may include obtaining or attempting to obtain aid from law enforcement or medical personnel." Violation is a misdemeanor.

The Wisconsin statute, Wis. Stat. Ann. par. 940.34 (West 2005), states: "Any person who knows that a crime is being committed and that a victim is exposed to bodily harm shall summon law enforcement officers or other assistance or shall provide assistance to the victim." The statute then specifies that compliance is not necessary if it would place the individual in danger or interfere with duties owed to others, if assistance is being summoned or provided by others, or if the crime has already been reported by others.

One case now in the courts under this statute, *State v. LaPlante,* 521 N. W.2d 448 (Wis. 1994), cites a failure to aid the victim of a beating.

Several other states have imposed limited duties to report crimes: Florida, in Fla. Stat. Ann. par. 794.027 (West 2000), in regard to reporting sexual batteries; Hawaii, in Haw. Rev. Stat. Ann. par. 663–1.6 (LexisNexis 2002), applying to all crimes in which the victim suffers "serious physical harm"; Massachusetts, in Mass. Gen. Laws. Ann. ch. 268, par. 40 (West 2000), requiring the reporting of aggravated rape, rape, murder, manslaughter, or armed robbery to the extent that the person can do so without danger to himself or others, and Mass. Gen. Laws Ann. ch. 269, par. 18 (West 2000), requiring the reporting of hazing; Ohio, in Ohio Rev. Code Ann. par. 2921.22 (West 1997), requiring the reporting of a felony; and Washington, at Wash. Rev. Code. Ann. par. 9.69.100 (West 2003), applying to certain crimes against children and violent offenses.

19. See also M. Bava Meẓia 7:2 and that chapter generally.

20. Maimonides, *Guide for the Perplexed,* part III, chap. 27.

21. M.T. Laws of Ethics (De'ot) 1:7. See also M.T. Laws of Slaughter 14:16 and M.T. Laws of Shemitah and Yovel (Cancellation of Debts in the Sabbatical Year and the Jubliee) 13:13, in both of which Maimonides identifies "the ways of God" not as the commandments themselves but as the paths of righteousness.

22. T. Avodah Zarah 8:4; B. Sanhedrin 56a, 60a. See Novak, *The Image of the Non-Jew in Judaism.*

23. For more on Judaism and pluralism, both among the various forms of Judaism and in interfaith relations, see Dorff, *To Do the Right and the Good,* chaps. 2 and 3.

24. B. Sanhedrin 59a.

25. B. Sanhedrin 57b. The same teaching is taught in the name of Rabbi Hanina in Genesis Rabbah 34:14.

26. M. Oholot 7:6. This Mishnah declares that the exact moment that the fetus attains the status of a full human being, equal to that of its mother, is when its head emerges. T. Yevamot 9:9 and B. Sanhedrin 72b concur. J. Shabbat 14:4, however, reads "its greater part," presumably referring to a breech birth, and J. Sanhedrin 8, end, reads "its head or its greater part," presumably referring to either a normal birth (head first, and so the head appearing is the decisive moment) or a breech birth (when "its greater part" appearing outside the body of the mother is the decisive moment). On this topic generally, see Feldman, *Birth Control in Jewish Law,* chaps. 14 and 15, esp. pp. 254–262.

27. Tosafot to B. Sanhedrin 59a, s.v., *leka;* Tosafot to B. Hullin 33a, s.v. *ehad;* but see Tosafot to B. Niddah 44b, s.v. *ihu;* and, in general, Feldman, *Birth Control in Jewish Law,* p. 262.

28. *Lawrence v. Texas* 539 U.S. 558 (2003).

29. For more on this, see Dorff, *The Way into Tikkun Olam,* chap. 4.

30. For at least two children: M. Yevamot 6:6 (61b). For preferably more: B. Yevamot 62b. For more on these rabbinic standards, see Dorff, *Matters of Life and Death,* p. 336, nn. 9 and 10, and on this topic generally, chaps. 3 and 4.

31. For parental duty to teach sons Torah and a trade: B. Kiddushin 29a. For the curriculum: M. Avot (Ethics of the Fathers) 5:23 (5:24 in some editions). For a general discussion of parental and filial duties in Jewish law and practice, see Dorff (2003), chap. 4.

32. See, for example, Dorff, *Love Your Neighbor and Yourself,* chap. 7 and bibliography therein.

33. B. Nedarim 28a; Gittin 10b; Bava Kamma 113a; Bava Batra 54b–55a. For more on this, see Dorff and Rosett, *A Living Tree,* pp. 515–523.

34. For a good treatment of the evidence for the Documentary Hypothesis in nontechnical and very clear style, see Friedman, *Who Wrote the Bible?* For a history of acceptance of biblical scholarship, see Sperling, *Students of the Covenant.* For examples of Orthodox writers who reject biblical scholarship, see Lopes Cordozo, "On Bible Criticism and Its Counterarguments," and Ross, *Expanding the Palace of Torah.*

35. Fishbane, *Biblical Interpretation in Ancient Israel.*

36. For a thorough discussion of the motives suggested by the Bible and Rabbis, see Dorff, *Mitzvah Means Commandment.* For a shorter version of that, see Dorff and Rosett, *A Living Tree,* pp. 82–123 and 246–249. For some medieval discussions of rationales for observing the commandments, see Saadia Gaon, Book of Doctrines and Beliefs, chap. 3, and Maimonides, Guide of the Perplexed, part 3, chaps. 25–49.

37. *Lawrence v. Texas* 539 U.S. 558 (2003).

38. See Dorff, *To Do the Right and the Good,* chap 4., esp. pp. 105–107.

39. For more on the relationship between God, the law, and morality in the Bible and in rabbinic literature, see Dorff and Rosett, *A Living Tree,* pp. 110–122, 249–257.

40. The Sifrei, both Talmuds, and Maimonides all maintain that only men may serve as witnesses as a matter of biblical law. That, however, is founded on reading the masculine plural word for "witnesses" (*edim*) in Deut. 19:15 or Deut. 17:6 as exclusively male in reference, even though the text of the Torah itself can just as easily be read to include women as to exclude them and even though the Sifrei itself interprets the masculine plural words for the litigants in these verses to include women. Thus Sifrei Devarim Piska 104, sec. 190 (ed. Finkelstein, p. 230), bases the restriction of testimony to men on a linking (*gezerah shavah*) of the word *shenei* (two) in Deut. 19:17 to Deut. 19:15, claiming that the former is clearly referring only to men and so the latter is too. The truth is that neither is necessarily referring to men, for *anashim* (men) in verse 17 can just as easily be "people," as the Sifrei itself

interprets it! Compare also the Jewish Publication Society translation, "the two parties to the dispute." In M. Shevu'ot 4:1 women are excluded from testifying; and the Talmud (B. Shevu'ot 30a), in trying to justify that ruling, offers a variety of arguments to make *shenei ha-anashim* (two men) in Deut. 19:17 refer to witnesses rather than litigants. But all those efforts are disputed, and so it ultimately relies on the Sifrie's linking of *shenei* (two—two witnesses and two men) in the two verses. Apparently dissatisfied with that proof, or possibly basing his thoughts on J. Shevu'ot 4:1 (35b), Maimonides (M.T. Laws of Testimony 9:2) instead bases the restriction on "the mouth of two witnesses" (Deut. 17:6), where "witnesses" is the masculine form of the noun. Karo, however, in Kesef Mishneh, objects to this justification on the grounds that the masculine form of the noun there also does not necessarily mean men alone, and so, in S.A. Hoshen Mishpat 35:1, 14, he just asserts the rule that women are barred from serving as witnesses without attributing the rule to the Bible. I discuss this further in Chapter Seven herein.

41. Novak, *Covenantal Rights*.

42. Borowitz, *Renewing the Covenant*, esp. pp. 189–204.

43. See note 33.

44. Fackenheim, *God's Presence in History*, chap. 3.

45. Dorff, "God and the Holocaust."

46. Gillman, "What Do Americans Believe? Symposium," p. 39.

47. B. Makkot 24a. This teaching is identified as that of the school of Rabbi Ishmael in B. Horayot 8a.

48. The talmudic tradition is in B. Haggigah 6a–6b, B. Sotah 37b, and B. Zevahim 115b. See Heschel, *Heavenly Torah*.

49. Maimonides, *Guide for the Perplexed*, part 2, chap. 33.

50. In an excellent article on this whole question, Benjamin Sommer identifies this with Naftali Tzvi Horowitz of Ropshitz (d. 1815), who quoted his teacher, Menachem Mendel of Rymanov (d. 1815); see Sommer, "Revelation at Sinai in the Hebrew Bible and in Jewish Theology."

51. Rosenzweig, *The Star of Redemption*, pp. 176–178.

52. I think that this effectively answers Yehudah (Jerome) Gellman, who claims in "Conservative Judaism and Biblical Criticism" that presence cannot produce authoritative commands; in many places it does. I would like to thank my friend Rabbi Michael Graetz for suggesting this article to me.

53. B. Shabbat 88a; B. Avodah Zarah 2b.

54. Levinas, *Nine Talmudic Readings*, pp. 30–50. See also Aronowicz, "Emanuel Levinas' Talmudic Commentaries."

55. B. Bava Meẓia, 59b.

56. Heschel, *God in Search of Man*, p. 185. On the similarities and differences between Rosenzweig and Heschel on revelation, see Gillman, *Sacred Fragments*, pp. 24–25.

57. Balaam (Num. 22–24) is the non-Jewish prophet described in the

Torah as having true revelations from God, and the Rabbis recognize that there are more non-Jewish prophets (B. Gittin 57a). The Rabbis speak of *tzadekei umot ha-olam*, "the righteous of the nations of the world" (B. Hullin 92a; Batei Midrashot II 46:76). The Talmud also establishes a blessing to be said when a Jew sees one of the *hahmei umot ha-olam*, "the wise people of the nations of the world" (B. Berakhot 58a). These passages indicate that the Rabbis recognized that righteous and wise people do indeed exist outside of the People Israel. That non-Jews need only obey the seven laws of the Noahide covenant and not the full Sinai Covenant: T. Avodah Zarah 8:4; B. Sanhedrin 56a–b; Genesis Rabbah 16:6; Song of Songs Rabbah 1:16; *Pesikta de-Rav Kahana*, Bahodesh 202–203. Those who do so inherit the world to come: B. Sanhedrin 95a; M.T. Laws of Repentance 3:5; see M.T. Laws of Kings 8:11, for his definition of *hasedei umot ha-olam*, "the pious of the nations of the world," as those who abide by the Noahide covenant.

58. This is a composite formulation of what I wrote in my article "Revelation" and later, in a different articulation within an expanded context, in my book *Knowing God*, pp. 99–113, and see chap. 4 generally; with a few sentences added to bridge the two.

59. I develop this more in Hoffman, *My People's Prayer Book.* Vol. 4, *The Torah Service*, p. 107.

60. Numbers Rabbah 13:15–16.

61. M. Avot 5:22.

62. Dorff, *Conservative Judaism*, pp. 98, 117–119, 133–139.

63. Dorff, "Two Ways to Approach God," and see my *Knowing God*, pp. 113–127 ("Experiencing Revelation," in contrast to the first part of that chapter, "Understanding Revelation") and, more broadly, see chaps. 1 and 2. See also how another exponent of this objectivist approach—namely, Rabbi Jacob Agus, formerly rabbi of Beth El Congregation in Baltimore, a member of the Committee on Jewish Law and Standards and an important philosopher of Jewish law—interweaves the personal with the objective: Agus, *Guideposts in Modern Judaism*, part 2, sec. 2.

PART II

The Core Concepts of My Theory of Jewish Law

CHAPTER TWO

The Body of Jewish Law: How It Resembles Other Legal Systems

A STATEMENT OF MY OWN THEORY OF JEWISH LAW

Now that I have explained what a theory of law is, I can describe my own theory of Jewish law. In my 1992 book, *Knowing God: Jewish Journeys to the Unknowable,* I described Jewish law as a way to know God.[1] Here, I would like to go further: Jewish law is not only a way to know God but also an important way in which we relate to both God and human beings. Specifically, I view Jewish law as *an expression of the love that we Jews have for both God and other human beings.* Like all forms of human love, our love of God and other human beings and God's love of us ideally involve all of our being— body, mind, emotions, will, and interactions with others. Putting this another way, our love is best expressed in both body and soul, for then it can be both physically active and intellectually and emotionally compelling.

To be a meaningful expression of both forms of love—the mutual love among people and that between God and us—Jewish law must, therefore, have both a body and a soul. I consequently see Jewish law very much like a human being, the entity that we most associate with the capacity to love. Some of the features of Jewish law resemble a human body, and some are like a human soul—that is, the mind, emotions, will, and the ability to interact with others. Just as the body and soul of a person constantly interact and affect each other, so too do the body of the law (literally, in the Latin term for it, the *corpus juris*); and its beliefs, values, emotions, and goals continually interact and affect another. (Sometimes that is expressed as the intermingling of law, [*halakhah,* and lore or theology, *aggadah;* but that way of characterizing this interaction seems to me to be too limited and imprecise.) Furthermore, just as people are very much affected by the physical, political, economic, social, and moral environment in which they live, both the body and the soul of Jewish law are influenced by their ongoing interactions with God, with other peoples and cultures, and with the various aspects of the environment in which they function.[2]

Every human being has a body, and although each of our bodies is unique in some ways (for example, its DNA), we share a great deal—so much so, that a physician can treat people from widely varying genetic backgrounds. Analogously, in its bodily functions Jewish law resembles other legal systems. Even here, Jewish law is different in some ways from other legal systems, just as we each walk and talk a bit differently and just as people from varying genetic stock are more or less susceptible to certain diseases, and so the similarities, while real, should not be overstated.

The same is true for the soul of Jewish law. The religious convictions at its heart make it markedly different from secular and other religious legal systems. At the same time, just as all people wrestle with some of the same emotional and psychological issues, and thus the disciplines of social work, psychology, and psychiatry can exist, so too Jewish law has some similarities in its assumptions and approaches to other legal systems. Even so, although the uniqueness of Jewish law should not be overstated, the real differences between Jewish law in its perceptions, values, and style do make it distinctive in degree if not in kind. In general, the similarities between Jewish law and other legal systems will be more a function of the bodily features of all legal systems, the aspects of law that enable it to function in the world, while the uniqueness of Jewish law will be primarily a function of its soul.

Why do I see Jewish law this way? In large measure, it is because doing so helps me to understand how Jewish law has functioned in the past and how I think it should function now.

I could have simply said that Jewish law is like other legal systems in certain ways and distinctive in others, but the image of body and soul gives me a way of understanding the phenomena of Jewish law in the past and present and of helping plan its future. In the language explained in Chapter One, I am comparing Jewish law to a human being not to justify any assertions but to help understand and explain the nature and functioning of Jewish law. In all of the rest of the book, but especially in this chapter and the next, this model will help to explain *why* all legal systems act in some of the ways Jewish law does and why, on the other hand, legal systems, for all their similarities, can be and are distinctive. The model, in other words, helps me go from simple assertions comparing legal systems to an understanding of why and how legal systems in general, and Jewish law in particular, do what they do. The extent to which my theory does this is rightfully open to the judgment of all who read it.

Because one's thoughts are inevitably connected to one's personal experiences, however, it may help to understand any theory by knowing a bit about the experiences of the person proposing it. So, briefly, I view Jewish law as an expression of love for, and commitment to, both God and other people in part because I grew up in a warm, supportive home and I was influenced heavily by Camp Ramah, in both of which I experienced Jewish law in an immensely positive way. Jewish law was the vehicle that enabled us to celebrate Shabbat with great joy and to mourn the tragedies of the Jewish people on Tisha b'Av with real sorrow. It also demanded that we think hard about the serious issues of life, behave with others in ways that respected their inherent dignity as human beings created in the image of God even if we did not like them or what they did, and act continuously to make human lives better. The last piece of this explains why I have done so much scholarly work in Jewish ethics. It also explains why I have been so active in Jewish Family Service of Los Angeles, ultimately serving as its president, because that organization does acts of loving kindness for others in over sixty programs each and every day. I know that most Jews have grown up in environments that did not take Jewish law seriously, whereas others have experienced Jewish law as authoritative but also burdensome, anal, pointless, obsequious, and/or demeaning. Readers should know at the outset, then, that my theory grows out of a very different experience with Jewish law, a very happy and meaningful one in which Jewish law has immensely enriched my life, and it should not be

47

surprising that my theory reflects this. Given my background, read-ers should also understand how I take Jewish law seriously and even see it as being authoritative for my life but also think that we should apply our own sense of judgment to change it in the few places where the received law causes harm to people.

In this chapter, I will first indicate why I do not believe in one very popular legal model of law generally and of Jewish law in par-ticular—namely, legal positivism. Then I will spell out the first part of my own legal theory—namely, how Jewish law operates like an organism in ways that are parallel to, although not identical with, other legal systems. Then, in the next chapter, I will discuss the other side of my model, the part that makes it like a unique human soul—namely, the internal and interpersonal aspects of Jewish law—as I use the covenantal model to augment the organic one.

WHY I AM NOT A LEGAL POSITIVIST

This book's goal is to formulate my own theory of Jewish law. Sometimes it is helpful to understand something not only by seeing what it is, but also by understanding what it is not. I will thus clarify why I do not subscribe to one legal theory as applied to Jewish law—namely, Jewish law as a deductive system (a form of what is called legal positivism). I have chosen this as my illustration of what I do *not* assert both because lawyers as well as nonlawyers commonly think of law in a deductive way and also because my own theory is, in some ways, a distinct alternative to that theory. Legal positivism will, therefore, serve as a clear contrast to my own theory.

Probably the most explicit and sophisticated description of Jewish law as a deductive system is that of Joel Roth in his book *The Hal-akhic Process: A Systemic Analysis*[3] As the subtitle of his book indi-cates, Roth seeks to understand Jewish law as a deductive system, much like geometry, with foundational definitions and axioms and everything else—or almost everything else—following deductively from those. The beauty of such a system, of course, is that it is self-contained, and so if one accepts the premises and if a conclusion is validly deduced from those, then it follows with 100 percent certain-ty. That is a major lure of any deductive system: It promises order and certainty. Furthermore, because conclusions are connected in clear, deductive lines with the original grounds of the theory, if one accepts the authority of the foundations of the system, then one will see the conclusions from those grounds as authoritative as well. The twin advantages of order and authority explain why many people yearn to understand law (and not just Jewish law) in this way.

The continental European systems of law—as, for example, the French Napoleonic Code, the Prussian Code, and the codes governing France and Germany to this day—are largely deductive in their nature and functioning. That is, to know what the law is you consult the code; judges may make decisions based on the code, but it is the code—and therefore legislators—who hold ultimate legal authority, not judges. As my friend and teacher Rabbi Uziel Weingarten has suggested, this may explain why Ashkenazic legal writing during the last several centuries makes the individual rabbi's role as someone who could shape the law in new ways very limited because, similar to continental law, authority rests in the book rather than in the people using the book to decide cases. My basic claim is that that move is very problematic, that we need to interpret and apply Jewish law much more along the lines of talmudic and Anglo-American models.

Specifically, in contrast to code-based, continental law, both talmudic and Anglo-American law are mostly case based ("casuistic").[4] English law does not even have a constitution. American law does include a federal Constitution, state constitutions, and collections of legislated laws. In both English and American law, however, the meaning and application of laws (including the U.S. Constitution) is ultimately determined by the courts. In doing so, the courts can sharply narrow or expand the scope of the law, and they can even declare a law unconstitutional (according to either the federal or state constitution) and therefore null and void.

Roth chooses the former, continental model for his interpretation of Jewish law. He thus adopts what legal theorists describe as legal positivism—that is, the doctrine that the law is totally encompassed by what the legislators say it is in the law they posit (hence the term "legal positivism"). They may have had all kinds of reasons to enact a particular law—moral, social, economic, political, or simply the pressure of time—but none of that matters in interpreting and applying the law; what counts is what the law says. The only way that those factors can influence a judge is if there are two streams of legal precedents going in different directions; then the judge's own perspective on life may influence which of the streams he or she chooses to follow. That is what might happen in fact. In law, however, the judge's decision must be based on the authority of the legal precedents, not on his or her own personal convictions.

Roth's positivism is not as pure as that of some legal theorists because he introduces the notion of "extralegal" factors in determining the law and even in interpreting it. Like all positivists, however, Roth gives much less weight to these factors than to the stated law itself. This is evidenced by the very term he uses: by describing such factors as extralegal, he clearly asserts that for him they are, literally, *outside* the law.

Roth borrows the German term *"grundnorm"* from the legal theorist H. Kelsen[5] to name what Roth takes to be, the deductive ground for the Jewish legal system. In the opening pages of his book, he describes what he takes to be the grundnorm of Jewish law in three separate ways: (1) "The document called the Torah embodies the word and will of God, which it behooves man to obey, and is, therefore, authoritative"; (2) "The document called the Torah embodies the word and the will of God, which it behooves man to obey, as mediated through the agency of J, E, P, and D, and is, therefore, authoritative"; and (3) "The document called the Torah embodies the constitution promulgated by J, E, P, and D, which it behooves man to obey, and it is, therefore, authoritative." In the latter two formulations, Roth is taking into account modern biblical scholarship, according to which the text of the Torah that we have in hand was edited from (at least) four different sources, which scholars have designated J ("the Jahwist source," in which God is described by His proper name, the tetragrammaton), E ("the Elohist source," in which God is described by the generic word for God, *Elohim*); P (the priestly source), and D (the Deuteronomist). Roth's first articulation of the grundnorm asserts that God's will as articulated in the Torah is the source of authority of Jewish law, accepting as a faith statement that the Torah does in fact express God's will and leaving aside all questions of how the Torah was composed; the second articulation explicitly acknowledges J, E, P, and D as the mediators of God's will but continues to ground the authority of the Torah in God; and the third says that even if one has doubts about God's role in the creation of the Torah but accepts it as authoritative on other (presumably human) grounds, the Jewish legal system can still be completely authoritative and function as a system on that basis.

Some may fault Roth for admitting the second and, especially, the third possibility for his grundnorm, for those options seem to distance the authority of the Torah from God. I, however, see his alternatives as a distinct strength of his theory, for it then does not depend on any specific beliefs regarding God or the composition of the Torah. However one understands God—even if one is a complete atheist—and however one understands the Torah—from its being the direct and accurate transcription of the word of God to its being a totally human document—Jewish law is authoritative, according to Roth's theory, if one accepts the Torah as authoritative for whatever reason one has.

The grundnorm, though, is not all that one must accept to make all of Jewish law authoritative: one must also accept the methods by which Jewish law historically has interpreted and applied the Torah. After all, classical Reform thinkers (Abraham Geiger, J. W. Schorr, Kaufman Kohler, and so on) accepted the Torah as authoritative for its time but then maintained that revelation has progressed over the centuries and should now be interpreted by individual Jews according to their own conscience. One might even say, as the Karaites did, that the Torah is indeed the word of God but that it must be interpreted without the Oral Tradition. Or, as Christians and Muslims assert, one might say that the Torah is authoritative but later texts like the New Testament or the Koran are more authoritative. So Roth's theory involves some crucial extra steps that he clearly assumes but does not identify as part of his grundnorm—namely, that the Torah was and remains the sole basis for Jewish legal authority, where "Torah" here refers to both the Written and Oral Torah.

Although most Orthodox rabbis are also legal positivists, Roth's legal positivism is clearly not Orthodox in that he provides for biblical scholarship in defining his grundnorm. Virtually all Orthodox proponents of legal positivism (with David Hartman a prime exception) would insist that the Torah is the literal word of God as heard on Mount Sinai, and it is for that reason that the Torah has divine authority. Furthermore, Roth's divergence from Orthodox belief is evident in his recognition of factors other than the texts of the Torah and the Oral Torah that shape Jewish law. Although a few modern Orthodox thinkers (again, Hartman most specifically, but also Emanuel Rackman, Eliezer Berkovits, and others) would acknowledge this as well, most modern Orthodox leaders (such as Norman Lamm, J. David Bleich, Moshe Tendler, and Yeshayahu Leibovitz) would be wary of admitting such factors external to the texts of the tradition in interpreting it. Leibovitz, in particular, who, like Roth, sees Jewish law as a closed system, would see consideration of human factors outside the system as sullying the divine authority of the Torah. Orthodox rabbis might, of course, consult experts in modern science, economics, politics, and other areas to understand the issues that these disciplines raise for any given decision, but ultimately Orthodox rulings are based solely on applying the received texts to the current situation. Roth goes beyond this in acknowledging that at times the classical tradition itself introduced such elements into the decision-making process, sometimes even to the point of overturning received texts, as, for example, in maintaining— as some medieval rabbis do—that the Talmud's medical cures are not to be followed in other times and places. Roth provides a number of examples of such changes "because the times have changed" (*nishtanu ha-itim*) as well as other rationales for changing the received law. In doing so, and in recommending that modern rabbis do so as well, he sees himself, as he says, as one who must "persevere as a member of a minority"[6] that takes both Jewish law and these extralegal elements seriously.

Roth's theory is thus consciously more open than most Orthodox legal positivists are to considering influences outside the texts of the law on the shaping of the law historically and in our own time. Specifically, he describes four categories of such elements: (1) medical/scientific, (2) sociological/realia, (3) economic, and (4) ethical/psychological. Moreover, Roth maintains that even if such factors lead a contemporary rabbi to interpret the Torah itself at variance with the way it has been interpreted in the past, this would not undermine the grundnorm demanding allegiance to the Torah. Rabbis should clearly do such things only sparingly and carefully, lest the continuity and divine authority of the law be undermined; but when a contemporary rabbi interprets and applies Jewish law in a new way, the authority that adhered to the original rabbinic interpretation of the Torah now transfers to its contemporary understanding.

Even though Roth demonstrates the considerable scope that such factors have had in the past, he notes several limitations on their functioning. First, "our emphasis on the widespread use of extralegal factors in the halakhic system is in no way meant to imply that they play a part in every legal decision; there are many decisions reached on the basis of legal sources alone."[7]

Second, such factors—and the experts who know about them—do

THE BODY OF JEWISH LAW

not, in and of themselves, determine the law; only the rabbi does that. Rabbis may, and probably should, consider such expertise in their decisions, but Roth uses a vivid talmudic passage (B. Sanhedrin 75a) to point out that even if doctors affirm that a person's life is at stake, only rabbis can determine whether the remedy that the doctors are recommending accords with Jewish law. Thus the proper role for these extralegal factors is to help rabbis think about their decisions so that they might, for example, put more weight on a given stream of Jewish legal thinking rather than another when both appear within Jewish legal sources. So, to give my own example of how his theory would work in practice,[8] even though a strong case can be made, based on the Talmud's understanding of fetal development, to allow not only the "morning-after pill" but even abortifacients like RU486 that work as late as six or seven weeks after fertilization, the rabbi may want to forbid such pills because of the major demographic problem that the Jewish community is currently having. Whether the rabbi chooses to be lenient or stringent, however, is solely the rabbi's decision and not that of doctors, demographers, or even the woman herself.

Third, "it would seem to be true that the more systematically severe the legal procedure, the more reticent *posekim* are (and should be) to make use of extralegal material."[9] That is, the more a given extralegal factor would cause a disruption to the established legal system, the more serious the justification must be for using it to change the law and the more wary the rabbi should be in using it for that purpose.

The most important limitation on using these factors, though, is the very term Roth uses to describe them—"extralegal," outside the law. This immediately identifies the law with the received, written tradition. Other theorists of Jewish law, myself certainly included, would disagree with this completely, pointing to the oral nature of most of the tradition from its very origins and the immense role that custom, morality, economics, politics, and even style have played in the history of Jewish law, especially as Jews spread all over the world. As a result, despite Roth's conscientious effort to demonstrate the role of such extralegal elements in the law in the past, his theory seems to limit the scope and the methods of the law far too much to be historically accurate, and many would find his definition of Jewish law too narrow to form a wise basis for making Jewish legal decisions in our own time.

This is especially so because of another characteristic of Roth's system. Roth is very liberal in defining what the grundnorm is, allowing even those who believe the Torah to be a totally human document to count as accepting it as long as they also accept its legal authority. Those who do not accept that, however, are then completely out of the system; as with all deductive systems, you are either in or out, depending on whether you accept the definitions and premises. But in our own day, the vast majority of the world's Jews would be defined out of Roth's system from the very beginning. This is a major problem, not only because it makes Roth's theory irrelevant to the vast majority of the world's Jews but also because it leaves out many Jews who in fact practice Jewish law but not because they see the Torah as legally binding. From the point of view of the tradition, that is surely not optimal; in fact, there is a long debate within the tradition as to whether one must have the proper intention to fulfill one's legal duties or whether doing the action required is enough.[10] There are many Jews who keep kosher, some form of Shabbat, engage in Jewish study and social action, and so forth, but do so for many reasons other than accepting the legal authority of the Torah. They want any Jew to be able to eat in their homes; they like how Shabbat affects themselves and their family; they enjoy the intellectual give-and-take of Jewish sources or study them to deepen their ties to the tradition; they are morally committed to Jewish norms of social action. Roth's theory would include some Jews that classical sources would not—namely, those who do not see the Torah as divine but who accept the Torah as legally binding—but, more pervasively, it would exclude Jews who in fact abide by Jewish law to a great extent but for many other reasons. Roth's theory thus seems to be factually inadequate in leaving out many Jews who observe Jewish law and would be seen by others as observant. It also makes it very difficult to have a genuinely pluralistic discussion because only those who accept Roth's premise have a voice in shaping Jewish law, leaving out those who obey the law for other reasons.

Another objection to Roth's theory concerns his methodology. Although continental systems of law do indeed operate in much the way that Roth describes, Jewish law has historically been much closer to Anglo-American law in its methods. Although the Torah does include codes that govern the building of the sanctuary and sacrifices similar in style and comprehensiveness to European codes, its primary legal sections on other matters (especially Exod. 19–24 and Deut. 16–25) look much more like collections of judicial precedents. That becomes especially clear when one realizes, as biblical scholar Umberto Cassuto pointed out, that the Torah does not provide laws for many everyday occurrences, like how to conclude a business deal or how to get married. Moreover, the form of the Torah's laws is not always that of a complete statute. In particular, the Torah's laws do not always state the penalty to be imposed on the transgressor, as a complete law would; sometimes only an absolute command or prohibition is enjoined as an expression of God's will.

Contrariwise, sometimes the Torah adds the reason for the law, from a religious or ethical point of view, unlike the European continental codes mentioned earlier, which give no reasons. Moreover, the Pentateuch includes religious and ritual regulations alongside legal ordinances governing everyday life without differentiation, which is not the case in those legal codes. The Torah's ethical intent creates further disparity between it and standard legal codes. The entire concern of the aforementioned codes of European continental law is to determine what is due to a person according to the letter of the law, whereas the Torah seeks on many an occasion to go beyond strictly legal requirements and to grant people what is due them based on morality and the love that people should have for each other when seen as fellow Jews and even fellow human beings, since we all have one Father.[11]

For these reasons, Cassuto describes the Torah's collection of laws as "only notes on the existing laws" that were part of the king's laws, the oral tradition, and the accepted customs of biblical society. Furthermore, Menachem Elon, former chief justice of the Supreme Court of Israel and creator of the curriculum in Jewish law in Israeli law schools, has pointed out that systematic codes never fared very well in Jewish legal history, for as much as their authors specifically intended to make Jewish law clear and indisputable, the major codes of Jewish law are all published with numerous commentaries, limitations, and objections surrounding them, thus indicating that Jewish law is not nearly as systematic as Maimonides, Yosef Karo, or Roth have tried to make it out to be. As Elon says with reference to Maimonides' *Mishneh Torah*:

It would be difficult to find in all of halakhic literature another instance of a work that produced results so contrary to the avowed purpose of its author. Far from restoring to the halakhah its uniformity and anonymity, "without polemics or dissection . . . but in clear and accurate statements" (Mishneh Torah, Introduction), Maimonides' pursuit of that very aim became the reason for the compilation of hundreds of books on his work, all of them dissecting, complicating and increasing halakhic problems, resulting in a lack of uniformity far greater than before.[12]

Indeed, virtually every page of the Talmud is one argument after another, hardly the tone or product of a group that thinks in terms of established, defined, deductive, and authoritative legal systems. Rather, the history of Jewish law from its very beginnings in the Torah has been much more casuistic in nature, with all the unsystematic chaos that this entails. Even when the Mishnah gives a few examples of a legal principle and then says, "this is the general rule" (*zeh ha-kelal*), the Talmud often rejects even that amount of systematization by claiming that the Mishnah is actually referring to another case that you would not have known from the previous ones.[13] The Talmud goes further: it states as a general principle, in the name of Rabbi Yohanan, that "we may not learn [that is, derive legal conclusions in specific cases] from general rules, even when those rules specify exceptions."[14] In rejecting a systematic approach, Jewish law loses the clarity and neatness that a system would have, but, like most Anglo-American law, it gains a much clearer connection to reality and to the way that law actually functions in societies.

Another serious drawback of Roth's theory affects all forms of legal positivism: If the law is identified with texts, and if all considerations outside those texts are extralegal, and therefore secondary in authority and import, change will happen very slowly, if at all. It is all the more unlikely that those who adopt this theory would be proactive in adapting Jewish law to the needs of modern times. Indeed, in one area in which Roth himself tried to be proactive, in advocating for women to be ordained as rabbis, he was able to find sources within the tradition that could be read to validate a woman's acceptance of commandments from which she is normally exempt as sufficiently powerful legally to enable a man listening to her lead services to fulfill his obligations to pray by saying amen to her blessings. The only way Roth could imagine removing the barriers in traditional Jewish law preventing women serving as witnesses, though, was through a *takkanah*, a conscious change of the system as it has come down to us.[15] In that same rabbinic ruling and in his subsequent book, however, he worries that those who would make such a change lack the legal authority to do so,[16] and that stance, of course, makes such changes completely impossible.

Finally, with Roth's understanding of the nature of the law, there can be no serious moral or social critique of the law. Instead, either the law is accepted forever as the criterion of what it means to be moral or it loses any claim to morality. Those are clearly results that Roth tries to avoid by introducing his extralegal category, but in the end, his classification of morality as extralegal makes it far too weak a component of Jewish law if it is indeed to be what a moral God demands of us. This was clearly in evidence, for example, in his method for justifying the ordination of women, by which he based his argument solely on what he could find in precedents without mentioning morality as even one of several motivating factors for the change, in sharp contrast to, for example, the approaches of Rabbis Robert Gordis and Simon Greenberg.[17]

In the end, to understand the problems with this kind of deductive approach, one must remember what the Rabbis of the Talmud and Midrash knew full well—namely, that texts must be interpreted and applied and that in doing so rabbis make choices. Most of the classical Rabbis probably followed Rabbi Akiva in affirming both that the revelation at Mount Sinai was in discreet, Hebrew words and that the Torah that we have in hand is an accurate transcription of that revelation, rather than Rabbi Ishmael's view that only general rules were given at Sinai.[18] They nevertheless maintained that the Jewish tradition was not going to be literalist, for "there are seventy faces to the Torah."[19] Therefore one cannot base law on the text of the Torah itself but must rather use the Sages' interpretation of it in each generation, for "one cannot give a proper decision from the words of the Torah, for the Torah is shut up [cryptic and therefore ambiguous] and consists entirely of headings. . . . From the words of the Sages, however, one can derive the proper law because they explain the Torah."[20] Thus even the classical Rabbis maintain that the Torah must be interpreted by the rabbis of each generation. This process inevitably involves judgment, for the text of the Torah is generally not monolithic and often not even clear in its meaning. That is, rabbis' construction and application of the halakhah is a choice of a path taken; and that choice is inevitably, and correctly, made with the moral, social, and economic implications of the various possible ways to rule in mind.

Justice Oliver Wendell Holmes made a similar point about American law. Judges do not and cannot make important decisions simply by "doing their sums right"—that is, by merely citing precedents or scientific data. Rather, in what Justice Benjamin Cardozo later called "the serious business cases of the law," where the issue is not one of fact (who owes whom money, who killed a person) but of law (that is, how the law should be determined when it could be construed or applied in several different ways), judges inevitably invoke the entire panoply of their worldview, their values, and their goals:

> I once heard a very eminent judge say that he never let a decision go until he was absolutely sure that it was right. So judicial dissent often is blamed, as if it meant simply that one side or the other were not doing their sums right, and, if they would take more trouble, agreement inevitably would come.
>
> This mode of thinking is entirely natural. The training of lawyers is a training in logic. The processes of analogy, discrimination, and deduction are those in which they are most at home. The language of judicial decision is mainly the language of logic. And the logical method and form flatter that longing for certainty and for repose which is in every human mind.
>
> But certainty generally is an illusion, and repose is not the destiny of man. Behind the logical form lies a judgment as to the relative worth and importance of competing legislative grounds, often an inarticulate and unconscious judgment, it is true, and yet the very root and nerve of the whole proceeding. You can give any conclusion a logical form. You always can imply a condition in a contract. But why do you imply it? It is because of some belief as to the practice of the community or of a class, or because of some opinion as to policy, or, in short, because of some attitude of yours upon a matter not capable of exact quantitative measurement, and therefore of founding exact logical conclusions. Such matters really are battle grounds where the means do not exist for determinations that shall be good for all time, and where the decision can do no more than embody the preference of a given body in a given time and place. . . . No concrete proposition is self-evident, no matter how ready we may be to accept it. . . .
>
> It is revolting to have no better reason for a rule of law than that it was laid down in the time of Henry IV. It is still more revolt-

ing if the grounds upon which it was laid down have vanished long since, and the rule simply persists from blind imitation of the past.[21]

Nobody doing Euclidean geometry speaks in terms of the choices to which Holmes refers. The proof is either valid or it is not. That is why advocates of a deductive approach to law must assert that those who come to another conclusion must be wrong because they "were not doing their sums right."

This is indeed what Roth asserts about the alternative approaches to homosexuality that were proposed to the Conservative movement's Committee on Jewish Law and Standards on December 6, 2006. After arguing against the alternatives that would have permitted rabbis to perform commitment ceremonies for homosexuals and Conservative seminaries to ordain homosexuals as rabbis, he then wrote, "What is at stake here, for me, and I believe for the Committee on Jewish Law and Standards as a body, is whether the Law Committee can continue to be seen as an halakhic decision-making body"[22]—that is, that none of the other approaches could claim to be within the bounds of Jewish law as he conceives it, that it was "his way or the highway"— and then he resigned from the committee when one of the permissive rulings was adopted along with his. To his credit, on other matters he has been a defender of halakhic pluralism for a very long time. In that pluralism, though, he was acting differently from the way his philosophical model would suggest, for if law is really deductive, then there should be only one right answer, just as there is in Euclidean geometry.[23] In this case, though, he remained consistent with his theory in claiming that no pathway from the received tradition could be justified other than his, despite the other papers that claimed to create just such a linkage to the received tradition to permit commitment ceremonies and ordination for homosexuals, including one that garnered the same number of votes as his did.

Moreover, in his paper he indicates quite clearly the secondary place that extralegal considerations hold in determining the law:

Is theology the dog which wags the tail called halakhah, or is halakhah the dog which wags the tail called theology? It cannot be both ways.

There can be no real doubt that normatively speaking the halakhic tradition is the given, and theology is required to fall into place behind it. Theology can, indeed, should, provide the narrative which makes the halakhic tradition intellectually persuasive and emotionally acceptable and satisfying, and that narrative can change as needed, and it need not be the same for everyone. . . . Whatever narrative works is fine, so long as the narrative does not reverse which is the dog and which is the tail.[24]

But if the law is not a deductive system but rather a living organism, then, in fact, every system within it will influence every other system, and sometimes one will be determinative and sometimes another will be (for example, your reproductive system or your digestive system in stimulating growth; your immune system or your respiratory system in identifying and treating breathing problems), and so sometimes the law will override theology (or moral, economic, social, or political concerns), sometimes the reverse will happen, and sometimes (most of the time, we hope) they will pull in the same direction. Jewish law has been and continues to be applied deductively in the vast majority of cases, when the question is simply a straightforward application of clear precedent to a particular case. In the "serious business cases" of Jewish law, however—that is, when any of several possible precedents might be invoked, leading to different results; when no precedent exists because of new developments that previous rabbis could never have imagined (e.g., embryonic stem cell research); or when clear precedent does exist but raises major moral, theological, social, economic, or political problems— rabbis have not reasoned deductively in the way Roth's theory describes. They rather have given—and should give—much greater weight to the considerations that he calls extralegal than his deductive model permits. To capture both the ongoing, direct applications of previous Jewish law and its innovative, revisionary rulings over the ages and in our own time, we must abandon the deductive model and think of Jewish law instead as a living organism—the model that I will now develop.

JEWISH LAW AS A LIVING ORGANISM

Because Jewish law functions not only in the world of theory but also in the real world, it has many features that enable it to work in that world. As a living legal system, it is much more like living organisms than it is like rocks. The Latin term captures this aspect of the law: it is a *corpus juris*, a body of law. In fact, law is simply one expression of a particular culture, and human cultures in all their parts resemble living organisms in many ways. Further, because Jewish law is very much shaped by its internal perceptions and values, among organisms it is most like a human being. As noted earlier, the remainder of this chapter will explore the similarities between Jewish law and the human body, and the next chapter will discuss the soul of Jewish law.

There are several features of the human body that will be most suggestive to understand the functioning of Jewish law in the past and how it should function now:

1. Change: Its Existence, Rate, Functions, and Methods

With the possible exception of our brain cells and a woman's egg cells, all of the cells in the human body not only change with time but actually die and are replaced. Some, like skin cells, change very rapidly: We lose thousands of skin cells every day and gain thousands more. Near the other end of the spectrum, bone cells change much more slowly, and thus a bone break takes months to heal. Some injuries, such as a severed spinal cord, cannot be repaired at all, at least with current medical techniques. Most of our cells change at rates in between these two extremes. After one donates a pint of blood, for example, one's red blood cells replenish themselves within about two months, and so one can (and should!) safely donate blood four or five times a year. Platelets replenish themselves much more rapidly, and so one can donate platelets for cancer patients every three or four days, if that is needed, and certainly every month. Molecules replace themselves even more rapidly than cells do.

These changes are critical not only for the ongoing life of the organism but also for its functioning. One must become an adult, for example, in order to be able to reproduce. The changes in our neural connections and arrangements that occur over time are the basis for our new experiences, learning, attitudes, and memories.

The analogy to Jewish law is clear. Jewish law, like any legal system, has historically added, subtracted, and modified specific laws, and it continues to do so today. Sometimes this happens intentionally and officially when a rabbi writes a responsum (*teshuvah*) that narrows or broadens precedents or applies them in new ways. It occurs most dramatically when rabbis intentionally and publicly institute a change in the law (*takkanah*). The equivalent in my analogy would be a clear direction in the DNA of a person to grow or destroy some tissue or even a decision and plan of action by a person to lose weight when that is followed by a successful and significant diet.

At other times, modifications of Jewish law happen more haphazardly through changes in circumstance or custom. These include customs that add new practices (such as Holocaust Remembrance Day, Israel Independence Day), modify old ones (for example, performing a wedding right after betrothal rather than waiting a year, as the Mishnah prescribes[25]), and drop others as laws and customs fall into disuse for one reason or another (such as many of the Mishnah's requirements for business transactions when Jews found themselves in countries that handled business matters differently). My point here is simply that change has occurred in a variety of ways in Jewish law, just as it does in organisms; in both cases we are talking about living organisms, the nature of which is not static but dynamic.

Moreover, some changes in the human body are sudden and striking ("metamorphic" in that sense), although most are slow and evolutionary. Metamorphic changes include birth, puberty, pregnancy, the loss of a faculty or limb through an injury or accident, and death. Some important changes in the human organism do not change its form (in that sense are not metamorphic) but nevertheless significantly change the nature of how the organism functions as new stages of organic development take place—walking, toilet training, first ejaculation or menstruation, and menopause. Some significant changes occur because of both organic development and social influences—speaking, increasingly sophisticated interactions with others, reading, abstract thinking, moral development, and so on. Social institutions are often constructed in recognition of these major changes, including religious ceremonies to mark life-cycle events, legal definitions of the age of responsibility before the law, and, at least until recently, mandatory retirement ages.

Most modifications of the human organism, however, occur slowly, often so slowly that nobody notices them. That is why it is hard, if not impossible, to feel any difference in yourself the day before and the day of any birthday, despite the fact that you are now officially a year older. Still, these organic and developmental changes are real and significant, and so one often does recognize them between now and last year or between now and 5 or 10 years ago.

The same holds true for Jewish law. Some changes are sudden and metamorphic in that they change the shape and nature of Judaism. For example, after the destruction of the Second Temple, Rabbi Yohanan ben Zakkai issued nine legislative changes (*takkanot*) to shift Judaism radically from a religion centered on sacrifices in the Temple in Jerusalem to one centered in the synagogue.[26] Similarly, modern developments have brought about sudden and significant changes in how people approach questions such as respect for privacy (how does that work on the Internet?), honoring parents (when is a nursing home acceptable?), and maintaining life (when, if ever, may we detach someone from a life-support system?).

More commonly, we are not thrust into new situations requiring immediate response but gradually evolve into them, and the law follows suit. It took a full century for social and educational developments in both the Jewish and non-Jewish communities to make women equal to men in American law, and this has yet to happen fully in Jewish law and practice in the Orthodox world and even in places in the Conservative movement. Women still strive for equality in the workplace and in society generally.

This example also illustrates that evolutionary changes ebb and flow, with changes in one direction in one area often producing other changes in the same or another area in the opposite direction—more or less Newton's Third Law of Motion (For every action there is an equal and opposite reaction) applied to the organic and legal spheres. Thus, even as the effort to equalize salaries for women doing the same jobs as men continues, the opposite concern now affects education, in which boys as a group are consistently doing worse than girls. In fact, American universities, whose students a generation ago were predominantly men, are now populated by a majority of women and are finding it hard to recruit academically qualified men. Similarly, in the Jewish arena it has taken many Jews and Jewish institutions some time to adjust to women taking on new roles in the synagogue and in Jewish life generally, and men are still trying to define their roles in this changing environment. This has produced a renewed interest in men's spirituality and in synagogue men's clubs. Although some of these developments in gender roles in Jewish life have resulted from specific decisions in Jewish law, most of them, as

I discuss at some length in Chapter Seven, have occurred through changing customs. This pattern of slow, evolutionary change in Jewish law, punctuated by occasional, profound changes, parallels the functioning of living organisms.

2. Internal and External Influences on the Law

Some organic changes are internally generated. The genes, DNA, and other parts of a human being lead to specific developments according to a timetable that is itself inborn. That is what makes it possible for scientists to describe normal development in human beings, physically, mentally, morally, and in the tasks they are able to do, from birth through the teenage years into adulthood in its various stages. For example, the ability to walk, which is truly amazing when one thinks about it, is nevertheless expected of a child, usually in the first half of the second year of life. Further, exactly when the child will walk seems completely independent of the degree of parental involvement in the process; the child just begins to walk when he or she is ready to do that. Although nutrition undoubtedly plays a role in growth patterns and the onset of puberty, these developments too seem to be caused primarily by the person's genetic structure.

Other changes in organisms, however, stem mainly from factors external to the organism itself. Physically, a lack of water or food will prompt animals to abandon their homes to seek sustenance elsewhere. It may also make animals much more bellicose, as they fight for scarce resources. In fact, we adjust daily to viruses and bacteria of all sorts, seek to protect ourselves against other physical dangers to our lives or welfare (such as extreme heat or cold, hurricanes, earthquakes, tornadoes, poisonous plants,), and use parts of the environment to sustain ourselves and enhance our lives.

For humans, it is not only the physical environment that produces changes, but the social, moral, and cultural context as well. A person's community and culture have an immense influence on what he or she sees as important or trivial and as acceptable, forbidden, or desirable. Indeed, the process of growing up is not just a physical event, but an educational, social and moral one, in which the person's society does its best to implant its own concepts and values in its young. This continues through adulthood, as communities play an extensive role in shaping adult behavior. Think, for example, of the varying degrees to which Judaism, Christianity, Islam, Buddhism, and Hinduism encourage or discourage individuals to engage in independent thinking—and the varying degrees to which Western, Arabic, Chinese, and Indian cultures do that.

Moreover, groups of animals are influenced not only by the other members of their own herd but by other groups of animals of the same species to the extent that they come into contact with them. Because of a superior ability to communicate, this is particularly true of human beings. Especially in the context of modern communication and transportation but even in the past, when less interaction of nations occurred, human communities and cultures have always influenced each other.

Individuals react to the influences of their own community, and communities react to the influence of other cultures, in different ways. Sometimes individuals rebel against their community's norms with all their might. Similarly, sometimes communities do all they can to resist the influence of another culture. At the other end of the spectrum, many individuals assimilate completely into their own culture and may become intensely loyal to it as they become convinced of its view of the world and do what they can to defend it. On a communal level, at times one culture blends completely into another. Most often, though, both individuals and cultures will eclectically accept some aspects of the external influences on them and reject others. Even when individuals or communities do this, they may shape the new view or behavior in their own distinctive way.

Law definitely follows this organic pattern of change due to both internal and external influences, and Jewish law is no exception. Some developments in Jewish law are at least primarily, if not exclusively, the product of the initial texts and concepts of the tradition found in the Bible. So, for example, biblical laws demanding that adults learn the tradition and teach it to their children (Deut. 4:9, 6:6–7, 11:18–19, 31:10–13) quite naturally produced ways in which Jews could fulfill those demands, including the practice of reading the Torah publicly four times each week. Ultimately, when it became clear that many adults did not know how to teach it or did not know enough about the tradition to transmit it well to their children, Jews created schools:

Rabbi Judah said in the name of Rav: Rabbi Joshua ben Gamla should be remembered for good, for had it not been for him the Torah would have been forgotten in Israel. At first, the boy who had a father was taught Torah by him, while the boy who had no father did not learn. Later, they appointed teachers of boys in Jerusalem, and the boys who had fathers were brought by them [to the teachers] and were taught; those who had no fathers were still not brought. So then they decreed that teachers should be appointed in every district, and they brought to them lads of the age of sixteen or seventeen. And when the teacher was cross with any of the lads, the lad would kick at him and run away. So then Rabbi Joshua ben Gamla ordered that teachers should be appointed in every district and in every city and that the boys should be sent to them at the age of six or seven years.[27]

Even some radical changes in Jewish law undoubtedly grew out of some of the ideas and laws embedded in the tradition from the beginning. For example, although the Torah prescribes the death penalty for many violations of the law, including not only violent acts like murder and rape but also such infractions as breach of the Sabbath and practicing idolatry,[28] the Rabbis introduced so many restrictions on these laws and so many evidentiary requirements that they themselves say that "A court that has put a person to death once in seven years is called "a hanging court" [literally, "a destructive court"].[29] Another rabbi in that Mishnah immediately accuses his fellow rabbis "of multiplying murderers in Israel," presumably because he thought that capital punishment deters crime, but in the end the majority shaped the law to make a capital conviction all but impossible to achieve.

Why did they do that? In part, no doubt, because they did not want to take the responsibility of taking a life, for they were well aware of the limited knowledge that judges have of any given case (a factor very much in evidence in our own times as many capital convictions are overturned on the basis of new DNA evidence). They thus say this:

Two people once came to be tried before Rabbi Jose bar Halafta. They said to him, "[We agree to be tried by you] on the condition that you try us in accordance with strict law." He answered, "I do not know the strict law, and in any event, only He who knows man's thoughts [God] is able to punish those people who make false statements." When a person would come to Rabbi Akiva with a lawsuit, he used to say to them (the litigants), "Know before whom you stand, before Him who spoke and the world came into being, as it is written, 'the case of both parties shall come before God' (Exodus 22:8), (implying) but not before Akiva ben Joseph." It was taught: Forty years prior to the destruction of the Temple capital punishment was abolished, and in the days of Simeon ben Shetah civil suits were abolished. Said Rabbi Simeon bar Yohai: "Blessed be the Lord that I am not wise enough to act as judge."[30]

Another factor in this development derived from their strong conviction of the sanctity of human life, expressed especially in the early chapters of Genesis (1:27, 5:1, 9:6) that we are created in the image of God. That conviction is reflected in the Rabbis' ruling that a man without children of his own was eligible to judge a capital case,[31] presumably because his lack of experience in having children makes him insufficiently appreciative of the value of human life. Children bring a renewed sense of the preciousness of life, both that of the victim, in the case of someone accused of murder, and that of the culprit.

Some developments in Jewish law, however, are not primarily the result of concepts and convictions within the Jewish tradition but rather emerge from outside influences. For example, as comparative studies reveal, much of biblical and talmudic commercial law is based on how other nations in the region arranged to seal a deal, rent a house, or do other business. Ultimately, Jewish law recognized this openly when the 3rd-century sage Samuel gave permission to merchants to ignore Jewish law in declaring that in regard to business dealings, "the law of the land is the law."[32] Similarly, the fact that Rabbenu Gershom banned polygamy for Ashkenazic Jews beginning in the 10th century was undoubtedly because Jews began living in large numbers among Christians who also prohibited it; Sephardic Jews, in contrast, who lived primarily among Muslims, continued to allow polygamy, just as Muslims did.

Finally, as in biology, most developments in Jewish law are the product of both nature and nurture—that is, factors both internal and external to the organism itself. To take the last example, although it was clearly living among Christians or Muslims that determined for Ashkenazic and Sephardic rabbis whether they would permit polygamy, the move to ban it also had internal roots in the talmudic

Rabbis' insistence that a man who married more than one wife had to fulfill his financial and sexual responsibilities to each of them separately,[33] thus making polygamy quite burdensome for the man. This talmudic requirement—and, indeed, the Rabbis' expansion of what a man owes his wife through the vehicle of the wedding contract (ketubbah)[34]—were, in turn, undoubtedly rooted in the biblical view that both men and women were created in the image of God.

These same roots of respect for women (as well as men) in biblical and talmudic sources, documented fully in Judith Hauptman's book, Rereading the Rabbis,[35] were important grounds also for the decisions in the Reform, Reconstructionist, and Conservative movements in the 1970s and 1980s to ordain women and to extend to them both the right and the responsibility to take a fully equal role with men in synagogue services and in synagogue life. These internal foundations, however, were not the only motivating factor for equalizing the role of women in Jewish life, for if they were, women would have been rabbis and active lay leaders long ago. The non-Orthodox movements used these sources as grounds to ordain women and expand their role in the synagogue only when at least two external factors existed: (1) that in the 20th century girls and then women for the first time began to receive the same Jewish education that boys and men did and (2) that feminism became a major force in American society, beginning with Betty Friedan's 1963 book, The Feminine Mystique. These internal and external factors have even produced some limited changes favorable to women in some Orthodox communities, including their synagogues, schools, and organizational structures.

This continuing interaction between received Jewish law with both internal and external factors is the reason that Joel Roth's claim that law must be the dog wagging the tail of theology cannot be right. It is rather that Jewish law, theology, morality, and political, social, technological, scientific, and economic developments in the Jewish community and in the larger communities within which Jews live are all intertwined, and each affects each other in critical ways on an ongoing basis. It is true that some features of the Jewish legal organism will be more persistent than others, just as our bone structure changes more slowly than our skin cells do. In that sense I myself would claim, as Roth does, that Jewish law needs to be changed, if at all, slowly and deliberately. Moreover, just as it is hard to recognize someone whose bone structure has changed rapidly (teenagers growing a foot in a year, for example), so too radical changes in Jewish law make it hard to recognize Jewish practice as Jewish, as having any sense of identity with what Jews did in the past. Therefore significant changes in Jewish law do need to be considered even more thoroughly and deliberately than smaller changes. At the same time, however, just as the hormonal system leads to the metamorphic growth during the teenage years and just as external, environmental events can lead to someone losing a limb, so too all features of the Jewish tradition and of the broader world in which Jews live are involved in these changes, and any one of them can produce a metamorphic change. Conversely, Jewish law does and should affect how we Jews think, feel, and act in our theology, morality, politics, social action, economics, and even in our science (e.g., in honestly reporting research results, even when they are disappointing). These ongoing interactions of all parts of the Jewish experience and their effect on any one of them, including Jewish law, are an important part of what it means for Jewish law to be a living legal system.

3. Resistance to Outside Factors

The processes by which legal systems assimilate influences from outside sources may be compared to an organism learning to live with only those nutrients it finds in its environment or adjusting to the weather patterns common in a particular area. In contrast, sometimes legal systems actively resist outside influences. They do everything in their power to defend themselves against such influences, similar to the defense mechanisms built into every animal's body to protect it from prey or other dangers.

This too can be easily demonstrated in the history and contemporary practice of Jewish law. The Hanukkah story as told in the Book of Maccabees is clearly one example of the Jewish community militarily fighting off Hellenistic influences, including both Greek beliefs and practices. Another example of defending Judaism from outside culture—this time using the law to do the work—is the set of 18 decrees that the Rabbis of the houses of Hillel and Shammai established in the first century C.E. to prevent socializing between Jews and Gentiles, lest it lead to Jews assimilating into the Roman culture, abandoning their Jewish commitments, and ultimately intermarrying and practicing idolatry.[36]

In modern times, with Jews intermingling with non-Jews much more pervasively and marrying non-Jews at high rates, many Jewish leaders have engaged in various forms of outreach to intermarried couples while still doing what they can to discourage intermarriage in the first place. Some, though, especially among the Orthodox, have resisted all change in this matter, making conversion to Judaism very hard, if not impossible. Some Orthodox Jews also isolate themselves in their own communities (for example, Kiryas Joel in Monroe, New York) and dress in the black garb of Polish gentry of the 18th century so as to reject modern culture as staunchly and as graphically as possible.

Outright rejection of the outside world and invoking all of one's defenses against it is frankly a questionable way to sustain the life of Jewish law; after all, animals and other organisms rarely succeed in continuously warring against the elements of their environment. Certainly, though, some element of resistance is a common phenomenon as both organisms and cultures seek to maintain their own integrity. The trick is striking a balance between assimilating to the outside environment or culture and asserting one's own distinctiveness. With animals, this happens primarily, or perhaps purely, on the level of instinct; with humans, deciding what influences to welcome or reject, to what extent, and how all are matters of judgment, often one that is difficult to make. Such decisions, in fact, test the mettle of both a society and its leaders, for nothing less than the future of the society and its culture is at stake.

4. Identity

Identity is the other side of the picture from the characteristics that I noted in the sections above. Despite the fact that organisms change regularly in response to both internal and external forces, we still think that they are the same in important ways—the same tree, the same dog, the same person. Moreover, if the organism is conscious, it has a sense of its own identity through all the changes it experiences.

What, though, makes any given organism the same organism through all these changes? A second, separate but related question specifically for conscious animals like humans, is this: What gives the organism a sense of identity through all these changes? That is, on what grounds do I have the conviction that I am the same person I was when I was a boy or even 10 years ago, even though many things have changed since then in my body, let alone my activities, relationships, thoughts, and feelings?

These and many other conundrums about identity are discussed at length in several fields of philosophy, most especially in logic and philosophy of mind.[37] For our purposes, suffice it to say that our untutored sense of a person's identity combines factors of both body and mind. Normally, we identify Max as Max when we see the body we have known as Max and find that when we interact with him, he has the same characteristics that we have come to expect in him. Problems arise in our identification of Max only when one or more of these factors go awry—when there are major and sudden changes to his body or mind, or when he responds in a way that, given our previous experience with Max, completely mystifies us. Much earlier in his life, let us say, Max lacked seriousness about anything intellectual, and suddenly a high school or college teacher piqued his interests, and Max suddenly became an A student. Or perhaps Max was a vibrant, intellectually alive, gregarious adult but now suffers from dementia. Even then, if either the body or the personality is recognizably the same as the one we knew as Max, we adjust our image of him but still call him Max.

The same factors apply to Jewish law. Jewish law has changed substantially from the time of the earliest biblical texts to our own time. It is still recognizable to both Jews and non-Jewish observers as Jewish law, however, in part because most of the changes that have occurred have happened gradually, and those that were metamorphic could be expected in an organism like a legal system. To use a metaphor suggested by Robert Cover,[38] the Jewish legal tradition has been an ongoing narrative in which each new chapter is an understandable continuation of the previous chapter, even if the story could have continued in other ways and even if, in later moments, the characters of the story and their interactions become quite different from what they were at the beginning. Moreover, with all the changes, one can still recognize some of the same content and underlying concepts that have characterized the DNA of Jewish law from the beginning.

What, though, gives Max a sense of himself? That is, how does Max understand his own identity, especially as all his physical, mental, emotional, and conative factors change over time as well as his activities and friendships?

There are at least three factors in Max's self-identity. First, except for the metamorphic changes mentioned earlier, his body changes slowly, and so an important element in his sense of self is tied to his body—the one he sees in the mirror each morning and feels throughout the day. As he gets a sense of others, he can even understand his continuing identity through metamorphic changes, for he can see (and be told by his parents) that others are, for example, beginning to use the toilet, attending school for the first time, or going through puberty.

A second factor is his memory of his past and his identification with it. That memory is not continuous, for he loses consciousness each night as he sleeps. Yet, when he awakes, he has a distinct sense that today is a continuation of his yesterday, that what he remembers thinking, feeling, and doing yesterday and during many yesterdays past will affect him today and through his future and that, further, there is a distinct "he" who is remembering all these things and creating new experiences and memories each day.

Finally, a third important element in his sense of identity stems from his recognition that others see him as the same person that they knew in the past, they call him by the same name, and they expect that their interactions with him today will reflect their interactions with him in the past. These three factors—bodily integrity, mental and emotional connectedness with his past, and social expectations about who Max is—all contribute to giving both Max and his community a sense of who he is and what kind of person he is.

The same three factors affect Jewish law. Although specific laws change over time, the body of the law (*corpus juris*) must remain largely the same through time for the law to function as law—that is, for the law to provide the people living by it knowledge of what they can expect of others and what others can expect of them. Without that continuity, people would live in constant fear that they could be accused and punished for something they did not know violated the law, and they would never be able to trust that the community would support them in demanding that others, for example, honor their contracts.

Sometimes, though, radical changes in society require major changes in the law. Physical insults to the society—war, drought, hurricanes—often require emergency legislation (the draft, curfews, rationing), and technological developments make new law necessary (on Internet privacy, end-of-life decisions in the context of new medical technology, ownership of embryos). Jewish law has experienced in the past and is experiencing today just such major changes. All of the laws governing the Temple rites—a full third of the Mishnah—ceased functioning with the destruction of the Second Temple in 70 C.E. Although the underlying commitment to having a spiritual life did not change, its form changed completely from sacrifices to prayer. Similarly, the rules governing the transfer of ownership of movable objects as stated in the Talmud require the actual transfer of the object to the domain of the buyer before the deal is legally sealed, but by the Middle Ages a handshake was enough to do that.[39] These examples are the equivalent of performing a lobotomy on the Jewish legal corpus, excising a major piece of it, and, in the case of Jewish commercial law, replacing it with something else. On the other hand, Jewish legal norms governing medical procedures at the beginning and end of life have increased exponentially over the last 50 years as major medical breakthroughs have raised new questions. This is analogous to the kind of rapid growth that people experience during puberty. Even such radical eliminations or replacements of old laws or introductions of whole new areas of the law can be understood both by the members of the society and by those outside it through comparisons to other societies going through similar circumstances. Still, most of the laws must remain the same from year to year for people both to be able to recognize and identify it as Jewish law and for Jews to have a sense that their legal system is indeed the same that it has always been, despite a few major changes and more ongoing, minor alterations of it.

This sense is strengthened through a community's memory of its laws. A large part of the authority of both law and custom is the memory that people have of always having done it (whatever it is) this way. Part of the power of a traditional wedding ceremony, for example, is the knowledge that your parents, grandparents, and their ancestors all followed the same procedures. Couples certainly may and do add to that ceremony to give it their own distinctive flavor, but experiments in the 1970s to create completely new ceremonies largely failed for lack of a sense of continuity.[40] In many areas of the law, it is not only the authority of the law but its claim to justice that depends on the community's consciousness of continuity. Without a specific change in the law that everyone knows or can discover through public media and to which everyone is subject, it would be grossly unfair, for example, to punish a person for a crime today in a radically different way from that applied to people who have committed the same crime in the past. Similarly, unless the parties to a business deal specifically agreed to another arrangement, courts judging commercial disputes must presume that the parties intended that the rules that generally govern such business dealings would apply to theirs as well; to rule otherwise would be unfair to one or both of the parties, for both of them have a right to expect that the commonly accepted customs in their society would apply to them.

Thus communal memory and the continuity, authority, and justice it brings with it are important factors in enabling people to identify a body of law through changes in its substance: specifically, it is the set of laws recognized as authoritative and practiced by a group of people whose membership changes as people are born, convert, and die but who see themselves as part of the same group (in the case of Jewish law, Jews) whose lives have been and continue to be shaped by that body of law. In addition, communal memory enables that group of people to have a sense of their own identity, for it links them and their perspectives, values, and practices to those who have believed and done many of the same things in the past.

Finally, a society's legal system is also identified by how it perceives the laws of other nations and, on the other hand, how other communities perceive its laws. American immigration laws, for example, provide for refugee status for those who would be unfairly prosecuted in other countries. Conversely, many countries with no capital punishment refuse to extradite their citizens to states within the United States that do execute people. A recent U.S. Supreme Court case on executing minors included a sharp difference of opinion between Justice Kennedy and Justice Scalia on the advisability of considering the moral standards built into other Western legal systems in deciding matters in American law.[41] On the other hand, despite the fact that there are cases in which one country looks askance on the laws of another, at least in a given area of the law, most countries recognize and treat as legally binding the marriages and commercial contracts that take place validly in other nations. Part of a community's identity and its sense of itself as the same throughout changes in its life and its laws, then, comes from how others perceive it and how its members perceive others as being distinct from themselves.

5. Periods of Relative Rest and Activity

Every organism has periods of relative rest and activity. Comparing an animal's sleeping vs. waking hours each day is one clear example of this, as are hormonal and activity fluctuations throughout the day (for example, postprandial, afternoon sluggishness), but one can even see this pattern of behavior at various periods of a person's life. The changes that occur, for example, between a human being's birth and his or her 1st birthday are truly breathtaking, much more dramatic than those that occur, say, between a person's 30th and 31st year of life.

Legal systems manifest the same pattern. In Jewish law, one immediately thinks of the eras when the classic texts of Jewish law were written as times of great activity—the Torah, the Mishnah, the Talmud, Maimonides' *Mishneh Torah*, Karo's Shulhan Arukh. On the other hand, other periods were less productive, even though responsa and other legal materials continued to be written at those times. Just as growth does not cease in an animal during sleep or periods of latency, so too Jewish law did not stop developing during periods of lesser creativity, but one can clearly see the highs and lows of the sine curve of Jewish legal creativity.

6. The Birth and Death of Whole Organisms

Although most of the legal systems of the distant past have died, a few—like Jewish and Confucian law—continue to exist. These few defy the usual pattern in nature, in which organisms usually are born, live their lives, and die, with most species having a limit to their life span. That Jewish law still exists after a history of millennia is thus nothing short of a miracle.

What is interesting, though, is that some members of these cultures have sought to kill off their legal systems. In organic terms, they have sought to commit cultural suicide. That was certainly true for Mao Tse-tung in the middle of the 20th century and is still true today to a slightly lesser degree for the government of China. It is also true for some modern expressions of Judaism that question the accuracy and wisdom of seeing Jewish law as a functioning legal system altogether.

The classical Reform movement of the 19th and early 20th centuries, articulated by such thinkers as Abraham Geiger in Germany and Kaufman Kohler in the United States, is one clear example of this. These thinkers asserted that Jewish ritual laws were not laws at all but, at best, customs, and that most of those customs should be dropped in our times because they isolate Jews from non-Jews and make it difficult for Jews to engage fully in the modern world. The moral laws of Judaism still apply, but as universal moral norms and not as Jewish law, per se. For most of the Reformers, greatly influenced as they were by the philosopher Immanuel Kant, such moral norms gain their authority from, and are known through, reason. The 1885 Pittsburgh Platform of the American Reform Rabbis makes clear their evaluation of Jewish law as a dead legal system, one that governed an ancient state but not a modern one, with only Jewish moral commitments and the "spirit of Mosaic legislation" relevant to modern Jews as demonstrated in the specific items noted below taken from the document:

- We recognize in the Mosaic legislation a system of training the Jewish people for its mission during its national life in Palestine, and today we accept as binding only its moral laws, and maintain only such ceremonies as elevate and sanctify our lives, but reject all such as are not adapted to the views and habits of modern civilization.
- We hold that all such Mosaic and rabbinical laws as regulate diet, priestly purity, and dress originated in ages and under the influence of ideas entirely foreign to our present mental and spiritual state. They fail to impress the modern Jew with a spirit of priestly holiness; their observance in our days is apt rather to obstruct than to further modern spiritual elevation.
- We recognize, in the modern era of universal culture of heart and intellect, the approaching of the realization of Israel's great messianic hope for the establishment of the kingdom of truth, justice, and peace among all men. We consider ourselves no longer a nation, but a religious community, and therefore expect neither a return to Palestine, nor a sacrificial worship under the

sons of Aaron, nor the restoration of any of the laws concerning the Jewish state. . . .

- In full accordance with the spirit of Mosaic legislation, which strives to regulate the relation between rich and poor, we deem it our duty to participate in the great task of modern times, to solve on the basis of justice and righteousness, the problems presented by the contrasts and evils of the present organization of society.[42]

Mordecai Kaplan is another thinker who considered Jewish law as law to be dead. Jews living in Western countries have freedom of religion, and so may choose any form of Judaism they wish, including abandoning it altogether. In such a voluntaristic society, the state does not enforce Jewish law, and the Jewish community lacks legal power to do that, even if it wanted to do so. Because Jewish law in such societies is unenforceable, it is, for Kaplan, no longer sensible or helpful to speak of it as law. Instead, the moral parts of the Jewish tradition are built into nature and, as such, are universally binding on all human beings. (He does not deal with the question of whether the specifically Jewish way of defining and applying moral norms is or should be the universal one or not; he simply assumes that moral norms are universal.) He calls Jewish ritual laws "folkways," which Jews should obey only to the extent that, and only in contexts in which, they want to identify as Jews. So, for example, Jews might keep kosher at home but not in a public restaurant or when having dinner with non-Jews. In an open rejection of Robert Gordis's attempt to understand Jewish law as law despite its lack of state enforcement, Kaplan argues that to portray it as law is false, misleading, and counterproductive.[43]

The organic model of Jewish law, then, explains how not only individual laws and customs can come to be and fall into disuse but how whole legal systems, including Jewish law, might do so.

7. "A Horse of a Different Color": Similarities and Differences among Legal Systems

All animals have means of eating, eliminating bodily wastes, moving, procreating, and defending themselves, but they do those tasks in very different ways. Similarly, legal systems share some features with each other and differ in others, even in the way they accomplish common tasks. All legal systems, for example, have ways of creating laws, judging disputes, and enforcing both laws and judgments, but they differ markedly in how they do these things.

Jewish law, as a religious legal system, shares with secular legal systems a number of functions. Jewish law is remarkably like American law in emphasizing the authority of judicial rulings over codes, in developing the law through human agents (despite original authorship by God, however that process is understood by particular Jews), and in covering the breadth of topics of civil law (including not only contracts and business practices but wills and estates and even maritime law), criminal law, procedural law, and family law. Many of the specific provisions of the two legal systems on these topics vary, but the fact that Jewish law addresses all these subjects indicates that its progenitors and followers intended it to be a fully functioning legal system. Furthermore, like American law, Jews assumed, at least until the Enlightenment, that Jewish law would be enforced; even during the many centuries when Jews lived under the aegis of non-Jewish rulers, they often had a degree of autonomy to enforce Jewish law on the Jewish community, including not only matters like zoning and taxes but also criminal penalties (fines, lashes, excommunication) and, in a few places and times, even capital punishment. This was reinforced by Jewish laws prohibiting Jews from taking their disputes with other Jews to the non-Jewish courts and punishing those who did, and it was also often reinforced by the tendency of non-Jewish courts to rule unfairly against Jews— and then, sometimes, to punish the whole Jewish community for bothering the state's courts with their affairs. Jewish sources make clear that both the creators of the law and those who were supposed to follow it intended, at least until the Enlightenment in the 18th century, that Jewish law would in fact govern them in all these ways, with the sole exception of the commercial law that governed business transactions between Jews and non-Jews.

The situation is more complicated when it comes to origins. All organisms share much of our own, human genetic endowment, for many of our genes are the same as those of a paramecium, a starfish, or an ant. Life was "invented" or created only once. The genetic endowment of all living creatures has been elaborated and has branched out in all kinds of novel ways, but there has never been a different, parallel genetic system. In this way, legal systems are importantly different from living organisms, for the legal systems of the Incas, the Chinese, and the Mesopotamians seem to have arisen independently; and later legal systems (including Jewish law) blended and borrowed from them and from each other. Another way to look at this, though, is that all legal systems are the product of the image of God within us, an image that was created only once, and then the development of differing legal systems all from one source would parallel events in nature.

The substance of legal systems, though, is much more diverse than the genetic endowment of all organisms. In criminal law, for example, both the definitions of crime and the punishments prescribed for it vary markedly among the world's many legal systems, much more so than the genetic code of the world's organisms, even though the latter are much more numerous than the former.

The biological analogy that I have developed in this chapter is useful for calling attention to the traits of legal systems delineated above and for illustrating how these characteristics interact with each other. They illustrate my thesis that Jewish law in some significant ways is like many other legal systems and that legal systems in general, and Jewish law in particular, resemble human bodies. This analogy is not a perfect fit—just as one would expect from an analogy that does not pretend to be an equivalence. The other important contributions of this analogy, though, have yet to be explored—namely, the ways in which Jewish law is like a human being in combining body and soul. It is to the soul of Judaism that we turn in the next chapter.

ENDNOTES

1. Dorff, *Knowing God,* chap. 3.
2. Western philosophy beginning with Plato makes a sharp distinction between the body and the mind—so much so that the way that the two are connected is a stock issue in Western thought (the mind–body problem). Similarly, Christianity, influenced heavily by Gnosticism, makes a sharp distinction between the body and the soul, with the ideal person (the priest, nun, or monk) denying the body as much as possible to cultivate the soul. Judaism acknowledges the distinction between our bodily functions and

those of our soul; but in sharp contrast to both Western thought and Christianity, it asserts the integration of body and soul. Here is one graphic illustration of that:

> Antoninus said to Rabbi [Judah, the President, or "Prince," of the Sanhedrin]: "The body and soul could exonerate themselves from judgment. How is this so? The body could say, 'The soul sinned, for from the day that it separated from me, lo, I am like a silent stone in the grave!' And the soul could say, 'The body is the sinner, for from the day that I separated from it, lo, I fly like a bird.' "
>
> Rabbi [Judah] answered him: "I will tell you a parable. What is the matter like? It is like a king of flesh and blood who had a beautiful orchard, and in it was lovely, ripe fruit. He placed two guardians over it, one lame and the other blind. Said the lame man to the blind man: 'I see beautiful ripe fruit in the orchard. Come and carry me, and we will bring and eat them.' The lame man rode on the back of the blind man, they reached the fruit and ate it. After a while the owner of the orchard came and said to them, 'Where is my lovely fruit?' The lame man answered, 'Do I have legs to go?' The blind man answered, 'Do I have eyes to see?' What did the owner do? He placed the lame man on the back of the blind man and judged them as one. So also the Holy Blessed One brings the soul and throws it into the body and judges them as one (B. Sanhedrin 91a–91b).

This interaction is not only a matter of personal responsibility: it is also at the heart of the Rabbis' recipe for a good life: "An excellent thing is the study of Torah combined with a worldly occupation, for the labor demanded by both of them causes sinful inclinations to be forgotten. All study of the Torah without work must, in the end, be futile and become the cause of sin" (M. Avot [Ethics of the Fathers] 2:1). For more on this, see Dorff, *Matters of Life and Death,* pp. 20–26; and Dorff, *Love Your Neighbor and Yourself,* pp. 20–26.

3. Roth, *The Halakhic Process.*

4. One important exception to this is the American tax code, which functions very much like a continental code.

5. Kelsen, *General Theory of Law and State,* p. 115. See also Kelsen, *Pure Theory of Law,* pp. 194ff.

6. Roth, *The Halakhic Process,* p. 310.

7. Ibid., p. 302.

8. This is my example, not Roth's.

9. Roth, *The Halakhic Process,* p. 304.

10. See, for example, B. Berakhot 13a (in regard to saying the *Shema*); B. Eruvin 95b–96a (in regard to the use of phylacteries); B. Pesaḥim 114b (in

regard to the need for two dippings at the Seder); B. Rosh Hashanah 27a–29a (especially 28b, in regard to blowing the Shofar); and see my discussion on *keva* and *kavanah* in prayer in my *Knowing God,* pp. 177–191. Maimonides takes the extreme position of imposing a requirement of proper intention even on non-Jews when he rules that they have not fulfilled the seven duties of the Noahide covenant unless they do so intentionally to fulfill a commandment of God as announced by Moses in the Torah and not mere-ly as acts their own reason requires: see *Mishneh Torah, Laws of Kings and Their Wars* 8:11. See also B. Shabbat 72b in regard to the related question of whether one needs to have intention to be held liable for violating a law. This latter question had yet a further development that even those who claimed that unintentional violation did not make one liable nevertheless held that one would be liable if one's violation of the law in doing an act was, though unintentional, an inevitable consequence of acting as one did (*ps'ik reisheh v'al yamut,* "Can you cut off its [a chicken's] head and expect that it will not die?"); see B. Shabbat 75a, 103a, 111b, 117a, 120a, 133a, 143a; B. Sukkah 33b; B. Ketubbot 6b; B. Bekhorot 25a.

11. Cassuto, *A Commentary on the Book of Exodus,* pp. 260–264.

12. Menachem Elon, "Codification.", pp. 642–643.

13. Umberto Cassuto has made this point with reference to biblical law codes, which, he says, "should not be regarded as a code of laws, or even as a number of codes, but only as separate instructions on given matters" (Cassuto, *A Commentary on the Book of Exodus,* pp. 260–264). The Babylonian Talmud in Eruvin 27a and Kiddushin 34a expressly objects to treating the Mishnah's general rules as inviolable principles; moreover, in practice it recurrently interprets general principles announced in the Mishnah (with phrases like *zeh ha-klal*) not as generalizations at all but rather as additions of further specific cases. See Efrati, *Tekufat ha-saboraim v'sifrutah,* part 2, pp. 157–278, who points out that the Talmud interprets the phrase this way explicitly 16 (or possibly 18) times among the 85 unrepeated instances in the Mishnah where this expression occurs and who claims that these discus-sions, limited to the Babylonian Talmud, are Saboraic in origin (that is, from 500 to 689 C.E.). (I want to thank my colleague at the University of Judaism, Dr. Elieser Slomovic, z"l, for this reference.) Sometimes this effort by the Babylonian Talmud to apply the Mishnah's announcement of a general rule to a specific case not yet covered by the Mishnah is specifically introduced by the phrase, *zeh ha-kelal l'atuyei mai?* "[When the Mishnah says] 'This is the general rule,' what [specific case] does it come to include?" That occurs 8 times in the Talmud: B. Shabbat 103a; B. Eruvin 70b; B. Megillah 21a; B. Shevu'ot 37b; B. Avodah Zarah 73b; B. Hullin 41b, 54a; B. Niddah 57a. In regard to the genre of Jewish codes, its methodological pros and cons, and its origins in medieval systematics, see Dorff and Rosett, *A Living Tree,* pp. 366–401.

14. B. Eruvin 29a; B. Kiddushin 34a.

15. Roth, "On the Ordination of Women as Rabbis."

16. Ibid., pp. 149–174, esp. pp. 161–162 and 171–174, where he recommends "the exercise by the faculty of the ultimate systemic right of the learned who are committed to the *halakhah* to openly and knowingly abrogate the prohibition against women serving as witnesses." In oral comments at meetings of the Committee on Jewish Law and Standards, however, and on pp. 376–377 of his book *The Halakhic Process,* he maintains that we may not make women eligible to serve as witnesses in Jewish legal matters because we lack authority to make the change.

17. Gordis, "The Ordination of Women," and S. Greenberg, "On the Question of the Ordination of Women as Rabbis by the Jewish Theological Seminary of America."

18. For a thorough discussion of this debate and its ramifications for Jewish law today, together with excellent commentary by Gordon Tucker, see Abraham Joshua Heschel, *Heavenly Torah.*

19. Numbers Rabbah 13:15–16.

20. Numbers Rabbah 14:4.

21. Holmes, "The Path of the Law."

22. Roth, "Homosexuality Revisited," p. 29; see also p. 31.

23. As I am claiming here, the fundamental problem with any deductive system—in law and even in mathematics—is that life often does not fit into neat categories with deductive consequences. Thus most of us are convinced of two postulates of Euclidean geometry—namely, that the shortest distance between two points is a straight line and that there can be only one line drawn parallel to any given line through a particular point external to it. In fact, your geometry teacher during the very first week of class may have sent you out, as mine did, to measure the distance between any two points with a string and a ruler to see for yourself that the former postulate is true, and the same rough-and-ready technique might well have convinced you of the second postulate as well. In the nineteenth century, however, Nikolai Ivanovich Lobachevsky (1826) and independently Janos Bolyai (1832) proved that the second postulate is false, and they generated a wholly different geometry (hyperbolic geometry) based on the assumption that more than one parallel to a given line could be drawn through a fixed point and that the shortest distance between two points was a concave line. Later (1854) Georg Friedrich Bernhard Riemann created yet another non-Euclidean geometry by assuming that the shortest distance between two points is a convex line. These new geometries shattered the confidence that most people had in the inevitability of Euclidean geometry, but it was only an intellectual game until some 50 years later, when Albert Einstein demonstrated in his general theory of relativity that at the speed of light, lo and behold, the shortest distance between two points is in fact a convex line.

These discoveries, of course, do not undermine the accuracy or usefulness of Euclidean geometry for most of the things we do in life; and indeed, as I shall state, most decisions in Jewish law follow a straightforward, deductive model; but these developments in geometry do demonstrate that even in mathematics a deductive system does not adequately encompass and explain all of reality, especially when things are not "normal" and our assumptions and precedents need to be stretched or changed altogether.

24. Roth, "Homosexuality Revisited," p. 30.

25. M. Ketubbot 5:2 (57a).

26. B. Rosh Hashanah 32b.

27. B. Bava Batra 21a.

28. The death penalty for murder: for example, Exod. 21:12; Num. 35:16–21. For rape: Deut. 22:25–27. For violation of the Sabbath: Exod. 31:14. For idolatry: Exod. 22:19; Lev. 20:2–6, 27; Deut. 13:2–6; see also Exod. 20:4–61; Deut. 5:8–10, 11:16–17.

29. M. Makkot 1:10.

30. J. Sanhedrin 1:1 (18a).

31. T. Sanhedrin 7:3; B. Sanhedrin 36b; M.T. Laws of Courts (Sanhedrin) 2:3.

32. For comparative studies, see, for example, B. Cohen, *Jewish and Roman Law.* For a discussion of the talmudic principle declared in the name of Samuel that "the law of the land is the law" (B. Nedarim 28a; B. Gittin 10b; B. Bava Kamma 113a; B. Bava Batra 54b–55a), see Dorff and Rosett, *A Living Tree,* pp. 515–523.

33. B. Yevamot 65a, a ruling of Rava; cf. B. Yevamot 44a; B. Ketubbot 80b; B. Pesaḥim 113a; M.T. Laws of Marriage 14:3–4; S.A. Even ha-Ezer 1:9–10; 76:7. The M.T. and S.A. (E.H. 76:7) use the same words in saying: "A man may marry multiple wives, even a hundred, whether all at once or one after the other, and his [first] wife cannot prevent him from doing so on condition that he is able to provide food, clothing, and sexual satisfaction to each and every one of them. He may not force them to dwell in the same courtyard, but [he must rather provide housing for] each and every one of them by herself."

34. M. Ketubbot 4:7–12; 5:1–2.

35. Hauptman, *Rereading the Rabbis.*

36. M. Shabbat 1:4 (13b). See B. Shabbat 17b for the rationales of preventing intermarriage and idolatry. See also B. Avodah Zarah 31b, 35b, and 36b for those same rationales.

37. This is different from another problem associated with identity—namely, recognizing unity amid diversity, as two red spots that have the "same" color, giving rise to questions about individual instantiation of abstract qualities or ideas, or the relationship between individuals and universals. Because other issues the philosophers raise in regard to identity do

not affect the points I am trying to make here about Jewish law, I am not discussing them, important as they are. These include, among others:

- Frege's point about the difference between meaning and reference ("Venus is the morning star" and "Venus is the evening star" have the same reference to the planet Venus, but the sentences mean different things, just as "Elliot Dorff is a teacher" and Elliot Dorff is a father" are two sentences with the same reference but different meanings).
- The questions surrounding identity in a life after death (in what sense, if any, am I the *same* person if I live in some sense after my physical death, even though in that state I presumably have a different body or none at all?).
- Moral and legal responsibility for what I have done in a different stage of my life (how long do I bear responsibility for, say, an insult I uttered at age 15?) or in a different mental and physical state (am I the same person as I was when I was drunk or on drugs and therefore morally and legally responsible for what I did in those altered states?).
- Comparative vs. numerical issues of identity ("He is the same man" can mean either that he now has characteristics very much *like* the ones I knew him to have before, or it can mean the he is *numerically* the very person I knew before).
- Group identity (Is a Jew someone who asserts that he or she is, or are there communal criteria for asserting that, and, if the latter, which ones?).

For a clear, thorough, and yet reasonably brief description of how philosophers have dealt with the various aspects of the problem of identity and with personal identity in particular, see Stroll, "Identity," and Penelhum, "Personal Identity."

38. Cover, "Nomos and Narrative."

39. The original law sealing the transfer of property only when the property has been moved to the domain of the buyer: M. Bava Meẓia 4:2. The replacement of that law through the custom of shaking hands: Piskei ha-Rosh, Bava Meẓia, chap. 5, #72, citing Rabbenu Hananel; S. A. Hoshen Mishpat 207:19. On this generally, see Elon, *Jewish Law,* 2:913–917.

40. Two poignant articles wistfully expressing the power of traditional weddings over individually created ones appeared in the height of the period of experimentation. One was published without ascription in *The New Yorker* on August 30, 1976, and the other was Morrow's "The Hazards of Homemade Vows." Both are reprinted in Dorff and Rosett, *A Living Tree,* pp. 489–492 and 510–511.

41. *Roper v. Simmons* 543 U.S. 551 (March 1, 2005).

42. This and the three subsequent platform statements of the Central Conference of American Rabbis can be accessed at www.ccarnet.org /documentsandpositions/platforms/. For discussions of later platform statements in the light of this one, see Borowitz, *Reform Judaism Today;* Smith, ed., *Where We Stand;* and Washofsky, *Jewish Living.*

43. Kaplan, "Reply," in his *Questions Jews Ask,* pp. 264–276; reprinted in Dorff, *The Unfolding Tradition,* pp. 121–128. See also Kaplan, *The Future of the American Jew,* pp. 387–401.

CHAPTER THREE

The Covenantal Soul of
Jewish Law: How Jewish
Law Is Unique

THE BODY AND SOUL OF THE LAW

Jewish thinking and living can only be adequately understood
in terms of a dialectical pattern, containing opposite or contrasted properties. As in a magnet, the ends of which have opposite magnetic qualities, these terms are opposite to one another
and exemplify a *polarity* which lies at the very heart of Judaism,
the polarity of ideas and events, of mitsvah and sin, of kavanah
and deed, of regularity and spontaneity, of uniformity and indi-
viduality, of halacha and agada, of law and inwardness. . . .
Taken abstractedly, all these terms seem to be mutually exclusive, yet in actual living they involve each other; the separation
of the two is fatal to both. There is no halacha without agada,
and no agada without halacha. We must neither disparage the
body, nor sacrifice the spirit. The body is the discipline, the pattern, the law; the spirit is inner devotion, spontaneity, freedom.
The body without the spirit is a corpse; the spirit without the
body is a ghost.

—Abraham Joshua Heschel[1]

Human beings are body and soul, and the two constantly interact and affect each other. What we think, feel, and desire and our relationships with other people—what I am collectively calling our "soul"—has major effects on our bodies, and the reverse is true as well. Jewish law has the features described in the last chapter, properties that define the body of every legal system. Just as people's bodies differ, however, the body of each legal system has distinctive features, including its particular way of addressing the issues common to all human beings (its substance) and its particular mode of operation (its methods).

The most significant differences among people, however, are functions of their personalities—their thoughts, emotions, aspirations, and associations. The same is true for communities and their legal systems: Law has not only the organic features discussed in the previous chapter but also properties rooted in its community's philosophical vision and its emotions—that is, the particular way the members of a society understand and feel about themselves, others, and the world in which they live. These internal qualities determine the role of law in their lives. So, for example, as described in Chapter One, the Enlightenment's view of human beings as individuals with rights leads Western countries to think of law as preserving rights, with major implications for law's limits and methods. In contrast, the Jewish tradition understands Jews as members of a thick, organic community that has chosen to respond to God's commandments and fulfill its mission of fixing the world. This underlying perception of the source and purposes of the law directly affects it scope, content, procedures, and tone, and it makes Jewish law significantly different from Western legal systems like that of the United States.

Stories are a good way to get to the heart of a civilization and its laws. The first Jewish story is that of Abraham. Unlike the beliefs of all the other peoples in the ancient world, for whom the gods ruled on the basis of their power alone, where "might makes right," Abraham discovers that the ways of God are "to do what is just and right" (Genesis 18:19). It is that which later prompts Maimonides to characterize Abraham as "the pillar of the world,"[2] for everything after that in the Jewish tradition, including the law given by God to and through Moses, is based on that fundamental premise. God is moral, even if we do not always understand how, and we therefore must be moral too (*imitatio dei*).

The other Jewish story that defines the consciousness of Jews as

Jews is the Exodus from Egypt followed by the Revelation at Mount Sinai (Horeb) and the trek to the Promised Land. In that story, the model for understanding Jewish law is the covenant between God and the People Israel. Although the Torah records that God previously entered into covenants with Noah and Abraham and had renewed the latter with Isaac and Jacob,[3] it is at Mount Sinai that the covenant is specifically with the whole People Israel, and it is only there that both the basic assumptions about the relationship between God and Israel and its underlying values are articulated. Israel's covenantal relationship with God thus expresses the soul of Jewish law. "Covenant" is not a word or concept that is imposed on Jewish law from external sources: It comes from the very roots of the Jewish tradition. It is one of the primary ways in which the tradition expressed and understood itself.

Self-perceptions may be mistaken, however, and so it is important to spell out the ways in which the covenantal terminology reports the facts about Jewish law. To do that we must first clarify what understanding of covenant we mean to apply to Jewish law, for even in the Bible the word "covenant" (*brit*) is used for a wide variety of relationships.

THE MEANINGS OF "COVENANT"

When the word "covenant" denotes a bond among human beings, it sometimes describes ties of commitment, with no legal dimensions whatsoever (1 Sam. 18:3, 20:8, 23:18), or the deeper bond of marriage (Mal. 2:14, Prov. 2:17). It is more commonly used, however, to designate a legal tie, sometimes a contract between two individuals (Gen. 14:13, 21:22ff., 31:44ff.) but more often a pact between nations (Exod. 23:32, 34:12,15; Deut. 7:2; Josh. 9:6,7; 1 Sam. 11:1; 1 Kings 5:26; Ezek. 17:13–19; Ps. 83:6).

The political connotations of the term are also evident in its use as a constitution between a monarch and his subjects (2 Sam. 5:3; 1 Chron. 11:3; Jer. 34:8–18), similar to ancient Near Eastern suzerainty treaties between kings and their vassals.[4] Such agreements are probably the model for the biblical covenants that God contracts with Noah (Gen. 9:9–17; Isa. 54:10; Jer. 33:20,25), the Patriarchs (Gen. 15:18, 17:2–21; Exod. 2:24, 6:4,5), Joshua and the people (Josh. 24:25), David (Ps. 89:4, 29,34,39, 132:12; Jer. 33:21), Jehoiada and the people (2 Kings 11:17; 2 Chron. 23:3), Hezekiah and the people (2 Chron. 29:10), Josiah and the people (2 Kings 23:3), Ezra and the people (Ezra 10:3), and—especially—Moses and the people at Sinai (Exod. 19:5, 24:7,8, 34:10,27, 28). In a number of these cases the "covenant" is not strictly a contract in the common law sense of the term since God promises something without specifying the consideration to be received from human beings in return, but whatever is missing in one context is unambiguously supplied in others.

The importance of remembering the historical origins of the biblical idea of covenant is underscored by the fact that the Rabbis use that common biblical theme very little. By their time, it was not the practice of kings to write covenants with their subjects; they simply insisted that those whom they ruled accept the yoke of their reign. Consequently, the Rabbis expressed the covenant idea in language appropriate to their times—that is, as "giving the Torah" (*mattan Torah*) and "accepting the yoke of the Kingdom of Heaven" (*kabbalat ol malkhut shamayim*), parallel to, but also in contrast with, accepting the Roman yoke.[5] The idea, however, remains the same: Jewish law was to be seen as the product of the interaction of God with the People Israel, including God's gift of the Torah and Israel's acceptance of it, including all its obligations.

From the time of Abraham, however, the Jewish tradition has understood God to be not only powerful but good. Therefore the relationship with this Sovereign, powerful though He be, is not based on might makes right. On the contrary, as Moses tells the people, the point of the covenant is to help us flourish: "The Lord commanded us to observe all these laws, to revere the Lord our God, for our lasting good and for our survival. . . . It will be therefore to our merit before the Lord our God to observe faithfully this whole Instruction, as He has commanded us" (Deut. 6:24–25). God informs us that there will be negative consequences if we fail to abide by the Covenant (Lev. 26; Deut. 28, 29), but the Torah gives us the clear message that God did not enter into this covenant primarily to demonstrate and exert His authority. He rather created this covenant with the People Israel *for their good*—specifically, so that they can be "a kingdom of priests and a holy nation" (Exod. 19:6). As the Psalmist put it:

Come, my sons, listen to me:
I will teach you what it is to fear the Lord.
Who is the man who is eager for life,

who desires years of good fortune?
Guard your tongue from evil,
your lips from deceitful speech.
Shun evil and do good,
seek peace and pursue it. (Ps. 34:12–15)

In more contemporary terminology, the soul of the covenant with God is *tikkun olam*, "fixing the world," where the morals of the Jewish tradition apply directly to this task, and its rituals bring together and identify the community, remind it of its mission and moral obligations (Num. 15: 37–41), and make life an art.[6]

This underlying purpose and tone of the covenant leads the prophet Hosea in the eighth century B.C.E. and subsequent prophets to use another covenantal model—namely, the covenant of marriage. Just as couples have duties to each other, a few of which are spelled out in legal documents but most of which emerge from their ongoing relationship, so too God and the People Israel have an eternal relationship. That relationship produces duties, the most important of which is to be loyal to each other. That is why the Torah spells out in the Sinai Covenant that "You shall have no other gods besides Me" (Exod. 20:3) and why Moses proclaims, "Hear O Israel, the Lord is our God, the Lord alone" (Deut. 6:4).[7] Hosea uses the metaphor of marriage to complain bitterly about Israel's unfaithfulness but in the end, in verses used for donning phylacteries (*tefillin*) for daily morning services, he promises that God will take Israel back:

I will espouse you forever:
I will espouse you with righteousness and justice,
And with goodness and mercy,
And I will espouse you with faithfulness;
Then you shall be devoted to the Lord. (Hosea 2:21–22)

In that day, Hosea says, God will take Israel "back with favor," declaring, "You are my people," and Israel will respond, "[You are] my God" (Hosea 2:23–25). Similarly, Jeremiah, in rebuking the people for whoring after other gods, recalls earlier, more innocent times in their marital relationship:

I accounted to your favor
The devotion of your youth,

Your love as a bride—
How you followed Me in the wilderness,
In a land not sown.
Israel was holy [special, separated out from all others] to the Lord,
The first fruits of His harvest. (Jer. 2:2–3)

Second Isaiah uses the marital metaphor to comfort the Jews exiled to Babylonia:

Nevermore shall you be called "Forsaken,"
Nor shall your land be called "Desolate";
But you shall be called "I delight in her,"
And your land "Espoused." . . .
As a bridegroom rejoices over his bride,
So will your God rejoice over you. (Isa. 62:4–5)

Sometimes yet another kind of covenantal love is invoked—namely, that between a parent and child. The Bible does not explicitly use the term "covenant" (*brit*) for this relationship, just as it does not explicitly use that term for marriage, but it asserts that God's relationship with the People Israel is like both a marriage and a parent–child relationship. Each of the latter brings with it its own concept of the nature of the relationship and the duties that come with it. So, for example, Moses uses the image of Israel as the nestlings of an eagle who takes good care of them:

For the Lord's portion is His people.
Jacob His own allotment.
He found him in a desert region,
In an empty howling waste.
He engirded him, watched over him,
Guarded him as the pupil of His eye.
Like an eagle who rouses his nestlings,
Gliding down to his young,
So did He spread His wings and take him,
Bear him along on His pinions;
The Lord alone did guide him,
No alien god at His side. (Deut. 32:9–12; see Exod. 19:4)

Similarly, God tells Moses to describe the People Israel to Pharaoh as "My first-born son" (Exod. 4:22), and Moses tells the Israelites that "You are children of the Lord your God" (Deut. 14:1). When the Israelites abandon God and worship other gods or act immorally,

The Lord saw and was vexed,
He spurned His sons and His daughters.
He said,
"I will hide My countenance from them,
and see how they fare in the end.
For they are a treacherous breed,
Children with no loyalty in them." (Deut. 32:19–20)

Similarly, Isaiah complains, in God's name,

"I reared children and brought them up—
And they have rebelled against Me!
An ox knows its owner,
An ass its master's crib:
Israel does not know,
My people takes no thought."
Ah, sinful nation!
People laden with iniquity!
Brood of evildoers!
Depraved children! (Isa. 1:2–4)

On the other hand, the Psalmist is convinced that God will have mercy on His children as human parents do: "As a father has compassion for his children, so the Lord has compassion for those who fear Him" (Ps. 103:13).

Parental love and the love that children have in return are, of course, of a different character than the love of lovers or spouses. Parents created the children (or adopted them) and provide for them when they cannot fend for themselves. (Later in life, the situation reverses, as the parents depend on their adult children, but the Bible never uses the image of adult children for Israel, presumably because God does not grow old.) Spouses depend on each other as well, but they choose to create their relationship voluntarily, and they usually are more or less at the same stage of life. Duties arise in both kinds of love, but they are different ones. That is undoubtedly why the Bible uses both kinds of love as images of the relationship between God and Israel.

The covenant between God and Israel establishes the basis for the love that Jews should have for each other. The verse "Love your neighbor as yourself" ends with "I am the Lord" (Lev. 19:18), indicating that this social bond is to be rooted in the recognition that God created and reigns over us all. Rabbi Akiva identifies this verse as "a fundamental principle of the Torah,"[8] and Hillel maintains that all of the rest of the Torah is simply commentary to this central value: "Hillel said: 'What is hateful to you, do not do to your neighbor. That is the whole Torah; the rest is commentary. Go and learn it.'"[9] Although many modern Jews understand this to refer to all human beings and although, as we shall see later in this chapter, the Rabbis did indeed require that Jews care for non-Jews as well as Jews, most classical commentators limited the scope of this particular verse to Jews. Furthermore, as usual in Jewish thought and practice, the Rabbis understood this verse to require not merely that we have a positive attitude toward our neighbor but also that we fulfill specific obligations toward all other Jews. This leads to the rabbinic assertions that "all Israelites are responsible for one another"[10] and that one may not separate oneself from the community.[11] As I shall describe in the last part of this chapter, the Rabbis spell out exactly what the community must provide for its needy members, framing the duty to give and the eligibility to receive in terms of the extent to which the poor person is rooted in the community.

Israel's covenant with God also establishes the standard that Jews as a community should relate to non-Jews with love. Although the primary focus of Jewish duties concerns fellow Jews, just as every society cares most for its own citizens, the Jewish tradition is remarkably concerned for non-Jews as well. I say "remarkably" because one must remember that the Torah and the Rabbis articulated these obligations during periods when non-Jews were more likely to be persecuting Jews than aiding them. In sharp contrast, the Torah demands that "You shall have one standard for stranger and citizen alike, for I the Lord am your God" (Lev. 24:22), a rule made even more explicit here: "There shall be one law for you and for the resident stranger; it shall be a law for all time throughout the ages. You and the stranger shall be alike before the Lord; the same ritual and the same rule shall apply to you and to the stranger who resides among you" (Num. 15:15–16).

No less than 36 times, by the Talmud's count—and some say 46—the Torah warns Jews not to wrong a stranger.[12] One must even "love the stranger, for you were strangers in the land of Egypt" (Deut. 10:19), again made even more explicit here: "When a stranger resides among you, with you in your land, you shall not wrong him. The stranger who resides with you shall be to you as one of your citizens; you shall love him as yourself, for you were strangers in the land of Egypt; I the Lord am your God" (Lev. 19:33–34). As I shall delineate at the end of this chapter, these principles lead the Jewish tradition to require Jews to fulfill a number of concrete duties toward non-Jews.

Thus the Bible uses at least three covenantal models to describe the relationship between God and Israel and its inherent obligations: suzerainty treaties, marriage, and the parent–child relationship. Even the suzerainty treaty is not imposed on Israel by a powerful and bullying God: God is instead depicted as both powerful *and good*. As a result, Israel *voluntarily accepts* to be in covenant with God at Mount Sinai (Exod. 24:3) and reaffirms that commitment in the time of Joshua (even when Joshua gives them the opportunity to abandon it and worship other gods; Josh. 24), again in the time of Esther (Esther 9:27), and yet again in the time of Ezra (Neh. 8–10). The marital model of the covenant with God certainly presumes that Israel consented to the marriage; and the parental model suggests that, although Israel did not have any say in engaging with God (children do not choose their parents), God is a good, caring parent, who knows how to discipline children when they stray from the proper path for their own good and then resume the relationship with full love. All three are models for an eternal relationship, for even when Israel engages in adulterous relationships with other gods and God responds in anger, ultimately God declares that He will persist in the relationship and take Israel back (Lev. 26:44–45). Furthermore, because God created all human beings and is a loving and moral God, the covenant that Israel has with God requires Jews to take care of each other and non-Jews as well.

In the remainder of this chapter, then, I shall first describe the aspects of Jewish law that the Jewish covenant with God helps us understand and briefly respond to some important problems with this model. Then I shall discuss what the Jewish covenant with God requires of Jews in their relationships to other Jews and to non-Jews. Although the covenant analogy is not perfect, it is, in my view, the best available to describe the soul of Jewish law as the expression of our love for God and for other people.[13]

OUR RELATIONSHIP WITH GOD: THE COVENANT MODEL

These three concepts of covenant—a suzerainty treaty, a marriage, and a parent–child relationship—form the basis of how Israel understands its relationship with God. Like any relationship, duties arise from these three relationships, duties spelled out, at least in part, in Jewish law. The covenant theme, then, pinpoints and clarifies at least the aspects of the nature and practice of Jewish law discussed in the following sections.

1. Love of God as a Motivation for Fulfilling the Obligations of the Covenant

To convince most people to follow the rules, societies must create feelings of pride, respect, and even love for their community and its laws. That is hard to accomplish because government and law are abstract and inanimate. It is much easier to relate to people. Therefore secular societies typically teach the history of the group, its songs, stories, and exemplary personalities to instill strong commitments to social institutions, and they reinforce those commitments through recurring rituals.

   Jews do that too: Jewish education usually includes a study of the same subjects just listed, and Jewish ritual patterns provide ample opportunity to renew national ties. But there is a difference. Jews adhere to Jewish law out of a sense of kinship and loyalty not only to other Jews but to God. God is the covenanted partner, and that relationship provides the context for covenantal obligations.

The Bible develops the personal implications of the covenant fully. It speaks of God having chosen Israel as His special people out of an act of love, and Jews should observe the commandments because of that love:

> Abraham is to become a great and populous nation, and all the nations of the earth are to bless themselves by him. For I have singled him out, that he may instruct his children and his posterity to keep the way of the Lord by doing what is just and right." (Gen. 18:18–19)

> For you are a people consecrated to the Lord your God; of all the peoples on earth you are the smallest of peoples; but it was because the Lord loved you and kept the oath He made to your fathers that the Lord freed you with a mighty hand and rescued you from the house of bondage, from the power of Pharaoh king of Egypt. Know, therefore, that only the Lord your God is God, the steadfast God who keeps His faithful covenant to the thousandth generation of those who love Him and keep His commandments. . . . Therefore, observe faithfully the Instruction, the laws, and the norms, with which I charge you today. (Deut. 7:6–11)

Just as God chose Israel, Israel chose God. They proclaim their promise of fealty to the covenant at Mount Sinai, declaring "All that the Lord has spoken we will faithfully do!" (Exod. 24:7), and they renew their commitment even when Joshua offers them a way out (Josh. 24) and again during the times of Esther (Esther 9:27[14]) and Ezra (Neh. 8–10).

One important way in which Israel expresses its love for God is through fulfilling the commandments, the acts that God has specified that He recognizes as tokens of Israel's love. "Love the Lord your God, and always keep His charge, His laws, norms, and His commandments" (Deut. 11:1). As indicated earlier, the prophets picture God and Israel as husband and wife, joined in a covenant of marriage (Jer. 2:2, 3:20; Ezek. 16:8; Hosea 2). One should observe the law, then, as a loving response to God's love for us and to what God represents—"what is just and right." Most legal theories that have been proposed to explain either Jewish or American law do not speak to this important foundation of love in Jewish law. The covenant model does.[15]

2. Promise Keeping as Another Source of Obligation

Another aspect of the personal relationship between God and Israel affects Jewish law significantly. Legal systems commonly hold native-born citizens liable for violating the law (once they achieve the age of majority) without ever asking them for their consent to abide by it. Society may justly impose its obligations on those who enjoy its benefits on two grounds: fairness (those who derive benefit from a community must follow its rules for living within it and contribute to meeting the needs of its other members) and "tacit consent" (even without specific verbal confirmation you indicate that you consent to a society's terms if you continue to be a part of it).

Judaism goes much further. First, the people standing at Mount Sinai promised God to obey the law not out of fear alone but for ample consideration. God made His will known to the people of Israel; redeemed them; would give them the land of Israel; and would make them God's treasured, model people. Therefore, the promise that they made is clearly warranted and binding:

> Israel encamped there in front of the mountain, and Moses went up to God. The Lord called to him from the mountain, saying, "Thus shall you say to the house of Jacob and declare to the children of Israel: 'You have seen what I did to the Egyptians, and I bore you on eagles' wings and brought you to Me. Now then, if you will obey Me faithfully and keep My covenant, you shall be My treasured possession among all the peoples, although all the earth is Mine. And you shall be to Me a kingdom of priests and a holy nation.' These are the words that you shall speak to the children of Israel." Moses came and summoned the elders of the people and put before them all the words that the Lord had commanded him. All the people answered as one, saying, "All that the Lord has spoken we will do!" And Moses brought back the people's words to the Lord. (Exod. 19:2–8; compare Deut. 4:32–40)

Furthermore, even though the next generation did not stand at Sinai, Moses maintains that the covenant binds them and all future generations too: the later generations may not have been there physically, but they were there spiritually and took part in the promise made there. All Jews must see themselves as if they left Egypt, as the Haggadah will later proclaim, and God spoke to all future generations at Mount Sinai, where we promised along with our ancestors:

> It was not with our fathers [alone] that the Lord made this covenant, but with us, the living, every one of us who is here today. Face to face the Lord spoke to you on the mountain out of the fire. (Deut. 5:3–4)

> I make this Covenant, with its sanctions, not with you alone, but both with those who are standing here with us this day before the Lord our God and with those who are not with us here this day. (Deut. 29:13–14)

> Concealed acts concern the Lord our God; but with overt acts, it is for us and our children to all eternity to apply all the provisions of this Teaching. (Deut. 29:28)

Furthermore, as noted, the promise to live by the covenant was reconfirmed by subsequent generations in the times of Joshua, Esther, and Ezra.

As I shall discuss in the next chapter, this justification for the authority of Jewish law is problematic in a number of ways, but it is an important feature of Jewish law: We are obligated to follow Jewish law because we ourselves promised to do so when we all stood at Sinai and several times in the Bible subsequently. Moreover, by remaining faithful to the covenant, Jews throughout the ages have demonstrated in action, if not in word, that they consider themselves bound by these promises, even in times of doubt that God was fulfilling His end of the bargain. This promissory element of Jewish legal theory is best explicated through the concept of a covenant established by two parties, each of whom promises some things to the other to form the basis of their relationship, just as sovereigns did in ancient times with their subjects and just as married couples do at the time of their wedding.

3. God as Legislator

As I noted in the last section of Chapter One, the Torah presents the Sinai covenant as limited to the Decalogue; the rest of the Torah's laws God gives through Moses. Moreover, the Torah texts themselves and later rabbinic and philosophic treatments of revelation variously depict the way in which God communicated the Decalogue and the other laws of the Torah; but most are at pains to retain God's legislative role, even if they must explain it in untraditional ways. In any case, the Torah certainly presents God as Legislator, whether God delivers His laws directly to the People Israel or through Moses.

Modern critical scholarship asserts that the Torah consists of four documents that were written at different times during the biblical period and were later edited together (the Documentary Hypothesis), and this suggests that the laws of the Torah developed over the entire biblical period. In what sense, then, are the laws divine? There are many theories about this; in my book *Conservative Judaism,* I describe Orthodox, Reform, and four Conservative responses to this question,[16] and I describe my own theory of revelation in Chapter One herein. Briefly stated, I believe that the Torah consists of documents written by human beings who were describing their awareness of God and their experiences with Him as well as their understanding of the nature of our relationship with God. In formulating the Torah's laws, then, they were delineating their conception of what that tie demands of Jews.

Why did Jews of the past and why do I think that the Torah and subsequent Jewish law to our own day are not simply human creations but also the record of Jews' response to God? In part because the Torah portrays it as such, leading our ancestors to believe that God is the source and authority of the law. In addition, as Simon Greenberg has pointed out,[17] several phenomena of the ongoing practice of Jewish law can only be adequately understood if we presume God's involvement in some way. Specifically, the Jews' "sense of overwhelming awe when they contemplated the grandeur and majesty of the Law"[18] is certainly part of the religious feeling motivating those who observe it. Another element in the Jews' commitment to Jewish law is their conviction that through it they perform a cosmic role in helping God complete creation. The strength of these perceptions of God's role in creating Jewish law is especially evident in the numerous sacrifices that Jews have made to uphold it; only their belief that Jewish law expresses the will of God can explain their persistence in following it and their willingness even to die for it. Finally, Jews of the past and I myself attach divinity to Jewish law because, as God told Abraham, it helps define "the way of the Lord by doing what is just and right" (Gen. 18:19)—that is, it defines a path for life that is spiritually and morally rich, so rich that it is hard to believe that human beings in the ancient past would have been able to formulate it on their own.

4. Love Balanced by Fear: God as Judge and Enforcer

Our ancestors were also, of course, motivated by their faith in divine reward for those who obey Jewish law and divine punishment for those who disobey it. In other words, God, in their view, enforces Jewish law and acts as an infallible Judge in doing so, for God "knows the secrets of the world," as the High Holy Day liturgy asserts. That God is the ultimate Enforcer and Judge of the terms of the covenant is so central a tenet to Judaism that the rabbis defined a heretic as one who claims that "there is no justice and no Judge."[19] The covenant makes this clear: God creates His covenant with Israel amid thunder, lightning, and earthquakes at Sinai (Exod. 19–24), and he announces that He will avenge breaches of the covenant with vigor (Lev. 26, Deut. 28).

Like the promise-keeping element of Jewish law, this feature of it raises major problems. Does a link exist between faithfulness and flourishing and between sin and punishment? Even before the biblical period was over, Job and Kohelet (Ecclesiastes) raised questions about whether God justly rewards those who are loyal to the covenant and punishes only those who are unfaithful, as earlier books had maintained. The Rabbis of the Talmud go further: They honestly and straightforwardly observe that "righteous people suffer, and evil people prosper" (*tzadik v'ra lo, rasha v'tov lo*).[20] Those who suffered or died during the Crusades, Inquisition, pogroms, and, especially, the Holocaust have questioned even more sharply the link between loyalty to the covenant and one's fate in life. I will address these issues in the next chapter. For now, suffice it to say that, for all of its problems, the linkage between faithfulness and flourishing and between sin and punishment has historically been one important underpinning of Jewish law, and an element that the covenant model as well as most other models of Jewish law include.

How, though, can one balance the love of God with the fear of God? This balance of love with fear is not as strange as it may sound. In both king–subject relationships and parent–child relationships there is an element of voluntary acceptance and love, and both a king and a parent would like to maximize compliance out of love for both practical and moral reasons. Practically, it is simply easier to gain adherence to the rules if there is willing acceptance. Moreover, enforcement procedures can never be totally effective, even if God is the Enforcer. Thus the Bible describes many instances when Israel disobeys God, including the Golden Calf incident a bare 40 days after the thunder, lightning, and earthquakes of the Sinai Revelation! Morally, it is easier to justify the authority of the rules if they are accepted voluntarily and fulfilled out of love. Free acceptance is thus not only a nice adornment for a legal system but is absolutely crucial to its viability and moral authority.

But neither Jewish law nor any other legal system can exist if it is totally dependent on voluntary compliance; there must be some means of enforcement when people stray or fail to fulfill the duties of their relationships. Moreover, there are situations in life in which there are no choices about accepting a set of rules. Subjects of an absolute monarchy are one good example of this, and young children's duty to follow their parents' directions are another. In the passages noted earlier, the Bible maintains that Israel's special status and even her continued existence depend on her adherence to the Torah because that was the mission God assigned her.

Thus Israel's voluntary and loving acceptance of the Torah was good and proper, for the ways of God delineated in the Torah for us to follow are just and righteous. Further, love of God should ideally be one's primary motive for fulfilling its terms. Nevertheless, the authority of the Torah's laws does not depend completely on the Jewish community's willingness to observe them, for God, even more than a human sovereign or parent, has both the power and moral authority to dictate and enforce His rules. Again, whether and how God does this I leave for the next chapter, but the faith that God does this—that evil deeds do not go unanswered—has historically been and continues to be an important feature of Jewish law in both theory and practice, a feature captured by the covenant model at least as much as it is by other theories.

5. The National Domain of Jewish Law

The covenant is specifically between God and the Jewish people; its terms do not apply to others. The Rabbis make this explicit by claiming that non-Jews are subject to only the seven commandments that apply to all descendants of Noah,[21] but the Bible is also quite clear in restricting the jurisdiction of its commandments to Israelites. So, for example, at Mount Sinai, God announces His intention to make Israel alone "a kingdom of priests and a holy nation," and later God says, "I hereby make a covenant. Before all your people I will work such wonders as have not been wrought on earth or in any nation" (Exod. 19:5–6, 34:10)[22] The prophets look forward to a time when the other nations will learn Torah from Zion (Isa. 2:2–4; Mic. 4:1–5), but for now the covenant is limited to God's relationship with Israel— even though, as the Rabbis later interpret it, it demands that Jews care for needy non-Jews. Although positivist theories (those that identify the law with the decrees of the lawgiver) could account for this, theories that base Jewish law on universal phenomena like natural law and reason would be hard pressed to do so.

During the 19th century and the first third of the twentieth, some Jews tried to minimize the national character of Jewish law because of the danger of producing a narrow, chauvinistic outlook, thus undermining the universal, messianic goals of Judaism. Those who have taken this view have found the covenant problematic precisely because of its nationalism. Hermann Cohen, for example, bitterly attacked the cliquish consequences of a national covenant and stressed that its restriction to Israel was to be temporary in the messianic sweep of biblical historiography;[23] Franz Rosenzweig was more sanguine about Israel's special covenant with God but claimed that Christians had one too (albeit an inferior one) in his famous "dual-covenant" theory.[24] Since the 1930s, the value of ethnic roots has been recognized even by those who would deny that the Jewish people are specially chosen, and so the covenant has been reinterpreted but reasserted. Probably the best example of this is Mordecai Kaplan, who conscientiously denies that God chose the Jewish people for both theological and moral reasons but who affirms the covenant because it is only through national affiliation that one can contribute creatively to humanity. Jews are not chosen to serve God over and above any other nation of the world, according to Kaplan, but they do have a unique calling to serve God in their own specific circumstances and their own unique way:

> If we regard God as the Life of the universe, the Power that evokes personality in men and nations, then the sense of the nation's responsibility for contributing creatively to human welfare and progress in the light of its own best experience becomes the modern equivalent of the covenant idea. In it is implied that reciprocity between God and the nation that the term covenant denotes.[25]

The ability of the covenant theme to express the national character of Jewish law is thus increasingly being recognized as an advantage for both historical and philosophical reasons.

6. The Relationship of Jewish Law to Nature

Although Jewish law is specifically the law of the Jewish people, classical Jewish texts picture it as a manifestation of God's wisdom, parallel to the wisdom God used in creating the world. Psalm 19, for example, describes God's ordering of nature and then easily shifts to God's ordering of human life through the Torah to make the point that the two acts of God are complementary. Psalm 119:89–93 does the same thing more briefly:

> The Lord exists forever;
> Your word stands firm in heaven.
> Your faithfulness is for all generations;
> You have established the earth, and it stands.
> They stand this day to [carry out] Your rulings,
> for all are Your servants.
> Were not Your teaching my delight
> I would have perished in my affliction.
> I will never neglect Your precepts,
> for You have preserved my life through them.

Similarly, the prophets complain that animals know and follow the rules that God has set for them, but Israel does not know or obey

God's commandments, which should be equally as obvious to them (Isa. 1:3; Jer. 8:7). Moses invokes heaven and earth as witnesses to the covenant (Deut. 4:26; 32:1), and Jeremiah proclaims that the heavens are astounded when Israel flagrantly breaks the covenant (Jer. 2:12, compare 4:22–28, 6:19). The Land of Israel itself will "spew out" the Israelites if they violate the Torah's sexual laws (Lev. 18:26–30). Israel's covenant thus spells out rules that enable Jews to live wisely and successfully in the world that God has created in ways that no other legal system does, and that is part of the reason Israel is warned not to follow other nations' laws (Lev. 20:22–26; Jer. 10:1–5). The Rabbis, in fact, claimed that the very existence of the world depends on Israel's acceptance of the Torah:

> What is the meaning of the words, "The earth feared and was still" (Ps. 76:9)? Before Israel accepted the Torah, the earth was afraid; after they accepted the Torah, it was still. . . . For the Holy Blessed One stipulated a condition with the earth: If Israel accepts the Torah, you may exist, but if not, I will return you to the state of being unformed and void.[26]

What should we make of these claims? I find it hard to believe that the world's hospitality and, indeed, its very existence depends on whether Jews observe Judaism's ritual commandments. I think that Judaism's rituals are important expressions of our love for God, that they identify us a community, and that they make an art of life, and so I have made them part of my life. I do think, though, that the claims that the Bible and Rabbis are making here do apply to the tradition's moral laws, that violating the basic norms of how we treat each other does indeed undo society and that our very existence depends on comporting with them. As Micah put it: "What does the Lord require of you? To do justice, to engage in acts of loving kindness, and to walk humbly with your God" (Mic. 6:8). Thus although I would not go as far as David Novak has gone in interpreting all of Jewish law as based in natural law,[27] I would aver that the moral parts of Jewish law are indeed so.

In direct contrast to the previous section, natural law theories (and perhaps other absolutist approaches) can account for this element of Jewish law, while positivist views cannot. The covenant expresses both the particular, national character of Jewish law and its universal, natural roots: God, who created the world, enters into a covenantal relationship with Israel so that the law of at least one human society may reflect divine purpose just as natural law does and so that it can serve as a model and magnet for others to follow the divine paths of justice and righteousness.

7. The Scope and Specifics of the Law

Because God is our covenantal partner and because God cares about all aspects of our lives, Jewish law can and does speak to every facet of life, including many that fall outside of the jurisdiction of other legal systems. It sets an order not only for society but also for the private lives of individuals and families. So, for example, it specifies with remarkable particularity the duties incumbent on spouses to each other, including even the number of times that a man must offer to have sex with his wife.[28] The Talmud bans oppressing one's neighbor in speech, forbidding much more than American laws against libel and slander do, and it also maintains that those who intend to give a gift to a needy person carry out that intention even if they never overtly promised to do so.[29] These are all areas that legal systems do not dare touch, let alone regulate, but Jewish law speaks on these subjects because it is a spiritual legal system, one that requires us to model ourselves after God and to act in ways that demonstrate that we are fitting covenantal partners with God.

Because human beings are all part of nature, natural law theories could presumably have equally expansive scope and detail. In practice, however, they vary widely, ranging from a few general rules (as in Aquinas and Thomas Hobbes) to the very detailed list that 20th-century Catholic theologian Jacques Maritain provides.[30] Positivist theories would find it easier to account for the specificity of Jewish law, for in such theories the legislator can legislate anything, including personal matters. China's experiment to restrict the number of children per couple to one is an example of that. The covenant model, however, more adequately describes both the wide range of concerns treated by Jewish law and the specificity of its rules: A covenant has specific clauses, and when a caring God is involved, they can and should cover the whole gamut of human experience.

8. The Legal Techniques Used in Jewish Law

The biblical picture of God giving the Decalogue amid thunder, lightning, and earthquakes at Sinai (Exod. 19:20) misleads many into thinking that Jewish law does not operate as other legal systems do. Even though God can and does directly amend the law several times (Lev. 24:10–23; Num. 15:32–36; 27:1–11), the Torah, as the later tradition interpreted it, not only implies but explicitly states that the Israelites are never to do so (Deut. 4:2; 13:1). Human legal systems do not include such prohibitions, even in regard to their constitutions.

If one accepts the Documentary Hypothesis and modern biblical scholarship as I do, however, it is clear that without specific divine intervention biblical law developed over time, adding a number of things, ignoring others, and changing the form of previous norms. Indeed, Michael Fishbane has documented many instances of later strands of the Torah reinterpreting or revising earlier strands.[31] Furthermore, the Rabbis interpreted the biblical mandate to judge in Deuteronomy 17 very broadly, with the result that Jewish law in fact has changed over the centuries through normal legal techniques—to the point that a number of medieval rabbis grapple with the question of how to interpret the verses in Deuteronomy that they understand to forbid adding to, or subtracting from, the law given to Moses in light of these developments.[32]

For some readers these ongoing changes in Jewish law over the centuries are no doubt a surprising phenomenon. After all, however we understand the origins of the text of the Torah today, Jews have historically believed its commandments to be God-given law, and one might think, as fundamentalist Protestants do, that God's rules should be constant, that they can be changed, if at all, only by new revelations directly from God. The covenant model, however, provides the basis for Jewish legal development, for God not only commands but enters into a *relationship* through the covenant. Therefore, legal techniques like interpretation, narrowing or broadening the scope of precedent, subsidiary regulations to put the law into effect, administrative rules, customs, and even new legislation (*takkanot*) became appropriate for giving meaning to the parties' continuing relationship. This would not be true—at least not as clearly so—if Jewish law were only God's commands (a theological form of legal positivism) or natural laws outside the framework of a covenant, for then God's rules would not be amenable to human interpretation and change. The covenant makes them law rooted in an ongoing relationship with God and thereby makes them subject to human legal reasoning as we strive to determine what God wants of us now.

9. Jews' Attitudes toward the Law

Jews since Abraham have complained bitterly in times of distress or apparent injustice. This demonstrates Jews' presumption that Jewish law is based on mutual covenantal promises with God and an ongoing relationship with the Eternal, and thus Jews can call God to account for failing to uphold the covenant just as much as God can rebuke Jews for doing that. Complaints against God are hard to reconcile with either natural law theory (which sees Jewish norms as what nature requires of us), realism (which sees Jewish law as what we must do lest we be punished), or positivism (for which Jewish law consists of the Monarch's decrees with no underlying relationship with the Sovereign).

The Jewish tradition also created ways repeatedly to celebrate the covenant, something that those who interpret Jewish law in a naturalistic, realistic, or positivistic mode would have a hard time explaining. The talmudic Rabbis, for example, connected the festival of Shavuot with the Sinai Revelation,[33] and medieval Jewish tradition initiated the festival of Simḥat Torah (Rejoicing over the Torah) and used all of the symbolism of a couple (in this case Israel and God) entering into a marital relationship. The verses from Hosea (2:21–22) that are prescribed for putting on *tefillin* each morning are explicit, daily reaffirmations and celebrations of the covenant.

10. The Messianic Goal of Jewish Law: Tikkun Olam (Fixing the World)

Preambles to constitutions commonly spell out noble purposes for the law, but they do not aspire to transform human nature. Judaism does this, at least as it was developed by the prophets and Rabbis. Moses declares that the law "will be *for our lasting good*" (Deut. 6:24), and the Rabbis later articulate this ultimate aim of the law in a phrase that they use to explain some of their own rulings—namely, *mipnei tikkun ha-olam* (for the fixing of the world).[34] Thus biblical prophets maintain that in some future time, all people will worship God (Isa. 2:2–4, Zeph. 2:11, 3:8), resulting in universal justice and peace among people (Isa. 2:2–4,11–12). Toward that end, Israel is to be "a light unto the nations" (Isa. 49:1–6, 51:4). Jeremiah experienced the failure of Israel to perform its role of moral leadership and the consequent destruction of the First Temple wrought by God's tool, the Babylonians, but he promises that God will not destroy Israel completely (Jer. 5:18, 30:11, 46:28) and looks forward to a time when the law will be so natural to us that it will be written on our hearts (hard-wired into us) and thus totally internalized:

> See, a time is coming—declares the Lord—when I will make a new covenant with the House of Israel and the House of Judah. It will not be like the covenant I made with their fathers, when I took them by the hand to lead them out of the land of Egypt, a covenant that they broke, so that I coerced them—declares the Lord. But such is the covenant I will make with the House of Israel after these days—declares the Lord: I will put My Teaching into their inmost being and inscribe it upon their hearts. Then I will be their God, and they shall be My people. No longer will they need to teach one another and say to one another, "Know the Lord," for all of them, from the least of them to the greatest, will know Me— declares the Lord—for I will forgive their sins and I will no longer remember their transgressions (Jer. 31:31–34; compare 3:14–18).

The Bible and most rabbinic opinion assume that the Torah is immutable and eternal and that in messianic times it will be better understood and better fulfilled than ever before; but some rabbinic sources envisage a world so improved that the Law itself—or at least parts of it—will be completely altered.[35] In later Jewish history, the doctrine of a radically new Torah was popular in those times and places in which Jews expected the Messiah to be coming soon or already here; the more conservative notion of a more complete observance of the present Torah held sway when the messianic idea was a distant abstraction.[36] In any case, all Jewish sources agree that Jewish law is necessary now to teach us how to fix the world and to motivate us to do that.

The covenant theme accommodates both the anticipated changes in human nature and the possible revision of the law. As Creator of our present world, God can presumably change the nature of creation and, along with it, the terms of the covenant with Israel to better fit new conditions. Moreover, the covenant incorporates the Messianic goals of Jewish law to fix the world, for God has chosen Israel specifically to be a model and magnet for other nations of how to live justly and righteously. Indeed, the covenant brings God and Israel together to work as partners in the ongoing task of fixing the world.

THE PROBLEMS WITH THE COVENANT THEORY

An analogy by its very nature must compare two different things: If the objects of comparison were the same, we would have not an analogy but an equivalence. Analogies are useful for the philosophical and educational purposes described in Chapter One, but they inevitably involve the danger of drawing false comparisons on the basis of the analogy. The only way to prevent this is constantly to keep in mind that the analogy is just that—a comparison that may illuminate certain features of an object or phenomenon but may be downright misleading in regard to others.

Both the advantages and the problems with using analogies are heightened in speaking about God. The only language available to us is derived from human experience, and so to talk about God we must use symbols and analogies. However, if such metaphors can never be translated to words used literally, how can we ever be sure about what the symbols and analogies mean—let alone whether they make true claims? These philosophical problems have been discussed by a number of medieval and modern philosophers,[37] and theologians consistently warn us that any discussion about God is inevitably limited by the constraints of our human abilities and experience.

With this in mind, we should not be surprised that the problems with analogical thinking in general and the extra problems in using analogies with reference to God are all very much in evidence when we try to talk about a set of laws that are understood to express God's will and to link us with God. No analogy to human relationships is going to be totally satisfying. At the same time, because the Jewish tradition presents Jewish law as divine in character and origin, we must find some way to understand and articulate the divine aspect of Jewish law if we are ever going to make sense of its nature and operation. The real question, then, is the extent to which covenantal theory—or any other—illuminates the fundamental beliefs and methods of Jewish law and, on the other hand, the extent to which it is misleading.

My contention is that the covenant analogy is the least misleading of the available theories and that, in fact, it is not very misleading at all because the places where Israel's covenant with God deviates from human covenants are rather obvious. In an earlier essay, I consider nine arguments against describing Jewish law in covenantal terms.[38] Because most of them are issues more of theology than of legal theory, I will not repeat that discussion in this book. In the following sections, though, I discuss some legal difficulties with covenant theory.

If the Covenant Is Not a Social Contract in the Modern Sense, How Does It Explain Jewish Law at All?

If the covenant model is based on ancient suzerainty treaties and marriages rather than modern social contracts, how does it help to communicate the essence of Jewish law to moderns? The point of this challenge can be taken even further: Is not the term "covenant" downright misleading to modern people because they most likely would understand it as a social contract similar to other "covenants" that have established modern legal systems?

Theories are always subject to misunderstanding, of course, but the question is whether the use of the covenant model to explain Jewish law promotes misconceptions. I think that it does not, because the very assertion that the covenant is *with God* should alert people to the fact that the covenant is not a social contract in the usual, human sense.

If anything, it is the opposite error that is more likely: People may conclude from the Sinai event that Jewish law is not a legal system in any normal sense at all, that it is entirely composed of immutable, apodictic commands spoken in awesome circumstances. The covenant model actually helps prevent such misconceptions, for it indicates that the Sinai event is not simply the revelation of divine dictates but the occasion in which God and Israel establish an agreement and a continuing relationship. Immediately after the description of the Revelation on Mount Sinai in chapters 19 and 20 of the

Book of Exodus, chapters 21 through 23 speak in a very different tone. They announce a number of judicial precedents (*mishpatim*) to govern specific cases, precedents that beg for normal legal analysis. Consequently, although use of the word "covenant" to describe our relationship with God may be somewhat misleading, it is not seriously so because of its divine partner and its legal content. On the contrary, the covenant model can aid people in recognizing that Jewish law is a set of norms emerging out of a relationship, similar to the way that most of our duties arise.

Is the Covenant Authoritative Because Israel Willingly Embraced It, or Because God Forced Israel to Accept It? If the Latter, Is It Simply an Instance of Might Makes Right?

The biblical and rabbinic traditions were both ambivalent on the issue of why the covenant is authoritative. As noted earlier, the Bible clearly records Israel's agreement to the covenant both at Mount Sinai (Exod. 19:8; 24:3, 7) and during the reaffirmation of the covenant in the times of Joshua (Josh. 24), Esther (Esther 9:23), and Ezra (Neh. 10). In addition, as we have seen, it asserts that the covenant was made with the people Israel of all generations who at least tacitly agree to it through fulfilling its demands. The Bible also speaks, however, of God's "commanding" the clauses of the Torah amid thunder, lightning, and earthquakes, it describes the people's fear at the time (Deut. 5: 19ff.), it expresses God's wish that the people fear Him enough to obey the commandments (Deut. 5:26), and it confirms the covenant in a ceremony that is designed to inspire awe in the people (Deut. 11:26–32, 27:11–26). All of this certainly does not sound like voluntary acceptance of the covenant!

The Rabbis continue this theme. One popular homily describes God's fruitless search among the mighty nations of antiquity for a people to accept the Torah. Failing to convince any one of them, He finally turns to puny Israel, who said, "We shall faithfully do" (Exod. 24:7)—or, as the Rabbis interpreted it, "we shall do and we shall hear," indicating that Israel trusted God so much that they committed themselves to follow the commandments even before they knew what they were.[39] Even though this is not informed acceptance, it is certainly voluntary. On the other hand, another equally popular story pictures God picking up Mount Sinai and holding it over the people as He tells them that He will bury them under the mountain unless they accept the Torah.[40] This portrays a People Israel with no choice but to accept the Covenant or face death.

The situation is not as strange as it sounds. In both king–subject relationships and parent–child relationships there is an element of voluntary acceptance, and, as noted earlier, both the king and parent would like to maximize this for both practical and moral reasons. Practically, it is simply easier to gain adherence to the rules if there is willing compliance; indeed, enforcement procedures can never be totally effective. Morally, it is easier to justify the authority of the rules if they are accepted voluntarily.

But, as also noted earlier, neither Jewish law nor any other legal system can exist if it totally depends on freely chosen adherence. Some people will flagrantly and often violate the law, and some will do so less seriously and less often, and so there must be some means of enforcement. Moreover, there are situations in life in which there are no choices about accepting a set of rules in the first place. Israel's acceptance of the Torah was therefore good and proper, but the authority of its laws does not depend on that alone, for God, even more than a human king or father, has both the power and moral authority to dictate the rules.

Do Human Beings Have the Power and/or the Right to Revoke the Covenant Unilaterally?

The question of whether people can revoke the covenant unilaterally arises in a variety of different contexts, and it has a different meaning in each one of them. I shall consider three.

1. Since human beings can change provisions of the law, does not that ultimately amount to the power and/or right to revoke the covenant entirely? When the question is put this way, the answer is definitely no, at least as far as the Jewish tradition has understood things. The interpretive mandate was always to be used to further the observance and objectives of the law, not to abrogate it. A Jew is even permitted to violate all the laws of the Sabbath to save his or her life or that of another person, but the purpose of setting aside the law in this way is explicitly so that the person saved might live and then observe many future Sabbaths.[41] Interpretation of the law for the

purpose of abolishing it would be a gross abuse of the legal methodology of the system.

This becomes much murkier in modern times, however, when people like Spinoza, the leaders of the Reform movement, and many secular Jews affirm Jewish values but not necessarily the specific laws that Judaism has developed to express them, let alone Jewish rituals that are not directly connected to those values. Rabbi Robert Gordis maintained in his 1960 book, *Faith for Moderns,* that such Jews are living off the capital of the tradition they learned in religious contexts but will not be able to transmit those values across generations without structuring them in Jewish religion and law.[42]

I would not go as far as he does in this. I do think, though, that it is much harder to articulate and apply Jewish values apart from the structure of Jewish law, for then one is not likely to study Jewish law in any depth and thus loses the deep thinking that our ancestors have devoted to applying those values to concrete cases. The recent trend in Reform movement publications to translate talmudic texts and later codes into English rather than just cite general moral principles proclaimed in the Torah or elsewhere in Jewish sources indicates that Reform educators have realized that a serious Jewish discussion of moral values must invoke Jewish legal discussions over the ages. I still remember a lecture given by Reform Rabbi Steven Passamaneck in the early 1970s at Hebrew Union College in Los Angeles, where he served then and ever since as a professor of rabbinics, in which he claimed that the Reform movement's fundamental vision of Judaism as ethical monotheism should prompt Reform Jews to study codes and responsa so that they can see how the Jewish tradition has understood moral mandates. Thus while there are certainly Jews who deny the authority of Jewish law but affirm Jewish values, I, like Rabbi Gordis, wonder how deeply that can be held and how long such an approach can be sustained.

2. This brings us to the second formulation of this question: Since no country in the world requires Jews to live by Jewish law (except Israel in matters of personal status), what prevents Jews from abandoning it completely? Jews certainly do have the power in this post-Enlightenment world to invalidate the covenant for themselves, and many in fact do. Whether they have a *right* to do so depends on one's understanding of the authority of the covenant in the first place. The situation is thus directly parallel to civil legal systems. A citizen of

Israel, for example, has the power to avoid army service if he lives outside of Israel, beyond the power of Israel to enforce its law; whether he has a right to evade the law in that way depends on how one construes the basis of authority of Israeli law on him in the first place. Is it only a matter of enforcement? Are there moral obligations or other reasons to abide by the law? If so, to what extent, and why? The exact same questions apply to Jewish law: Does our covenantal relationship with God require us to abide by Jewish law even when no government forces us to do so? If so, why, and to what extent? If not, how shall we understand the covenant?

It is interesting that several modern Reform thinkers have addressed this question explicitly. Rabbi Jakob Petechowski, who taught Jewish thought at Hebrew Union College in Cincinnati until his death, and Rabbi Eugene Borowitz, who does the same at Hebrew Union College in New York, have both maintained that the Reform emphasis on individual autonomy must be balanced by our duties to God and to the Jewish tradition. Borowitz phrases this explicitly in covenantal terms. Although both stop short of saying that Jewish law should be seen as binding on contemporary Jews, they both have reinserted into Reform thought a demand that Jews take the tradition seriously and incorporate into their lives as many traditional Jewish practices as they can, a call made official Reform policy in the 1999 Pittsburgh platform statement of the Reform rabbinate.[43]

3. After the Holocaust do Jews have the right to abandon the covenant because God seems to have reneged on His part of the bargain? The answer to this troubling question depends, in the first place, on how one construes the relationship of God to the Holocaust. Was it exclusively an atrocity created by human beings, for which God shares no blame? Was God actively involved in creating it as the "Creator of good and evil" (Isa. 45:7)? Was God at least passively implicated for not stopping it sooner? Can we know? Even if God is to blame, does that free us of our covenantal obligations to God?

There are those who claim that God's failure to stop the Holocaust does in fact release us from our covenantal duties to God. Rabbi Irving Greenberg,[44] for example, argues that after the Holocaust Jews must voluntarily choose to adhere to the covenant if they are to uphold it at all. In part this is because, for Greenberg, no divine punishment could be worse than the Holocaust was, and so the long lists of threatened punishments in Leviticus 26 and Deuteronomy 28 have lost their punch, as it were. In part, though, it is not a matter of power but of right: Did God not lose the right to ask us to follow His rules when He let so many innocent people suffer so?

There are no clear-cut answers to these questions. Some will in fact construe the Holocaust as a justification to abandon Jewish law. Those who continue to adhere to it, however, may well find the covenant to be a good expression of their commitment for all of the reasons listed in the first part of this chapter and in Chapter Four. They may admit that the Holocaust is a major problem for their faith, but in that they are in no worse a position than those who understand Jewish law through other analogies. On the contrary, the degree to which the Holocaust is problematic for a continued dedication to Jewish law is best understood when we see the law as the product of a covenant between a benevolent, loving God and Israel, for that articulates graphically the poignant and personal aspects of the problems that the Holocaust poses for our relationship to God and to Jewish law.

The covenant model also makes this question both stark and balanced: even assuming that God is totally responsible for the Holocaust and thus completely reneged on His part of the bargain to reward good people and punish evil ones, should we nevertheless remain faithful to the covenant, just as He promises to do when we have completely failed to fulfill our part of the bargain (Lev. 26:44–45)? Is that what lovers do for each other even after adultery? The Holocaust, of course, is not only God's doing; humans were very much complicit in fomenting it. Thus continuing our covenantal relationship with God would seem more warranted than couples continuing their marriage after a clear case of adultery where one partner was totally responsible for the breach of faith. Even in those cases, in some circumstances continuing the marriage is both warranted and wise; how much the more so when God is at worst only one of the parties culpable for the Holocaust.

Is the Covenant Model Inherently Ambiguous?

The relationships of subjects to their sovereign, of spouses to each other, and of parents to children are certainly not the same. By articulating God's link to Israel in all three of these ways, can the covenant clearly define that connection and its legal implications?

The covenant model would indeed be clearer if it depicted the relationship between God and Israel in only one of these ways. Doing so, however, would also make the covenant less adequate as a representation of Israel's connections to God, for our relationship to God involves features that are similar to each of those three connections. Sometimes that causes confusion—for example, the High Holy Day liturgy constantly shifts from depicting God as infallible Judge to merciful Father. Even so, because our relationship to God does in fact resemble all three of these relationships in certain respects, the covenant serves us well by calling attention to all three of these relationships and their implications for the mutual duties that they create.

COMPARING THE COVENANTAL MODEL
TO OTHER POSSIBLE ONES

This brings us to the second part of my claim: whatever the weaknesses in my arguments in defense of the covenant model, I would claim that alternative theories are no better; often, in fact, they are worse. We cannot reasonably expect an absolutely adequate analogy, but we can rank-order the ones available, and when we do, we find the covenant to be the best of the lot.

A complete analysis to prove this point would take us well beyond the confines of a book such as this, for it would require a full critique of each of the alternatives in addition to a comparison of their relative strengths and weaknesses. In addition to the comparisons with other theories that I drew above, however, I would make one more observation to provide warrant for my assertion. It calls attention to the transcendent thrust of Jewish law that is at the root of many of the strengths of the covenant model discussed in the first part of this chapter.

Probably the most important advantage of the covenant theory over the alternatives is that it clearly expresses the relationship between God and the Jewish people on which Jewish law is built. The ultimate attraction of Judaism in general and Jewish law in particular is that it enables the Jewish people to relate to God and to other human beings. Through Judaism they aspire to incorporate holiness in their lives, to capture the divine element that gives direction to life and makes it worth living. Judaism has historically claimed that the relationship with God is best expressed through observance of the terms of the covenant as detailed in Jewish law, but even non-halakhic approaches to Judaism like those of Buber[45] and Borowitz[46] have used the covenant model because of its powerful affirmation of the bond between God and Israel. People vary widely in their understanding of how and what God communicates to us, but some link to God is necessary if many of the phenomena mentioned in the first part of this chapter are going to make sense. It is this transcendent thrust that the covenant conveys: It is this relationship with God and with other people that provides much of the *raison d'être* of Jewish law.

OUR RELATIONSHIP TO OTHER HUMAN BEINGS: THE DUTIES OF COVENANTAL LOVE

Human societies have routinely established laws delineating the duties of their members to each other and to the community as a whole without invoking God. The Jewish tradition, however, bases its laws governing human interactions on God's commands. It is God who commands us, for example, to "love your neighbor as yourself," emphasizing the divine foundation for that commandment by ending this verse with "I am the Lord" (Lev. 19:18). Similarly, in the Torah it is God who commands Moses to announce prohibitions like those banning oppression of one's fellow Jew and the stranger as well as dishonest weights and measures,[47] and it is God who commands Moses to declare positive duties such as those that require us to educate our children and provide for the poor.[48] This gives commandments that govern our human relationships a transcendent dimension: They come to be and gain authority not only because they are compatible with our own aims but also because they express how we understand God's will for us so that we can become the "kingdom of priests and holy nation" (Exod. 19:6) that God wants us to be.

In *To Do the Right and the Good* and *The Way into Tikkun Olam (Fixing the World)*, I discuss at some length the duties that the Jewish tradition imposes on us as a result of the love we should have for our fellow Jews and for people of other faith communities. I will not repeat those materials here. Indeed, in my view *all of the laws that govern our relationships with other human beings should be seen as the* *fruits of the love we are supposed to have toward both God and other* *human beings.* Judaism spells out in law at least some of the duties that love demands because that makes clear what is expected of us and gives those responsibilities authority and continuity—some of the advantages of articulating moral duties in legal form that I describe in Chapter Six herein and elsewhere.[49]

Here, then, I will limit myself to describing some of the specific demands that the tradition derives directly from "Love your neighbor as yourself" (Lev. 19:18) and "You shall love the stranger" (Lev. 19:34; Deut. 10:19). This should demonstrate that our covenantal love, although based in our relationship with God, is intended to affect our interactions with human beings as well. Both are the heart and soul of Jewish law.

A rabbinic statement expands on the biblical verse governing Jews' interactions with other Jews: "What message did the Torah bring to Israel? Take upon yourselves the yoke of the kingdom of Heaven, vie with one another in the fear of God, and practice loving deeds toward one another."[50] The Rabbis spell out exactly what the Jewish community must provide for its needy members, framing the duty to give and the eligibility to receive in terms of the extent to which the poor person is rooted in the community:

> One who settles in a community for thirty days becomes obligated to contribute to the charity fund together with the other members of the community. One who settles there for three months becomes obligated to contribute to the soup kitchen. One who settles there for six months becomes obligated to contribute clothing with which the poor of the community can cover themselves. One who settles there for nine months becomes obligated to contribute to the burial fund for burying the community's poor and providing for all their needs of burial.[51]

Hillel famously summarized the whole of the Torah by articulating the converse of the commandment to love one's neighbor, an implication that is clearly entailed in the Torah's verse. When a heathen offered to convert to Judaism on condition that Hillel could teach him the whole Torah while standing on one foot, "Hillel said: What is hateful to you, do not do to your neighbor. That is the whole Torah; the rest is commentary. Go and learn it."[52] A variant of this story illustrates that this general principle was intended to have practical consequences. An ass-driver asked Rabbi Akiva to teach him the Torah all at once. He replied:

> "My son, Moses our teacher stayed on the Mount forty days and forty nights before he learned it, and you want me to teach you the whole of it all at once? Still, my son, this is the basic principle of the Torah: If you wish that nobody should harm you in connection with what belongs to you, you must not harm him in that way; if you wish that nobody should deprive you of what is yours, you must not deprive your fellow man of what belongs to him." The man rejoined his companions, and they journeyed until they came to a field full of seed-pods. His companions each took two, but he took none. They continued their journey, and they came upon a field full of cabbages. They each took two, but he took none. They asked him why he had not taken any, and he replied, "Thus did Rabbi Akiba teach me: 'What is hateful to you, do not do to your fellow man.' "[53]

The Rabbis thus clearly did not understand the command to "Love your neighbor as yourself" as merely a matter of attitude or feeling. They instead interpret it to require specific actions of us. They derive this from the phrase that follows the command to love one's neighbor: "Why does the Torah say, 'Love you neighbor as yourself; *I am the Lord*'? I, the Lord, created him for My honor. Therefore if you act justly and righteously toward him, you love him, and if not, you do not love him."[54]

The Rabbis derive from this command a number of specific duties. For example, the Torah specifically forbids injuring one's parents (Exod. 21:15), but may one do that, the Talmud asks, to let blood from one's father in an attempt to cure him? Rav Mattnah answers that one may and should on the basis of "Love your neighbor as yourself."[55]

On the basis of this verse, the Talmud also rules that a man may not marry a woman until he sees her, lest he marry her unseen and then find her undesirable, thus subjecting her to rancor and maybe even divorce.[56] Similarly, a couple may not have sexual intercourse during the day lest the man see something that he does not like about his wife's naked body, making her undesirable to him.[57]

This verse is used additionally to require that those executing a person by stoning use a high place from which to throw him on the stones so that he dies instantly on hitting the ground, and it also requires that those executing a culprit by the sword do so at the neck so that he dies instantly and as painlessly as possible, for loving one's neighbor, even one deserving of the death penalty, requires that we "choose for him a pleasant death."[58] Later, Nahmanides determines that we must provide health care for those who cannot afford it on the basis of this verse.[59]

Maimonides maintains that this commandment is the basis for a number of requirements instituted by the Rabbis:

> It is a positive command instituted by the Rabbis to visit the sick, comfort mourners, take the dead [to their place of interment], bring the bride to the wedding canopy, accompany guests [on the way to their residence], and to deal with all the needs of burial, [including] to carry [the coffin] on one's shoulders, to walk before it, to eulogize [the deceased person], to dig [the grave], and to bury [the person]. [The Rabbis also required us] to bring joy to the bride and groom and to provide for all of the needs of their wedding banquet. These are acts of kindness that have no limit. Even though these commandments are of Rabbinic origin, they come under the category of "Love your neighbor as yourself" (Leviticus 19:18), [meaning that] all the things that you want others to do for you, do them for your brother in Torah and observance.[60]

In addition to the command to love our neighbor, there is a command not to hate him or her: "You shall not hate your brother in your heart" (Lev. 19:17). On this the Rabbis comment: "It is possible to think that [all that the Torah requires is] you should not curse him or smite him or slap his face; therefore the verse adds "in your heart," the intention being to forbid hatred that is in your heart."[61] Hatred of one's fellow is one of the three vices that "put a man out of the world."[62] Conversely, "Who is mighty? He who turns an enemy into his friend."[63]

Although the primary focus of Jewish duties concerns fellow Jews, just as every society cares most for its own citizens, the Jewish tradition requires that Jews care for needy non-Jews as well, that Jews must not oppress the strangers in their midst but indeed must love them. Thus in many places the Rabbis speak not of "your broth-er" (*ahikha*) or "your neighbor" (*ra'ekha*), both of which the tradition usually interprets as referring to fellow Jews, but God's "creatures" (*beriyyot*), which clearly refers to all human beings. So, for example, as the Torah commands us to "love the stranger" (Lev. 19:34; Deut. 10:19), Hillel exhorts us to "love your fellow creatures."[64]

Based on this principle, the Jewish tradition insists on a number of things. The Torah itself requires that in court Jews apply the same rules to non-Jews as they do to Jews.[65] The Rabbis say that "One may not deceive one's fellow creatures, not even a Gentile."[66] Further, "More serious is stealing from a Gentile than from an Israelite because it involves, in addition [to the ban on stealing], pro-faning God's Name."[67] The Torah asserts, "If you meet your enemy's ox or ass going astray, you shall surely bring it back to him again" (Exod. 23:4). On this the Rabbis comment, "'Your enemy's ox,'" this refers to a Gentile who is an idolater; from this we learn that idol-aters are everywhere designated enemies of Israel."[68] That is, even though the Jewish tradition would clearly have us oppose idolatry and therefore idol worshipers, this must not undermine the demand to act humanely toward them.

In a number of cases, the Rabbis insist that Jews extend them-selves to non-Jews "for the sake of peace." One instance of this is the Mishnah that states "We do not prevent the poor of the Gentiles from benefitting under the Torah's laws concerning gleanings, forgotten sheaves, and the corner of the field" (Lev. 19:9–10).[69] The Talmud expands this to require Jews to provide for the needs of non-Jews when they cannot fend for themselves:

> Our Rabbis have taught: We support the poor among non-Jews along with Jews who are poor, and visit the sick among non-Jews along with Jews who are sick, and bury the dead among non-Jews [if their families do not, or cannot afford to, bury them] along with Jews who have died, [all] in the interests of peace.[70]

The upshot, then, is that the Jewish covenant with God directly and profoundly affects our relations with fellow Jews and non-Jews as well as our interactions with God. The soul of the covenant is thus not only love and respect for God but also love for our fellow human beings as we work together to fix the world.

ENDNOTES

1. Heschel, *God in Search of Man*, p. 341. I would like to thank my friend Rabbi Aaron Mackler for reminding me of this passage.

2. M.T. Laws of Idolatry 1:2 (end). Maimonides uses the same term for Abraham in his *Guide for the Perplexed*, part 3, chap. 29.

3. For the covenant with Noah: Gen. 9. For the covenant with Abraham: Gen. 15, 17. For the covenant with Isaac: Gen. 26:2–5. For the covenant with Jacob: Gen. 28:13–15.

4. For examples of such documents, cf. Pritchard, ed., *Ancient Near Eastern Texts Relating to the Old Testament*, pp. 159–161 (Lipit-Ishtar Lawcode) and at pp. 163ff. (the Code of Hammurabi—see esp. Prologue on pp. 164–165 and Epilogue on pp. 177–180). Good secondary reading on this includes McCarthy, *Old Testament Covenant;* and Hillers, *Covenant.*

5. I am indebted to Seymour Rosenberg, formerly a master's student at the University of Judaism and a member of its board of directors, for pointing this out to me.

6. For a description of at least some of what is entailed in *tikun olam*, see Dorff, *The Way into Tikkun Olam (Fixing the World)*.

7. This is the new translation of the Jewish Publication Society, with a note pointing to the medieval commentaries of Rashbam and Ibn Ezra as well as Zech. 14:9. The more common translation is "the Lord is one," which would not deny the uniqueness of the Lord as God but would affirm something else about Him. Louis Jacobs has listed no less than 30(!) different interpretations of this verse in rabbinic literature from the time of the Rabbis to modern translations, some reasonable interpretations of the plain meaning of the text and some more homiletical; see Jacobs, *Principles of the Jewish Faith*, chap. 2, esp. pp. 96–117.

8. Sifra Kodashim, 4:12; Genesis Rabbah 24:7.

9. B. Shabbat 31a. A. Cohen cites "Professor Kittel," who argues convincingly that even though some people today might derive different lessons from this negative formulation of the value than from the positive form in the Torah (and cited by Jesus), the people of his time would have derived the same meaning from both formulations; see A. Cohen, *Everyman's Talmud*, p. 214. He cites an instructive article on this by Brockwell King, "The 'Negative' Golden Rule," who traces it to several pre-Christian sources, including Tobit 4:15, which Hillel may well have been quoting.

10. Sifra Behukkotai 7:5; B. Shavu'ot 39a; Numbers Rabbah 10:5; Tanhuma (Warsaw), Netzavim 2:2; Tanhuma (Buber) 5.

11. M. Avot 2:4.

12. B. Bava Meẓia 59b. Examples include Exod. 22:20, 23:9; Lev. 19:33, 25:17; and Deut. 24:14–15.

13. Readers may be interested in three of my previous essays in which I describe various aspects of the covenant analogy—namely, "Judaism as a Religious Legal System"; "The Meaning of Covenant"; and "The Covenant."

14. The Rabbis understood this to refer to all of Jewish law, not just Purim. B. Shabbat 88a: "Rava said: '[Although Israel originally accepted the Torah through the coercion of having the mountain overturned on them like an overturned cup,] even so Israel again accepted it in the days of Ahashverosh, as it is written, "They confirmed and accepted" (Esther 9:27), that is, they confirmed what they had already accepted.' "

15. William Moran has argued, in "Ancient Near Eastern Background of the Love of God in Deuteronomy," that the root "*ahv*" is a technical, political term in the Bible denoting loyalty rather than love. Even if he is right, later generations of Jews understood it to designate the full gamut of emotions that we call "love." Thus the Rabbis accepted Rabbi Akiva's interpretations of Song of Songs as love poetry between God and Israel (M. Yadayim 3:5; cf. M. Eduyyot 5:3, T. Sanhedrin 12:10, and T. Yadayim 2:14), and Rabbi Akiva said: "Beloved is Israel, for they are called the children of God, and it was a special token of love that they became conscious of it" (M. Avot 3:18).

16. For a summary of the range of modern interpretations of God's legislative role, see my *Conservative Judaism,* chap. 3, sec. D.

17. Greenberg, "A Revealed Law," (reprinted in Siegel, ed., *Conservative Judaism and Jewish Law;* hereinafter cited as Siegel), discussed in Dorff, "Judaism as a Religious Legal System," pp. 1348–1349.

18. Greenberg, "A Revealed Law," p. 41 (Siegel, p. 182).

19. Genesis Rabbah 26:6.

20. B. Berakhot 7a.

21. See T. Avodah Zarah 8:4; B. Sanhedrin 56–60; B. Avodah Zarah 64b; Genesis Rabbah 34:4. The Torah (Gen. 9:8–17) speaks about a covenant between God and all living beings; but the Rabbis do not connect their doctrine of the seven Noahide Laws to that covenant. They derive it instead from Gen. 2:16 (R. Yohanan on B Sanhedrin 56b) or seven separate verses from Gen. 6 and 9 (school of Menasheh on B. Sanhedrin 56b–57a). The Book of Jubilees 7, which has a slightly different list, derives it from Gen. 9 on the death of Noah. On this doctrine generally, see Novak, *The Image of the Non-Jew in Judaism.*

22. Other biblical passages that make it clear that the covenant (that is, the Decalogue, including its provision of the Sabbath) is limited to the relationship between God and Israel: Exod. 31:12–17; Lev. 20:22–26, 25:39–46; Deut. 7:1–11, 10:12–22, 33:4; Jer. 11:1–13.

23. H, Cohen, *Religion of Reason out of the Sources of Judaism,* pp. 52–54, chap. 13, pars. 35, 38, and 40; p, 271, chap. 14, par. 4; p. 353, chap. 16; and H. Cohen, *Religion and Hope,* pp. 46–50, 168ff., and chap. 6; see also my dis-

cussion of his doctrine of covenant in Dorff, "The Meaning of Covenant," pp. 46–50.

24. Rosenzweig, *The Star of Redemption,* part. 3, books 1–2. For the Bible is a revelation of God but not the only one because revelation is also to the individual; see ibid., part 2, book 1, p. 309, and book 2, esp. pp. 167–188. For consequently, other claims to revelation might well be true:

> Did God wait for Mount Sinai or, perhaps, Golgotha? No paths that lead from Sinai and Golgotha are guaranteed to lead to Him, but neither can He possibly have failed to come to one who sought Him on the trails skirting Olympus. There is no temple built so close to Him as to give man reassurance in its closeness, and none is so far from Him as to make it too difficult for man's hand to reach. There is no direction from which it would not be possible for Him to come, and none from which He must come; no block of wood in which He may not take up His dwelling, and no psalm of David that will always reach His ear (Glatzer, *Franz Rosenzweig,* p. 29).

25. Kaplan, *The Meaning of God in Modern Jewish Religion,* p. 102. See also his *Judaism as a Civilization,* pp. 258ff. See also my discussion of Kaplan's doctrine of covenant in Dorff, "The Meaning of Covenant," pp. 40–46 and, in general, in Dorff, *The Unfolding Tradition,* pp. 67–77.

26. B. Shabbat 88a.

27. Novak, *Covenantal Rights.*

28. On the duties incumbent on spouses to each other, see M. Ketubbot 5:5–7:9 and M.T. Laws of Marriage 12:10,11,14,15, 13:3–6. On sexual obligations, see M. Ketubbot 5:6.

29. On oppression through speech, see M. Bava Meẓia 4:10 and B. Bava Meẓia 58b–59b. On carrying through with an intended gift see Kitsur Shulban Arukh 62:17.

30. Aquinas, *Basic Writings of St. Thomas Aquinas,* "*Summa Contra Gentiles*" pp. 3–4, 5, 59–60, 85 and "*Summa Theologica,*" pp. 226–227, 234–238, 335–342, 356–357, 748–750, 774–775, questions 6, 19, 20, and 91; reprinted in Denise et al., eds,, *Great Traditions in Ethics,* pp. 86–104. Hobbes, *Leviathan,* chaps. 14–15; reprinted in Denise et al., eds,, *Great Traditions in Ethics,* pp. 137–141. Maritain, *The Rights of Man and Natural Law,* pp. 111–114.

31. Fishbane, *Biblical Interpretation in Ancient Israel.*

32. For a summary of how several medieval rabbis reconciled Deut. 4:2 and 13:1 with the obvious fact that Jewish law had changed dramatically over the centuries, see Dorff and Rosett, *A Living Tree,* pp. 403–404.

33. B. Pesaḥim 68b.

34 For rabbinic uses of *tikun olam:* M. Gittin 4:2–7, 9, 5:3, 9:4; M. Eduyyot

1:13; T. Ketubbot 12:1; T. Gittin 3:12–13; 6:10; T. Bava Batra 6:6; B. Ketubbot 52b; and J. Pesaḥim 14b. For a fuller exposition of this theme in Judaism, see Dorff, *The Way into Tikkun Olam (Fixing the World)*.

35 For example, Midrash Psalms, par. 4, on Psalm 146:7, God "frees the bound (*mattir assurim*)."

36. See Klausner, *The Messianic Idea in Israel*, pp. 444–450; Patai, *The Messiah Texts*, pp. 247–257 (a convenient selection of primary texts in translation); W. Davies, *Torah in the Messianic Age*; Scholem, *The Messianic Idea in Judaism*, pp. 49–77.

37. For example, Maimonides, Guide of the Perplexed, part 1, chaps. 51–61; Hume, *Dialogues Concerning Natural Religion*, part 2; Tillich, *Dynamics of Faith*, pp. 41–54; Edwards, "Being-Itself and Irreducible Metaphors"; and Mascall, *Existence and Analogy*, pp. 97–121. The last three articles are reprinted in Santoni, ed., *Religious Language and the Problem of Religious Knowledge*.

38. Dorff, *Matters of Life and Death*.

39. Sifrei Devarim, par. 343; Numbers Rabbah 14:10.

40. B. Shabbat 88a; B. Avodah Zarah. 2b; and so on.

41. Mekhilta Ki Tissa on Exod. 31:12. Later sources debate whether this applies to saving the life of a non-Jew as well.

42. Gordis, *A Faith for Moderns*, p. 23:

> Our modern age has been the spendthrift heir of virtuous, hard-working ancestors, who created the heritage that their children have now all but squandered. All the decencies of human nature today were nurtured by the creeds of yesterday. Justice, mercy, and truth became human imperatives, because they were felt to be the attributes of God, whom men were commanded to imitate. Ethical culture is possible only in a soil rendered fertile earlier by religious faith. . . . All too often, they [men] have been heedless of the fact that their moral standards derived from habits of thought and patterns of action inculcated by religion and that these values could survive the decay of faith only for the brief interval of a generation or two or less.

43. Petechowski, "Some Criteria for Modern Jewish Observance." See also his *Ever Since Sinai*, pp. 108–113. Borowitz, *Renewing the Covenant*, esp. chaps. 16–20. The 1999 Pittsburgh Platform of the Central Conference of American Rabbis can be found at www.ccarnet.org/documentsandpositions/platforms/. See Dorff, *The Unfolding Tradition*, pp. 444–456, for my discussion of the emerging commitment to Jewish law in the Reform movement as evidenced by the positions they have taken in their four platform statements between 1885 and 1999, and see my interchange of letters with

Rabbi Borowitz on his theory of covenant in contrast to mine on pp. 463–480 therein.

44. I. Greenberg, "Cloud of Smoke, Pillar of Fire." See also the discussion of post-Holocaust theologies in Chapter Four of the present volume.

45. Buber, *On Judaism,* pp. 112–113; and his *Israel and the World,* pp. 170–171. Buber is not a complete antinomian: every I–Thou experience with God involves a demand on the individual having the experience, but those demands are specific to the individual and not necessarily the requirements of Jewish law; see *Israel and the World,* p. 209, and Rosenzweig's "The Builders.".

46. Borowitz, *Renewing the Covenant,* pp. 284–299.

47. For do not oppress one's fellow Jew: Lev. 25:14, 17; Deut. 24:14–15. For do not oppress the stranger: Exod. 22:20, 23:9; Lev. 19:33; Deut. 24:14–15. For honest weights and measures: Lev. 19:35–36; Deut. 25:13–16.

48. For educate our children: Deut. 4:9, 6:7, 11:19. For care for the poor: Lev. 19:9–10, 25:25–46; Deut. 14:27–15:18.

49. Dorff, *To Do the Right and the Good,* pp. 262–282, esp. pp. 272–282; Dorff, *Love Your Neighbor and Yourself,* pp. 311–344, esp. pp. 337–344.

50. Sifrei Devarim, par. 323.

51. M.T. Laws of Gifts to the Poor 9:12. Cf. T. Pe'ah 4:9; J. Bava Batra 1:4; B. Bava Batra 8a.

52. B. Shabbat 31a.

53. Avot d'Rabbi Natan, second recension (Schechter, ed.), chap. 26, p. 53.

54. Avot d'Rabbi Natan, chap. 15. See also B. Pesaḥim 113b.

55. B. Bava Kamma 84b.

56. B. Kiddushin 41a.

57. B. Niddah 17a.

58. B. Sanhedrin 45a; B. Ketubbot 37b.

59. Nahmanides, Kitvei ha-Ramban (Chavel, ed.), 2:43; this passage comes from Nahmanides' *Torat Ha-Adam* (The instruction of man), *Sha'ar Sakkanah* (Section on danger), on B. Bava Kamma 8, and it is cited by Joseph Karo in his commentary to the Tur Bet Yosef, Yoreh De'ah 336. Nachmanides bases himself on similar reasoning in B. Sanhedrin 84b.

60. Maimonides, M.T. Laws of Mourning (A'vel) 14:1.

61. Sifra on Leviticus 19:17

62. M. Avot (Ethics of the Fathers) 2:16.

63. Avot d'Rabbi Natan 23.

64. M. Avot (Ethics of the Fathers) 1:12.

65. For example, Lev. 18:26, 19:33–37, 24:22; Num. 15:15–16; Deut. 10:17–19.

66. B. Hullin 94a.

67. T. Bava Kamma 10:15.

68. Mekhilta on Exod. 23:4.
69. M. Gittin 5:8.
70. B. Gittin 61a; M.T. Laws of Gifts to the Poor 7:7 According to B. Gittin 59b, obligations that are for the sake of peace have Pentateuchal authority.

PART III

Implications of My Theory for Key Aspects of Jewish Law

CHAPTER FOUR

Motivations to Live
by Jewish Law

MULTIPLE MOTIVES

Why should I live my life in accordance with the law? Most people immediately think of enforcement: I must follow the law because if I do not, I will be punished. Mordecai Kaplan, in fact, thought that Jewish norms should no longer be seen as law precisely because they would not be enforced in modern societies that guarantee freedom of and from religion.[1]

The threat of punishment does indeed play a role in producing compliance in most legal systems, including religious ones that govern countries like Pakistan and Saudi Arabia, but no legal system can rely on that alone. If only enforcement prompted people to stay in line, society would need three police officers for every citizen, assuming that a police officer works an eight-hour day, and then police officers to watch over the police officers. One clear demonstration that punishment alone will not suffice is Prohibition: most people obeyed it, but because a small minority flouted it, it had to be repealed. Even the full power of the U.S. Armed Forces could not make a constitutional amendment work if any more than a tiny minority refused to obey it without being forced to do so.

For the law to govern effectively, most people must adhere to it for other reasons. Then the police can enforce it on the 1 or 2 percent of the population who routinely violate it, and they can remind the rest of us to watch our speed while driving and to avoid other temptations.

The Torah already understands that the threat of punishment, even at the hand of God, will not be enough to produce compliance. As I noted earlier, at Mount Sinai the Israelites were exposed to this rationale in the most powerful way possible. Thunder, lightning, and earthquakes accompanied God's revelation of the law; if that did not impress the people of the power of God to enforce His law, nothing would. And yet, just 40 days later, the Israelites were worshiping the Golden Calf. This certainly demonstrated to the leaders of biblical Israel that the threat of punishment alone—even by God—would not suffice.

No wonder, then, that the Torah itself describes many other reasons to obey the commandments, and the Rabbis of the Talmud and Midrash add yet more. In this chapter, we shall examine the rationales for living by Jewish law that the Torah and the Rabbis suggest, and then I will ask which, if any, of these motivations might work for us today as well.

Before exploring these motivations, it is important to note that in law, as in most things in life, people's motivations to do something or to refrain from doing something are often multiple. There may be one primary motive that a person has in mind, but a little probing often reveals that other factors also play a role, sometimes consciously and sometimes unconsciously. If I agree to give a lecture, for example, it may be because they are paying me to do so, because I love to teach, because a friend asked me, because I want to sell my books, because I want to meet someone who is participating in the same program, because I want to try some new ideas on an audience to get their reactions, and so on. Any or all of those motives might play a role, one or more of them may be more prominent in my decision than others, and some may not motivate me at all to give the lecture. I may also have some unconscious motives—the quest for approval, for example, or for attention.

The same thing applies to people's motives for adhering to law. At any one time, multiple motives may be at work in my deciding to do or refrain from some action. Put another way, motivation to adhere to the law (or to break it) is often *overdetermined,* shaped by many factors acting in tandem.

Furthermore, at any given moment, I may abide by the law primarily because of fear of punishment, hope for reward, or any of the motives listed in the following sections. Exactly which factor determines my behavior varies with the circumstances and even my mood. Furthermore, what prompts me to be guided by one law may be different from what leads me to follow another. In both of these ways, my reasons for following various laws are *eclectic,* with some determining my behavior in regard to one law at one time and others producing my actions in regard to another law or even the same law at another time.

MOTIVES SUGGESTED BY THE BIBLE

1. Wisdom

Why, then, should I live my life in accordance with Jewish law? One of the rationales the Torah suggests is self-interest: A person should fulfill the commandments because that is a smart way to live, one that enables a person to succeed in life. Wisdom in the Bible does not refer to two other kinds of knowledge—namely, the accumulation of information or the intellectual ability to analyze things; it is rather the knowledge that comes from experience, *savoir faire,* "street smarts." The Torah maintains that the law is so wise that even non-Jews, who have a vested interest in touting their own ways of life, will recognize the superior wisdom of Jewish teaching:

> See, I [Moses] have taught you laws and statutes, as the Lord my God has commanded me, for you to do in the land that you are about to enter and inherit. Observe and do them, for it is your wisdom and discernment in the eyes of other nations, who will hear of all these laws and say, "Surely that is a great nation of wise and discerning people." For what great nation has gods close to it as the Lord our God whenever we call out to Him? Or what great nation has righteous laws and statutes as this entire teaching that I set before you this day? (Deut. 4:4–8).

In the following passage, the Psalmist goes without a beat from extolling creation to praising the Torah, indicating by this juxtaposition that the laws fit the world and that both the world and the Torah are expressions of God's loving wisdom:

The heavens declare the glory of God,
The vault of heaven proclaims His handiwork.
One day speaks to another,
Night to night speaks its knowledge,
And this without speech or words,
Their voices are not heard.
Their word goes out to the entire earth,
Their words to the end of the world.
He placed in them [the heavens] a tent for the sun,
Who, like a groom coming forth from his wedding canopy,
Rejoices like a mighty man to run the path.
His rising is at one end of the heavens,
His circuit reaches the other,
And nothing escapes his heat.
The teaching of the Lord is flawless, restoring life.
The covenant of the Lord is trustworthy, making the simple wise.
The precepts of the Lord are just, rejoicing the heart.
The commandment of the Lord is clear, giving light to the eyes.
The fear of the Lord is pure, abiding forever.
The judgments of the Lord are true, righteous altogether.
More desirable than gold, than much fine gold,
Sweeter than honey, than drippings from the comb,
Your servant pays them heed,
In obeying them there is much reward. (Ps. 19:2–12)

Similarly, Psalm 147 goes to great lengths to praise creation and then compares God's commands of nature to God's commands of the People Israel:

He sends forth His word to the earth;
His command runs swiftly.
He lays down snow like fleece,
scatters frost like ashes.
He tosses down hail like crumbs—
who can endure His icy cold?
He issues a command—it melts them;
He breathes—the waters flow.
He issued commands to Jacob,
His statutes and rules to Israel.
He did not do so for any other nation;

of such rules they know nothing.
Hallelujah. (Ps. 147:15–20)

Furthermore, the biblical Books of Proverbs and Psalms spell out recipes for living life based on the experience of those who have come before. Although Proverbs in particular does not speak directly of obeying the law but rather of following the lessons of experience (wisdom), many passages in Proverbs and Psalms encourage a way of life that is shaped by the values underlying many of the laws, including respect for God and for one's parents and elders; honesty; telling the truth; and fidelity to one's spouse, friends, and business partners. They even promise that one who lives by these values and laws will be happy. For example:

Who is the man who is eager for life,
who desires years of good fortune?
Guard your tongue from evil,
your lips from deceitful speech.
Shun evil and do good,
seek peace and pursue it. (Ps. 34:13–15)

Happy is the man who fears the Lord,
who is ardently devoted to His commandments.
His descendants will be mighty in the land,
a blessed generation of upright men.
Wealth and riches are in his house,
and his beneficence lasts forever.
A light shines for the upright in the darkness;
he is gracious, compassionate, and beneficent.
All goes well with the man who lends generously,
who conducts his affairs with equity.
He shall never be shaken;
the beneficent man will be remembered forever.
He is not afraid of evil tidings;
his heart is firm, he trusts in the Lord. (Ps. 112:1–7)

The Lord grants wisdom;
Knowledge and discernment are by His decree.
He reserves ability for the upright

And is a shield for those who live blamelessly,
Guarding the paths of justice,
Protecting the way of those loyal to Him.
You will then understand what is right, just,
And equitable—every good course.
For wisdom will enter your mind
And knowledge will delight you. . . .
It will save you from the way of evil men,
From men who speak duplicity. . . .
It will protect you from the forbidden woman,
From the alien woman whose talk is smooth,
Who forsakes the companion of her youth
And disregards the covenant of her God. . . .
So follow the way of the good,
And keep to the paths of the just.
For the upright will inherit the earth,
The blameless will remain in it.
While the wicked will vanish from the land
And the treacherous will be rooted out of it.
(Prov. 2:6–10,12,16–17,20–22)

All of these sources maintain that it is wise to live by the Torah's values and laws because they fit the structure of nature and, therefore, work well. Ample experience demonstrates that following the laws enables one to accomplish one's goals in life and attain happiness; the laws are tried and true. Conversely, as the closing verses in the last selection indicate, if you lead a corrupt life and live in a corrupt society, both you and society will suffer. It is as if nature had an allergic reaction to such deeds.

On the other hand, Job and Kohelet (Ecclesiastes) have enormous existential angst in confronting the reality that following the law is not always accompanied by good fortune. As a result, Kohelet concludes that one should not exert oneself to be good. At the same time, one should not abandon the Torah's rules for life, lest one get into trouble. Thus in the end he too thinks that it is wise to live moderately within the Torah's values. Furthermore, one should enjoy life as much as possible and live it with gusto:

In my own brief span of life, I have seen both these things: sometimes a good man perishes in spite of his goodness, and sometimes a wicked one endures in spite of his wickedness. So do not overdo goodness and do not act the wise man to excess, or you may be dumbfounded. [On the other hand,] do not overdo wickedness, and do not be a fool, or you may die before your time. It is best that you grasp the one without letting go of the other, for one who fears God will do his duty by both. . . . Go, eat your bread in gladness, and drink your wine in joy; for your action was long ago approved by God. Let your clothes always be freshly washed, and your head never lack ointment. Enjoy happiness with a woman you love all the fleeting days of life that have been granted to you under the sun—all your fleeting days, for that alone is what you can get out of life and out of the means you acquire under the sun. Whatever it is in your power to do, do with all your might, for there is no action, no reasoning, no learning, no wisdom in Sheol [the grave], where you are going. (Eccles. 7:15–18, 9:7–10)

Even though the following passage speaks of the benefits of following wisdom, Jewish liturgy has us sing the last several verses as we return the Torah to the ark after reading it publicly. In that context, in saying (singing) these lines we are asserting that the Torah is one important expression of God's wisdom and that it is simply smart to follow its laws:

Happy is the person who finds wisdom,
The person who attains understanding.
Its value in trade is better than silver,
Its yield greater than gold.
It is more precious than rubies,
All of your goods cannot equal it.
In its right hand is length of days,
In its left, riches and honor.
Its ways are pleasant ways,
And all its paths, peaceful.
It is a tree of life to those who grasp it,
And whoever who holds on to it is happy. (Prov. 3:13–18)

2. Moral Knowledge and Motivation

By following the Torah's laws, one can attain not only success in life but moral virtue. This is because the Torah's laws define what it means to be moral, thus enabling us to know how to live morally. In some cases, as the Rabbis later say, we might learn moral traits from the other animals (humility from the cat, honesty from the ant, forbidden intercourse from the dove, and good manners from the cock),[2] but in many areas of life we need instruction about how to live morally. Furthermore, most of us need willpower to avoid immoral activities and to dedicate ourselves to fulfilling positive moral duties, and Judaism reenforces our desires to be moral people. Thus we might follow Jewish law for both the knowledge it provides us of how to act morally and the motivation it reinforces in us to be moral in the first place.

How do we learn how to be moral? We learn that first from our parents and later from our teachers and classmates in school and from our interactions with society at large. Robert Fulghum famously asserted this in the very title and in the content of his popular book, *All I Really Need to Know I Learned in Kindergarten.*

How, though, do all those people know what is right, and why should we trust them as moral teachers, especially when we know that every human being is fallible? Secular systems of ethics maintain that the source of authority of moral norms is not particular human beings but rather reason, custom, emotion, intuition, or nature. Western religious systems of ethics maintain that all these human factors should play a role in discerning the moral thing to do, but so should our understanding of God and what God wants of us—indeed, a more important role than any of the other factors.

This, of course, assumes that God is moral in the first place. The Bible and the Rabbis repeatedly affirm that that is the case, but they are also open to questioning some of the acts and even the laws of God as recorded in the Bible. These broader issues of the morality of God and theodicy, both in Jewish classical literature and in my own view, I have discussed elsewhere,[3] and in Chapter Six I shall discuss at some length the relationships between law and morality.

Here, then, suffice it to say that the Torah is the first attempt of our ancestors to define what it means to walk in the ways of God, a God whose paths are, as Abraham already discerns, "what is just and right" (Gen. 18:19). This produces a robust wrestling with God and with the law whenever a law appears to be immoral, motivated by the conviction that a moral God could not plausibly be understood to desire what is patently immoral. Historically, this has led to narrowing a number of laws (such as the death penalty, the stubborn and rebellious son of Deut. 21;18–21, the illegitimate child of Deut. 23:3)[4] so that they rarely if ever apply; imposing restrictions on other laws so that they become so onerous that nobody would want to take advantage of them (for example, slavery);[5] expanding other laws (for example, applying the ban against putting a stumbling block in front of a blind person in Lev. 19:14 to prohibit deceiving those who are intellectually or morally blind as well);[6] reinterpreting others (such as an "eye for an eye" to mean not retribution but compensation);[7] and adding others (like the entire institution of the *ketubbah*, the marriage contract, to increase the protections of women in marriage).[8] All of these rabbinic modulations of the law stem from their strong conviction that God would not want the law to allow, much less require, immoral things.

Thus there is a *dialectic process* by which the Torah instructs us on what is moral; and we, in turn, bring our own moral sensitivities, influenced by the Torah and by the other elements in our lives, to the task of interpreting and applying the Torah. To the extent that rabbis and the Jewish community in every generation succeed in shaping the law to articulate what it means to be moral, the moral guidance that Jewish law provides is a compelling reason to live by it.

Moreover, the places where we have moral difficulties with the Bible's laws and stories, while real and troubling, are rare. They should not blind us to the fact that over and over again we look to the Torah and to its rabbinic interpretations to teach us the very meaning of what it is to be moral. This includes some very broad principles, applying to almost everyone and every circumstance: for example, "Justice, justice shall you pursue" (Deut. 16:20) and "Love your neighbor as yourself" (Lev. 19:18); some more specific principles, applying to specific groups of people and circumstances: "You shall not mistreat any widow or orphan" (Exod. 22:21) and "Honor your father and mother" (Exod. 20:12); and some very specific rules: "When you build a new house, you shall make a parapet for your roof, so that you do not bring bloodguilt on your house if anyone should fall from it" (Deut. 22:8).

When we think of the moral component of the Bible and of the Jewish tradition generally as reasons to obey the law, we probably think first of the sweeping principles it describes in such sections as the Decalogue (the Ten Commandments). The glory of the Jewish tradition, however, is that it not only announced the principles of morality that are at the root of Western civilization but also spelled out in detail what it means to abide by these principles. We, after all, do not live in a world of abstract principles; we live instead in a world of concrete realities. The only way in which general principles can have an effect on our lives is if they are translated into specific commandments governing the details of our conduct in everyday life.

The Torah begins this process, but it is the rabbis over the generations who have given detailed instructions as to how to live by the Torah's principles. For example, the Torah states a simple, but important rule: We must return lost objects to their owner. When this is first announced in Exodus, it is already in a specific context, one common to the nomadic community in which most Jews lived at the time: "When you encounter your enemy's ox or donkey wandering, you must take it back to him" (Exod. 23:4).

Scholars generally date the Book of Deuteronomy approximately four centuries later than the Book of Exodus—specifically, in the late seventh century B.C.E. By that time, many questions had arisen as to the extent of finders' obligations under this rule. Must they, for example, return anything other than animals? If the owner lives far away, does the finder have to travel a long distance to return the lost object? What if the owner is unknown? Deuteronomy addresses all these questions, at least in a preliminary way, and makes the principle of returning a lost object a general one, applying to any kind of loss:

> Do not see your brother's ox or sheep straying and ignore them. You must return them to your brother. If your brother is not near you or you do not know him, you shall bring it home and it shall be with you until your brother claims it; then you shall return it to him. So shall you do with his donkey; so shall you do with his garment; and so shall you do with anything your brother loses and you find: you may not ignore it. (Deut. 22:1–3)

The first rabbinic collection of laws, the Mishnah (edited about 200 C.E.), and the continuing rabbinic discussion of the Mishnah found in the Talmud (edited about 500 C.E.) include an entire chapter (Bava Mezia 2) on the subject of lost objects! It investigates yet further questions that arise in fulfilling this obligation. Do finders' obligations have a time limit? That is, if they do not find the owner within, say, a year, may they stop trying? May finders use the object in the meantime? Who is responsible for paying for the costs and the lost time in reaching the owner? All these questions, and many more, must be resolved if the finder and owner are to know their respective duties and privileges under the moral obligation to return a lost object. This is the only way that the principle can guide us morally.

Returning a lost object is a relatively simple moral principle, where the duty is clear and generally not too burdensome to fulfill. Yet, as soon as we seek to apply it to actual situations, many questions arise. Even if we assume that the finder and the owner genuinely *want* to act morally in this situation, they need guidance to tell them specifically how to do so.

If this is necessary in regard to a generally accepted and relatively uncomplicated principle like returning a lost object, it is even more needed in regard to the more controversial and difficult areas of business, medicine, family life, and communal life. So, for example, the Torah itself defines whose claim takes precedence between a burglar and a home owner who wounds him during the burglary (Exod. 22:13) and between a lender collecting a loan and a borrower's dignity (Deut. 24:10–13). Contemporary examples in which the morally right thing to do is not clear, such as removing life support systems from a dying patient or genetic testing and selection, call all the more for moral guidance from our tradition.

In addition to establishing moral standards and giving moral values and ideals concrete application, the law helps us determine what is moral in at least two other ways that I describe in fuller detail elsewhere. It provides a public forum for adjudicating moral conflicts. It also affords moral norms continuity and authority at the same time that it provides methods for changing moral norms or their applications.[9]

The law furthermore helps motivate us to act morally. In part, it does this by giving voice to our moral sensitivities. That is, it assumes that we *want* to be moral human beings, and it appeals to that desire within us in motivating us to do what is right. So, for example, the Torah has clauses like these:

If you lend money to My [God's] people, to the poor among you, do not act toward him as a creditor; exact no interest from him. If you take your neighbor's garment in pledge, return it to him before the sun sets; for it is his only covering, it is his only garment for his skin. In what shall he sleep? If he cries out to Me, I will listen, for

> I am compassionate. . . . Do not oppress a stranger, for you know
> the soul of the stranger, because you were strangers in the land of
> Egypt. (Exod. 22:24–26, 23:9)

Here the reasons to abide by these rules are not only that they will
be enforced by God or by human authorities but that they also appeal
to our own sense of fairness and to the compassion our historical
experience should have taught us. We must return the poor man's
clothing because "in what shall he sleep?" Even before it asserts that
we should do this because ultimately God will listen to the poor
man's cry of desperation and punish us for being heartless, the Torah
states that we ourselves should have sufficient compassion to act in
this way. Moreover, we should know better than to oppress a
stranger, for we ourselves have known what it means to be strangers;
we have ourselves tasted the needs and the dangers of being a for-
eigner. We should, therefore, be sensitive to others who are now
strangers and treat them fairly and empathetically.

The law also hones our moral sensitivities and motivates us to be
moral by requiring us to do specific acts that embody moral norms.[10]
This minimally provides the benefit that the moral action achieves.
It may also, as the Talmud suggests, teach us to do the right thing for
the right reason, even if we did not have that motivation now: "Rab
Judah said in Rab's name: A person should always occupy himself
with Torah and good deeds, even if not for their own sake, for out of
[studying Torah and doing good] with an ulterior motive, he will
come to [study Torah and do good] for their own sake."[11] Furthermore, the law tests and preserves the integrity of our moral intentions, for it requires us to act on them and thus see exactly how sin-
cere they are. In addition, the law gives us a means to make amends
for what we have done wrong and repair moral damage so that we
are not bogged down in guilt and can instead go on with our lives to
do good things. Finally, the law creates a community in which moral
ends can be attained. Many moral norms require more than one person to produce, and both the ritual and moral components of the law
help create communities that can accomplish these ends.

One important reason to live by the commandments, then, is that
we look to them to define what is moral and to motivate us to do
what is moral. We all want to see ourselves as moral people; this is
an important part of our self-image. The Torah's commandments tell
us *how* to do that in very specific—and therefore practical—terms.

They also remind us of our desire to be moral people and recharge our moral motivation in the other ways delineated earlier. We ought to live by the commandments, then, because they instruct us in how to think, feel, and act morally.

3. Covenantal Promises

We have moral duties not only to other human beings but also to God. The Torah articulates these obligations as those of the covenant between God and the People Israel. As described in Chapter Three, the Torah's covenant between God and the People Israel is modeled on both marriage covenants between two equals and also ancient suzerainty treaties between a ruler and his people. Even the latter type includes mutual promises by the parties as well as the clear intent to create an ongoing relationship between them. Creating relationships is a prime goal of covenants in contrast to contracts, which are instead focused on completing a specific task or providing a particular service.

Why should Jews adhere to the terms of the covenant together with all the laws that developed later on the basis of it? In part, of course, to gain its rewards for abiding by it and avoid its penalties for not doing so. But the reasons for compliance go deeper than that. They include at least three grounds for abiding by the terms of the covenant: (1) because we promised to do so, and we should keep our word; (2) because our relationship with God imposes obligations on us, just as all relationships do; and (3) because we owe God in gratitude for the favors God has done for us. We shall examine the first of these in this section and the other two in the sections that follow.

Part of the authority of the laws of the covenant derives from the promises the People Israel made at Mount Sinai to abide by its laws. "Moses went and told the people all the words of the Lord and all the statutes; and all the nation answered with one voice, saying, 'All the things that the Lord has spoken we will do!' Moses then wrote down all the words of the Lord" (Exod. 24:3-4). In context, this is a promise to be loyal to the God of Israel and not others and to follow the laws delineated in Exod. 20-23. The later tradition, however, expanded the content of the promise to include the later biblical and rabbinic tradition as well.

The morality of promise keeping thus binds us to the laws of the

Torah. If one gives one's word, one should fulfill it. This is an important mark of personal integrity and moral worthiness—that, as the Rabbis will later say, "one's yes should be yes, and one's no should be no."[12]

Although this seems clear on its face, it actually raises two significant questions. First, when the covenant was first made at Mount Sinai, promises were made under anything but ideal moral circumstances. Thunder, lightning, and earthquakes certainly make it seem that the people were coerced in promising what they did (to say nothing of the children who were too young to be held responsible for what they said then). The overpowering nature of the Sinai event undermines the binding quality of what the Israelites said there, for promises must be kept only when they are voluntary.

In defense of the covenant's morality, one might say that the promises that our ancestors made were authoritative for them because it was not just at Sinai that they promised God to adhere to the terms of the covenant; later in Moses' life and during the times of Joshua, Esther, and Ezra new generations repeated this commitment under conditions that were not at all threatening and that included full knowledge of what they were promising to uphold.[13] Thus even if their original promise was coerced, it was followed by a pattern of repeated, voluntary commitments under much calmer conditions.

Even if the Israelites made binding promises to adhere to the law during biblical times, however, why and how does this bind later generations? The Torah itself is sensitive to this problem. When Moses addresses the Israelites at the end of his life, the children and grandchildren of those who left Egypt and stood at Mount Sinai, he says this:

> The Lord our God made a covenant with us at Horeb. Not with our fathers [alone] did the Lord make this covenant, but with us, the living, every one of us who is here today. Face to face the Lord spoke to you on the mountain out of the fire. (Deut. 5:2–4)

> You stand this day, all of you, before the Lord your God—your tribal heads, your elders and your officials, all the men of Israel, your children, your wives, and even the stranger within your camp, from your woodchopper to your waterdrawer—to enter into the covenant of the Lord your God and His oath, which the Lord your

God is concluding with you this day, so that He establish you this day as His people and He will be your God, as He has spoken to you and as He swore to your fathers, Abraham, Isaac, and Jacob. I make this covenant, and this oath, not with you alone, but with those who are standing here with us this day before the Lord our God and with those who are not with us here today. (Deut. 29:9–14)

In other words, the Torah claims that even though the second and the newly emerging third generation were not physically at Mount Sinai, they were there in spirit and are bound by the promises made there.

The same issue, of course, arises in secular law. How can Americans, for example, be morally bound by the promises made by the Founding Fathers and the state legislatures that approved the Constitution long ago, especially because the ancestors of most Americans were not even living within its borders at the time?

There are at least two answers that philosophers have proposed. One hearkens back to the 17th-century thinker Thomas Hobbes. He argues that if you are still part of a nation on the day you become an adult (however the nation defines that), then you have given your *tacit consent* to all of its laws and can be held responsible to obey them.[14] Of course, immigrants to a country who become naturalized citizens give conscious, public, and articulated consent to the laws when they pledge allegiance to their new country after studying at least some of its laws and taking an examination to ensure that they know to what they are agreeing. That is clearly informed consent. Citizens by birth may never make such a public declaration, but they nevertheless have done it silently, says Hobbes, if they have learned about the legal expectations of the society while growing up in it and have remained in it upon achieving adulthood. This silent consent provides the moral grounding for enforcing the laws on such citizens, for they have communicated with their bodies (if not also verbally) that they have given their informed consent to abide by the nation's laws.

In secular societies, those who do not want to abide by the promises of their ancestors or follow their nation's rules can leave and escape its jurisdiction—at least if they have not committed a felony while there. May Jews similarly leave the Jewish people and stop abiding by Jewish law? That is, may they actively indicate that they are not tacitly consenting to Jewish law and choosing to live under some other legal system instead? The Rabbis claim that Jews may not do so. Hillel articulates the norm: "Do not separate yourself from the community."[15] The Rabbis then prescribe harsh penalties for those who violate this norm by consciously deciding to abandon Jewish law: Such people lose their place in the world to come—apparently even if they abide by the commandments—and the community is not obligated to set aside time from work to mourn them. Even those who separate themselves from the community in lesser ways—by, for example, refusing to pay taxes—suffer the latter fate.[16] Thus Hobbes's theory of tacit consent, which assumes the ability of citizens to leave the country and thus actively deny consent to its laws, cannot apply to Jewish law, which does not grant Jews the right to leave the Jewish community or its laws.

In fact, in the context of freedom of and from religion, even express consent to be part of a religious community is unenforceable. For example, part of the Bar (and usually Bat) Mitzvah rite involves young adults publicly pronouncing the blessings over the Torah that praise and thank God for "choosing us from all the nations and giving us His Torah." In chanting these blessings, they publicly and specifically identify with the People Israel and accept the Torah as binding—much as Americans do when they take a Pledge of Allegiance orally or in writing upon registering for the draft or applying for a government job. Those applying for American citizenship, however, are 18 years old or older. Even though Jewish law maintains that 13-year-olds become responsible for following the commandments, it is not clear that their praise of God at this age for making them part of the Jewish People and for giving Jews the Torah is a pledge at all, little less a pledge to which a person of that young age can be held.

In sum, then, the promises made by our ancestors cannot alone morally bind us because we did not make those promises and, by the terms of Jewish law, we cannot leave its jurisdiction if we choose to do so. Therefore the force of this reason to adhere to Jewish law—that you promised to do so—applies only to those Jews who, like our ancestors of old, restate the promise themselves, either orally or tacitly in the way they live their lives. This is not a small group; it applies not only to those who consciously and explicitly promise God to abide by Jewish law but also to Jews who observe Jewish law in practice. This consideration then provides yet another reason to observe the commandments—namely, one's explicit pledge or one's behavior demonstrates that one has personally confirmed the promises made long ago, and one should fulfill one's own promises.

4. Our Covenantal Relationship of Love with God

There is another, more compelling way to justify the authority of law to govern those who never consciously and voluntarily agreed to it. As discussed in Chapter One, Americans, more than any other group, think of society as a *voluntary association of individuals* who can choose to belong or to give up membership in any group, including even American citizenship itself.

More modern thinkers in other parts of the world and even in the United States, however, have shown that such thinking is in error. Whether we want to be or not, we are part of small and large communities from our very birth. Our responsibilities to the members of our family, community, and even to humanity at large exist before we are ever asked to agree to anything. These thinkers assert that human beings are inherently *social* by nature: Regardless of our desires, we are related to each other, with the rights and responsibilities such ties entail. Human beings are *not* isolated and independent in nature any more than atoms are; we are related to each other as soon as we are born. Our primary relationships—to our family, our people, to humanity as a whole, to the environment, and to God—do not depend on our desires; they arise out of the nature of our being in relationship with others.[17]

The same kind of reasoning applies to our ties to God. We have a bond from the moment we are born through our entire lives. This relationship imposes duties on us, just as our human connections do. The duties we have toward God do not derive alone—or perhaps even primarily—from any specific promises we made. They instead arise as an immediate and direct result of the relationship we have with God, just as our duties to our family, friends, and community emerge.

The deeper the relationship, the more extensive the duties that follow from it. As a result, except in abusive situations, family ties to parents and siblings are our deepest human relationships and bind us most extensively, even though they originally arose out of biological events rather than voluntary choice. The duties that accompany our other relationships grow out of our feelings of caring, affection,

147

and—at their most intense—love. In those situations, the obligations of the relationship, while definitely real, are not felt so much as duties that one must do but rather as expressions of love that one wants to do for the loved one.

The Jewish tradition applies this kind of analysis to the relationship between God and the People Israel: God gives us the commandments not only (and maybe not primarily) as an act of power but rather out of love. Whether God's love for us is as parent or as lover, the *Ahavah Rabbah* prayer recited each morning and the *Ahavat Olam* prayer recited each evening, both immediately before *Shema,* eloquently express the Jewish tradition's conviction that God's giving us the Torah is in itself a prime act of love on God's part.

Ahavah Rabbah

You have loved us with great love, Lord our God, boundless is Your tender compassion. Our Father, our King, because our ancestors trusted in You, You taught them life-giving laws; graciously teach us as well. Our Father, compassionate Father, have mercy on us and enable us to understand and discern, to listen, to learn, and to teach, to observe, to do, and to fulfil all the words of Your Torah with love. Open our eyes to Your Torah, help our hearts cleave to your commandments. Unite all our thoughts to love and revere You. . . . Praised are You, Lord, who chooses His People Israel in love.

Ahavat Olam

With everlasting love You have loved Your people Israel, teaching us Torah and commandments, statutes and laws. Therefore, Lord our God, when we lie down to sleep and when we awake, we shall think of Your laws and speak of them, rejoicing in Your Torah and commandments always. For they are our life and the length of our days; we shall meditate on them day and night. Never take away your love from us. Praised are You, Lord, who loves His people Israel.

This is the polar opposite from Pauline Christianity, for Paul depicts the law as impossible to fulfill and, worse, the vehicle through which we learn how to sin. God, therefore, frees us from the law, according to Paul, through sending Jesus so that we can live by the spirit instead (Rom. 7–11). In sharp contrast, the Jewish tradition sees the law as a great gift from God, as the prayers just cited affirm, for the law is nothing short of "life-giving," "our life and the length of our days."

How is the law a gift of love? The easiest way to understand this is to think of human analogies. A society without law is in chaos. Moreover, as Kafka depicted graphically in his story "The Trial," without the law people cannot know what they can expect of others and what others can expect of them; this produces sheer terror, for you may be held responsible and punished at any time for you-know-not-what. A good suzerain, then, gives you laws to bring order to society and to define mutual expectations.

If we return to the parent–child analogy in the Bible rather than the suzerainty treaties of old to understand our relationship with God, the same outcome occurs. Good parents are those who set reasonable limits for their children and enforce them fairly and yet compassionately. Children whose parents set no boundaries for them understand this—rightly—not as love but as neglect. Anyone with children understands immediately why this is so: it takes considerable energy to create rules for your children and stick by them, but loving them requires that.

In response to God's love of us, the People Israel feel love for God as well; in fact, they have a duty to do so:

> Hear O Israel! The Lord is our God, the Lord alone. You must love the Lord your God with all your heart, with all your soul, and with all your might. Take to heart these words with which I charge you this day. Teach them diligently to your children. Recite them when you stay at home and when you are away, when you lie down and when you get up. Bind them as a sign on your hand, and let them serve as a symbol on your forehead; inscribe them on the doorposts of your house and on your gates. (Deut. 6:4–9)

> Love, therefore, the Lord your God, and always keep His charge, His laws, His rules, and His commandments. (Deut. 11:1)

The imperative to love God in these passages is problematic, for how can you command someone to love someone else, even God? One way to respond to this problem is to note that these verses may not require love at all because in covenantal contexts scholars understand the Hebrew root "*ahv*" as used in the Bible to mean not love but loyalty. These verses thus command us to be faithful to God alone, abstaining from worshiping any other gods. (Hence the translation of the first line in the new translation of the Jewish Publication Society, "Hear O Israel, the Lord is our God, the Lord *alone.*") Alternatively, Maimonides does indeed see these verses as a command to love God, but he restricts the command to those who can worship God out of love rather than fear.[18] Yet another possibility is that the verses are not an imperative at all but a future indicative—that is, a statement of the fact that in response to God's love of Israel, Israel will love God. In any case, an important way that Israel expresses its love or loyalty for God is through following the commandments.

Beyond the problem of commanding love, there may be some ambiguity as to exactly what the obligations of love entail, just as there is in our love relationships with human beings. This ambiguity can lead to misunderstandings and hard feelings between the partners, and so the partners need from time to time to spell out what each expects of the other and to negotiate any disagreements they have. That such duties exist, however, is not a function of such agreements and promises; it rather is a feature inherent in the very fact of the relationship.

Part of the meaning and pleasure of human relationships is that people see each other, talk with one another, and do things together. Some relationships can continue and even be quite close despite the fact that the parties do not live in the same city and thus do not see each other often; modern techniques of communication make this more possible today than in the past. Still, one has to expend extra effort to make such relationships last, for normally we crave the companionship that relationships afford. Conversely, when friends or family members offend one another, one of the primary ways in which they express their displeasure is by staying away from the other party. Spouses who are spatting sometimes deny sex to one another, children are sent to their rooms for a time-out, and friends refuse to answer phone calls.

The Bible depicts our relationship with God in similar terms. The greatest of rewards is that God sees humanity as fit to live with. God agrees to abide with His Chosen People, and the tabernacle in the wilderness and later the Temple in Jerusalem are the signs of His presence: "The Lord spoke to Moses, saying: . . . Let them make me a sanctuary that I may dwell among them." (Exod. 25:1–9)

When people do things that depart from the divine path of honesty, kindness, and holiness, however, they lose touch with God. The people of the early biblical era assumed that once God agreed to dwell among us, God would never abandon them, no matter what. Jeremiah (7:1–15), however, makes clear that their trust in the Temple to keep God among them is ill-founded: God's willingness to dwell among the Israelites is conditional on their acting in accordance with God's paths. God is even willing to destroy His Temple, if necessary, if they fail to do that. Such behavior also pollutes the land and thus makes it impossible for God to continue to dwell among His people because of the impurity of the habitat; accepting a ransom for a murderer, for example, would do just that, and "You shall not defile the land in which you live, in which I Myself abide, for I the Lord abide among the Israelite people" (Num. 35:34; see also Lev. 18:17–30).

Even if specific violations do not drive away God's presence completely, they may lead God to stop talking to us. A number of biblical prophets describe just such a pulling away by God, where God's refusal to communicate with them makes them dumb:

A time is coming—declares my Lord God—when I will send a famine upon the land: not a hunger for bread or a thirst for water, but for hearing the words of the Lord. Men shall wander from sea to sea and from north to east to seek the word of the Lord, but they shall not find it. (Amos 8:11–12)[19]

Note that Amos and the other prophets who talk in this way assert that we have a *desire* to hear God's word and dwell with God. For our desire to be fulfilled, however, we must love God just as God loves us, demonstrating our love by walking in the paths that God has taught us. Preserving and nurturing the mutual covenantal love between God and us, then, is a powerful reason to live by the commandments.

5. Gratitude

Gratitude is one of our most potent motivators. When people do good things for us, we feel the strong need to do something good for them

151

in return. This is certainly true for lovers, and it is true for parents and children as well. In a more extended way, it is even true for citizens who have a sense of owing their country and express this by volunteering to serve in the armed forces, the Peace Corps, Teach for America, or some other form of public service.

The Torah maintains that God has done multiple things for the People Israel in its infancy and childhood as a nation, gifts for which the Children of Israel owe God gratitude. This is not because the parties have promised anything to each other contractually. It is not even because the parties love each other. It is rather that during their history together God has helped Israel time and time again, and hence Israel has incurred obligations of gratitude. This is not the morality of promise keeping or the duties of love, much less the fear of punishment; it is the recognition of a debt owed for a favor done.

> Ask, please, about bygone ages that came before you, ever since God created man on earth, from one end of heaven to the other. Has anything as grand as this ever happened, or has its like ever been heard? Has any people heard the voice of God speaking from out of the fire, as you have, and survived? Or has any god ventured to go and take for himself a nation from the midst of a nation by prodigious acts, by signs and portents, by war, by a mighty hand and an outstretched arm and awesome power, as the Lord your God did for you in Egypt before your eyes? You have been shown to know that the Lord alone is God; there is none beside Him. From the heavens He let you hear His voice to discipline you; on earth He let you see His great fire; and from amidst that fire you heard His words. And because He loved your ancestors and chose their offspring after them, He Himself, in His great might, led you out of Egypt to drive from your path nations greater and more populous than you, to bring you to and give you their land as a heritage, as is now the case. Know therefore this day and take to heart that the Lord is God in heaven above and on earth below; there is no other. Observe His laws and commandments, which I [Moses] command you this day, that it may go well with you and your children after you, and that you may long remain in the land that the Lord your God is giving you for all time. (Deut. 4:32–40)

Notice, first, the tone of this passage. Moses asks the Israelites standing in front of him many rhetorical questions as if to say that anyone in his or her right mind should recognize the obvious necessity to be grateful to God. This is not a situation in which special sensitivity is necessary; anyone with the least moral sense should recognize how unusual God's favors to us have been and how obliged we therefore are to do what God wants in return.

Note also the many favors that Moses lists. God has spoken to us out of the fire and yet let us survive. God has redeemed us from the midst of another nation, which itself is unprecedented. What makes it even more surprising is that the nation from which God redeemed us is Egypt, arguably the mightiest nation on earth at that time. God therefore had to use awesome power to accomplish this. Moreover, God provided signs and portents (in the form of plagues and Moses' warnings to Pharaoh) to make it absolutely clear that the Israelites' redemption was not due to the displeasures of the Egyptians' gods with them or the military skill or luck of the Israelites; it was God who acted to free the Israelites. God did not do this through an intermediary; God personally led us out of Egypt. Furthermore, after freeing us, God did not abandon us. On the contrary, God brought us to Mount Sinai, where God spoke directly to us to give us rules to govern our lives. And now God is about to lead us to the Promised Land. What a list of favors!

Along the same lines, the popular Passover hymn *Dayenu* spells out the many divine favors included in God's leading us from Egypt to the Promised Land, asserting that any one of them would be enough for us. The truth, of course, is that without following through with all the rest God would not have done enough to redeem us, but the point of the hymn, as with this biblical passage, is that we should appreciate each and every favor that God has done for us.

Finally, in the biblical passage just cited , note the obligations that these favors impose on us. We must recognize the source of our good fortune—God. We must keep in mind that the Lord alone is God in heaven above and on earth below. We must additionally observe God's laws and commandments. We must do these things in recognition of, and in response to, God's remarkable kindnesses to us. Simple justice requires that we acknowledge and thank God in these ways.[20]

This may look like returning favor for favor (quid pro quo), but the Torah's point is not as mechanical as that. That is, it is *not* that, as it were, there is some cosmic balance sheet in which God's acts on our behalf create a debt for us to repay. The point, rather, is that we owe God because *decent and just people* should recognize when acts of kindness (*hesed*) are done for them, and they should then respond in kind. In other words, it is not a matter of equalizing the good that each party gives each other; the Israelites could never equalize a balance sheet with God. It certainly is not that we must somehow compensate God for the material benefits God has bestowed on us, for we never could. The Torah is rather concerned that our relationship with God be an honorable one, in which we show gratitude for what God has done for us. It focuses on our *character* as people: We should be sensitive enough to recognize God's acts of caring for us and to respond appropriately—namely, by living our lives in the ways God has taught us.[21]

In the rabbinic mind, the mutual relationship between God and Israel means that God also owes us for what we do for God. Here is one example of that:

> It was taught: Abraham said before the Holy Blessed One: "It is revealed and known to you that at the time You told me to offer him [Isaac] as a burnt offering, I had grounds to object: Yesterday You said to me that your posterity will be through Isaac (Genesis 17:15–19), and now You tell me to offer him as a burnt offering? I, however, overcame my inclination [to disobey] (other version: I overcame my compassion for my son) to do Your will. So too, may it be Your will that when Isaac's children have troubles and there is no one to defend them, You should be their defense attorney. (Other version: When Isaac's children sin and do evil, this binding should be remembered on their behalf, and You should be filled with mercy for them.)[22]

Jewish liturgy brings all of this from the past to the present. It is not just God's boons for our ancestors in antiquity that should lead us to follow in God's ways now; it is, as we say three times each day in the *Amidah,* to thank God "for the miracles that are with us each and every day." The liturgy helps us do that by calling attention to the many things we might otherwise take for granted and instructing us to bless God for them. The blessings of the morning (*Birkhot ha-Shaḥar*), originally said as one was awaking and dressing, thank God for enabling us to recognize the difference between day and night, for making us Jews and free, for giving us sight, for clothing the naked, for enabling us to sit up in bed ("for releasing the bound," *mattir a'surim*), for making it possible for us to stand straight, for creating land so that we can stand, for providing for our needs, for enabling us to walk, and for restoring vigor to the weary. Especially as we are just regaining consciousness, we are prone not to notice any of these things and to take them for granted; the blessings serve to call our attention to these many necessities of our lives and to thank God for them, as is appropriate. Indeed, the tradition requires us to utter 100 blessings each day scattered throughout the day so that we cultivate a strong sense of gratitude.[23]

Other elements of Jewish law also engender gratitude for current features of our lives. The blessing of God before meals for bringing bread from the earth (ha-Motzi) and Grace after Meals (Birkat ha-Mazon) are clear examples of this: They require us to stop before and after we eat to thank God for the food we have, an expression of gratitude that the Rabbis ascribe to Abraham:

> Abraham caused God's name to be mentioned by all the travelers whom he entertained. for after they had eaten and drunk, and when they arose to bless Abraham, he said to them, "Is it of mine that you have eaten? Surely it is from what belongs to God that you have eaten. So praise and bless Him by whose word the world was created."[24]

Indeed, the dietary laws (kashrut) may also be an expression of our gratitude to God. We accede to the limitations on the animals that we may eat (only about 4 percent of the animal kingdom); we slaughter the animal as painlessly as possible; we drain the blood, the sign of life, out of the meat; and we separate meals for which we take an animal's life from those in which we consume mammals' paradigmatic life-giving substance (milk). All four of these steps are an expression of both our respect for animal life and pain as well as our gratitude to God for allowing us to eat meat.

Another example of law as an expression of gratitude is the Torah service. We do not just open the Torah scroll and read it; we first thank God for giving us the Torah and then do so again after each portion has been read. In this way we express our thanks for the continuing guidance God gives us through His Book of Instruction (the literal meaning of the word "Torah").

Yet another example is niddah, the laws that forbid couples to engage in sexual intercourse during the woman's menstrual period and for a few days thereafter. The Torah presents these laws as a matter of purity, but they also can be seen as a way of thanking God for the pleasures of sexual relations and of calling attention to the miracle of our ability to procreate. For a period of time each menstrual month we abstain from conjugal relations to take note of, and thank God for, its awesome potential for procreation when we resume. This also makes us appreciate each other: We are not simply each other's objects for sexual release but rather partners in the most intimate, deepest, and most extensive way possible. As the Talmud puts it from the man's point of view, these laws ensure "that she does not become disgusting to her husband"[25] but rather appreciated for the woman and mate she is. The same idea undergirds the Sabbath: We desist from work one day each week to recognize that the earth is the Lord's and we need to thank God for providing us with the means to earn a living the other six days.

In sum, as the Psalmist says it, "It is good to give thanks to the Lord" (Ps. 92:1).[26] The Prophet Micah famously said: "He has told you, O man, what is good, and what the Lord requires of you: Only to do justice, and to love goodness, and to walk humbly with your God" (Mic. 6:8). The medieval philosopher Judah Halevi interprets the last of those demands as a requirement to express gratitude for God's bounty:

> The divine law cannot become complete till the social and rational laws are perfected. The rational law demands justice and recognition of God's bounty. What has he, who fails is this respect, to do with offerings, Sabbath, circumcision, etc.? These are, however, the ordinations especially given to Israel as a corollary to the rational laws.[27]

Some of the commandments also express gratitude to other human beings. For example, the Jerusalem Talmud maintains that the Torah's command to honor one's parents is to thank them for bringing you into the world and raising you.[28] Another talmudic passage maintains that "One who quotes something in the name of the person who [first] said it brings salvation to the world."[29] Although the tradition is not as forthcoming in its insistence that we recognize the boons that other people have done for us as we might expect, it does articulate the value of acknowledging such boons and thanking our benefactors for them (hakkarat ha-tov).

Like many of the other motivations I am describing in this chapter, gratitude is not the rationale for acting in accordance with all of the commandments, but it is a motive for many of them. We recognize the benefits that God and other people provide, and we express our thanks, especially to God, by fulfilling the commandments.

6. Preserving God's Reputation—and Ours

Because the covenant links Jews to God, and because we have a long history together, we affect each other's reputation. This, in fact, is one of Moses' arguments when he pleads with God not to destroy the Israelites after they made and worshiped the Golden Calf: If the Israelites suffer, God's own good name will be tarnished in the eyes of the other nations:

> Moses pleaded with the Lord his God, saying: "Why, God, does Your anger blaze forth against Your people, whom You took out of the land of Egypt with great power and with a mighty hand? Why should the Egyptians say, "With evil intent He took them out, to kill them in the mountains and annihilate them from the face of the earth"? (Exod. 32:11–12)

In like manner, both Second Isaiah and Ezekiel quote God as saying that He withheld his wrath from the People Israel "for the sake of My name" (l'ma'an shemi). For example, even though the Israelites sinned in Egypt, "I acted for the sake of My name, that it might not be profaned in the sight of the nations among whom they were. For it was before their eyes that I made Myself known to Israel to bring them out of the land of Egypt" (Ezek. 20:9; see also Isa. 48:9, 66:5; Ezek. 20:14, 22,44).

If God must preserve Israel for His own name's sake, we Jews must similarly protect God's good name—and our own—by acting in a godly way. We need to adhere to the commandments because our actions reflect not only on ourselves but our families, our friends, our people, and our partner in the covenant and in history, God.

Acting in a way that sanctifies God's name is called kiddush ha-Shem; acting in a way that desecrates God's name is called hillul ha-Shem. The former term can also designate martyrdom,[30] but its original and broader meaning is acting in any way that brings glory to God.

It is not enough for behavior simply to be good to be an act of *kiddush ha-Shem;* the behavior must be *recognized by others* as flowing directly from one's commitments as a Jew. Similarly, bad behavior is not, in and of itself, *hillul ha-Shem;* to be so others must assume, rightly or wrongly, that it is a product of one's Jewish identity and commitments.[31] In other words, both terms are not strictly moral terms; they refer rather to one's reputation as a Jew.

These terms were not applied to all Jews in their everyday lives until rabbinic times, but the Bible provides the basis for the rabbinic concept in a variety of places.[32] Although the following verses were addressed to Aaron and his sons, the priests, they express what later Judaism expected of all Jews who, after all, were to be "a kingdom of priests" (Exod.19:6):

> You shall faithfully observe My commandments: I am the Lord. You shall not profane My holy name, that I may be sanctified in the midst of the Israelite people—I the Lord who sanctify you, I who brought you out of the land of Egypt to be your God, I the Lord. (Lev. 22:31–33)

Similarly, the man (or angel) who comes to Eli, the *kohen,* tells him in God's name, "For I honor those who honor Me, but those who dishonor me shall be dishonored" (1 Sam. 2:30).

This is a powerful reason to observe the law. When nobody knows who we are, we may be willing to do things we are not proud of. On the other hand, when we know that we will be identified, we are less willing to behave badly, not only because we fear being punished but also because we do not want to embarrass ourselves and those whom we know and love.

Conversely, when we know that others know who we are, we are often motivated to extend ourselves to do what is right. Ideally, we do the right thing even if nobody knows about it, and many people do just that. Even so, people commonly take special care to do the right thing if they know they are being noticed, for then their own reputations and those of their relatives and friends are at stake. We want to add to the honor of our own reputation and of those close to us. In his commentary on the Torah, Nahmanides applies "Love your neighbor as yourself" (Lev. 19:18) to this: You should act honorably so that your neighbor is honored by his or her association with you. The desire for a good reputation is thus not only a matter of self-love; it grows also out of love of others.

These feelings extend to our people as well—even those we do not personally know. There is a sense of shame Jews feel when a fellow Jew commits a crime or is otherwise publicly embarrassed. We feel our own self-image diminished by such an event. Even if the act had nothing to do with Judaism, we sense that the people with whom we associate and the faith we hold have been tarnished. We might also worry that non-Jews would improperly think that all Jews behave this way or that Judaism itself encourages such behavior. Depending on the circumstances, we might even worry that, as a result of the act in question, harm will come to fellow Jews—and perhaps even to ourselves. Here again our motives are a combination of self-regard and love of our group.

Conversely, when some Jews excel in a worthy endeavor, all Jews take pride. We love to hear about the Jews who have been awarded Nobel Prizes, the Jews who have been elected or appointed to important government positions, the Jews who have achieved fame in sports and entertainment, and the Jews who have given of themselves to help others. Even if we had nothing to do with these achievements, they add to our own self-image. This is *our* brother or sister who did that, and we are as proud as we can be!

The Bible and, even more, the Rabbis extend this line of thinking and feeling to God. Because God has linked Himself through the covenant with the People Israel, God's own reputation depends on how Jews behave. For example,

Rabbi Haninah said: Better that a man should commit a sin in secret than that he should profane the Name in public.[33]

The Lord said to Moses and Aaron: "Because you did not trust Me enough to affirm My sanctity in the sight of the Israelite people, therefore you shall not lead this congregation into the land that I have given them" (Numbers 20:12). Hence Moses was not allowed to enter the land. But did Moses never show a greater lack of faith? Did he not say, "Could enough flocks and herds be slaughtered to suffice them [the Israelites in the wilderness]?" (Numbers 11:22). Why did God not pass sentence on him then? It is like a king who had a friend who behaved overbearingly to him in private, but the king paid no attention to him. Some days afterwards, he acted similarly to him in the presence of his legions. Then the king sentenced him to death. So God said to Moses: "I took no account of your first action because it was in private; but now I cannot overlook it, because this sin was in front of the multitude," as it says, "because you did not trust Me enough to affirm My sanctify in the sight of the Israelite people." (Numbers 20:12)[34]

"You shall not render an unfair decision" (Leviticus 19:15). A judge who perverts justice is called unrighteous, hateful, abominable, a cursed thing, and abhorred. [These terms are all derived from biblical quotations.] Moreover, he is the cause of five misfortunes: he defiles the land, profanes the Name of God, and causes God's Presence to depart and Israel to fall by the sword and be exiled from their land.[35]

Other nations will judge God by the actions of His People, those whom He has chosen to teach His own Instruction (Torah) about how to behave. Therefore, "More serious is defrauding a non-Jew than the defrauding of a fellow Israelite on account of the profanation of the Divine Name [involved in the former]."[36]

We, therefore, should follow God's paths and do what is right not only because our own reputation (name) and that of our loved ones depend on it but also because God's reputation (name) is at stake. This clearly applies directly to Jewish laws that affect our interactions with other people and to those rituals that specifically sanctify God (for example, *Kiddush* on Sabbaths and festivals, the *Kaddish* prayer in all its versions) and less so to other elements of Jewish law that govern our relationships with God (such as, refraining from eating unkosher food, the laws of family purity). Still, sanctifying God's name, both in its social and theological meanings, is another important motivation to follow many parts of Jewish law.

7. Making Our Lives Holy

This motivation to fulfill God's commandments actually consists of three different, but related ideas: obeying God's commandments (a) makes God especially interested in us as God's special people, (b) enables us to become like God in our character traits, and (c) gives us a mission.

God's Special People

"Holy" is a word that we do not use very often. Moreover, when we do use it, English speakers—even Jewish ones—might well have Christian notions in mind, such as "Holy Ghost." Moreover, when we think of holy people, it is quite likely that the first thing that comes into our minds is Christian examples of such people, who tend to be ascetic; they are holy in that they deny themselves the pleasures of life. This is because English is a Christian language. It was created by Christians, and well over 90 percent of the people who speak it as their native language are Christian. It should be no surprise, then, that a religious word like "holy" sounds Christian to us and carries with it connotations of spiritual (in opposition to concrete and material), superhuman, and even otherworldly.

The Hebrew word that we translate as "holy" is *kadosh*. Its root means "set apart," "separate." In describing the Jewish People as holy, the Torah is thus asserting that in observing the commandments, Jews become a people set apart, different from all other peoples. The distinctions between Israel and other nations, though, are not just a matter of style, taste, or the accident of where they happen to live; it is based on Israel's willingness to live by God's laws and thereby be a model people. God deeply wants all nations to fulfill His commandments, and the Bible's prophets look forward to a time when all people will.[37] When the Bible was written, however, only Israel had promised to adhere to God's commands, and this makes Israel not only different from all other nations, but special—indeed, God's "treasured possession":

> Moses went up to God. The Lord called to him from the mountain, saying, "Thus shall you say to the house of Jacob and declare to the children of Israel: 'You have seen what I did to the Egyptians, how I carried you on eagles' wings and brought you to Me. Now, then, if you will listen to Me and keep My Covenant, you shall be My treasured possession among all the peoples, for all the earth is Mine. You shall be to Me a kingdom of priests and a holy nation.' These are the words that you shall speak to the children of Israel." (Exod. 19:3–6)

This passage clearly defines "holy" as "special," "chosen," "picked from among others." Note, however, that the Israelites are to be God's holy people, his "treasured possession," only if they are indeed a "kingdom of priests," a nation devoted ardently to God. Holiness is not a privileged status that one inherits and keeps, no matter what one does; one must *deserve* that distinction by living up to what God expects of a people associated with His name.

What is involved in being a holy people? The Torah defines this in two ways, specifying what Jews are *not* supposed to do as well as what they *are* supposed to do. We are not supposed to follow the abhorrent rituals or morals of other nations. This includes, as Leviticus 18 and 20 state, Egyptian and Canaanite practices of consigning their children to fire as a sacrifice to Molekh, their use of sorcery and magic, and many of their sexual practices. Instead, we are to abide by God's commandments:

> The Lord your God commands you this day to observe these laws and statutes; observe and do them with all your heart and soul. You have made God your king this day to walk in His ways, to observe His laws and commandments and rules, and to obey Him. And the Lord has elevated you this day to be His treasured people, as He promised you, and to observe all His commandments, and to elevate you in fame and renown and glory, above all the nations that He has made, that you shall be, as He promised, a holy people to the Lord your God. (Deut. 26:16–19)

As I noted in the previous chapter, this doctrine has come under considerable attack in modern times. It has produced hostile feelings toward Jews, for it seems as if Jews are claiming special merit and privilege. Richard Rubenstein maintains that it was one of the factors that produced the Holocaust and that we should learn from that terrible time to present ourselves as being normal, a nation like all others.[38] Mordecai Kaplan also repudiates the Chosen People concept and removed references in the liturgy to it in, for example, the blessing before reading the Torah. He nevertheless affirms the importance of national identity, and so he speaks of each nation's "vocation" to live life in its own unique way and thereby contribute to world civilization. Thus Kaplan asserts that we should follow Judaism's ritual laws as the folkways to reinforce our sense of identity as a people, and both Jews and non-Jews should act morally because, for him, moral standards are built into nature.[39] Thus for some modern Jews, this rationale to adhere to Jewish law is very troubling, and it will not be part of their motivations to do so. Even those who find this concept compelling, either along Kaplan's line of argument or in its traditional form, must recognize that it denotes that we are chosen for special status with God only on the condition that we fulfill the many more requirements that God makes of Jews through the 613 commandments of the Torah and all subsequent rabbinic legislation in contrast to just the seven laws required of non-Jews as part of the Noahide covenant. As early as the eighth century B.C.E., Amos made this clear: "You alone have I singled out of all the families of the earth; that is why I will call you to account for all your iniquities" (Amos 3:2).

Becoming Godly

By fulfilling God's commandments, we not only retain our special status in God's sight; we actually become godly, imitating the very nature of God. We stretch our humanity to its limit and become as close to being like God as possible. This is not only an ideal; the Torah makes it a command. That is, Jews are *required* to try to become godly. As Maimonides puts this:

> We are commanded to go in these middle paths, which are the good and right paths, as the Torah says, "and you shall go in His paths" (Deuteronomy 28:9). . . . The Prophets called God all these names: long-suffering and extremely kind, righteous and honest, pure, mighty and strong, and so on, to teach that these are the good and right ways to live, and each person is required to guide himself by them and to aspire to be like Him as much as he can.[40]

The clearest expression of this in the Torah is Chapter 19 of Leviticus, in the beginning of which God says, "You shall be holy, for I, the Lord your God, am holy." This sentence serves as a header for the rest of the chapter, which then specifies some of what it means to imitate God. The chapter includes many kinds of laws. Thus one becomes holy in part through ritual practices that one does, like observing the Sabbath, and that one refrains from doing, like the pagan ritual practices of making gashes in one's flesh in memory of the dead. One also becomes holy through moral actions, like respecting one's parents, loving one's neighbor, providing for the poor, and doing business honestly. By obeying these laws, one becomes and then remains not only special to God, but like Him.

This in and of itself is a powerful motivation to abide by Jewish law, especially those parts of it that ask us to strive for high moral standards and for deep compassion, for this call to imitate God appeals to our deeply felt desire to be and do our best. We *want* to strive for noble goals; we *want* to be as good as human beings can be. When we strive to be more like God and—even more—when we succeed in some measure, our lives gain meaning. We feel good about ourselves and enjoy the good opinion others have of us, especially because these feelings and impressions are based on important achievements.

In the following passage, the themes of being a special people to God and becoming more like God are closely linked, and both ends are to be accomplished by acting in accordance with God's commandments:

> And now, O Israel, what does the Lord your God ask of you? Only to revere the Lord your God, to walk in all His ways, to love [or be loyal to] Him, and to serve the Lord your God with all your heart and all your soul to keep the Lord's commandments and laws that I [Moses] command you today so that it be good for you. The heavens to their uttermost reaches belong to the Lord your God, the earth and all that is on it! Yet it was only your ancestors that the Lord desired and loved, and He chose you, their descendants, from among all peoples—as is now the case. Circumcise the foreskin of your hearts and stiffen your necks no more. For the Lord your God is God of gods and Lord of lords, the great, the mighty, and the awesome God, who shows no favor and takes no bribe, but does justice for the orphan and widow, and loves the stranger, giving him food and clothing. Love the stranger, for you were strangers in the land of Egypt. (Deut. 10:12–19)

We are to "circumcise the foreskin of our hearts and stiffen our necks no more"—both metaphors for removing our self-centered barriers to seeing the needs of the less fortunate. Instead, we are to be like God, who "shows no favor and takes no bribe, but does justice for the orphan and the widow, and loves the stranger, giving him food and clothing."

This theme of obeying the commandments to be more like God is articulated even more clearly in what the Rabbis later said:

"To walk in all His ways" (Deuteronomy 11:22). These are the ways of the Holy One: "gracious and compassionate, patient, abundant in kindness and faithfulness, doing kindness for thousands, forgiving iniquity, transgression, and sin, and granting pardon . . ." (Exodus 34:6). This means that just as God is gracious and compassionate, you must be gracious and compassionate. . . . The Holy One is called righteous, as it says, "For the Lord is righteous, He loves righteous deeds" (Psalms 11:7); you too must be righteous. The Lord is called kind, as it says, "For I am kind, declares the Lord; I will not bear a grudge for all time" (Jeremiah 3:12); and you too must be kind.[41]

Rabbi Hama said in the name of Rabbi Hanina: What is the meaning of the verse, "Follow the Lord your God" (Deuteronomy 13:5)? Is it possible for a mortal to follow God's Presence? After all, it is said, "the Lord your God is a consuming fire" (Deuteronomy 4:24). The verse rather means to teach us that we should follow the attributes of the Holy Blessed One. As God clothes the naked, . . . you should clothe the naked. The Holy Blessed One visited the sick . . . ; you too should visit the sick. The Holy One comforted mourners . . . ; you too should comfort mourners. The Holy Blessed One buried the dead . . . ; you too should bury the dead.[42]

Note that this motivation is not only distinct from what we have discussed earlier; it has a wholly different tone. We should follow in God's paths not only out of love and not because of the moral duties arising from promises, our relationships, or the benefits that God has bestowed on us. We should follow God's paths because we *aspire* to be like God. This motivation appeals not to external factors but to our internal sense of the kinds of people we can and should be. In trying to emulate God's attributes we elevate and effectuate the best parts of ourselves. In Jewish religious terms, we actualize our potential for *kedushah,* for holiness.

A Holy Mission

We become holy as individuals if we abide by the law, but we also become holy as a people when we act in an exemplary manner. This theme runs through the Bible, but the Book of Isaiah gives this conviction its most famous expression. The People Israel are to be a model people, "a light of the nations":

This is My servant, whom I support, My chosen one, whom I desire. I have put My spirit upon him. He shall teach justice to the nations . . . He shall not grow dim or be bruised till he has established justice on earth; and the coast lands shall await his teachings . . . I the Lord, have summoned you in righteousness, and I have strengthened you and I have fashioned you and appointed you a covenant-people, a light of nations—to open unseeing eyes, to rescue prisoners from confinement, from the dungeon those who sit in darkness.[43] (Isa. 42:1,4,6,7)

This is a powerful reason to obey the law: we have a *mission* to teach justice and righteousness to the entire world. This mission gives us purpose in life, a goal to change things for the better. In contemporary Judaism, we often call that *tikkun olam,* "fixing the world";[44] the classical Rabbis called the various parts of what we now mean by this term *gemillut hasadim* (acts of kindness), *tzedek* (fairness, or justice), and *kevod ha-briyyot* (honoring the dignity of God's creatures), as well as *kedushah* (holiness). To be holy is, on the one hand, a frustrating and never-ending task, for human beings are imperfect, self-centered, and morally flawed. This is why Maimonides was careful to say in the passage quoted in the previous subsection that a person should emulate God "as much as he can." On the other hand, striving to be holy makes life challenging, energizing, and meaningful; it gives life a purpose, a goal worth working and sacrificing for.

My friend and teacher Rabbi Uzi Weingarten told me that he once heard Rabbi Joseph Soloveitchik point out that the Bible often speaks about those who seek God, *dorshei ha-Shem.* The *search* for God sanctifies and hallows us, whether or not we find answers or succeed in fixing the world in the end. The very aspiration to be a holy people is uplifting. I would add that the specific, concrete steps we take in an effort to accomplish this aim are even more so.

8. Enforcement

As I mentioned at the beginning of this chapter, most people think of the authority of the law as a function of its enforcement and are unaware of the multiple motives that in fact make a legal system viable. In exploring the multiple motivations mentioned in the Bible for adhering to Jewish law, as I have to this point in this chapter, and in continuing to do so below with those that the Rabbis add, I trust that I have disabused my readers of the notion that enforcement is the only, or even the primary, source of its authority. Jewish classical texts assert that *all* these factors are crucial in motivating people to adhere to the law.

This is not to say, however, that Jewish law does not presume enforcement; quite the contrary, biblical texts make it clear that both God and human courts would make the law stick. Leviticus 26 and Deuteronomy 28, known as the chapters of rebuke (*tokhekhah*), spell out in more detail than other biblical passages both the rewards for living by God's laws and the punishments for violating them. The rewards include children, the Land of Israel, abundance of crops, victory in battle, and health. Violating God's laws leads to punishments delineated in much greater, excruciating detail. They include infertility, lack of rain, poverty, starvation, defeat in battle, destruction of the community's homes and institutions, and illness, all of which lead to desperate acts like eating the flesh of one's children (Lev. 26:29).

The benefits promised by secular systems for compliance and the punishments for disobedience are not nearly as extensive or graphic, but they nevertheless serve as one important reason to obey the law. In general, secular systems of law promise that people will attain the advantages of government. The Preamble to the U.S. Constitution, for example, maintains that the new government is being established "in order to form a more perfect union, establish justice, insure domestic tranquility, provide for the common defense, promote the general welfare, and secure the blessings of liberty to ourselves and our posterity."

Like secular legal systems, Jewish legal texts provide for human authorities to enforce parts of the law. This is an aspect of Jewish law that many contemporary Jews presume was lost to Jewish law long ago. Actually, Jewish authorities enforced Jewish law on most of the Jews of the world until the 20th century. That is because until then most Jews lived in Eastern Europe, North Africa, and the Middle East, all places untouched by the Emancipation. Enlightenment philosophers like John Locke, Jean Jacques Rousseau, and Charles Montesquieu maintained, to use Thomas Jefferson's formulation in the U.S. Declaration of Independence, that it is "self-evident that all men are created equal, that they are endowed by their Creator with certain unalienable rights, and that among these are life, liberty, and the pursuit of happiness." If everyone is understood to be an individual with rights, then Jewish individuals have no less claim to such rights than anyone else. Further, because Enlightenment countries perceive religion as a matter of individual conscience, freedom of religion is to varying degrees guaranteed, at least in theory and often, at least to an extent, in fact.

The vast majority of the world's Jews, however, did not live in countries governed by Enlightenment principles until the 20th century. The nations in which Jews predominantly lived instead functioned on the assumptions that had governed most countries from the time of the Romans—specifically, that Jews were a minority *group* living within, and at the tolerance of, the majority; that the legal status of individual Jews, including their rights, responsibilities, and legal limitations, was determined by the government's laws governing Jews as a group; and that Jews were to handle their own legal affairs and enforce their own courts' judgments, with the government powers of enforcement available as a backup.

In such societies, Jews had at least some degree of legal autonomy. This was not usually the result of magnanimity toward Jews; it was rather because governments did not want to be bothered by the problems Jews had. In fact, if Jews did go to the government's courts, they were likely to be treated unfairly. If two Jews brought their dispute to the government's court, often the court would effectively say "a plague on both your houses" and punish both parties as well as the Jewish community as a whole for bothering the government's courts. This—and the conviction that Jewish law was the law of God and should therefore have jurisdiction on Jews—led to the rule in Jewish law, as early as the time of the Mishnah, forbidding Jews to take their disputes with other Jews to government courts, together with harsh penalties for doing so.[45] It also meant that Jewish law was enforced by Jewish courts, which had the power to impose fines, lashes, and, most important, excommunication on those who failed to obey the decree of the court.

None of this applies, of course, to modern Jews, almost all of whom live in countries that grant freedom of and from religion. (In Israel, ironically, although non-Jews have full freedom of religion, Jews are restricted in their form of Jewish expression on some issues, such as who may marry them. Thus Israel has freedom of religion for everyone but Jews!) Freedom of religion means, for Jews, that human enforcement of Jewish law no longer exists.

That leads us to the threat of divine enforcement. The Torah in many places asserts that adherence to God's laws will bring physical and other blessings, and violation of them will bring physical and other forms of suffering. Job and Kohelet, however, already point out that life simply does not work that way. The Rabbis grapple with this in many ways, admitting openly that "the righteous suffer and the evil prosper" and creating multiple justifications of God's justice ("theodicies") despite this.[46] The need for such justifications is even more evident to Jews of today, who can look back at the Crusades, the Inquisition, the pogroms of the Middle Ages and of modern times, and the Holocaust to cast doubt on the Torah's assurances of just, divine enforcement of the law.

Contemporary thinkers have created a number of "post-Holocaust theologies" precisely to respond to the challenges the Holocaust poses for this traditional tenet. Some theologians deny the connection between faithfulness and flourishing outright by repudiating a God who acts in history and affirming only the God of nature (for example, Richard Rubenstein). Others go in the opposite direction, trying to justify God's role in the Holocaust either as just punishment for those who sinned (see Michael Wyschograd) or as vicarious punishment of the innocent to atone for the sins of the blameworthy, along the lines of Isaiah 53 (such as Ignaz Maybaum). Most formulate a response somewhere in between, struggling in various ways to define how Jews can have faith after the Holocaust, the God in whom one can have faith, and the proper terms of our relationship with God in light of the Holocaust (for example, Eliezer Berkovits, David Blumenthal, Emil Fackenheim, Irving Greenberg, Harold Kushner, and Harold Schulweis).[47]

I myself have written about this issue in my book *Knowing God*.[48] Because the present volume is a book on Jewish law and not on theology, suffice it to say here that it seems obvious to me, as it did to Job, Kohelet, and the Rabbis, that there is no one-to-one relationship between fulfilling the commandments and good fortune. At the same time, there are consequences for what we do, both individually and communally. For example, abusing our bodies by smoking raises the probability of contracting lung cancer; treating people fairly and graciously is likely to evoke the same kind of response by most of them (although there are no guarantees), while treating them badly will probably produce the opposite response; and polluting our environment will make it hard for our species to survive.

Thus, like the Rabbis, on some level I believe that we cannot expect a tie between good actions and good results, certainly as individuals and even as communities; that we instead should be satisfied with the fact that "the reward of fulfilling a commandment is that you are prepared to fulfill another one, and the result of committing a sin is that you are more likely to commit another one, for fulfilling commandments leads to fulfilling other commandments, and committing sins leads to committing other sins."[49] At the same time, also like the Rabbis, I believe that our actions have consequences, even if we cannot always see them or understand them. Minimally, acts of unfaithfulness to our covenant with God through violating its terms, and even failure to attend to that relationship by neglecting the positive commandments that nurture it, will weaken our relationship with God and with other human beings, thus distancing ourselves from the goals of the covenant. Like all relationships, our covenantal ties to God and to other people become as deep or as shallow as we allow them to be through our actions. It is in this sense that I understand traditional Jewish language of God as judge and enforcer of the covenant, the other laws that Moses announced in the Torah, and even subsequent Jewish law. Thus even if I have more qualms about these divine roles than some of my ancestors did, the traditional depictions of God as Judge and Enforcer are compelling metaphors for me in my own theology and in my understanding of Jewish law.

What is most important, though, is that *love and the other positive motives to follow the law* described here are by far the most important motives for me to do so; *fear of punishment* is only a back-up mechanism to produce compliance for those not motivated by all these other factors. I have much in the Jewish tradition to support my contention.

First, although the Torah speaks of both loving God and fearing Him in almost equal numbers of references and degrees of emphasis,[50] the very structure of two books of the Torah suggest that love is more important than fear. Leviticus begins with a long description of the sacrifices that are supposed to bring us near to God, even when we sin. (The Hebrew word for sacrifice is *korban,* whose root is *krv,* meaning "to bring close.") Leviticus then tells us how to be holy, expressed in both ritual events like celebrating the Sabbath and the festivals and in interpersonal relations, like fair weights and measures and extensive provisions for the poor. Only toward the end (Chapter 26) do we get the chapter that promises rewards if we follow God's laws and punishments if we do not—and even that is followed by the last chapter delineating the laws about vows to God made to come closer to Him and the rules of the Jubilee year, with the result that the book does not end on the theme of reward and punishment. Deuteronomy speaks of punishments for violating God's laws in many places, but it is only toward the end (Chapter 28) that the penalties for violating the covenant are spelled out in great detail—and this is followed by six further chapters so that this book also does not end with the theme of reward and punishment. Given that the structural basis for both of these books was the suzerainty treaties of antiquity, which routinely ended with rewards for those who adhered to the terms of the treaty and curses and punishments for those who did not, it is not surprising that the full delineation of the rewards and punishments is reserved for the end of Leviticus and Deuteronomy. This historical fact, however, only reenforces the theological one that I am making—namely, that all the other elements that are part of our relationship with God come first, for these are the primary foundation and justification for our adherence to the covenant; the rewards and punishments for maintaining or violating the laws are described only near the end, for they are definitely not the only, or even the primary, reason to live by the laws.

The Rabbis also make clear this preference for love over fear. The very first lesson in the Mishnah's tractate Avot (Ethics of the Fathers) is the teaching of Simeon the Just, who says, "The world rests on three things—on Torah, on service of God, and on deeds of kindness." No mention here of fear of punishment. This is followed by the saying of Antigonus, of Sokho, who brings in the fear of God but only after saying that we should ideally not be motivated by that: "Do not be like servants who serve their master expecting to receive a reward; be rather like servants who serve their master unconditionally, with no thoughts of reward. Also, let the fear of God determine your actions."[51] The Rabbis also constructed the *Shema* prayer by putting Deuteronomy 6, which asks us to love God and says nothing about reward or punishment, before Deuteronomy 11, which also asks us to love God but does speak of reward and punishment, thus indicating that following God's commandments out of love alone is preferable to adhering to the covenant out of fear.

This preference for love of God over fear of God is made most explicit, though, in Maimonides (with apologies for his sexism):

1. A person should not say, "I will observe the precepts of the Torah and occupy myself with its wisdom in order that I may obtain all the blessings written in the Torah or to attain life in the world to come; I will abstain from transgressions against which the Torah warns so that I may be saved from the curses written in the Torah or that I may not be cut off from life in the world to come." It is not right to serve God in this way, for whoever does so serves God out of fear. This is not the standard set by the Prophets and Sages. Those who serve God in this way are only the illiterate, women, or children, whom one trains to serve out of fear until their knowledge shall have increased such that they will serve out of love.

2. Whoever serves God out of love occupies himself with the study of the law and the fulfillment of the commandments and walks in the path of wisdom impelled by no external motive whatsoever, moved neither by fear of calamity nor by the desire to obtain material benefits. Such a man does what is truly right because it is truly right, and ultimately happiness comes to him as the result of his conduct. This standard is indeed a very high one; not every Sage attained to it. It was the standard of the Patriarch Abraham, whom God called His lover (Isaiah 41:8) because he served only out of love. It is the standard that God, through Moses, bids us to achieve, as it is said, "And you shall love the Lord your God" (Deuteronomy 6:5). When one loves God with the right love, he will straightaway observe all the commandments out of love. . . .

5. Whoever engages in the study of the Torah in order that he may receive a reward or avoid calamities is not studying Torah for its own sake. Whoever occupies himself with the Torah neither out of fear nor for the sake of recompense, but solely out of love for the Lord of the whole Earth who enjoined us to do so is occupied with the Torah for its own sake. The Sages, however, said, "One should always engage in the study of the Torah, even if not for its own sake, for he who begins thus will end by studying it for its own sake" (B. Pesahim 50b). Hence, when instructing the young, women, or the illiterate generally, we teach them to serve God out of fear or for the sake of reward until their knowledge increases and they have attained a large measure of wisdom. Then we reveal to them this mystic truth, little by little, and train them by easy

stages until they have grasped and comprehended it and serve God out of love.[52]

Thus, even though the desire for reward and the fear of punishment do play a role in Jewish law, it is only as a back-up mechanism to achieve compliance for those who have not been convinced by any of the other biblical motives described earlier as well as those in rabbinic literature, discussed next. Even in eras before the Emancipation, in other words, reward and punishment were not intended to be the main motive to prompt Jews to live by Jewish law; it was to be invoked only when nothing else worked. In our day, with the loss of Jewish courts with the power to enforce their decisions and with questions about God's enforcement made ever more acute by the Holocaust, this motive does and should fade even more into the background as a rationale to adhere to Jewish law. I have described the important, but limited sense in which I myself believe it, and I think, as Maimonides does, that we are much better off focusing on any of the other rationales described in this chapter, including especially the love of God and our fellow humans.

Although Maimonides clearly prefers love of God over fear of God as the motive to adhere to Jewish law, he nevertheless believes, as he indicates in this passage, that fear of God must be taught to the uneducated. I differ with him on this, both because the Holocaust has made fear of God's punishment practically ineffective and morally questionable as a motive to follow God's law and also because I believe that one need not be as learned as Maimonides claims to live by God's law out of love. Rather, along with David Hartman, I believe that "the capacity of love is related to the psychological maturity that comes with accepting one's finitude and self-limitation and to the productive use we make of this awareness in our interpersonal relationships. Although this type of maturity is a difficult achievement, it is not necessarily restricted to the few."[53]

ADDITIONAL MOTIVES DESCRIBED BY THE RABBIS

9. Refining Human Beings

Perhaps the most important rationale that the Rabbis suggest for following the laws is that they refine us:

> Rav said: The commandments were given to Israel only to purify people. Does it matter to God whether an animal is slain at the throat or at the neck?[54]

> What does God care whether a man kills an animal in the proper way [that is, according to Jewish laws of slaughter, called *shehitah*] and eats it, or whether he strangles the animal and eats it? Will the one benefit Him, or the other injure Him? Or what does God care whether a man eats impure or pure [that is, kosher] animals? "If you are wise, you are wise for yourself, but if you scorn, you alone shall bear it" (Proverbs 9:12). So you learn that the commandments were given only to refine God's creatures, as it says, "God's word is refined, a shield to all who take refuge in Him." (2 Samuel 22:31)

This is close to the biblical assertion that the commandments teach us what it means to be moral and motivate us to be so. This rationale, however, focuses more on the ends than the means: in learning moral values from the commandments and in acting in moral ways, we become purified as human beings—that is, we come much closer to the ideal of what it means to be human. The commandments call people to their higher selves.

This reason to obey the commandments, then, resembles the biblical claim that the laws can make us holy and more like God. Unlike that rationale, though, this one focuses not only on divinity but also on humanity: Following the commandments makes us more fully and honorably human. We are purified of our moral and emotional dross so that we can be the best that humans can be; the commandments help repair our flaws so that we can be whole.

It is not surprising that the Rabbis maintain that we should follow the commandments to improve ourselves as human beings. What is absolutely astonishing in these passages, though, is that in claiming this, the Rabbis assert that God does not benefit from our adherence to His laws, that God, in fact, does not care whether we act according to His laws or not.

This clearly is a rabbinic flourish, an exaggeration to emphasize the commandments' effectiveness in functioning for our human benefit. After all, the Torah announces many, many times that God cares a great deal about whether we obey the commandments. Only then would it make sense for God to promise generous rewards for doing so and threaten excruciating punishments for failing to do so, and only then would God bother to establish laws for us in the first place as an act of love. *God in Search of Man* is the title of a book by 20th-century Jewish theologian Abraham Joshua Heschel, and it correctly suggests, as he demonstrates in the book, that classical Judaism portrays a God who is very much interested in what human beings do. God does not need any physical sacrifice, as the pagans of old thought, but God "rejoices in His creatures," as the Psalmist says (Ps. 104:31).

The Rabbis were nevertheless able to step back from this theological foundation of the commandments to maintain that even without the religious reasons to obey them, there are good reasons of self-interest to do so—namely, that Jewish law calls us to become our higher selves, to improve our character and our human relations. The Rabbis thus sound in these passages as if they were speaking to many 21st-century Jews!

10. Maintaining the World

On the other hand, the Rabbis asserted the exact opposite claim too. You should obey the commandments not for your own benefit, but for God's. God, in fact, cares very much that Jews observe the commandments—so much so that God has made the continued existence of the world contingent on whether Jews fulfill the Torah's commands:

> What is the meaning of the words, "The earth feared and was still" [Psalms 76:9]? . . . Before Israel accepted the Torah, the earth was afraid; after they accepted the Torah, it was still. . . . For the Holy Blessed One stipulated a condition with the earth: If Israel accepts the Torah, you may exist, but if not, I will return you to the state of being unformed and void [as before Creation, according to Genesis 1:2].[56]

> God said, "If you read the Torah, you do a kindness, for you help to preserve My world, for if it were not for the Torah, the world would again become 'without form and void.' " . . . The matter is like a king who had a precious stone, and he entrusted it to his friend and said to him, "I pray you, pay attention to it and guard it, as is fitting, for if you lose it, you cannot pay me its worth, and I

175

have no other jewel like it, and so you would sin against yourself and against me; therefore, do your duty by both of us, and guard the jewel as is fitting." So Moses said to the Israelites, "If you obey the Torah, not only upon yourselves do you confer a benefit, but also upon God," as it is said, "And it shall be a benefit for us" (Deuteronomy 6:5). [The Midrash takes "us" in this biblical verse to mean God and Israel, and the word *tzedakah*—"righteousness"—it takes to mean benefit, which led to its later, more familiar meaning as charity.][57]

To believe that God would never have created the physical world without the Jews' acceptance of the Torah—that is, to take this rabbinic comment literally—not only tests the limits of our credulity but is disgracefully chauvinistic. Furthermore, it flies in the face of Judaism's appreciation of people of other faiths being in the Noahide covenant with God.

The comment, though, can have credible meaning, indeed, very important meaning, if we read it in the context of other things the Rabbis said. The first chapter of the Mishnah's tractate *Avot (Ethics of the Fathers)* contains two passages that suggest that the Rabbis thought that the continued existence of the world as we know it functionally depends *on the foundational values* embedded in Jewish law: "Shimon the Just . . . used to say: 'The world stands on three things: on Torah, on worship, and on acts of kindness' " (1:2); "Rabban Shimon ben Gamliel taught: 'The world exists on the basis of three things: on justice, on truth, and on peace' " (1:18). It is not the physical world that depends on these things; rather it is human society that depends on these values inherent in Jewish law. Without Torah, we would not have the gift of God's guidance for our lives; without worship, we might think that only we matter, making it impossible to escape the self-centered way in which we are all-too-prone to think and act; and without acts of kindness none of us would be able to survive, either physically or emotionally. Similarly, without justice and a government that enforces it, people would "kill each other alive,"[58] as another passage from *Avot* proclaims; without truth, nobody could know whom or what to trust; and without peace, as the Rabbis say elsewhere, none of the blessings of life matter.[59] In the Jerusalem Talmud, Rabbi Shimon ben Gamliel continues his teaching thus: "And all three are intertwined: when justice is done, truth is served, and peace ensues."[60] It is in this sense that the world—and especially human societies—depend on these values underlying Jewish law.

11. Identifying as Members of a Distinct Community

As discussed earlier, the Bible states a number of times that the Israelites are not to do what the nations around them were doing, both ritually and morally. In this way, the Israelites were to define themselves negatively—that is, by what they do *not* do. At the same time, the Bible talks of God choosing the Israelites to be covenanted partners with Him so that they would be a model people. In that way, the Bible defines the People Israel positively—that is, in what the Israelites *were supposed* to do.

Identity as a separate people became all the more important in rabbinic times. No longer were Jews concentrated in Israel or in any specific area of the world like Egypt or Babylonia. They were scattered all over the earth. Even in Israel, they lived among Romans. Geography no longer united the Jews into one easily identifiable people. As a result, Jewish law became ever more important as the identifying mark of the Jewish people, and Jews adhered to the law to identify as Jews.

> "Yet, for all that [that is, all the punishments that God visits on the Israelites for violating His law], when they are in the land of their enemies, I have not rejected them utterly" (Leviticus 26:44). All the good gifts that were given them were taken away from them. And if it had not been for the Torah that was left to them, they would not have differed at all from the nations of the world.[61]

> If it were not for My Torah that you accepted, I should not recognize you, and I should not regard you more than any of the idolatrous nations of the world.[62]

But it is not only God who recognizes Jews by their holding fast to Jewish law. In creating a relationship between the Jewish People and God, the covenant also binds the Jewish people to each other. Throughout most of Jewish history and still to this day for many

Jews, these two relationships are understood and deeply felt as inter-twined. That is, my duties to my fellow Jews are in response to what God expects of me as a member of God's Chosen People, who are to be "a kingdom of priests and a holy nation" (Exod. 19:6). Conversely, my duties to God, as articulated in Jewish law from the Torah to our own time, include numerous obligations to my fellow Jews.

With the rise of secularism in modern times, many Jews (in fact, probably a majority of the world's Jews) feel connections with the Jewish People, even deep ones for some, but they do not connect those ties to God. The absence of God in the self-understanding of these Jews usually means that they do not engage in Jewish wor-ship or ritual practices, but not always. Ahad Ha-Am, for example, one of the great early theorists of cultural Jewish identity, is famous for, among other things, noting that "More than Israel has kept [guarded, preserved] the Sabbath, the Sabbath kept Israel." He writes:

> A Jew who feels a real tie with the life of his people throughout the generations will find it utterly impossible to think of the existence of Israel without the Sabbath. One can say without exaggeration that more than Israel has kept the Sabbath, the Sabbath has kept Israel. Had it not been for the Sabbath, which weekly restored to the people their "soul" and weekly renewed their spirit, the week-day afflictions would have pulled them farther and farther down-ward until they sank to the lowest depths of materialism as well as ethical and intellectual poverty. Therefore one need not be a Zionist in order to feel all the traditional sacred grandeur that hov-ers over this "good gift," and to rise up with might against all who seek to destroy it.[63]

The Los Angeles Jewish Federation Council, like many other fed-erations, insists that all its public events be kosher, not for religious reasons per se, but to ensure that all Jews can participate. It closes its offices on the Sabbath and Jewish festivals (including the second day observed in the Diaspora) for the same reason. This parallels the reasoning of some secular Jews in their personal lives as well. Their homes may be kosher to enable all Jews to eat there, even if the fam-ily eats nonkosher food when dining out, and they may observe some of the rituals of the Sabbath or Jewish holy days or invent their own to mark these occasions as part of their Jewish cultural heritage. The same applies to life-cycle events, including circumcision, Bar or

Bat Mitzvah celebrations, weddings, and funerals. This motive for living by Jewish law—or at least some parts of it in either the traditional way or a new, creative way—is to retain and reinforce one's ties to the Jewish community.

12. Making Life Beautiful

Although the idea of making life beautiful as a rationale for fulfilling the commandments is not nearly as prominent in rabbinic thought as many of the ones discussed in this chapter, it does appear. Abiding by the commandments makes the People Israel beautiful in the eyes of God.

The Bible does not hesitate to talk about the relationship between God and the People Israel as one of lovers. Hosea (2:4–18,21–23) does this specifically. The biblical book Song of Songs is a series of love poems, probably intended simply to express the love between human lovers. The Rabbis included it in the biblical canon, however, largely because Rabbi Akiva interpreted it as the love poems between God and the People Israel.[64] This means, of course, that God and the Jewish People enjoy each other and find each other beautiful. How, according to the Rabbis, does Israel make herself beautiful in God's eyes? By observing the commandments:

> "You are beautiful, my love" (Song of Songs 1:15). You are beautiful through the commandments, both positive and negative [that is, what one is to do and what one is to avoid doing]—beautiful through good deeds; beautiful in your house with the heave offerings and tithes; beautiful in the field through gleaning, the forgotten sheaf, and the second tithe [gifts the Torah requires be left for the poor]; beautiful in the law about mixed seeds, the edges of the field, first fruits, and the fourth year planting; beautiful in the law of circumcision; beautiful in prayer, in the reading of the Shema, in *mezuzot* and tefillin, in the *lulav* and *etrog*; beautiful too in repentance and in good deeds; beautiful in this world and beautiful in the world to come.[65]

It is as if the jewelry and perfumes with which Israel adorns herself for God, her lover, are the commandments. Jews should obey the commandments, then, to appear beautiful in God's sight.

The enjoyment and beauty experienced in Israel's observance of the commandments, however, are not restricted to God. The Torah says specifically, in regard to the festivals, "And you shall be happy in your Festival . . . and be only happy" (Deut. 16:14–15). This includes, according to the Rabbis, eating well and buying new clothes to be worn for the first time on the festival.[66] According to the Rabbis' interpretation of another verse in the Torah, it is a special duty to make one's observance of the law aesthetically beautiful (*hiddur mitzvah*). One should choose a pretty *etrog* and decorate one's sukkah for the festival of Sukkot; one should use an attractive prayer shawl (tallit) and tefillin while praying; one should tidy up and decorate the place of worship.[67] The reason for these rules, of course, was to honor God and the occasion, but their *effect* (even if not their motive) was to make observance of these events enjoyable and aesthetically pleasing to all who participated.

Because the commandments are a way of honoring God, the nature and manner of fulfilling them had to fit this purpose. Specifically, aesthetic considerations could never violate the very commandments they were meant to honor. So, for example, one should preserve modesty in dressing up for weddings or worship. Similarly, using Shabbat to paint a picture, although undoubtedly an aesthetic experience, would violate the Sabbath in the very act of trying to honor it.

This aesthetic ground for obeying Jewish law, while certainly not at the center of the Jewish tradition's understanding of itself, is often the first factor that prompts Jews to become more observant. The Friday night table—with family and friends, singing, good food, and protracted conversation—is often mentioned by people as the experience that drew them to greater interest in Judaism, including recreating the experience in their own homes. The music of worship can draw to the synagogue people who like singing, including participating in the choir. The distinctive music, foods, and artwork of the festivals, together with their ability to pull family and friends together, stimulate people to get involved in this aspect of Jewish life. The same is true for Jewish life-cycle events. So although this motive probably will not suffice on its own for most people, many begin a serious commitment to Judaism on this basis. It also serves as a significant element in the ongoing commitment of religious Jews to Jewish law.

MOTIVATIONS TO LIVE BY JEWISH LAW

THE IMPLICATIONS OF THESE MOTIVES FOR MODERNS

One reason I have discussed the varying motives for observing Jewish law is to point out the fallacy in our common assumption that law is authoritative only if it is enforced. From biblical times to our own, Jews have adhered to Jewish law for multiple reasons, only some of which are tied to either human or divine enforcement. For that matter, Americans obey American law for multiple reasons as well, and if it were only enforcement that gave American law authority, it would have ceased functioning long ago.

This means, among other things, that Mordecai Kaplan was wrong about the status of Jewish law—and, along with him, many other Jews as well. As I have demonstrated, people have always abided by Jewish laws for many reasons other than enforcement. Therefore, even in a voluntaristic society, where no government officials force Jews to abide by Jewish law, treating Jewish law as fully law makes great sense. This means not only that we should see Jewish law as authoritative but also that we should apply to the rules of Jewish law all of the legal techniques of interpretation and application that Jews have used for millennia to plumb its guidance for our lives.

Another important implication of the analysis carried on in this chapter is that modern Jews may be motivated more by some of the factors discussed in this chapter than by others. Those who have trouble with belief in God will clearly be more attracted to the motives that do not refer to God than by those that do. For such people, the moral, communal, and aesthetic import of Jewish law will count for much more than any of the facets of our relationship with God, and they will probably observe only those laws in which they find these meanings. They may well think, however, that the laws that govern the practices they follow are indeed authoritative laws, for if one is to observe Shabbat, for example, Jewish law defines how to do that.

On the other hand, those who relish their relationship with God may find the theological motives described above—our relationship with and promises to God, embodied in the covenant idea, and our gratitude for what God has done for us and continues to do for us each day—much more central in their reasons for making Jewish law an important part of their lives. Even for those who believe in God, the Holocaust, earthquakes, hurricanes, and illness may make us question, as a number of theologians have, whether God has kept His part of the bargain in our covenant with Him and thus whether our promises to God are still binding and whether our gratitude to God is still warranted. So the plethora of these motives enables people with different depths and kinds of Jewish commitments to find Jewish law meaningful.

Further, what prompts a Jew to obey Jewish law at any given time may be different now from what it was yesterday or will be tomorrow, for our own thoughts, desires, emotions, and associations change constantly, just as the cells in organisms do. As a result, the availability of many different motives for obedience means that even if a given rationale that I found compelling yesterday seems emotionally pale and intellectually unconvincing to me today, I may observe Jewish law nonetheless for some other reason. It is thus a strategy of strength that Jewish law invokes multiple mo-tives for obedience so that it can be authoritative for people with varying religious commitments and for the same person from one day to the next.[68]

ENDNOTES

1. Kaplan, "Reply to Robert Gordis."
2. B. Eruvin 100b.
3. For the biblical and rabbinic materials on the morality of God, see Dorff and Rosett, *A Living Tree,* pp. 110–123, 249–257. For my own view of these matters, see Dorff, *Knowing God,* chap. 5.
4. The Rabbis make the evidentiary procedures necessary to convict someone of a capital offense so rigorous that they themselves admit that a court that decrees such a sentence once in seven years is "a bloody court" (M. Makkot 1:10). They narrow the eligibility for qualifying as a "stubborn and rebellious son" so much that they ultimately maintain that there never was or will be such a person (B. Sanhedrin 71a). The Rabbis narrow the definition of an illegitimate child (a *mamzer*) as much as possible, such that the product of a married man having sexual relations with an unmarried woman is not one, and neither is a child born out of wedlock to two unmarried people. Further, in practice, rabbis do everything in their power to free a person from this category, including retroactively invalidating conversions and first marriages.
5. "'Because he is happy with you' (Deut. 15:16): he must be with [that is, equal to] you in food and drink, such that you should not eat white bread and he black bread, you [should not] drink old wine and he new wine, you

[should not] sleep on a feather bed and he on straw. Therefore it was said, "He who buys a Hebrew slave is like one who buys a master for himself " Sifra, Behar 7:3; B. Kiddushin 20a, 22a; B. Arakhin 30b. The quoted version follows the reading in B. Kiddushin 20a.

6. Sifra on Lev. 19:14 (that one may not mislead people in giving advice); B. Pesaḥim 22b (that one may not offer wine to a Nazarite, who has foresworn wine); B. Bava Meẓia 75b (that one may not lend money in the absence of witnesses less that encourage the borrower to claim that the loan was never made).

7. M. Bava Kamma 8:1, and the Talmud on that Mishnah. Even if the Torah is interpreted literally, it represents a moral advance from Hammurabi's code, according to which a person of a lower class who punches out the eye of a person of a higher class is put to death. In contrast, the Torah was saying *only* an eye for an eye, not death for an eye, and it removes all class considerations. The Rabbis, writing some 1,200 years after the Exodus law code was probably formulated, take this one step further by reinterpreting this to mean—through 10 separate proofs!—not retribution at all but rather monetary compensation. See Dorff and Rosett, *A Living Tree,* pp. 152–173, for a translation of the Mishnah and Talmud on this law.

8. M. Ketubbot 4:7–12.

9. Dorff, *To Do the Right and the Good,* append. B, esp. pp. 275–276.

10. I describe the import of this more fully in ibid., pp. 276–282, and in Dorff, *Love Your Neighbor and Yourself,* pp. 341–344.

11. B. Pesaḥim 50b; B. Sanhedrin 105a; B. Arakhin 16b; B. Sotah 22b, 47a; B. Horayyot 10b; B. Nazir 23b.

12. B. Bava Meẓia 49b.

13. See Deut. 27, 29:9–14, 30:11–20; 1 Kings 8; Josh. 24; Esther 9:27; Neh. 8–10 (esp. 8:6 and 10:1–30). These passages describe varying degrees of "persuasion" by God and varying degrees of informed consent.

14. Hobbes, *Leviathan,* "Review and Conclusion," (following Part 4), p. 292; see also part 2, chap.. 19, pp. 159, 161, and part 2, chap. 21, p. 176. However, John Locke, a later 17th-century philosopher, draws a distinction between being what we would now call "a resident alien" in contrast to being a citizen. Tacit consent indicates only our willingness to abide by the country's laws while we enjoy its benefits; as soon as we leave the country or cease to enjoy its benefits for some other reason, we no longer are obligated to see ourselves as tied to that country or morally required to abide by its rules. In contrast, according to Locke, if we expressly swear allegiance to a country, then we "perpetually" and "unalterably" remain citizens no matter where we live, including the duties of citizenship. See Locke, *Two Treatises of Government,* Second Treatise, chap. 8, pars. 116-122, pp. 390–394. Tacit consent makes people liable even for the laws they do not know, for their experience within the society should be enough to teach them how to

behave within it, and they can always ask if they have a question as to whether something is permitted or not.

15. M. Avot (Ethics of the Fathers) 2:4.

16. B. Rosh Hashanah 17a; M.T. Laws of Repentance 3:6, 11; 4:2. S.A. Yoreh De'ah 340:5 (gloss), 345:5.

17. This is one of the primary themes, for example, of Emanuel Levinas (1906-1995), a French Jewish philosopher whose writings in French have now been largely translated into English. See, for example, *Face to Face with Levinas*. Ronald Dworkin, a contemporary American philosopher of law, has similarly emphasized the underlying communal nature of human beings in criticizing the powerful individualism of American legal thought; see, for example, his *Law's Empire,* esp. pp. 206–216.

18. M.T. Laws of Repentance 10.

19. See also Isa. 29:10; Hosea 3:4, 5:6; Mic. 3:6–7; Lam. 2:9; and Ezek. 7:23–27, who all announce similar punishments of being cut off from God's word if the Children of Israel fail to obey God's commandments.

20. Other biblical passages that express this theme include Deut. 6:20–25, where the Torah describes how parents should respond to children asking why they should obey the commandments, and Deut. 26:1–10, where the Torah records a formula that an adult is supposed to recite when bringing the first fruits of the land to the Temple as an expression of his own gratitude.

21. This *may* also be the rationale for obeying the Ten Commandments. The Torah introduces them with "I, the Lord, am your God who brought you out of the land of Egypt, the house of bondage" (Exod. 20:2; Deut. 5:6). In beginning this way, God may simply be identifying Himself so that the Israelites would have no doubt that the God at Sinai was the same God who had brought them out of Egypt. In that case, it is as if God were saying this: "I am not strange to you; I was there with you in Egypt, and I was the one who brought you here."

God, alternatively, may be pointing to His power as a reason to obey the commandments He is about to announce. Then the introductory verse would mean something like this: "I had the power to redeem you from slavery in a country as powerful as Egypt, and so you had better obey what I am about to command."

One *can,* however, read this introductory sentence in line with the passage from Deut. 4 that I have been discussing in this section, as if God were saying, "I am the God who redeemed you from slavery in Egypt, and you should obey My commandments out of a sense of *gratitude* for My having done so." If this last reading is correct, God's power to reward and punish would not be the primary—or, at least, the only—reason to abide by these central commandments; it would rather be the debt of gratitude we owe God.

22. J. Ta'anit 2:4; Genesis Rabbah 56:10

23. B. Menaḥot 43b.

24. B. Sotah 10b

25. B. Shabbat 64b. This was also the motivation for allowing a woman to wear sandals on Yom Kippur (B. Yoma 78b) and to take possession of any extra wornout clothing the family has so that she can wear that during her menstrual period and keep her other clothes in better shape for the times each month when the couple may engage in conjugal relations so that her husband is attracted to her and not repulsed by her (B. Ketubbot 65b).

26. For more on gratitude to God, see Dorff, *The Way into Tikkun Olam (Fixing the World)*, pp. 100–103.

27. Halevi, *The Kuzari*, part 2, par. 48, p. 112. I would like to thank my friend and teacher Rabbi Uzi Weingarten for pointing this out to me.

28. J. Pe'ah 1:1 (3b).

29. B. Megillah 15a; B. Hullin 104b; B. Niddah 19b.

30. Maimonides, for example, uses these very verses to justify and define the proper limits of martyrdom: M.T. Laws of the Foundations of the Torah 5.

31. For a discussion of this value concept in general, and this aspect of it in particular, see Kadushin, *Worship and Ethics*, chap 6, esp. pp. 131–151 and pp. 231–232. For a shorter, less technical discussion, see Garfiel, *The Service of the Heart*, pp. 78–80.

32. God is most commonly sanctified in the Bible through His own impressive acts of might rather than through the acts of individuals. Thus according to Isa. (8:13; 29:23), it is the Lord of Hosts—that is, the Lord who acts mightily with military legions—whom the Israelites will sanctify. But it is especially Ezekiel who links God's sanctity to His acts of might. These include punishing Ẓidon (Ezek. 28:22) and Gog (Ezek. 38:16,23) and also acts of redemption. Thus the very fact that Israel is dispersed among the nations desecrates God's name, and God's redemption of Israel will, conversely, sanctify God's name (Ezek. 36:16–38, esp. vv. 20–23, and 39:25,27).

Nevertheless, the Bible does contain some instances in which individuals' actions would *desecrate* God's name through illicit theological or ritual acts. So, for example, Moses and Aaron are blamed and punished "because you did not trust Me enough to affirm My sanctity in the sight of the Israelite people" (Num. 20:12, see 27:14; Deut. 32:51). Similarly, desecration of God's name occurs if someone sacrifices his children to the Moabite god Molekh (Lev. 18:21, 20:3), swears falsely by God's name (Lev. 19:12), offers idolatrous gifts to God (Ezek. 20:39), or engages in apostasy (Ezek. 43:7–8). *Kohanim* (descendants of Aaron who filled special roles in the Temple rites) must take special care to "be holy to their God and not profane the name of their God" (Lev. 21:6) by observing the special restrictions imposed on them in their personal lives (for example, not shaving smooth any part of their heads, cutting their beards, making gashes in their flesh, or marrying a har-

185

lot or a divorcee [Lev. 21:5–8]) and in their professional services in the Temple (see Lev. 22, esp. vv. 2 and 32). The prophet Amos applies this also to moral offenses: "Oh, you who trample the heads of the poor into the dust of the earth and make the humble walk a twisted course! Father and son go to the same girl and thereby profane My holy name" (Amos 2:7).

The Bible does not specifically speak of *people sanctifying* God's name, although it does refer to other positive acts by which people treat the name of God. So, for example, the Psalmist and/or Chronicler praise or bless God's holy name (Ps. 103:1, 105:3, 145:21; 1 Chron. 16:10), acknowledge it (Ps. 106: 47; 1 Chron. 16:35), and trust it (Ps. 33:21).

Thus while the concepts of *kiddush ha-Shem* and *hillul ha-Shem* have antecedents in the Bible, their full usage to characterize the acts of individuals begins with the Rabbis. See M.T. Laws of the Foundations of the Torah 5:1,10–11.

33. B. Kiddushin 40a. On the same page (and in B. Hagigah 16a), Rabbi Ilai applies this to a man who cannot control his sexual urges. He says, "let him go to a place where nobody knows him, dress and cover himself in black, and act as his passion desires, but let him not profane the Name of God in public." On the other hand, M. Avot 4:5 asserts that one is punished even if the profanation of God's name takes place in private and even if done unintentionally.

34. Tanhuma, Buber Hukkat 61a on Num. 20:12.

35. Sifra 88d (end) on Lev. 19:15.

36. T. Bava Kamma 10:5.

37. For example, Isa. 2:1–4; Zech. 14:8–9,16.

38. Rubenstein, *After Auschwitz,* chaps. 2 and 3.

39. Kaplan, *The Meaning of God in Modern Jewish Religion,* p. 102. See also Kaplan, *Judaism as a Civilization,* pp. 258ff. See also my discussion of Kaplan's doctrine of covenant in "The Meaning of Covenant," pp. 40-46, and, in general, in my "The Covenant: How Jews Understand Themselves and Others." For Kaplan's views of rituals as folkways, see Kaplan, *Questions Jews Ask,* chap. 4. For his view of Jewish law as a combination of moral norms and folkways, see *Questions Jews Ask,* pp. 263–276, reprinted in Dorff, *The Unfolding* Tradition, pp. 121-129, and see my discussion of Kaplan's exchange with Robert Gordis on this matter in Dorff, *The Unfolding Tradition,* pp. 94–97.

40. Maimonides, M.T. Laws of Ethics (De'ot) 1:6.

41. Sifrei Devarim, Ekev #49.

42. B. Sotah 14a.

43. See also Isa. 49:6, 51:4. Many mistranslate this phrase as "a light to the nations," as if the Hebrew were *or la-goyim* rather than what it in fact is: *le-or goyim.* In Isa. 49:6, as the note on the passage in the new translation of the Jewish Publication Society suggests, this may actually mean "an agent of

good fortune"—that is, an agent to bring good fortune—rather than an instructor of peoples; but in Isa. 42:6, it does seem to mean the latter. (It also means that in Isa. 51:4, but there it is God who is the instructor of nations, not Israel.) Other biblical passages that similarly envisage a time when all nations would come to Jerusalem to learn Torah (instruction) from Israel include Isa. 2:2–3, Mic. 4:1–2, and Zech. 14:3–9.

44. See Dorff, *The Way into Tikkun Olam (Fixing the World)*, esp. chap. 1.

45. The ban against Jews taking their disputes to gentile courts: B. Gittin 88b; M.T. Laws of Courts (Sanhedrin) 26:7; S.A. Hoshen Mishpat 26:1.

46. A good summary of the Rabbis' attempts to do this can be found in A. Cohen, *Everyman's Talmud*, pp. 110–120.

47. Rubenstein, *After Auschwitz*; Wyschograd, "Faith and the Holocaust"; Maybaum, *The Face of God after Auschwitz*; Berkovits, *Faith after the Holocaust, Crisis and Faith*, and *With God in Hell*; D. R. Blumenthal, *Facing the Abusing God* and *The Banality of Good and Evil*; Fackenheim, *Quest for Past and Future, The Jewish Return into History*, and *To Mend the World*; I. Greenberg, "Cloud of Smoke, Pillar of Fire"; Kushner, *When Bad Things Happen to Good People*; Schulweis, *Evil and the Morality of God* and *For Those Who Can't Believe*; and Katz, *Post-Holocaust Dialogues*.

48. Dorff, *Knowing God*, chap. 5.

49. M. Avot (Ethics of the Fathers) 4:2.

50. For love of God as the motive: Deut. 6:4–5, 11:13,22, 19:9, 30:6,15–20. For fear of God as the motive: Deut. 4:10–14, 6:24–25, 10:12–13, 31:10–13— as well as the punishments delineated in greatest detail in Lev. 26 and Deut. 28 and the fearsome scene at Mount Sinai.

51. M. Avot (Ethics of the Fathers) 1:2–3.

52. Maimonides, Laws of Repentance, 10. In his Guide of the Perplexed 3.52, Maimonides has another theory about the relationship between love and fear of God—namely, "The love is the result of the truths taught in the Law, including the true knowledge of the existence of God, while the fear of God is produced by the practices prescribed in the Law. Note this explanation."

53. Hartman, *A Living Covenant*, p. 301.

54. Genesis Rabbah, Lekh Lekha 44:1 and Leviticus Rabbah, Shemini 13:3.

55. Midrash Tanhuma, Shemini (ed. Buber), 15b.

56. B. Shabbat 88a.

57. Deuteronomy Rabbah, Nitzavim 8:5.

58. M. Avot (Ethics of the Fathers) 3:2.

59. Numbers Rabbah 11:7.

60. J. Ta'anit 4:2.

61. Sifra 112c.

62. Exodus Rabbah, Ki Tissa 47:3.

63. Ha-Am, *Al Parshat Derakhim*, 3:30.

64. M. Yadayim 3:5; see M. Eduyyot 5:3; T. Yadayim 2:14; T. Sanhedrin 12:10. See also Schoville, "Song of Songs"; Gordis, *The Song of Songs*, pp. 1–44, esp. pp. 2–4, 43–44; and G. D. Cohen, "The Song of Songs and the Jewish Religious Mentality."

65. Song of Songs Rabbah on Songs 1:15.

66. B. Pesaḥim 109a.

67. The verse is Exod. 15:2. The rabbis used a play on the Hebrew word, *v'anvehu* (and I will enshrine Him) in that verse to make it mean "and I will glorify Him"—that is, make oneself beautiful before Him in carrying out the commandments; see Mekhilta, Beshalah-Massekhta d'Shirah, chap. 3 (ed. Horovitz-Rabin, p. 127); B. Shabbat 133b; B. Sukkah 11b; B. Nazir 2b; and so on. For a description of the many areas in which later rabbis applied the talmudic injunction, see *Enẓiklopediya Talmudit* 8:271–284 (Hebrew). A good treatment of this subject in regard to beautifying prayer can be found in Petuchowski, *Understanding Jewish Prayer*, pp. 26–34.

CHAPTER FIVE

Continuity and Change in Jewish Law

No legal system can exist very long without change. New issues emerge. Old assumptions no longer hold. Whether technological, scientific, economic, social, political, moral, or simply a matter of style, changes occur in life, and any legal system that does not adjust is doomed to become obsolete. This is especially true in our time, when changes occur much more rapidly than in the past.

On the other hand, a legal system that changes too rapidly or too extensively loses its ability to function as law. In his story "The Trial," Franz Kafka depicts a man on trial who does not know the charges against him, the consequences of being found guilty, the methods available to him to prove his innocence, or even the rules, if any, that bind the judges.[1] We feel the sheer terror of not knowing what we can expect of others and what others can expect of us or do to us. Avoiding such insecurity is one of the primary reasons for establishing a legal system in the first place, and it is the factor that distinguishes government by law from government with power unlimited by law. If the law changes too often, however, it loses its ability to tell us what we can expect of others and what others can expect of us. Furthermore, in losing its continuity and the security it brings, the law also loses an important source of its authority.

Every legal system, then, needs to balance continuity and change. This is a hard task to accomplish for any legal system, but it is especially hard for Jewish law. One reason is that, with the exception of the era of the Sanhedrin, Jews have lived throughout the world without a central legal body to determine the law. Maintaining enough continuity to keep Jewish law clear in its demands and yet flexible enough to accommodate vastly different social and commercial circumstances, then, has been quite a challenge. Furthermore, Jewish law bases its primary claims for authority on the belief that God gave us the law and continues to want us to abide by it. How, then, can human beings have the authority to make any changes in it?

THE ROLES OF GOD AND HUMAN BEINGS IN INTERPRETING AND APPLYING JEWISH LAW

To begin with the theological issue, some sections of the Torah declare that God gave the law, and no human tinkering—let alone a conscious change of the law—is or should be allowed.[2] This is how the Rabbis interpreted two passages in Deuteronomy (4:2 and 13:1) in which Moses tells the Israelites "not to add anything to what I command you or take anything away from it, but keep the commandments of the Lord your God that I enjoin upon you." Even though the context of both verses in the Torah is idolatry, the Rabbis understood this ban to apply to all of Jewish law. Furthermore, the Decalogue and the rules in Exodus 21–23 are given at Mount Sinai in an overpowering event, with thunder, lightening, and earthquakes to make one think, "Hands off! This is God's law, and don't you dare tamper with it!" The understanding of the origins and functioning of Jewish law that many Jews have is based on these biblical passages alone.

Other passages of the Torah, however, indicate that even in its earliest times Jewish law was subject to change. In three instances (Lev. 24:10–23; Num. 15:32–36, 27:1–11), Moses does not know what to do and seeks a new oracle from God. The Torah, though, does not rely on new divine revelations alone; indeed, shortly after the First Temple period, Zechariah (13:2–4) declares that people who claim revelations shall be made to feel ashamed for making such claims and their own parents will call them liars and will put them to death.

Why so? Jeremiah complains bitterly about the people's inability to distinguish true prophets from false ones, and indeed it is hard to judge who has heard God at all, let alone whether that person has interpreted God's words or vision correctly. Furthermore, prophecy has the potential to change the law radically at any moment: The prophet can simply announce that even though God has told us until now to do *x*, now we should do *y*. These problems inherent in prophecy made Zechariah and the later tradition abandon oracles as the way to determine the law. Claims to revelation persist after the close of the Bible, but the mainstream Jewish tradition denied their authority.[3]

Jewish tradition has instead depended on the other biblical method for determining the law—namely, human judges. In chapter 18 of Exodus, the chapter before the Decalogue is given amid thunder and lightning on Mount Sinai, Moses is depicted as judging cases "from morning until evening" (v. 13), and Jethro, his father-in-law, suggests that he delegate this responsibility to others for most cases and judge himself only "every major dispute" (v. 22).[4] This is an indication in the Torah itself that there was a body of common law that governed the Israelites even before the Revelation at Mount Sinai (that is, that the Oral Torah stretches back well before the Sinai Revelation, as events centered on accepted law in the lives of the Patriarchs also indicate) and that Moses had the power to make judgments under that law and even to delegate his authority to others. Later, Deuteronomy 17:8–13 specifically instructs Israelites faced with cases "too baffling for you to decide, be it a controversy over homicide, civil law, or assault, matters of dispute in your courts" to go to the Temple in Jerusalem, where "the levitical priests or the magistrate in charge at the time"—that is, in each generation—would render judgment and where contempt of court would be punished by death. This certainly empowers human judges not only to apply the law to specific cases but to interpret it in new ways when cases are "baffling." With judges we still are left with the problem of distinguishing good decisions from bad ones and with the possibility that judges might overturn precedent radically, but now the power to determine the law rests in the hands of human beings whose judgment can be evaluated by other judges and by the community itself.

Furthermore, *Judaism is not identical with the religion of the Bible.* Judaism is based on the way in which the Rabbis of the Talmud and Midrash and rabbis in all succeeding generations defined the contents of the Bible and interpreted it (in contrast to non-religious, Christian, and Muslim understandings of it) and on how the Jewish community has historically practiced it. In the same way, neither

Christianity nor Islam is the religion of their holy scriptures alone but rather each is a *tradition* based on those scriptures. Thus if one wants to get a sense of how any modern legal theory fits, or fails to fit, the ages-old and ongoing Jewish tradition, it is crucial to see how *the Rabbis* balanced tradition and change in Jewish law.

When we consult biblical and rabbinic sources, we discover some important and surprising things. First, the Bible claims that God spoke to Moses and the prophets directly, and it leaves open the possibility of future prophets (for example, Deut. 18:15–22). The Rabbis, however, claimed that God ceased to make the divine will known through prophecy shortly after the destruction of the First Temple:

> When the latter prophets, Haggai, Zekhariah, and Malakhi died, the Holy Spirit departed from Israel."[5]

> The Holy One, blessed be He, said: "Twenty-four books [the Hebrew Bible] have I written for you; beware and make no addition to them." For what reason? "Of making many books there is no end" (Ecclesiastes 12:12). He who reads a single verse that is not from the twenty-four is as though he read in "the outside books." Beware of making many books [to add to the Scriptures], for whoever does so will have no portion in the World to Come.[6]

Modern biblical scholarship has demonstrated that the Torah was not edited in more or less the form that we have it now until the time of Ezra (c. 450 B.C.E.), well after the time of the biblical prophets that we can date with assurance.[7] The Rabbis, however, gave greater credence to the Torah than to the prophets, claiming that Moses' prophesies were most authoritative because his vision was clearest and most inclusive:

> What was the distinction between Moses and the other prophets? The latter looked through nine lenses, whereas Moses looked only through one. They looked through a cloudy lens, but Moses through one that was clear.[8]

> Forty-eight prophets and seven prophetesses spoke prophecies for Israel, and they neither diminished nor added to what was written in the Torah, with the exception of the law to read the Book of Esther on the Feast of Purim.[9]

In place of prophecy, the Rabbis greatly expanded the judicial powers that the Torah had created in chapter 17 of Deuteronomy, and they claimed that *their interpretations were the new and only way in which God spoke to humankind:*

> Rabbi Abdimi from Haifa said: Since the day when the Temple was destroyed, the prophetic gift was taken away from the prophets and given to the Sages.—Is then a Sage not also a prophet?—What he meant was this: Although it has been taken from the prophets, it has not been taken from the Sages. Amemar said: A Sage is even superior to a prophet, as it says, "And a prophet has a heart of wisdom" (Ps. 90:12). Who is [usually] compared with whom? Is not the smaller compared with the greater?[10]

The following source demonstrates exactly how far this judicial authority goes: " 'According to the sentence . . . of the judges shall you act, you shall not deviate . . . to the right or to the left' (Deuteronomy 17:11). Even if they say that right is left and that left is right, listen to them."[11] On the other hand, another strain within the tradition maintains that judicial rulings, just like prophetic revelations, are to be evaluated for the propriety of their content before being obeyed as authoritative law:

> "You must not deviate from the verdict that they [the judges in your time] announce to you either to the right or to the left" (Deuteronomy 17:11). You might think that this means that if they tell you that right is left and left is right, you are to obey them; therefore [that is, to show you that that is not true] the Torah tells you, "to the right or to the left," [to indicate that] when they tell you that right is right and left is left [you are to obey them, but not otherwise].[12]

THE NEED FOR INTERPRETATION

Aside from the problems inherent in prophecy, the Rabbis expanded on the Torah's mandate for judicial activity because they were convinced that the Torah needs interpretation, that nobody could follow God's will on the basis of the Torah alone. There are sects of Christians who are "fundamentalists." They try to make their decisions in life on the sole basis of the Bible. Many Muslims do the same thing with the Koran. There also have been sects of Jews who have tried that, including the Karaites (who were strongest in the 9th and 10th centuries but who still exist today) and, to a lesser degree, the Sadducees. Even though these groups maintain that they are relying exclusively on Holy Scripture, which they take to be the only authentic word of God, what actually happens is that they are living according to their own particular convictions about what constitutes Scripture and what it means.

The Rabbis were much more conscious and honest about the necessity and process of interpreting Scripture to know what it means. They even indicate that they were aware that they were making the text mean what they wanted it to mean, shaping the law according to their value system. This is evident, for example, in their open recognition that they had made the Torah's many laws that demand capital punishment effectively inoperative, just as they had done with the Torah's law governing a stubborn and rebellious son.[13] It is also evident in how they shaped the law according to their own values—justice, kindness, study, sanctifying God's name—"value concepts," as Max Kadushin calls them, which are named many, many times in their interpretations and applications of Jewish law.[14]

In part, what justified their expansive use of their judicial mandate was the lack of a legislature to make changes in the law. Anther factor that justified this was their understanding that the text of the Torah itself is an open, rich one, susceptible to multiple understandings; and so no claim to one and only one possible reading made sense:

"Is not My word like a hammer that breaks a rock in many pieces?" (Jeremiah 23:29). As the hammer causes numerous sparks to flash forth, so is a Scriptural verse capable of many interpretations.[15]

There are 70 faces to the Torah.[16]

"The words of the wise are as goads. . . . They are given from one shepherd" (Ecclesiastes 12:11), that is, the words of the Torah and the words of the Sages have been given from the same shepherd [Moses]. "And furthermore, my son, be careful: Of making many books there is no end" (Ecclesiastes 12:12) means: More than to the words of the Torah pay attention to the words of the Scribes. In the same strain it says, "For your love is better than wine" (Song of Songs 1:2), which means: The words of the beloved ones [the Sages] are better than the wine of the Torah. Why? Because one cannot give a proper decision from the words of the Torah, since the Torah is shut up [cryptic and therefore ambiguous] and consists entirely of headings. . . . From the words of the Sages, however, one can derive the proper law because they explain the Torah. And the reason why the words of the Sages are compared to goads (*darvanot*) is because they cause understanding to dwell (*medayerin binah*) in people [a play on words].[17]

Interpretation is necessary not only because the Torah on its own is ambiguous, but also because Jewish law must retain sufficient flexibility:

If the Torah had been given in a fixed form, the situation would have been intolerable. What is the meaning of the oft-recurring phrase, "The Lord *spoke* to Moses?" Moses said before Him, "Sovereign of the Universe! Cause me to know what the final decision is on each matter of law." He replied, "The majority [of the judges] must be followed: When the majority declares a thing permitted, it is permissible; when the majority declares it forbidden, it is not allowed; so that the Torah may be capable of interpretation with forty-nine points *for* and forty-nine points *against*."[18]

In fact, the Rabbis considered new interpretations and expansions of the law not only necessary, but also desirable:

A king had two slaves whom he loved intensely. He gave each one a measure of wheat and a bundle of flax. The intelligent one wove the flax into a cloth and made flour from the wheat, sifted it, ground it, kneaded it, baked it, and set it [the bread] on the table on the cloth he had made before the king returned. The stupid one did not do a thing [with the gifts the king had given him]. After some time, the king returned to his house and said to them: "My sons, bring me what I gave you." One brought out the table set with the bread on the tablecloth; the other brought out the wheat in a basket and the bundle of flax with it. What an embarrassment that was! Which do you think was the more beloved? [Similarly] when the Holy Blessed One gave the Torah to Israel, God gave it as wheat from which to make flour and flax from which to make clothing through the rules of interpretation.[19]

Finally, human interpretation and application of the law are necessary because God required it in chapter 17 of Deuteronomy. Thus
not to interpret the law anew in each generation would be to disobey
God's law!

> Nobody should say, "I will not observe the precepts of the elders"
> [i.e., the Oral Torah], since they are not of Mosaic authority [liter-
> ally, contained in the Torah]. For God has said, "No, my child,
> whatever they decree for you, you must perform," as it says,
> "According to the Torah that they [i.e., the elders in days to come]
> *shall* teach you shall you do" (Deuteronomy 17:11): for even for Me
> do they [the Rabbis] make decrees, as it says, "when you [i.e., the
> rabbis] decree a command, it shall be fulfilled for you" [i.e., by Me,
> God, a playful interpretation of Job 22:28].[20]

RETAINING COHERENCE DESPITE MULTIPLE INTERPRETATIONS

These reasons to require interpretation are all well and good, but if
there are many interpretations of the law, how is it to have any
coherence—any sense that, despite the many different understandings and applications of the law, this is still one, reasonably consistent, system? And how are the various interpretations of God's word
to retain divine authority?

Those are hard questions, but the Rabbis faced them squarely.
They answered the question of coherence in three ways. First of all,
the tradition would remain coherent despite the many variations of
opinion because they are all based on the Torah.[21] In somewhat the
same way, American law is coherent because it all derives from the
framework and powers that were established in the Constitution—
however much it has changed since then and however many interpretations of it exist today.

Second, the tradition will be cohesive because there is a sense of
continuity within the tradition itself. There is a famous story in the
Talmud that illustrates this. When Moses visits the academy of Rabbi
Akiva, who lived some 1,400 years after him, he does not even
understand what Rabbi Akiva is saying, let alone agree with it.
Nevertheless, Moses is comforted when Rabbi Akiva cites one of the
laws in Moses' name because that indicates that Rabbi Akiva and his

contemporaries understood themselves to be part of the ongoing tradition that stretches back to Moses.[22] This story clearly indicates that the Rabbis realized that there had been changes in the law; and, at the same time, it illustrates the sense of continuity that the Jewish community has about its tradition, however much it has changed in form, a sense that imparts coherence and authority to it.

Third, Jewish law retains its coherence despite multiple, conflicting rulings because it includes a way of deciding which of them will be authoritative. All opinions could be aired in discussion; and in fact, all are to be considered "the words of the living God,"[23] but in the end the majority would prevail.[24] After all, although the Jewish tradition is remarkably tolerant and even encouraging of debate, Jews, like all other societies, must in the end have a way of deciding the law so that citizens know what to expect.

MAKING DECISIONS AFTER THE DEMISE OF THE SANHEDRIN: THE *MARA D'ATRA* AND REGIONAL COURTS

The situation became more complicated when the Sanhedrin ceased to exist and there was no longer a central authority in Judaism, but there are still ways in which decisions are made in Jewish law, thus preserving its continuity. First, each community is supposed to follow the decisions of its local rabbi, its *mara d'atra* (the teacher [master] of the place) and the court that he or she often chairs; for each community is *commanded* to establish a court:

> Courts should be established in Israel and outside it, as it says, "Such shall be your law of procedure throughout the generations in *all* your settlements" (Numbers 35:29), from which we learn that courts must be established in Israel and outside it. So why does the Torah say, "in all the settlements that the Lord your God is giving you" (Deuteronomy 16:18)? To teach you that in Israel you establish courts in every district and city, but outside Israel only in every district.[25]

Local rabbis gain their authority on the basis of two sources: their ordination, which indicates that they have achieved sufficient knowledge of the Jewish tradition and the ways it functions to make legal decisions for their community; and the community's hiring of a given rabbi to be its legal authority on the basis of their assessment of his or her erudition, wisdom, and insight. The former factor does not require that rabbis have expertise in every area of law; like American lawyers and doctors, rabbis now, as in centuries past, often consult with other rabbis known to have particular knowledge of, and experience with, a given area of the law. Hence the long history of responsa literature, in which one rabbi would ask another for advice on how to resolve an issue, and such consultations take place today by telephone and through e-mail. Ordination means, though, that the rabbi knows enough about Jewish law to answer most questions and to know whom to consult when something arises that he or she does not know and cannot determine through his or her own research.

The second factor that gives the rabbi authority—that a community has hired him or her—means, of course, that the rabbi must always be aware of the community's sensitivities, that, as the Talmud declares, "One must not institute a legal decree on the community that the majority of the community cannot bear,"[26] and that, in consequence, the content of the law itself is always an interaction of what the rabbis say and what the people do. I will discuss more about this feature of Jewish law in Chapter Seven on custom.

That local rabbis make decisions also means that there are many different decisions being made on any given issue in the various places in which Jews live, but even then there is a general rule to coordinate the decisions and give Jewish law coherence:

4. . . . After the Supreme Court [Sanhedrin] ceased to exist, disputes multiplied among the Jewish people: one person declared something impure, giving a reason for his ruling, and another declared it pure, giving a reason for his ruling; one forbade [something], the other permitted [it].

5. If two scholars or courts disagree with each other, when there is no Supreme Court in existence or before the Supreme Court had clarified the matter, whether they rule simultaneously or consecutively, one pronouncing pure what the other pronounces impure, one declaring forbidden what the other declares permitted, and it is impossible to determine the correct decision, then if a Scriptural law is involved, act according to the more stringent view and according to the more lenient view if a rabbinic law is at issue.[27]

Moreover, because Jews have lived under many different conditions in the scattered places in which they have found themselves, it probably is a good thing that the court in each area makes decisions appropriate to its particular setting. Jewish law thereby gains the necessary flexibility to enable it to work in many different times and places. Furthermore, in some places and times, Jewish communities have been sufficiently organized to have a centralized court system for a community or a group of communities. That was true for the synods of the Middle Ages and the Committee of Four Lands in Eastern Europe (1650–1850), and it is the precedent for the Conservative movement's Committee on Jewish Law and Standards today. Even without such centralized mechanisms to make decisions for whole groups of Jewish communities, the authority of the local rabbi provides a clear way of making decisions wherever Jews live; and that, together with the sense of continuity and the dependence on one Torah discussed earlier, gives Jewish law coherence and a reasonable degree of consistency.

RETAINING AUTHORITY DESPITE MULTIPLE OPINIONS AND CHANGES

The second question goes to the very root of the authority of Jewish law: With all of the various interpretations of the law and the new applications of it, how is it in any sense divine? After all, the Rabbis explicitly claimed that it is the *human* judges in each generation that have the authority to make decisions in Jewish law. Furthermore, in a famous Talmudic story in which the Rabbis quote God's own words that the law "is not in heaven" (Deut. 30:12), they audaciously assert that God no longer has the right or authority to determine the law even if God wants to do so—and then God, according to the story, laughs and says, "My children have bested (or perhaps eternalized) Me."[28] But then how is Jewish law as the rabbis interpret it God's word any more?

This is a crucial question, and it is important to remember why it arises in the first place. On the one hand, the Rabbis clearly wanted to retain divine authority for Jewish law: There are many reasons to observe it, as described in Chapter Four, but the most important one by far—at least as the Rabbis saw it—is that it is the will of God. On the other hand, the Rabbis had to assert the right of rabbis in each generation to interpret and apply the law for the reasons discussed earlier in this chapter: the difficulties of using prophecy as a legal guide; the ambiguity of the Torah, especially in regard to how it is to be applied to new situations; the need to retain flexibility in the law to enable it to function under new circumstances; and the commandment of God Himself that judges in each generation take on the responsibility of interpreting the law.

There is no simple way of affirming both the divine authority of the law and the right of human beings to interpret it. The Rabbis, in a style typical of them, claimed two opposite things to assert the truth of both of them. On the one hand, they maintained that all later developments in the law were already revealed at Sinai:

> What is the meaning of the verse, "And I will give you the tablets of stone, and the teaching and the commandment, that I have written, so that you may teach them" (Exodus 24:12)? "Tablets of stone," [refers to] the Decalogue; "teaching" [refers to] the Torah; "commandment" [refers to] the Mishnah; "that I have written" [refers to] the Prophets and Hagiographa [Writings]; "so that you may teach them" [refers to] the Gemara [Talmud]. The verse [thus] teaches that all of those sources were given to Moses on Sinai.[29]

> Even what a distinguished student was destined to teach in the presence of his teacher was already said to Moses on Sinai.[30]

Thus because all of the interpretations, extensions, and revisions of the law by the rabbis of all generations to come were already revealed at Sinai, they carry God's authority. On the other hand, the Rabbis were aware that many of their interpretations and laws were new—so new that Moses could not understand them—and they even held that it is God's desire that the law not be fixed, that the Rabbis instead apply the law anew in each generation. Moreover the Rabbis claimed that these new interpretations were the form in which God revealed His will to us in postbiblical times. They therefore also said this:

> When God revealed His presence to the Israelites, He did not display all His goodness at once, because they could not have borne so much good; for had He revealed His goodness to them at one time they would have died. . . . When Joseph made himself known

to his brothers, they were unable to answer him because they were astounded by him (Genesis 45:3). If *God* were to reveal Himself all at once, how much more powerful would be the effect. So He shows Himself little by little.[31]

Matters that had not been disclosed to Moses were disclosed to R. Akiva and his colleagues.[32]

How is it possible that everything was revealed at Sinai and yet new things are revealed each day? Actually, it is not as contradictory as it seems. Reading a good story as a child and then again as an adult is a good example of how this can happen. As a child, you understand the story in one way, but as an adult you might see completely new levels of meaning in it. For that matter, reading it at different times in adulthood may disclose new messages and significance. The text is the same, but it says something new to you because you are different. You experienced new things and can, therefore, relate the story to more areas of life. You also can appreciate more of the themes of the story. *Alice in Wonderland,* for example, is indeed an imaginative and even funny story about a girl who has a crazy dream, but it is not only that. It is also a satire on many different types of people and even includes some interesting problems of logic. You certainly did not see it that way when you read it (or saw the movie) at age seven or eight, but you may be able to understand it that way now. Similar things apply to the stories in the Bible. Those who read them in childhood and never again have missed a great deal of their meaning. The Bible is *at least* good literature, which must be studied and appreciated again and again throughout life.

Law operates in a similar way. On the one hand, with the exception of the last 16 amendments, the Constitution of the United States is the same as it was in 1791, when the Bill of Rights was ratified. Its meaning, however, has extended far beyond the intentions of its framers, for judges, lawyers, and scholars have carefully examined its every phrase in applying it to new problems and circumstances. It has even changed meaning a number of times as the Supreme Court reversed itself or greatly narrowed or expanded the application of its previous rulings. *Yet, in an important sense, all of the later developments were already inherent in the original Constitution because they all derived from the governmental bodies that it established and the general principles that it enunciated.* The Constitution is understood and applied in many novel ways each year—or, in more theological terms, many new, previously undiscovered meanings and applications are revealed in it as time goes on. But all of the new meanings gain authority because they are affirmed by the structures established by the Constitution (Congress, the courts, the executive) and because they extend or apply the Constitution and its subsequent interpretations, however much they stretch to do so. This is the sense of continuity that the law enjoys.

The exact same thing is true about Jewish law. Even though the description of the Revelation at Sinai in the Torah itself restricts the content of the Revelation to the Decalogue and the precedents in Exodus 21–23, the later tradition thought of the entire Torah as revealed there—and for that matter, the Oral Torah as well. As a result, every interpretation and application of Jewish law that has ever existed or will be created in the future was already revealed at Sinai because every one of them comes directly or indirectly from the procedures and principles that the Jewish constitution, the Torah, established. Even though Deuteronomy 17 authorizes judges in each generation only to interpret the law, the Rabbis read that passage to authorize them even to enact *takkanot* (revisions). *Takkanot* represent a change in the content of the law, as the word implies, but they nevertheless are part of Jewish law because they are enacted by its duly authorized representatives throughout the generations to our own day. Similarly, and more pervasively, each time a Jewish court or judge decides to interpret the Torah or Talmud in one way and not another, the meaning of those texts changes. Sometimes the texts are given meanings that they never had had before through this process of midrash (interpretation), and sometimes several possible alternative interpretations are cut off by this process.

In any case, it is possible to expand or contract the meaning or application of a given verse in the Torah only because the Torah ordained that judges in each generation do that. In this sense, *every* later development in Jewish law, no matter how far removed in content from the simple meaning of the Torah, was already revealed to Moses at Sinai because it comes from a judge ultimately authorized by the Torah to function as such. On the other hand, in every generation the Torah is given new meanings and applications, and in that sense "matters that had not been revealed to Moses were revealed to Rabbi Akiva and his colleagues." The authority of Jewish law does not diminish, then, as it is applied anew in every generation; on the contrary, speaking theologically, continuing interpretations and applications of the Torah and Talmud are nothing less than the way God talks to us in our time.

Moreover, the authority of Jewish law depends not only on its divine source but also on its relevance to modern circumstances. If it remains the same from one generation to the next, it may retain its strong link to the past, but it will lose its import for the present and future, thus becoming a delicate and well-preserved relic but not a tool for living today. The Rabbis clearly recognized this. So far we have seen how they did this in what they *said,* but the evidence is more overwhelming if we consider what the Rabbis *did.* Through using the methods of exegesis (interpretation) that they developed (some of which are contained in "The Baraita of Rabbi Ishmael," found in the early part of the daily Shaharit service in many prayer books), they, at one extreme, made some biblical laws totally inoperative and, at the other extreme, they created whole new bodies of law. For example, the Bible requires capital punishment for a whole variety of offenses, but the Rabbis created court procedures for capital cases that were so demanding that it became virtually impossible to obtain a capital conviction in Jewish law. To give you an idea of what they did, they instituted requirements that:

1. The culprit for a capital offense must be warned by two witnesses immediately before committing the act that it carries the death penalty. After all, the accused may not have known that the act is illegal or punished so severely, and how can you hold people liable for a penalty as severe as death if they did not know these things?
2. The accused must respond, "Even so, I am going to do it," for otherwise one cannot be sure that the culprit heard the warning.
3. The defendant must commit the act within three seconds after hearing the warning—the time it takes to say, "Greetings to you, my teacher, my master" (*Shalom alekha, rabi, mori*)— because people forget things, and if the culprit forgot the law, we should not hold him or her responsible for a penalty as serious as death.

4. The witnesses may not be related to each other or to the culprit.
5. There must be at least one judge on the court who votes to acquit the defendant, for otherwise the court might be prejudiced against him or her—which, by the way, is the exact opposite of the requirement in American law for a unanimous jury.

Some of these requirements—and some of the other things the Rabbis required for a capital conviction—are clearly implausible extensions of principles that are reasonable in a different form, and the Rabbis certainly knew that. The majority, though, had decided to abolish the death penalty, despite the numerous times the Torah requires it, and they used court procedures and limitations on those culpable under the laws that carry the death penalty to accomplish that. Put another way, they interpreted the death penalty out of existence, and their disputes with their colleagues about doing so made them realize the issues involved fully:

> A court that has put a person to death once in a seven-year period is called "a hanging court" [literally, a destructive court]. Rabbi Elazar ben Azariah says, "Even once in seventy years." Rabbi Tarfon and Rabbi Akiva say, "Were we members of the court, no person would ever be put to death." Rabban Simeon ben Gamliel retorted, "If so, they would increase those who shed blood [murderers] in Israel."[33]

On the other hand, while the Rabbis effectually nullified the death penalty, they created a whole structure of Sabbath laws far beyond those in the Bible—to the extent that they themselves said: "The laws of the Sabbath are like mountains hanging by a hair, for they consist of little Bible and many laws."[34] Thus the Rabbis of the Talmud and Midrash clearly and consciously changed Jewish law as evidenced both by what they said and by what they did, adding a number of laws, dropping some, and changing the form of some.

Two things must be emphasized about this. First, they considered their actions authorized by God because *they*—the Rabbis themselves—were the ones appointed by the Torah to interpret and apply it in every age. In other words, in Jewish law, as in American law, the original document (the Torah or Constitution) establishes some laws and authorizes communal officials to interpret and apply those laws. In both systems, the interpretations in later generations may vary widely from the original substance or intention of the constitutional laws—even to the extent of nullifying them—*but the new interpretations carry constitutional authority because they are made by the authorities established by the Constitution.* This is the reason why lawyers usually cite recent court decisions about the Constitution rather than the Constitution itself, and that is also the reason for the Geonic rule in Jewish law that *hilkhita kevatra'ai,* (the law is according to the last [that is, the most recent] authorities).[35] In both cases, it is the *forms* (institutions) established by the original document that determine its meaning, even to the point of effectively canceling sections of its contents, and it is because the new rulings issue from the duly authorized bodies that they carry constitutional authority.

Second, and perhaps more important, with all of the changes that the Rabbis instituted, they did *not* think that anything goes, that they could play completely fast and loose with the law. On the contrary, for them it was clearly a matter of "*tradition* and change." In fact, change in law is significant only if the law is taken seriously in the first place. Otherwise, the whole legal system is not a matter of practical concern, and changes in it are irrelevant.

TAKING JEWISH LAW SERIOUSLY AS THE PREREQUISITE FOR CHANGE

The Rabbis dared to make the changes that they did precisely because they took the law seriously. They practiced it, honored it, and were deeply concerned with its continuing authority and viability. For them it was clear that it is the law that defines Jews as Jews; without it there is no point to their separate identity:

["... They rejected My rules and spurned My laws. Yet even then, when they are in the land of their enemies,] I will not reject them or spurn them [so as to destroy them, annulling my Covenant with them]" (Leviticus 26:43–44). All the good gifts that were given them were taken from them. And if it had not been for the Book of the Torah that was left to them, they would not have differed at all from the nations of the world.[36]

Israel's acceptance of the Torah was the reason it had a special covenant with God: "If it were not for My Torah that you accepted, I

rabbinic tradition and the modern Conservative (Masorti) move-ment,[40] as it is *"tradition, which includes change."* It is for this reason—and also because the name "Conservative movement" misleads peo-ple into thinking that it is the equivalent to conservative Christians in its approach to tradition and social policies—that I suggested in 1980 that we change the name to "Traditional Judaism," for the Jewish tradition in and of itself includes procedures for change.[41]

CONTINUITY AND CHANGE IN OUR TIME

If the Torah is to retain a reasonable degree of consistency, it cannot be left to every individual to decide which laws to keep intact, which to change, and how. This must be done together as a community. At the beginning of Chapter Nine, which includes some samples of my rabbinic rulings for the Conservative movement's Committee on Jewish Law and Standards, I will discuss more fully the process by which communal decisions in Jewish law are made within the Conservative movement. In general, though, communal decisions emerge as the local rabbi interacts with his or her community to come to decisions that reflect the Jewish tradition as well as the com-munity's morals, customs, needs, sensitivities, and style. In this process, the community will hopefully find a way to live by the tra-dition that itself includes change.[42]

ENDNOTES

1. Kafka, *The Trial.*
2. In this section I will only summarize the thrust of the biblical and rab-binic sources that I present in full in both *Conservative Judaism,* pp. 79–110 (2nd rev. ed., pp. 69–95); and in *The Unfolding Tradition,* chap. 2.
3. As my friend and teacher Rabbi Uzi Weingarten has pointed out to me, claims to revelation nevertheless persist throughout Jewish history, includ-ing not only those ultimately judged not to be articulating a form of Judaism (Jesus, Shabbetai Zevi, Jacob Frank), but also some within the Jewish com-munity. So, for example, in the famous story of the oven of Akhnai (B. Bava Meẓia 59b), Rabbi Joshua and the rest of the Sanhedrin firmly deny the power of a voice from heaven to determine the law, but Rabbi Eliezer still thinks that such a voice rules. Furthermore, in B. Eruvin 13b, it is a voice

from heaven that determines that the law is according to the house of Hillel rather than that of Shammai. Later Rabbi Joseph Karo, the author of the Shulḥan Arukh—perhaps the most authoritative code of Jewish law—cites dreams and visions from his *maggid meisharim* as the reason that he rules in a particular way (for example, on why the cantor should not say *ga'al Yisra'el* before the *Amidah* aloud), and some in the Orthodox world now claim *das Torah,* a new kind of appeal to revelational authority, as the source and justification for their rulings. Moreover, as Joshua Trachtenberg has conclusively demonstrated, lay Jews and even some rabbis have historically depended on magic and superstition to guide what they do. See his *Jewish Magic and Superstition.* Furthermore, Gershom Scholem and contemporary scholars of Kabbalah have demonstrated that mystical experiences have shaped at least some Jewish practices; the *Kabbalat Shabbat* service is perhaps the most widespread example of that. Still, the mainstream tradition as interpreted by rabbis and practiced by most Jews did not confer authority on revelations after the biblical period, and even a Jewish legal figure as important as Rabbi Joseph Karo gains his authority from his legal reasoning, not from his revelations.

4. In the version of this story in Deut. 1:9–18, it is Moses who initiates the idea of delegating judicial responsibility to others, and he asks the people to pick from each of their tribes suitable judges whom Moses then appoints as their heads.

5. B. Sanhedrin 11a.

6. Numbers Rabbah 14:4.

7. See Friedman, *Who Wrote the Bible?,* for a clear and engaging summary of this scholarship.

8. Leviticus Rabbah 1:14.

9. B. Megillah 14a.

10. B. Bava Batra 12a.

11. Sifrei Devarim, Shofetim #154.

12. J. Horayot 1:1.

13. On capital punishment: M. Makkot 1:10. On the stubborn and rebellious son: B. Sanhedrin 71a.

14. Kadushin, *Organic Thinking,* and *Worship and Ethics.*

15. B. Sanhedrin 34a.

16. Numbers Rabbah 13:15–16.

17. Numbers Rabbah 14:4.

18. J. Sanhedrin 22a.

19. Seder Eliyahu Zuta 2.

20. Pesikta Rabbati 7b (ed. Friedmann).

21. Numbers Rabbah 14:4.

22. B. Menaḥot 29b.

23. B. Eruvin 13b.

24. The authority of the majority and their elected officials is illustrated dramatically by a story in the Mishnah Rosh Hashanah 2:8–9, in which Rabbi Akiva has good reason to doubt the correctness of the decision that Rabban Gamliel had made to set the new month on a particular day but ultimately acquiesces to his authority.

25. Tosefta Sanhedrin 3:5: cf. B. Makkot 7a.

26. B. Bava Batra 60b; B. Avodah Zarah 36a; B. Horayot 3b.

27. Maimonides, M.T. Laws Concerning Rebels 1:4–5.

28. B. Bava Meẓia 59b. Most interpreters understand *nitzhuni banai* in this talmudic text to mean "My children have bested [or overcome] Me," from the Hebrew root *naẓe'ah*, meaning to win. It is possible, though, that it comes from the Hebrew root *ne'ẓah*, meaning eternity, in which case the story would be asserting that through rabbis' interpretations and applications of the law in each generation they give eternal meaning to God and God's Torah.

29. B. Berakhot 5a. The Hebrew phrase *torah mi-sinai* literally means "Torah from Sinai," although here—and often—it is translated "on Sinai." Jose Faur, one of my professors of Talmud at the Jewish Theological Seminary of America, suggested another interpretation based on time rather than space: "Torah from (the time of) Sinai"—that is, beginning at Sinai and continuing through history.

30. J. Pe'ah 17a.

31. Tanhuma, Buber Devarim 1a.

32. Numbers Rabbah 19:6.

33. M. Makkot 1:10.

34. M. Hagigah 1:8.

35. See Elon, *Jewish Law,* pp. 267–272, 984–985, 1170, 1284–1287, 1345–1370, 1389–1394, 1504–1506, where he describes the establishment of the Geonic principle, opposition to it, and nevertheless the general embracing of it—especially in Ashkenazic authorities during the Middle Ages—as well as the guidelines that developed for use of the principle.

36. Sifra on Leviticus 26:43–44, p. 112c.

37. Exodus Rabbah, Ki Tissa 47:3.

38. Deuteronomy Rabbah, Nitzavim 8:5. Even though the direct meaning of the verse is that it will be to our merit as a people to obey God's law, the midrash takes "us" to mean God and Israel, not just the people of Israel, and the word "*zedakah*"—"righteousness"—it takes to mean benefit, which led to its later signification of "alms." Thus while Moses tells the Israelites to obey the Torah for their own merit before God, the midrash reinterprets it to mean that if the Israelites obey the law, it will be a benefit to both the People Israel and to God.

39. Song of Songs Rabbah I, #15, I, on 1:15; f. 12b.

40. Waxman, *Tradition and Change.* "Conservative Judaism" is the name

used for the movement in the United States and Canada. "Masorti" is the name used everywhere else (including Israel) for the same movement.

41. Dorff, "Traditional Judaism." As I point out in that article, aside from removing misconceptions about what the movement stands for, changing the name from "Conservative Judaism" to "Traditional Judaism" has the added advantage of making the name universal, for "Masorti," the name of the movement outside the United States and Canada means "traditional."

CHAPTER SIX

The Relationship of Jewish Law to Morality and Theology

THE THEORETICAL BASIS OF THE MORALITY OF JEWISH LAW

How does one make moral decisions?[1] If you are a Catholic, you ask your priest and, ultimately, the Pope. Catholics have room for individual conscience in their moral theology, and Protestants are to be guided in their use of conscience by the Bible and by the policy statements of their denominations. The emphasis among Catholics, however, is on institutional authority, and among Protestants it is on individual conscience. The American, secular way of making moral decisions, from abortion to welfare programs for the poor, is by majority vote of legislatures and courts.

Jewish tradition, in contrast, makes its moral decisions primarily through the instrumentality of Jewish law. It trusts the legal process to discern the moral path, teach it, and motivate people to follow it. Most Jews, like other westerners, accept the Enlightenment view that "you cannot legislate morality." The Jewish tradition, however, believes not only that we can legislate morality but that we should.

Why so? The basic reason Jewish tradition relies on law as the primary vehicle for discerning moral norms is because the law is seen as an expression of a moral God's call that we be moral and holy. "You shall be holy, for I, the Lord your God, am holy," Leviticus 19:2

211

proclaims, and what follows is a list of both ritual and moral commands that spell out what it means to be holy. "God is good to all, and His mercies extend to all His creatures" (Ps. 145:9), the Psalmist declares in a passage Jewish liturgy has us read three times daily, and the Rabbis spell out the implications of that conviction for our own human behavior: "Just as God is gracious and compassionate, you too must be gracious and compassionate. . . . As the Holy One is faithful, you too must be faithful. . . . As the Holy one is loving, you too must be loving."[2] "As God clothes the naked, you should clothe the naked. . . . As God visited the sick, you too should visit the sick. . . . As the Holy Blessed One comforted those who mourned, you too should comfort those who mourn. . . . As the Holy Blessed One buried the dead, you too should bury the dead."[3] God thus calls us to morality and holiness and teaches us how to fulfill that call through Jewish law.

Thus, the theological foundation of Jewish law in a moral God requires us to understand and apply Jewish law with moral norms clearly in mind. That is, Jewish law must be interpreted and shaped by moral considerations; to do otherwise would ignore and undermine both the roots of Jewish law in a moral God, and the aims of both God and God's law to produce a moral society.

THE PRACTICAL BURDENS AND BENEFITS OF USING JEWISH LAW FOR MORAL GUIDANCE

To be sure, using law to discern, teach, and motivate morality has drawbacks. Law tends to act as a conservative force within society, and so Jewish moral norms, encased in law as they are, may respond sluggishly, if at all, to changes in circumstances and in moral perceptions. This is because in a legal system the burden of proof rests on those who seek change, not on those who are content with things as they are. Moreover, Jewish law is not based on democratic, majority rule; it rather is determined by rabbis who qualify for that role by virtue of their education and acceptance by their communities. Jewish law is thus interpreted by an aristocracy of the learned, an aristocracy that is sometimes out of touch with current realities and sensitivities. Furthermore, resolving moral issues through Jewish law assumes that Jews intend to follow Jewish law in the first place. The very legal form of Jewish discussions of moral issues may alienate those unfamiliar with the law or unconvinced they should follow it at all.

Classical Christian texts have a very negative view of law for yet other reasons. The New Testament view of the Pharisees as narrow, legalistic, and downright mean, especially in Matthew, sets the tone for seeing Jews as concerned only with details of rules and not with the broader aims they have. Paul's description of law as leading people to sin and damnation and as the opposite of life lived by Spirit is another major source of Christians' negative views of the law.[4] Society may need laws to restrain bad people as long as we live in Augustine's City of Man; but, with the exception of the Decalogue and certain sexual prohibitions in Leviticus 18, law is not, for Christian writers, the way to know what is right and good.

Using law for moral purposes, of course, need not involve these problems; it depends on how the law is used, and Jewish law strives to correct for these risks. It does not always succeed; some aspects of Jewish law in the past and even today are legalistic,[5] and some, as Nahmanides noted, can even produce a *naval b'reshut ha-torah,* "a scoundrel within the bounds of the Torah" (or possibly, "a scoundrel with the permission of the Torah").[6] Nevertheless, when Jewish law functions as I have presented it in this book, these dangers are avoided, or at least diminished, through a constant interaction of the law with Jewish beliefs, lore (*aggadah*), customs, and morality, and through the interaction of rabbis with the lay Jews asked to abide by the law.

Furthermore, Jews use the law extensively to guide their moral sensitivities and actions in large part because they appreciate the *benefits* of legal methods. Some of these benefits are discussed in the following sections.

Law Defines and Enforces Minimal Standards

The most obvious contribution is that Jewish law establishes minimum standards of practice. This is important because many moral values can be realized only through the mutual action of a group of people; minimum moral standards tell people what is expected of them and thus enable society to secure the cooperation necessary for such moral attainment.

Furthermore, there is an objective value to a beneficent act,

213

whether it is done for the right reason or not. Unlike Christianity, which requires proper intention to characterize an action as moral, Judaism instructs us to do the right action regardless of our intention, both because the action benefits others and because "from doing an action for external motives one comes to do it for pure motives."[7] Consequently, legislating minimum standards of moral practice helps establish basic moral behavior in society.

In spelling out minimal moral standards there is always the danger that people will interpret them narrowly, as the ideal behavior rather than minimum requirements. This human fallibility, however, has nothing to do with a legal system. Christians operating in a spirit-based system are just as likely to cut corners. So are Buddhists and Hindus. It is a human characteristic, not stemming from law. Judaism guards against such abuse through its requirements of public and private study of the Bible and other morally enriching literature, through liturgy and sermons, and through making the minimal requirements of action rather demanding in the first place. It also does this through its call to holiness and its demand that we act morally even beyond the letter of the law (lifnim me-shurat ha-din). As Nahmanides points out, because no legal system can articulate the right or good thing to do in every situation, the verse, "Do the right and the good in God's eyes" (Deut. 6:18) instructs us to do the right and good thing even if it is not required by law. These overarching demands of morality and holiness built into the law help protect Jews from thinking they have fulfilled it if they abide by its letter but violate its spirit by becoming scoundrels within its bounds; the law itself requires more than the minimum.[8]

Law Helps Actualize Moral Ideals

But it is not just on a minimal level that law is important for morality; law is crucial at every level of moral aspiration to translate moral values into concrete modes of behavior. The Prophets enunciated lofty values, and we feel edified and uplifted when we read their words or those of other great moral teachers. On the other end of the spectrum, when we go through the often difficult self-examination of Yom Kippur, we come away feeling chastened and purified. But if that edification and chastening are to contribute to a better world, they must be translated into the realm of day-to-day activities. We ordinarily do not have sufficient time, knowledge, or self-awareness to think seriously about what we are doing, and hence a system of concrete laws that guide us in a variety of circumstances enables us to act morally in the course of daily life. Rabbi Morris Adler has articulated this point well:

> Religion is not a matter of living on the "peaks" of experience. That is for the saint and the mystic. More fundamentally, religion must mean transposing to a higher level of spiritual awareness and ethical sensitivity the entire plateau of daily living by the generality of men. Idolatry is defeated not by recognition of its intellectual absurdity alone, but by a life that expresses itself in service to God. Selfishness and greed are overcome not by professions of a larger view but by disciplines that direct our energies, our wills, and our actions outward and upward.[9]

Law Provides a Forum for Weighing Conflicting Moral Values and Setting Moral Priorities

Until now we have spoken about areas in which the moral norm is more or less clear and the issue is realizing those norms. There are many situations, however, in which there is a conflict of moral values, and it must be determined which value takes precedence and in what circumstances. Nonlegal moral systems usually offer some mechanism for resolving moral conflicts, but they typically depend on the sensitivity and analytic ability of an authority figure or of each individual. By contrast, the law provides a format for deciding such issues *publicly,* thus ensuring that many minds of varying convictions will be brought to bear on the issue. This does not guarantee wisdom, but it does provide a greater measure of objectivity and a more thorough consideration of the relevant elements.

Furthermore, law enables us to analyze a moral question with the sharp tools of legal analysis, thus enabling us to gain a broad and accurate picture of the issues at stake. Just as lawyers and judges do with cases before the courts, the moral case before us is compared and contrasted to situations that have been considered and resolved, for that enables us to understand the various aspects of the present case better. We can then decide the issue with greater appreciation of its facets, its possible resolutions, and their implications. That is, legal methods enable us to make moral decisions *intelligently.*

This case-based ("casuistic") method also means that moral reasoning is not based on a mere hunch or on obedience to some authority figure; it is rather based on the decisions of rabbis who must present *reasoned arguments* for their decisions, with the facts and logic of those decisions open to public scrutiny and criticism, including by other rabbis and lay Jews. The linkages to past decisions and the exposure to public debate strengthen the prospects that rabbinic decisions will be wise, having gained from the experience of many people in the past and present.

Law Gives Moral Norms a Sense of the Immediate and the Real

Issues are often joined more clearly in court than in moral discussions because the realities of the case are dramatically evident in the courtroom, and a decision must be reached. Moral essayists or theorists, on the other hand, do not face the immediate responsibility of having people act on their decisions, and hence they tend to be somewhat "ivory-towerish." Consensus statements on moral issues often suffer from the need to include the opinions of everyone in the group and thus lose sharpness and sometimes even coherence. In contrast, a court ruling is specific and addressed to a real situation. Although the Talmud contains many theoretical discussions, especially regarding laws governing Temple practice long after the Second Temple was destroyed, it also contains numerous concrete cases that have this element of immediacy to them, for which the people involved stand to lose a great deal. Much of the wisdom of the rabbinic tradition can be attributed to the fact that the Rabbis served as judges as well as scholars and teachers. Of course, how to apply precedent to a new case is not always clear, but the legal context adds a sense of immediacy and reality to moral deliberation.

Law Balances Continuity and Flexibility and Provides the Foundation for Pluralism

Because law operates on the basis of precedent, a moral tradition that is structured legally has a strong sense of continuity. By tying present decisions to those of the past, legal methodology makes it probable that moral decisions are not made by whim or the fashion of the day but are rather rooted in a long-standing system of norms and laws.

On the other hand, the fact that we have always done something in a particular way does not mean that it was right then or that is right for now. Circumstances change, and moral sensitivities evolve. Legal techniques such as analogies and differentiation of cases provide flexibility and adaptability. By contrast, moral decisions made on the basis of natural law or fundamentalist readings of Scripture lack sufficient malleability to retain relevance to new situations and to take advantage of new knowledge. They also have little tolerance for varying interpretations and applications of natural laws or Scripture to new questions. Legal methodologies of interpretation, analogy, and distinguishing cases provide the most effective way to balance tradition and change and to understand and appreciate multiple ways of doing that.

This does not mean that legal methodology always succeeds in these tasks. I am well aware that ultra-Orthodox Jews, who are clearly committed to Jewish law, read Jewish legal texts in fundamentalistic ways and do not balance the laws in those texts with modern sensitivities and concerns. They also have little tolerance for anyone (including other Orthodox Jews) who practice Judaism differently from their way. A legal methodology is thus no guarantee of a good balance of tradition with needed change. Much of the thinking and practice of such groups, however, derives from their fear of, and reactions to, Reform Judaism and secularism. As a result, their adherence to stated law without balancing it with modern realities and sensitivities is a modern aberration.

Sephardic Jews have been much truer to tradition in their willingness to balance tradition and change and to accept multiple forms of Jewish practice, and thus nothing like Reform Judaism has emerged among them. The Conservative movement, which for many years adopted Mordecai Waxman's book title of *Tradition and Change* as its motto, began in the United States as the product of Sephardic Jews.[10] Moreover, it has sought to be historically authentic by understanding Jewish legal texts in their historical context and then applying them to modern times with due regard for the differences between then and now. Individuals may disagree with specific decisions, but the process is the classical one intended to revise Jewish law as necessary so that it can make Jewish beliefs and values live in new circumstances. This is the classical tradition, and it is the view of Jewish law that I am presenting here. This traditional approach to Jewish law adeptly balances the law that has come down to us with needed change and provides for pluralism as this process unfolds.

Law Gives Us a Sense of Security in Knowing What Can Be Expected of Us and What We Can Expect of Others

The very same conservative tendencies of a legal system that may cause it to adjust to new circumstances too slowly may, conversely, be one of its strengths in handling moral issues. One of the main reasons we are interested in law in the first place is because law defines what I can expect of others and what others can expect of me. Law spells out what can and cannot legitimately be demanded of us by tying the present decision to past laws and precedents so that we can often say *stare decisis,* "it stands decided." This gives us not only a sense of continuity, as noted in the previous section, but also a sense of security.

Law Imparts Authority to Moral Norms

Because people might abide by Jewish law for all the reasons mentioned in Chapter Four, the moral norms embedded in Jewish law gain traction. It is not just my personal opinion of what is right, or even my community's opinion at this moment, but rather the law that has roots in our covenant with God and with Jews throughout the ages. Thus all the reasons for following that law apply to the morals defined by it. Moreover, because legal rulings must be accompanied by justifying reasons, they gain authority by convincing people on the grounds presented in the legal opinion.

Law Serves as an Educational Tool for Morality

Theories of education are obviously many and diverse, but by insisting that people act morally, the Jewish tradition has a clear methodology for moral education:

Rav Judah said in Rav's name: A man should always occupy himself with Torah and good deeds, even if it is not for their own sake, for out of [studying and doing good with] an ulterior motive he will come [to study and do good] for their own sake.[11]

Run to fulfill a minor precept and flee from transgression; for precept draws precept in its train, and transgression draws transgression.[12]

This behavioral approach to moral education has much to recommend it; for legally *requiring* people to act in accord with moral rules is a step in teaching them to do the right thing for the right reason. Experience of acting morally also helps people learn how to apply moral norms to situations in which the right thing is not obvious. Moreover, although spirit-based teaching may assert that action is the expected fruit of the spirit (as in Christianity), law has the advantages described in this chapter, including putting action before spirit—that is, insisting that one act in the right way even if one does not have the right intention. This produces beneficial results for society while also teaching and inculcating moral values.

Law Helps Preserve the Integrity of Moral Intentions

We usually construe ourselves as having good intentions; but actions test, clarify, and verify our intentions. Rabbi Abraham Joshua Heschel put it this way:

The dichotomy of faith and works which presented such an important problem in Christian theology was never a problem in Judaism. To us, the basic problem is neither what is the right action nor what is the right intention. The basic problem is: what is right living? And life is indivisible. The inner sphere is never isolated from outward activities. . . .

It would be a device of conceit, if not presumption, to insist that purity of heart is the exclusive test of piety. Perfect purity is something we rarely know how to obtain or how to retain. No one can claim to have purged all the dross even from his finest desire. The self is finite, but selfishness is infinite. . . . God asks for the heart, but the heart is oppressed with uncertainty in its own twilight. God asks for faith, and the heart is not sure of its own faith. It is good that there is a dawn of decision for the night of the heart; deeds to objectify faith, definite forms to verify belief.[13]

Concretizing moral values in the form of law is thus an important method for testing the nature and seriousness of our intentions so that we can avoid hypocrisy. By telling us to take action, law also graphically shows us the effects of our intentions, so that, we hope, we will alter those that are knowingly or unknowingly destructive.

Law Provides a Way to Make Amends and Repair Moral Damage

One goal of law is social peace. Legal systems therefore generally provide ways for dealing with antisocial behavior and for adjudicating disputes. A religious legal system like Jewish law also provides a way for overcoming guilt; making amends; and reconciling with God, with the aggrieved parties, and with the community as a whole. That process is *teshuvah,* "return," according to which assailants must do these things: (1) acknowledge that they sinned, (2) express remorse and apologize to the victim, (3) compensate the victim, and (4) take steps to ensure that when a similar occasion arises again, the wrongdoer acts differently. In defining this process, Jewish law makes moral repair demanding but possible.

Jewish law then goes another step—it teaches that the victim must respond in kind. So, for example, according to the Mishnah, assailants must compensate their victims for five losses—the injury itself, time lost from work, pain, medical expenses, and the embarrassment the injury caused. After describing how each of these payments is to be calculated, the Mishnah teaches that "Even though the assailant pays the victim, he is not forgiven until he asks the victim's forgiveness"; this is the apology required in the process of return. The Mishnah then states that if after all this is done the victim refuses to pardon the assailant, the victim is regarded as "cruel."[14] There clearly are cases when wrongdoers should not be forgiven, such as Hitler and Stalin; but, by and large, we must forgive those who have fulfilled the requirements of the process of return and have asked for forgiveness.[15] In most American states, felons who have been released from prison are barred from voting and from government jobs the rest of their lives and must reveal the past felony to any potential employer. In Jewish law, by contrast, it is prohibited even to mention a person's past crime unless it has direct bearing on a practical decision. Once the person has fulfilled the requirements of the process of return, to mention the past sin is, according to the Mishnah, verbal abuse.[16] Thus Jewish law aids and abets reconciliation and peace as well as moral change and improvement.

In all these ways, then, law contributes to morality. I have discussed this thoroughly to demonstrate that the interaction between law and morality involves contributions in both directions: moral norms must be used as an important component of how we interpret and apply Jewish law in order to be faithful to the moral God whose law this is, and, conversely, law can and should guide our understanding of morality and our practice of it. This is especially important when we are trying to understand Judaism, which went so far in seeking to deal with morality in legal terms.

As important as law is in shaping Jewish moral vision and behavior, however, it is not the sole vehicle that Judaism uses to create moral people and societies. As I discuss in detail elsewhere,[17] *stories, history, family and community, moral leaders and models, moral maxims and theories, theology, prayer, and study all play critical roles, along with law, in enabling Judaism to contribute mightily to creating moral individuals and communities.*

None of these methods separately, and not even all of them taken together, guarantees moral character or behavior, for life does not come with guarantees, especially for something as complex as moral sensitivity and action. Moreover, as described earlier in this chapter, there are aspects of Jewish law that impede moral vision and action. Furthermore, as I describe elsewhere,[18] other aspects of Judaism and of religions generally contribute to the negative effects that religion can have on morality—as, for example, the assumed power of God's human representatives, the social pressure of religious communities, the conservative tendency of religions, the focus on rituals in preference to—and sometimes in violation of—ethics, and the fearsome nature of religious topics like life and death and moral culpability.

People of all religions must therefore take steps to ensure that such factors do not lead to morally atrocious results. These steps include a system of checks and balances within the religious community to ensure that no one person or group of persons determine policy and law. So, for example, even though Conservative rabbis usually adopt one of the positions validated by the Committee on Jewish Law and Standards, they may instead follow their own interpretation, as many rabbis did for decades in enabling women to take roles in worship.[19] Other important steps include a social tone that encourages debate, recognition that God's word is always filtered by fallible human beings, and deliberate exposure to the world outside one's own community and tradition. That having been said, many of us, myself certainly included, are grateful for the moral contributions of Jewish law and Judaism generally to our lives, as we are for the many other ways Judaism makes our lives richer and more meaningful.

INTEGRATING JEWISH MORAL NORMS AND THEOLOGY INTO THE PROCESS OF MAKING JEWISH LEGAL DECISIONS

Theory

Setting moral norms within a legal context, though, means that Jewish moral standards, like all other areas of Jewish law, must come out of the *continuing interaction* of how rabbis interpret the tradition and how the people who see themselves bound by the law observe it. This interaction functions in both directions, but most often the tradition defines moral norms and calls us to try to live by them.

A major reason Jews are interested in Jewish heritage is that it informs us about what is moral, teaches us greater moral sensitivity, and motivates us to be moral. Thus the Torah announces major moral principles that have influenced all of Western Civilization— norms like those embedded in the last seven of the Ten Commandments, "Love your neighbor as yourself" (Lev. 19:18), and "Justice, justice shall you pursue" (Deut. 16:20). Beyond that, the Torah and the later Jewish tradition extend far beyond such generalities to the details of life, where such convictions gain their practical meaning. The Torah thus sensitizes us to the plight of the poor and the inherent indignity of poverty in requiring us to return a poor person's cloak taken in pledge before nightfall, for "it is his only covering, his cloak for his skin. In what shall he sleep?" (Exod. 22:26). Similarly, a creditor may not enter a debtor's home to collect a pledge. He must stand outside, and the debtor is to bring the pledge outside to the creditor (Deut. 24:10–13). This preserves the debtor's dignity before his family and also the sanctity of the debtor's home.

The Rabbis of the Mishnah and Talmud expand on the biblical base, providing a treasure house of moral instruction in the concrete, specific areas of our lives. So, for example, they forbid us to ask a merchant the price of an object if we have no intention of buying it, lest we play with the shopkeeper's hope to make a sale and also steal his time.[20] The Rabbis expand on the Torah's demands for charity for the poor, requiring each community to have a soup kitchen and a communal fund, but they also set limits to the amount of charity one may give.[21]

Moral instruction did not cease with the classical Rabbis. One critically important task of contemporary rabbis is to help shape the moral behavior of their fellow Jews through analysis of Jewish texts, other kinds of lessons, sermons, and their own actions. It also occurs when rabbis answer moral questions, sometimes through extensive analysis in responsa, articles, or books. Sometimes these writings push the envelope of our moral thinking as rabbis apply the Jewish tradition to new issues or articulate new views on old ones.

It is not just rabbis who are involved in achieving Judaism's moral goals: a significant part of the ongoing task of the Jewish community as a whole is to teach us how to be moral and to motivate us to be so. That is, all Jews have a duty to conduct communal affairs in a morally exemplary manner, with lay leaders having special responsibility to ensure that this happens.

Sometimes lay Jews function in another way crucial to Judaism's moral task: They motivate new moral awareness and change. This happens when new moral sensitivities emerge in society and require a change in the law. One recent example of this happened when people had sufficient funds to educate their daughters as well as their sons. This lead to substantial changes in the latter decades of the 20th century with regard to the status of women in both American and Jewish law and practice. American law banned discrimination against women in education and jobs, with the result that women's roles in society expanded considerably as did men's roles in the home. This inevitably affected how North American Jews practice Judaism, opening new places for women in education, the synagogue, the rabbinate, and Jewish communal life generally. That, in turn, led to highlighting some aspects of traditional Jewish law, and changing others. So, for example, the Conservative movement's Committee on Jewish Law and Standards has allowed for women to be called to the Torah, to be counted for a prayer quorum (minyan), and to lead services.

But it is not only Jews who affect the development of Jewish morality: changes in the environment in which Jewish law functions do so as well. For example, developments in science and technology that have affected life in general have forced rabbis to interpret and apply the law anew. Jewish norms of privacy had to be expanded to apply to the Internet, and Jewish norms asserting the sanctity of life and requiring us to preserve our health had to be applied in new ways to a whole host of advances in medicine. This includes the new assisted reproductive techniques, the new technologies of prolonging life, and embryonic stem cell research.

Political developments have led to other changes in Jewish moral stances. Undoubtedly the most pervasive such change grew out of the Enlightenment ideology that made Jews full citizens of Western European and North American countries, leading to a major reassessment among Jews of how to relate to people of other faiths. In certain forms of Orthodoxy, secular education was seen, at best, as a waste of time, and, at worst, as a lure to violate Jewish law. As early as the 1820s, however, Orthodox Rabbi Samson Raphael Hirsch argued for the *halakhic* legitimacy of studying secular subjects. If, however, what one learns in a university contradicts Judaism, then Judaism takes precedence; for God created Judaism and fallible human beings created secular subjects..

Sometimes new artistic forms affect Jewish law. As Chaim Potok's book *My Name Is Asher Lev,* clearly demonstrates, Jewish norms about modesty pose questions about nude figures, and the centrality of Christian themes in Western art (including films like *Star Wars* and the *Matrix* series) raise questions about whether Jews may see it, let alone be involved in producing it. Even Jewish ritual items are affected. In some modern Hanukkah menorahs, the candles are not on a level plane, in conflict with Jewish law.[22] May they be used?

Jewish law and the moral norms that emerge from it, though, are not only the products of the interactions between rabbis and laity and between the Jewish community with the world outside it. Jewish law is embedded in, and continually interacts with, Jewish views of God, humanity, the People Israel, the environment, and Jewish hopes for the future. In other words, Jewish law can be properly understood only in its context of Jewish theology, anthropology, history, and eschatology—in how we understand God, ourselves, the past, and the future. Putting this point in theological language, Jewish legal discussions are the result of our shared wrestling with God, our world, and ourselves.

My point here is that *morality is not extrinsic to the process of determining Jewish law;* morality, along with Jewish theology, anthropology, history, eschatology, economics, and social needs—together with what is happening in the larger world of science, arts, politics, and interfaith relations—all are integral parts of how Jewish law is determined and taught. Among these factors, *morality and theology are at the very heart of Jewish law.* Put another way, morality, theology, and all these other factors are not "extra-halakhic"; they are part and parcel of the meaning of the law and how it should be defined.

This follows directly from perceiving Jewish law as a living organism, as I do. In a human being, even relatively permanent structures like bones are affected by all the other functions of the body and also by the outside environment. Similarly, Jewish law is affected by its internal parts—moral principles, theology, lore (*aggadah*), history, hopes for the future, and so on—and also by what is happening in the environment in which it functions.

Please note that I am *definitely not* adopting the stance of early Reform thinkers who claimed that Judaism is nothing but ethical monotheism. I am instead maintaining that we should observe Jewish law in all its facets for all the reasons discussed in Chapter Four. I am also, however, saying that in interpreting and applying Jewish law in our day we must recognize that *its goals are moral and theological,* and those factors therefore test the mettle of any ruling we make. In saying this, I am simply reasserting what the Rabbis themselves maintained, for when looking for increasingly shorter summaries of the 613 commandments, they chose biblical verses that unanimously focus on the moral and the spiritual:

David came and reduced them [the 613 commandments of the Torah] to eleven, as it is written, "A Psalm of David. Lord, who shall sojourn in Your tent, who may dwell on Your holy mountain? [1] He who lives without blame, [2] who does what is right, [3] and speaks the truth in his heart; [4] whose tongue has no slander, [5] who has not done harm to his fellow, [6] or borne a reproach against his neighbor, [7] in his eyes a contemptible person is despised, but [8] he honors those who fear the Lord; [9] who stands by his oath to his hurt; [10] who has never lent money on interest, [11] or accepted a bribe against the innocent. The man who acts thus shall never be shaken" (Psalm 15). . . . Isaiah came and reduced them to six, as it is written: "[1] He who walks in righteousness, [2] speaks uprightly, [3] spurns profit from oppressive dealings, [4] waves away a bribe instead of grasping it, [5] stops his ears against listening to infamy, [6] shuts his eyes against looking at evil (Isaiah 33:15–16). . . . Micah came and reduced them to three, as it is said, "He has told you, O man, what is good, and what the Lord requires of you: [1] Only to do justice, [2] and to love goodness, and [3] to walk humbly with your God" (Micah 6:8). . . . Again came Isaiah and reduced them to two, as it is said, "Thus said the Lord: Observe what is right, and do what is just" (Isaiah 56:1). Amos came and reduced them to one, as it is said, "Thus said the Lord to the House of Israel: Seek Me and live" (Amos 5:4). . . . Habakkuk came and based them all on one, as it is said, "The righteous shall live by his faith" (Habakkuk 2:4).[23]

I am also following Hillel, who said, "What is hateful to you, do not do to your neighbor. That is the whole Torah; the rest is commentary. Go and learn it."[24]

Methodology

Perhaps the easiest way to demonstrate how my assertion that moral and theological factors can and should be prominent in our minds as we seek to apply Jewish law to our times is to describe how all these factors influence me in answering questions of Jewish law. In deciding what Jewish law should be today, I must, as Jewish codes over the centuries have done, take note not only of what the legal texts say but also how they have been put into practice by Jews who have sought to live in accordance with Jewish law.[25] That is, I must take account of custom, which I shall discuss in the next chapter.

I must also, as the Rabbis clearly understood, be concerned by the effect of any given ruling on the community. So, for example, even if a given way of deciding a matter seems clearly demanded by the texts and precedents of the tradition, I must not rule that way if such a decision will inflict undue economic hardship on the community (*hefsed merubbeh*).[26] Furthermore, unless I think a communal custom is immoral or dangerously foolish and I therefore choose to fight it, I must not make a decision that will simply be ignored by those who otherwise obey Jewish law.[27] That would be a disservice to both Jewish law and to the Jewish community because it would call into question the authority of Jewish law in the face of widespread violation, and it would simultaneously classify many Jews as sinners.

For that matter, I must be sure that any decision fits not only the community but also the individual for whom it is rendered. Rabbi Joseph Dov Soloveitchik, when asked about conflicting decisions he gave to different individuals, is quoted as saying *"eid ehad ne'eman b'isurin* [one witness is reliable in prohibitions] only applies to the facts of the case, not the *psak* [decision] that is given. Therefore, you cannot rely on any *psak* of mine that you hear from others."[28]

The first story I heard about Jewish law came from my father. My grandparents lived across the street from a large Orthodox synagogue, of which they were members. Because of the proximity, my grandparents often hosted guests of the congregation for the Sabbath. One Friday afternoon my grandmother sent my father, then a lad of 15, to ask Rabbi Solomon Scheinfeld when the guests for that week were expected. Rabbi Scheinfeld served that congregation from 1902 to 1943, and, according to the *Encyclopaedia Judaica,* was the "acknowledged rabbinic head of Milwaukee's Orthodox community during his tenure."[29] When my father entered the rabbi's office, Rabbi Scheinfeld was in the process of deciding whether a chicken was kosher. As he turned the slaughtered chicken over in his hands, he asked the woman who had brought it many questions about the physical and economic health of her husband and family. After he pronounced the chicken kosher and the woman left the room, my father asked him why he had asked so many questions about her family. The rabbi turned to my father and said, "If you think that the kosher status of chickens depends only on their physical state, you understand nothing about Jewish law!" If this is true for chickens, how much more so for decisions involving human beings.[30]

I must also take care to ensure that the law embodies high moral standards so that it challenges us to be as much like God, our Exemplar, as we can be. It would be a desecration of God's name, a *hillul ha-Shem,* to decide otherwise. This is easier said than done, for "high moral standards" is not automatically equivalent either to what was interpreted as such in the past or to what would seem to be the moral ideal. Human beings are not God, and the law must demand only that which it is reasonable to ask of human beings. As the Talmud says, "The Torah was not given to the ministering angels!"[31] Thus the content of high moral standards must be continually determined by difficult, but absolutely critical, acts of *judgment* in which we weigh and balance conflicting moral claims on us.

Along with morality, theology is probably the chief internal factor that influences Jewish law. We are engaged in this process of interpreting and applying Jewish law primarily because we want to do what God wants of us, assured that it will be "for our everlasting good and give us life" (Deut. 6:24) for it supports life by giving us a wise way to live and by honing our moral instincts. To do that, though, we must discern God's will. Thus when I write a ruling, I am acutely aware that my task is not only to describe what I personally would like the law to be, but what I think God would want of us. Jewish tradition has interpreted the Torah to put the privilege and responsibility of discerning God's will in the hands of the rabbis of each generation. As a rabbi, I may not shirk this duty on the grounds of humility in deference to the great minds and hearts of previous generations:

> Jerubaal in his generation is like Moses in his, Bedan in his generation is like Aaron in his, Jepthah in his generation is like Samuel in his, to teach you that the most worthless, once appointed a leader of his community, is to be accounted like the mightiest of the mighty. Scripture also says: "And you shall come to the levitical priests and to the judge who shall be in those days" (Deuteronomy 17:9). Can we then imagine that one should go to a judge who is not in his days? This shows that you only have the judge who is in your days. It also says, "Do not say, 'How has it happened that former times were better than these?' [for not in wisdom have you asked this."] (Ecclesiastes 7:10).[32]

Indeed, the Talmud says that it was just such rabbinic humility that led to the destruction of the Second Temple and the subsequent exile of Jews from Israel.[33]

In deciding to become a rabbi, then, I assumed the responsibility, along with other rabbis of my generation, of making Jewish law live by applying it to the needs and circumstances of our time. I take on the task of writing a ruling, however, with a deep sense of responsibility to God and to my people in the past, present, and future.

I am comforted that my mistakes in discernment will, I hope, be corrected by my colleagues on the Committee on Jewish Law and Standards and, ultimately, by the practices of all Jews serious about making Jewish law part of their lives. Indeed, this is precisely how I distinguish between another one of Dorff's crazy ideas and nothing less than the will of God for our time—it depends on whether a particular decision of mine is endorsed by at least a substantial portion of my rabbinic colleagues and followed by many lay Jews.

We may all, of course, be mistaken. Jewish faith, though, is that the Torah and its ongoing interpretation and application by rabbis and by serious Jews articulates the will of God and what we should do to imitate God. As one who shares that faith in this traditional Jewish methodology, the approach that I use in writing a ruling is one that *attempts to combine honesty about the past and present, humility about what we can know of God's will or nature, and passionate commitment to making Judaism's understanding of God's will and character the model of what we should do to fix our world.* I do this in line with Maimonides' comments as bookends toward the beginning and at the end of the many ritual laws in The Book of Times (*Z'manim*), in which he states the heart of what I take Judaism and Jewish law to be all about—namely, "The laws of the Torah are not vengeance in the world, but mercy and kindness and peace in the world" and "Great is peace, for the entire Torah was given to make peace in the world, as it says, 'Its ways are ways of pleasantness, and all its paths are peace' (Prov. 3:17)."[34]

Because the purpose of Jewish law is to create "mercy and kindness and peace," I must construe its demands in terms of these moral goals. As a result, if any of my rabbinic colleagues or I come to a conclusion that Jewish law requires us to insist on or to do something cruel or otherwise immoral, that result cannot stand, and we must go back to the drawing board.[35] The result of our legal deliberations must be moral; and if it is not, that very fact indicates that we have made a mistake, and we must go back to interpret Jewish law to produce a moral result.

This, though, raises the question of what I mean by "morality" in the first place. Because I wrote a doctoral dissertation in moral theory and have written and taught in this area ever since, I am well aware of the complexities of this issue. If one is using the Jewish tradition as the basis for one's morality, however, the problem is not nearly as great as it is without that foundation, for Judaism provides specific guidelines as to what is entailed in morality through the general principles that the Torah and the Rabbis teach and also through their detailed laws.

Because the Jewish tradition is evolving, however, we must recognize that some of the laws of the Torah itself may have been moral advances for their time but no longer fulfill our understanding of morality. For example, the law of the stubborn and rebellious son (Deut. 21:18–21) may have been a way to get him out of the house and into the community's jurisdiction, where the authorities could refuse to inflict the penalty described, just as the Rabbis later specified legal ways to make it inoperative; the law subjecting a woman whose husband suspected her of adultery to a water trial (Num. 5:11–31) may have been a way to ensure that her husband would not harm her, trusting that the trial would not harm her either; and scholars generally agree that "eye for an eye" (Exod. 21:24) represents an advance over Hammurabi's code, which required death for an eye if the perpetrator was from a lower class, and then the Rabbis went a step further and transformed even that, more measured retribution into compensation.

Following in the steps of the Torah itself and of the Rabbis thereafter, then, *the process of determining what is moral is dialectical.* That is, most of the time we can immediately understand and affirm the moral principle or practice that Jewish sources teach. Sometimes, however, we now see some of the specific laws in Jewish sources as violations of the Torah's or Rabbis' own principles, and the same may be true for contemporary interpretations and applications of those sources. Under those circumstances, we must have the courage to change the practice to reflect our own understanding of God's will for us in our time. Other times, the tradition should critique contemporary practices or beliefs. This dialectical process will undoubtedly displease those who seek a simple formula to determine what is moral, but it is honest to both the complexity of doing so and yet our ability to discern when we hurt people and when we help them. These are the critical acts of *judgment* to which I referred earlier.

So, for example, any Jewish teaching that fails to recognize the sacred and unique character of each human being as created in God's image would fail Judaism's own moral test. This certainly does not preclude holding people responsible for their actions and punishing them when appropriate; on the contrary, failing to hold people responsible for their actions would undermine the Torah's understanding that we have the ability to discern the difference between right and wrong and to act on that knowledge. It does mean, however, that punishments should fit their crimes. This immediately raises problems for the Torah's own laws: that the people of Amalek are to be obliterated in every generation for what their ancestors did 3,200 years ago (Exod. 17:16; compare Deut. 25:18), that we are to execute a rebellious judge rather than just challenge his arguments (Deut. 17:12), that we are to execute a stubborn or rebellious son (Deut. 21:18–21), and more. The Rabbis understood the problems raised by some of these verses and sought to minimize or totally eliminate the effect of these laws; in doing so they were engaged in just the kind of dialectic with the Torah's laws that I am advocating.

Similarly, any result that oppresses someone monetarily violates the Torah's ban on doing so (Lev. 25:14, 17), and any result that oppresses someone in other ways violates the Rabbis' interpretation and extension of those verses.[36] Any result that is not both just and loving violates the Torah's requirements that we be both just and loving (Deut. 16:20; Lev. 19:18). As the Torah itself makes clear, none of these principles, and many others like them, means that we cannot make judgments about proper and improper behavior, even to the point of punishing the latter; but these convictions must function as criteria for judging our own use of the law to guide our conduct.

There are those who object that this dialectical methodology is much too imprecise, that it undermines the authority of Jewish texts, and that it depends far too much on contemporary views and values. These objections are specious. They assume, first, that a literal reading of the text will always produce what we recognize to be a moral result for our time; the examples I gave here show that that is simply not true. Furthermore, the classical Rabbis themselves, as I have pointed out, engaged in the kind of dialectic that I am describing, narrowing some laws and expanding others. I have provided some examples of how they narrowed some laws to achieve that aim. An example of how they expanded the Torah's laws to promote morality is that they read the ban on putting a stumbling block before the blind in Leviticus 19:14 to include not only the physically blind but also those who lacked knowledge or moral resolve. The Rabbis certainly took the Torah seriously. Taking it seriously, though, did not mean for them, and does not mean for me, reading it uncritically. On the contrary, when we find laws immoral, we must, as they did, do what we need to do to change them, and when we find an opportunity to expand the law to improve our morality, we should take advantage of it.

Practice

One recent example will illustrate this approach and how it differs from a more positivistic theory. In the protracted discussion on homosexual relations conducted by the Conservative movement's Committee on Jewish Law and Standards between 1989 and 1992 and again between 2004 and 2006, Rabbi Joel Roth ruled that although homosexual attractions may be inherent, homosexual actions are prohibited, and so homosexuals should remain celibate throughout their lives.

I found this result to be downright cruel (although he himself is anything but cruel), for this conclusion means homosexuals can never have sexual relations condoned by Jewish law. Although the tradition clearly legislated such a ban, our ancestors assumed that all people can fulfill their sexual needs heterosexually and that homosexual acts were thus a rebellion against Jewish law in which participants were following the practices of the Greeks and other nations. We now know that everyone is born with a particular sexual orientation and that attempts to change it do not work. As a result, retaining the tradition's ban on any form of homosexual sex violates the Torah's command that we not oppress each other, certainly in spirit and probably in letter, and it undermines the theological conviction of the Psalmist that Jewish liturgy has us say three times daily, "God is good to all, and His mercies extend to all His works" (Ps. 145:9). Rabbi Roth disagreed with my assessment of celibacy, maintaining that a moral God could indeed create some people who would have to be celibate all their lives.

Because I found his stance both immorally cruel and theologically problematic, I participated in writing a ruling, together with Rabbis Daniel Nevins and Avram Reisner, that restricted the prohibition on homosexual sex to what the Rabbis understood Leviticus 18:22 and 20:13 to mean—namely, anal intercourse between men. We removed all the rabbinic extensions of those verses to women and to other forms of male–male sexual activity. This admittedly still imposes a restriction on homosexual men that many would find difficult to live by, but it at least provides legitimate forms of sexual expression and companionship for gay men and lesbians.

Furthermore, our responsum asserted that it is in the interest of Jewish society as well as the individuals involved for homosexuals to form committed unions, for promiscuity is socially and morally undesirable within Judaism and, especially in the case of men, medically dangerous. Our responsum therefore maintains that it is appropriate for rabbis to officiate at public ceremonies celebrating such unions. These ceremonies should not use the forms of traditional Jewish marriage, both because they do not apply (they speak of bride and groom) and also because if we are creating ceremonies for homosexuals *de novo* we should avoid some of the problematic features of traditional Jewish marriage and divorce—features that, for example, speak of the woman as being "acquired" by the man and that limit the ability to divorce to the man. (This raises the question of why we should maintain these traditional marriage laws for heterosexual couples. Conservative rabbis have indeed resolved the latter problem through invoking the talmudic authorization of rabbis to annul marriages, and the Rabbinical Assembly has created a language of marriage contracts that is more egalitarian. I discuss these matters more fully elsewhere.[37]) Our ruling also welcomes homosexual Jews to apply to the Conservative movement's rabbinical and cantorial schools.

In all this, we were motivated by the demonstrated physical and psychological harm that the traditional stance imposes on homosexuals and their loved ones. The rate of suicide is much higher among homosexuals than among heterosexuals, so this is literally a matter of life and death, surely a serious enough concern to abrogate rabbinic extensions of the Torah's ban.[38] Furthermore, the traditional stance creates serious psychological harm for homosexuals, requiring them to remain in the closet and lie about their identity to themselves and others. Furthermore, if homosexuals seek to act as heterosexuals, marry, and have children, and later find that they cannot continue the sham, as is often the case, the divorce hurts everyone involved—the homosexual, the spouse, and the children.

In the course of the discussion, Rabbi Roth said explicitly that in his view, the morality of the situation should have nothing to do with determining the law and that, even if it did, a moral God could demand celibacy of some of His creatures. This was a clear dispute not only on the issue of homosexual relations but on the theories of law undergirding our two approaches. For him, the texts of the received law supersede any moral considerations, which are "extra-halakhic." For me, morality is the very heart of the law, its purpose and function, and so every law—including those in the Torah itself—must be evaluated morally and changed, if necessary. At the same time, because I believe that law must *balance* tradition and change, I sought a way within the bounds of the received law to enable gays and lesbians to celebrate their unions in a Jewish way in front of their families and community, to engage legitimately in at least some forms of sexual expression, and to be eligible to become rabbis and cantors.

Three notes about this are important for understanding not only this particular responsum but the whole process of integrating morality into legal decisions. First, I began my research in this topic hoping to find a way to enable gay men to have anal intercourse, for I recognize that this is a form of sexual expression that the majority of them like and use. Several things became clear to me early in the process, however, that tempered my efforts. First, Leviticus 18:22 is ambiguous, and it may well ban only bisexual men from having sex with men and not refer to gay men at all.[39] The Jewish tradition, however, is based on how *the Rabbis* interpreted the Torah, and the Rabbis were convinced that the verse prohibited all anal sex by males. Thus whatever the biblical verse originally meant, this is how the precedent stands.

Second, because the received rabbinic tradition is unanimous in interpreting the Torah as banning anal sex by all men with other men, I knew that to permit that would mean overturning strong precedent. Truth to tell, rabbis in every generation have changed precedents through legal techniques such as narrowing or broadening their scope; they ask, "for what kind of case is this being said" (*ba-meh d'varim amurim*) and then define the precedent as narrowly or broadly as they see fit. Our approach did the same thing: We simply narrowed the scope of the ban on homosexual sex to what the Rabbis understood the Torah itself to prohibit, deleting all further bans subsequently imposed by the rabbis. Still, because the precedents on this issue were both unanimous and long standing, we ourselves were hesitant to overturn them, and we knew our colleagues on the committee would be as well. It would have been much different if there were a long legislative history on this issue in which rabbis of the past had differed; then we could simply choose to follow one line of precedent over another. Our case, though, with its use of modern science and the testimony of homosexuals themselves, was what lawyers sometimes call "a case of first impression." That always requires substantial analysis and argument, even when the law includes no previous discussion of the topic; if, as in our case, this is the first time a line of argument is being invoked to overturn long-standing precedent, the analysis and argumentation have to be even stronger.

Furthermore, we had to face the political reality that the committee would not support commitment ceremonies and ordination if they depended on uprooting the Torah's law. In such situations, one must keep one's eye on the ball and be sure *not to let the perfect undermine the good.* That is, sometimes rabbis trying to make the law more moral than it was must recognize that the perfect resolution is not politically or socially possible at this time. They then must not simply give up; they must rather do what can be done and take satisfaction from the progress that a partial step in the right direction achieves. In this case, that partial step is quite an accomplishment, for it permits lesbians to engage in sex, it permits gay men to engage in forms of sexual expression other than anal sex, it permits Conservative rabbis to perform commitment ceremonies for gay men and lesbians, and it permits the seminaries of the movement to ordain them.

Still, I am very much pained by the limits of what we did, and I know many gay men are angry about the restriction that we maintained in our responsum and that they may ignore it. I am comforted, at least to a degree, by two things. First, the few studies that have been done on anal sex among males indicate that a significant percentage of gay men do not engage in anal sex altogether for either health or aesthetic reasons. The percentage reported varies widely, from as many as 50 percent who refrain from anal sex to as few as 20 percent.[40] This means that our position is not a legal fiction, that gay men can and do find sexually fulfilling expression without using anal sex.

Second, in that same chapter of Leviticus, the Torah declares heterosexual sex during the woman's menstrual period also to be *to'evah,* "an abomination" (Lev. 18:19, 27), and yet most Conservative rabbis perform wedding ceremonies for heterosexuals without mentioning this unless they sense that the couple might observe the family purity laws.[41] Rabbis should employ the same wise silence when speaking with those gay couples who are unlikely to abstain from anal sex. Our responsum goes further: It says that it would be a violation of the men's dignity for rabbis to ask about their sexual practices. On the other hand, if gay men do ask what guidance Jewish law gives them about sex, rabbis should tell them the strictures of our position as well as its leniencies, together with all the other Jewish norms that apply to sexual activity, be it heterosexual or homosexual, as outlined in the Conservative movement's *Rabbinic Letter on Human Intimacy.*[42] This is exactly parallel to what rabbis do with heterosexual couples, advising those likely to observe the laws of family purity about them and refraining from mentioning them to those who are unlikely to observe them. As the Talmud says, "it is better that they violate the law unwittingly rather than intentionally" and "just as it is a commandment to speak about things that will be heard, so it is a commandment not to speak about things that will not be heard."[43]

Third, in the end both Rabbi Roth's ruling and ours were endorsed by a majority of the committee—each was approved by 13 of the 25 voting members of the committee on December 6, 2006. This means, of course, that within my own community of rabbis a substantial number do not attribute the same weight to moral claims to determine the law as I do. Those supporting Rabbi Roth's ruling either embrace his theory about how Jewish law has worked in the past and should function today, or they were simply not prepared to change Jewish law on this emotionally charged issue, no matter how compelling the moral arguments were against the traditional stance. Those who supported our ruling, on the other hand, were moved by the terrible burden that the traditional stance imposes on gays and lesbians, a burden that Jewish moral principles would demand that we relieve.

How can I square this debate about the place of morality in Jewish law within my own community with my theory? *Traditions develop by focusing on some sources, ignoring others, and changing the shape of yet others.* Rabbi Roth and I emphasize differing strands of the Jewish tradition that have been in competitive tension from the very beginning. Both of us intend to follow God's instructions for us. His strand puts obedience to God first; mine puts moral concerns first, even to the point of challenging God. As my friend and teacher Rabbi Uzi Weingarten pointed out to me, these strands are as old as Abraham.

The Abraham of the story of the binding of Isaac is depicted as the obedient servant; the Abraham of Sodom and Gomorrah, on the other hand, is portrayed as one who teaches "the way of God, to do what is right and just" (Gen. 18:19) and challenges God on these very grounds, "Shall not the Judge of all the earth do justice?" (Gen. 18:25). Along the latter lines, Isaiah speaks of Abraham as the paradigm of those who seek justice:

Listen to Me, you who pursue justice,
You who seek the Lord:
Look to the rock from which you were hewn,
To the quarry from which you were dug.
Look to Abraham your father
And to Sarah who brought you forth.
For he was only one when I called him,
But I blessed him and made him many. (Isa. 51:1–2)

Similarly, some sections of the Torah portray Aaron and Moses as arguing with God for a just or merciful revision of the law, in all of which God acquiesces (for example, Lev. 10:19–20; Num. 9:6–14, 27:1–11). Furthermore, the rabbinic sources I have cited on capital punishment, the illegitimate child, the stubborn and rebellious son, an eye for an eye, and a host of other issues demonstrate conclusively that the Rabbis were constantly narrowing or overturning precedent, including ones that had not been questioned before, to achieve a just result.

In the end, Jewishly committed, intelligent, and moral people can disagree about how to weigh conflicting factors in our tradition and still live within one movement and love and respect each other. As an early rabbinic statement asserts, even though the schools of Shammai and Hillel disagreed with each other on a host of issues, "the House of Shammai nevertheless did not refrain from marrying women from the families of the House of Hillel, nor did the House of Hillel refrain from marrying those of the House of Shammai. This is to teach you that they showed love and friendship towards one another, thus putting into practice the verse, 'Love truth and peace' (Zekhariah 8:19)."[44] In my view, though, only if we use Jewish moral norms and theology in making concrete judgments in Jewish law can we fully join with the Psalmist in extolling not only the sweetness and wisdom of living a life according to Jewish law but also the morality it helps us attain:

The Teaching (Torah) of the Lord is without blemish, restoring life.
The Covenant of the Lord is faithful, making the simple wise.
The precepts of the Lord are upright, giving the heart joy.
The instruction of the Lord is clean, enlightening the eyes.
The fear of the Lord is pure, enduring forever.
The judgments of the Lord are true, righteous together.
More precious than gold, than much fine gold,
Sweeter than honey, than drippings of the comb. (Ps. 19:8–10)

ENDNOTES

1. The relationship between religion and ethics and, in particular, between Jewish law and ethics, has been a long-term interest of mine, ever since I was thinking of a topic for my doctoral dissertation. For my previous writings on religion and ethics and, in particular, Jewish law and ethics, see Dorff, *To Do the Right and the Good*, chap 1, appends. A and B; *Love Your Neighbor and Yourself*, append.; and *The Way into Tikkun Olam (Fixing the World)*, chap. 3.

2. Sifrei Devarim, Ekev on Deut. 11:22.

3. B. Sukkah 14a.

4. On the New Testament's view of the Pharisees, see, for example, Matt. 3:7; chap. 23 and Luke 18:9ff., in which they are variously called "hypocrites" and "offspring of vipers." The Rabbis themselves recognized the insincere among their numbers, whom they called "sore spots" or "plagues on the Pharisaic party" (M. Sotah 3:4; B. Sotah 22b). With the exception of the relatively favorable depiction of Rabban Gamliel in the Acts of the Apostles, though, the New Testament paints the Pharisees with quite a broad, negative brush, particularly for being legalistic in their approach to Jewish law—and then, to make matters worse, for hypocritically acting in violation of that law (at least as the New Testament writers see things). For the dispute between Jesus and the Pharisees over the details of Sabbath laws, see Matt. 12:9–14; Mark 3:1–6; Luke 6:6–11, 13:10–17, 14:1–6; John 5:1–18. For Jesus' dispute with the Pharisees over divorce, see Matt. 19:1–14; Mark 10:1–14. For the replacement of law with spirit, see, in particular, Rom. 7:1–8:8, 9:30–33, and his 5:16–26.

5. My friend and teacher Rabbi Uzi Weingarten pointed out to me an egregious example of this. The Mishnah has some 30 chapters on the purity or

impurity of utensils and not a single one on the love of God and other people, honoring parents, or treating widows and orphans.

6. Naḥmanides' commentary on Lev. 19:2.

7. B. Pesaḥim 50b and many other places in the Talmud; see Chapter 4, note 11, herein. Given that the verb here is *"la-asok,"* which is usually used with studying Torah but not with fulfilling commandments, this source in its original version may refer only to studying Torah, which should be done regardless of motive. That seems to be the text Maimonides had in front of him because he speaks of the motivations for following the commandments in a different section from the ones for studying Torah and quotes this talmudic passage only in the latter. M.T. Laws of Repentance 10:1, 5. Still, he too says there that one should observe the commandments out of fear if one has not yet reached the level of observing them out of love, and so the theory of doing the right thing even if not for the right reason applies to both studying and fulfilling the commandments.

8. Naḥmanides' commentary on Lev. 19:2.

9. Adler, *The World of the Talmud*, p. 64.

10. M. Davis, *The Emergence of Conservative Judaism*, part 3; Waxman, *Tradition and Change*, sec. 1.

11. B. Pesaḥim 50b, and in parallel passages elsewhere; see Chapter 4, note 11, herein.

12. M. Avot 4:2.

13. Heschel, *God in Search of Man*, (pp. 296–297.

14. M. Bava Kamma 8:7.

15. I discuss Jewish law governing forgiveness among individuals in Dorff, *Love Your Neighbor and Yourself*, chap. 6, and among peoples in Dorff, *To Do the Right and the Good*, chap. 8.

16. M. Bava Meẓia 4:10.

17. Dorff, *Love Your Neighbor and Yourself*, chap. 1 and append.

18. Ibid., pp. 311–315.

19. The one exception to this is Standards of Rabbinic Practice, which all Conservative rabbis and synagogues must follow on pain of possible expulsion from the movement. See Dorff, *Conservative Judaism*, pp. 152–155 (2nd rev. ed.).

20. M. Bava Meẓia 4:10.

21. For the requirement for a soup kitchen and communal fund: T. Pe'ah 4:9; M.T. Laws of Gifts to the Poor 9:3. For limits on charity to one fifth of one's income: B. Ketubbot 50a; M.T. laws of Gifts to the Poor 7:5. See also the remarkable story of Elazar Ish Biratha, the man who could not stop giving charity, in B. Ta'anit 24a. For a general discussion of Jewish laws on poverty, see Dorff, *Love Your Neighbor and Yourself*, chap. 6, and *The Way into Tikkun Olam (Fixing the World)*, chap. 5.

22. S.A. Oraḥ Ḥayyim 671:4 (gloss) and Magen Avraham there, quoting

the Maharal. Kitzur Shulḥan Arukh 139:9 specifies that "in a row," as used in those sources, requires not only that the candles not be in the form of a circle, but also that one not be higher than another.

23. B. Makkot 24a.

24. B. Shabbat 31a. Rashi is not happy with the breadth of Hillel's words and tries to do an end-run around them by suggesting that by "your neighbor" Hillel meant God (and, therefore, you should love God and follow all of the commandments) or that Hillel did not mean "all" of the Torah but most of it. This must be recognized, though, for the narrowing that it is: the context of speaking to a potential convert demonstrates that Hillel clearly meant what he said.

25. Solomon Schechter called this group "catholic Israel," his translation of "kelal Yisra'el," the community of Israel; see Schechter, Studies in Judaism, Introduction, (reprinted with an analysis of his legal theory in Dorff, The Unfolding Tradition, pp. 57–67). This sensitivity to communal practice, however, was not new with him. It has always been an important part of how Jewish law took form, influencing rabbis who had to decide whether to give legal sanction to communal practice, to let it remain the custom without such legal backing, or to fight to change it. See Chapter Seven of this volume.

26. For example, S.A. Oraḥ Ḥayyim 467:11, 12 (gloss); Yoreh De'ah 23:2; 31:1 (gloss); 35:8 (gloss); 36:7 (gloss), 16 (gloss); and so on.

27. "We may not issue a decree unless most of the community can uphold it": B. Bava Kamma 79b; B. Bava Batra 60b; B. Avodah Zarah 36a; B. Horayot 3b.

28. Anonymous, "CJF and Rabbinic Alumni Sponsor New York Premiere of Film and a Conversation on Rav Soloveitchik," p. 16.

29. Encyclopaedia Judaica 14:952.

30. My friend and teacher Rabbi Uzi Weingarten tells a similar story. His grandfather, Rabbi Ḥayyim Yitzhak Weingarten, was the rabbi of Liege, Belgium. In another story of a woman with a chicken, he spent two hours looking up references in books and then pronounced the chicken kosher. When asked by his son how he could say so, given that the chicken obviously was not kosher, he said, "The chicken was kosher the moment she walked into the room because if I pronounced it unkosher, she and her family would have nothing to eat. If I had to choose between answering to her or to the Rama [Rabbi Moses Isserles, author of the Ashkenazic glosses on the Shulḥan Arukh], I would rather answer to the Rama!" He also pointed out to me that M. Nega'im 12:5 draws the same kind of conclusion that I do here, stating that "if the Torah had pity on a person's despised property, how much the more so on his treasured property; and if on his money, how much the more so on the lives of his sons and daughters; [and] if this is true for a wicked person, how much the more so for a righteous person."

31. B. Berakhot 25b; B. Yoma 30a; B. Kiddushin 54a; B. Me'ilah 14b.

32. T. Rosh Hashanah 1:17; B. Rosh Hashanah 25b.

33. B. Gittin 56a, the comment of Rabbi Johanan: "Because of the humility of Rabbi Zechariah b. Abkulas our House has been destroyed, our Temple burned, and we ourselves exiled from the land."

34. M.T. Laws of the Sabbath 2:3; Laws of Hanukkah 4:14. I want to thank my friend and colleague Rabbi Bradley Shavit Artson for calling my attention to the former passage and to my friend and teacher Rabbi Uzi Weingarten for calling my attention to the latter one.

35. This is akin to the answers in the back of some mathematics books, put there so that you know that if you reached a different result, you need to do the problem again.

36. M. Bava Mezia 4:10.

37. On enabling a woman to procure a divorce when her husband is not willing to grant her one, see Dorff and Rosett, *A Living Tree,* pp. 523–545. The Rabbinical Assembly, the organization of Conservative rabbis, has not changed the language of acquisition in the marriage contracts (*ketubbot*) it publishes, but it has made them more egalitarian. They can be accessed at www.rabbinicalassembly.org. Rabbi Gordon Tucker and Rabbi Ben Zion Bergman have created *ketubbot* that are fully egalitarian. Rabbi Bergman's was approved in principle by the Committee on Jewish Law and Standards, and, as of this writing, the Rabbinical Assembly's Liturgy Committee is working on an elegant version of that.

38. Traditional Jewish law (B. Sanhedrin 74a) maintains that a person should die rather than violate the sexual prohibitions delineated in Leviticus 18. That is the main reason that we did not abrogate the Torah's law, at least as the Rabbis understood it. Still, the much higher rate of suicide among gay men and lesbians provides ample ground to abrogate rabbinic extensions of that verse, for saving a life preempts all but three of the Torah's laws and all rabbinic legislation (B. Yoma 85b; B. Sanhedrin 74a). See Ruemafedi et. al., "The Relationship between Suicide Risk and Sexual Orientation: Results of a Population-Based Study" and Jay Paul, et. al., "Suicide Attempts Among Gay and Bisexual Men," the latter of which found that 12 percent of urban gay and bisexual men have attempted suicide in their lifetime, a rate three times higher than the overall rate for American adult males, and that younger men were attempting suicide earlier in their lives, usually before age 25. As Jay Paul, the principal investigator said, "These rates are staggering, and highlight the cost of pervasive anti-gay stigmatization and victimization. . . . We cannot take these suicide attempts lightly, as almost half of the men in our study [who attempted suicide] reported multiple attempts. Furthermore, a study such as this can only report suicide attempts; we can never enumerate the lives lost through completed suicides." Quoted on www.eurekalert.org/pub_releases/2002-08/uoc—sar080502.php, August 5,

2002; contact Jeff Sheehy, jsheehy@psg .ucsf.edu. Another study found that one in five gay men were likely to be abused by their partner, approximately the same percentage as heterosexual women; see Gregory Greenwood et. al, "Battering Victimization among a Probability-Based Sample of Men Who Have Sex With Men." The most likely are those under 40 and those who are HIV positive. Yet another study showed that 48 percent of gay men smoke, compared to an overall rate of 27 percent among U.S. men; see Stall, et. al., "Cigarette Smoking among Gay and Bisexual Men." Surely these findings demonstrate that the dishonor to which our society subjects gays and lesbians are literally matters of life and death.

39. The text in Lev. 18:22, "A man shall not lie with another man as a man lies with a woman; it is an abomination," is inherently ambiguous. Because a man does not have a vagina, a man physically cannot lie with another man as men usually have sex with women—that is, vaginally. As a result, modern biblical scholars have suggested many different meanings of this verse.

My own view as to the plain meaning of the verse is that first suggested to me by Dr. Shai Cherry, a rabbinical student at the Ziegler School of Rabbinic Studies at the American Jewish University. He pointed out that the Babylonian Talmud reads the Torah on the assumption that no word (and sometimes no letter) is superfluous. If we read this verse that way, it becomes evident that if the Torah wanted to ban gay sex, it could have simply said "A man shall not lie with another man." What should we learn from the additional clause, "as a man lies with a woman"? Dr. Cherry suggests that this indicates that the verse is not talking about gay men at all but rather bisexuals—that is, that it is prohibiting *men who lie with women to lie with men also.* Just recently, Rabbi Uzi Weingarten pointed out to me that Midrash Hagadol sees the verse in the same way, commenting that the reason for this verse is that "men would leave their wives and lie with men."

Even if the plain meaning of the verse is thus not about the sex that gay men have exclusively with other gay men but rather about the sex that bisexual men have with men, however, the Jewish tradition, as I point out in the text here, is based on how the Rabbis interpreted the Torah, and the Rabbis were convinced that the verse prohibited anal sex by males. Thus whatever the biblical verse originally meant, it is this interpretation that is controlling for Jewish law.

40. Ekstrand et. al, "Gay Men Report High Rates of Unprotected Anal Sex . . ." found that of a sample of 510 unmarried gay men who were 18 to 29 years at the beginning of the study, the prevalence of unprotected anal intercourse increased from 37% to 50% between 1993 and 1994 and 1996 and 1997; this does not include, of course, gay men who use condoms during anal sex. The British Medical Journal reported that "two thirds of gay men have anal sex"; see Robin Bell, "ABC of Sexual Health: Homosexual Men and Women," *British Medical Journal* 318 (7181) (Feb. 13, 1999): 452-455.

The Laumann study, *The Social Organization of Sexuality,* found that 20 percent of gay men never practice it.

41. Although Conservative rabbis almost never broached this subject during most of the 20th century, an increasing, but still very small, percentage of Conservative rabbis and laypeople are now observing some form of the family purity laws. In September 2006, the Committee on Jewish Law and Standards validated three different ways of doing that, including one that limits the period to seven days and another that makes special provision for infertile couples. These responsa by Rabbis Miriam Berkowitz, Susan Grossman, and Avram Israel Reisner are available at www.rabbinicalassembly.org under the link "Contemporary Halakhah."

42. See Dorff, " 'This Is My Beloved, This Is My Friend' (Song of Songs 5:16)," pp. 6–13. In Dorff, *Love Your Neighbor and Yourself,* pp. 73–82.

43. B. Shabbat 148b; B. Beitzah 30a; B. Bava Batra 60b. See also M.T. Desisting on the Tenth [of Tishre = Yom Kippur, *Shevi'tat Assor*] 1:7; S.A. Orah. H.ayyim 338:5 (gloss); 339:3 (gloss); and especially 608:2 (gloss).

44. T. Yevamot 1:3; B. Yevamot 14b.

CHAPTER SEVEN

Jewish Law and Custom

THE CHARACTER OF CUSTOM

Custom is slippery. By definition, *customs* are a set of norms that arise out of the practices of the people. (This is different from *practices,* which describe what people commonly do but do not establish any norms about what they may or must do.) Because customs are rooted in what people do, judges who must decide cases on the basis of custom cannot rely on a paper trail of laws and precedents. In fact, sometimes it is not clear whether a custom exists about a given matter or not. Furthermore, precisely because customs emerge from communal practices, they are unlikely to be clearly defined in either scope or content. Finally, judges may think that customs are wrongheaded. All of these factors often make judging on the basis of a custom very difficult.

In the context of the Jewish community, customs are not established at a specific time and place by recognized rabbinic authorities. Many times customs are not even acknowledged by the rabbis, let alone validated by them. Because customs are not clearly stated in a rabbinic ruling, others, especially those living at a different time and place, often cannot understand what they do and do not entail. The very genre of custom, coming as it does as a "fact on the ground"

FOR THE LOVE OF GOD AND PEOPLE

rather than a proposal to be considered, suggests that it is somehow illegitimate to evaluate its legal cogency. We follow the custom because it is the accepted practice. Customs are not, in a word, legally neat, with clearly stated rationales open to analysis, challenge, and change and with explicit details specifying to whom they apply and what they require. Instead, custom emerges from the masses—in our case, from the people Solomon Schechter called "Catholic Israel." As such, its rationales, its demands, and the scope of communities in which it functions are often not clear. Moreover, because it emerges from the populace in given times and places, it is likely to differ from one Jewish community to the next.

The ways in which customs remain or change are also hard to grasp and even harder to control. Customs that are never formalized in law but rather passed down in the form of "what we do here" may become so entrenched that they cannot be uprooted despite compelling reasons to do so. Rabbis sometimes denounce certain customs as foolish (*minhag shtut*), but rabbinic opposition, even if unanimous and forcefully expressed, does not always succeed in uprooting objectionable customs. Many customs, however, become every bit as normative as statutory laws or rabbinic rulings—so much so, that after a while rabbinic rulings often recognize a given custom and enforce it.

Before a given custom becomes well established, however, practices will differ, and so people who want to abide by the custom may not know how to do so. Moreover, in the early stages of the development of a custom, judges who adjudicate disputes based on differing understandings of the local practice will not know what the parties should have expected. This is especially problematic because customs can pass out of existence just as quickly and inexplicably as they appear. Custom as a legal genre, then, requires one to be flexible enough to adjust to ill-defined and changing practices and expectations.[1]

Custom, however, cannot be ignored. In commercial transactions it all but reigns supreme; as the Mishnah says in regard to labor relations, "Everything depends on the local custom."[2] Jewish rituals surrounding special days or the life cycle may be rooted in the law—some are described in the Torah itself—but almost all of them are shaped significantly by communal and even by family customs.

246

TWO TYPES OF CUSTOM

Custom can function in two very different ways. It can sometimes permit what might otherwise be forbidden. At other times, it can establish demands that the law does not. When customs permit actions, they are used as a *justification* for a practice: I do *x*, and I may do *x* because many, and perhaps most, people in this community do *x*. I wear casual clothes on airplanes now (in contrast to the 1950s) because that has become the accepted custom. In Italy, men kiss each other in public as a sign of greeting, even though that is not common in most other countries. This justificatory sense of "custom" is inclusive; it permits and justifies a form of behavior that is not specifically authorized by law but is less than the most demanding standard that one can imagine.

Note that custom in this sense is definitely not law. Thus because business attire is not legally required on planes, nobody has the legal authority to force me to wear that. Conversely, if I dress up for a plane ride, nobody has the legal authority to force me to change into more casual clothes, but someone might tell me that in the future I may dress more comfortably on airplanes if I want to do so. Looking around at how other people on the plane are dressed should also inform me of what is, and what is not, expected. Similarly, if men kiss each other as a sign of greeting in the United States, it may seem odd, but nobody could be arrested for doing so. Custom in this sense, then, is not law and thus has none of the consequences of law.

Sometimes custom is instead used in a second sense, as a *demand* for specific behavior. I must do *x* because that is the way people do things here. In some communities, weddings call for formal attire; in others, business suits and dresses are sufficient; in some (such as on Israeli kibbutzim), even dressy casual clothes will do; and in some, the people arranging the wedding may set the standard, announcing it in the invitation. It is seen as cold and standoffish in Mediterranean countries for people to stand at a distance from one another when talking, but in northern European countries and the United States, close contact is seen as invading one's space and intrusive. This second sense of "custom" is exclusive: It prohibits behavior out of line with the established custom.

Custom even in this sense, though, is not law. If I come improperly dressed to a wedding, people may look askance at me, and I may even be told to leave. If I refuse to leave, those making the wedding may call the police. The police, though, would not have the authority to eject me because I violated the custom for dress at this particular wedding; they may eject me only because I would be violating laws forbidding trespassing on private property. Put more abstractly, unless a custom has been written into law or the law itself gives a (usually commercial) custom authority of law, custom in this second, normative sense imposes demands that are social in origin and social in their consequences.

Because Jews have been scattered all over the globe for much of their history, one would expect that custom in both these senses would play an even larger role in Jewish law than it does in American law, and, indeed, it does. Especially in times past, when instant, worldwide communications did not exist, customs could be localized without much interference from outside the community or even any awareness of how people might do things differently. This, then, raises the question of how law and custom differ from one another—and, indeed, how one can tell whether a given norm is a law or a custom.

THE DIFFERENCES BETWEEN LAW AND CUSTOM

Law and custom differ in important ways. The following paragraphs discuss some of these differences.

1. *Source.* Law comes from, or is at least articulated by, legal authorities. Customs, by contrast, emerge from the practices of the people; and for that reason, their demands may be harder to identify and define than the requirements of law are.

2. *Scope.* Custom often fills in gaps left by the law (for example, exactly how to wrap the tefillin of the hand, or how to make glassware kosher for Passover, or the choice of foods to mark the holidays in various locales). Conversely, laws sometimes produce customary norms where none existed before. So, for example, as noted earlier, the *Brown v. Board of Education* decision produced the custom (in the first, permissive sense of that word) to enable advertisers to picture blacks and whites socializing together, and the Civil Rights Act of 1964 has led to the custom (in the second, demanding sense of that

word) requiring the inclusion of women and people of color in addition to white men in any serious discussion of social issues.

3. *Domain.* Jewish law governs—or, at least, claims to govern—every Jew, no matter where that Jew lives. Customs, on the other hand, are only local and sometimes just familial in their reach, so that people outside the community or family that has a particular custom are not affected by it and neither need permission to engage in the custom nor can be required to practice it.

4. *Rationales.* Both lawmakers and judges often explain the reasons for their enactments or decisions. Lawmakers want to gain the people's compliance and ultimately their support in the next election. Judges want to demonstrate that their judgments are not arbitrary whims but are rather based on a fair reading of established law and precedent so that the parties, and ultimately society as a whole, will comply with their decision. In contrast, customs may or may not be justified by expressed rationales. Because they arise from people's practices, the rationales offered for them, in fact, may be ex post facto justifications for something people started doing for other, often unknown, reasons. Why, for example, do Jews eat dairy products on Shavuot? A survey of the reasons offered makes one strongly suspect that all those rationales are really desperate attempts to justify a norm that in fact emerged for reasons unknown to anyone.

5. *Enforcement.* Law is enforced through the use of legal remedies. In times past, the remedies imposed by Jewish law included social pressure and ostracism, fines, corporal punishment, and even death. Those measures are not available to Jewish legal authorities today, when Jews live largely in countries governed by Enlightenment principles and so, as full citizens of the realm, are subject to its laws and punishments. Nevertheless, human authorities can produce compliance by teaching Jews the demands of Jewish law in the first place, by explaining the multiple motivations (as described in Chapter Four) that should prompt us to live by it, by refusing to allow certain practices or by insisting on others in congregational life (for example, by requiring that meals be kosher and by prohibiting photography on the Sabbath within the synagogue). Ultimately, still today rabbis sometimes issue an official court decree of excommunication for people who have abused others, for example, and Jews generally treat some people as outside the community, as all of the Jewish community has done with respect to Jews for Jesus or messianic Jews. The sanctions of customs, on the other hand, are not

official, but they may be just as effective in producing behavior in accordance with social norms, for people often will do what they must to be part of a group.

THE INTERACTIONS BETWEEN LAW AND CUSTOM

Despite these important differences, custom and law interact in all possible directions. Sometimes custom is the source of laws; sometimes it undermines law; sometimes law creates new customs; and sometimes law changes customs. One example of custom creating law in the United States is constitutional, indicating just how powerful custom can be. When the custom of presidents serving a maximum of two terms was violated by Franklin Delano Roosevelt, the Twenty-Second Amendment to the Constitution was adopted to ensure that this did not happen again.

A more pervasive set of customs contributed to the formulation of the Uniform Commercial Code (UCC), adopted in some form by 49 of the 50 states. Until the UCC was formulated in 1977, state laws were completely at odds with what people in business were actually doing. In the early 1960s, my father and I stopped at a lumberyard. My father, who was a civil engineer, ordered some lumber to be delivered to a certain site on a certain day, shook hands with the salesman, and then we left. I asked him how he and the lumberyard could do business that way; after all, he had nothing to prove that he had ordered the lumber, and neither did the salesman; and both stood to lose a considerable sum of money if either denied their agreement. In answer to my question, my father shrugged his shoulders and said, "That's just the way we do business." They clearly had a long business relationship, but this kind of informality drives lawyers and judges mad. Nevertheless, it was just such business practices that became the model law known as the Uniform Commercial Code, and that code specifically invokes the "usage of trade" as a criterion for judging cases.[3]

A parallel development in Jewish law is the case of wine merchants putting their markers on kegs of wine. This, according to the Talmud, does not normally effect a legal transfer (*kinyan*) unless that is the custom among merchants.[4] Indeed, Rabbi Yosef Karo, author of the authoritative 16th-century code of Jewish law the Shulḥan

Arukh, often defers to local custom. Rabbi Moses Isserles, who wrote glosses on that code—identifying practices of northern European Jewry that differ from those of Mediterranean Jewry, which Karo recorded—spends much of his time describing customary norms. Thus custom often serves as the source of laws or is recognized by the law as authoritative in lieu of a law.

Sometimes the reverse happens, such that laws establish customs. So, for example, even though the *Brown* decision applied only to schools, it led to social expectations, at least in some parts of the country, that blacks and whites could socialize together, leading, in turn, to the very first advertisement I saw (in 1963) depicting blacks and whites enjoying Salem cigarettes together. Thus the law altered not only the practices it sought to govern in schools but also social expectations, to the extent that advertisers thought it would help sell their products if they depicted blacks and whites using them together.

Sometimes, on the other hand, customs undermine laws. So, for example, American driving practices made the nationwide speed limit of 55 miles per hour, imposed in the mid-1970s, effectively null and void. Indeed, as I have mentioned, even though a small minority of Americans violated Prohibition during the years it was law, ultimately that was enough to force the repeal of nothing less than a constitutional amendment.

Finally, sometimes laws undermine customs. *Brown v. Board of Education* and the Supreme Court decisions that followed in its wake, for example, abrogated not only laws that discriminated against blacks but also a number of customs, especially in the South, that shaped how whites treated blacks and even talked to them.

In Jewish law, custom has interacted with law in all of the same ways. Indeed, in light of the widespread nature of the Jewish people, one would expect that custom would have an even greater effect in shaping the practices of the Jewish people than it has had in other communities. Because of the divine status ascribed to the Torah, however, rabbis have not allowed custom to countermand a prohibition of the Torah, especially in ritual matters (*issur v'heter*), but even there one first has to define which rules have Torah status and which are instead rabbinic in their level of authority to decide whether this restriction applies. Most often, the Torah cannot be claimed as the basis for a custom, and rabbis must confront the custom on its mer-

251

FOR THE LOVE OF GOD AND PEOPLE

its, deciding whether to wage war with it, confirm it, or just let it remain as the custom of some but not necessarily of all.

Living legal systems, then, incorporate not only law but custom, and each exercises a claim on the members of the society. Sometimes these dual claims pose no problems. On the contrary, law and custom can actually reinforce one another, as, for example, when customs augment and even beautify observance of the law or when one fills in gaps left by the other. Sometimes, however, custom and law oppose each other, and then which takes precedence over which is not always clear. Rabbis will generally prefer the law for its clarity and authority, but some customs become so widespread that they overwhelm the law such that it falls into disuse. In other cases, the close interaction between law and custom leads lawmakers and judges to be unsure as to whether they are articulating law or custom. This is especially true, I would argue, in many of the ritual and commercial sections of Jewish law as articulated in the Shulḥan Arukh and in other Jewish codes and rabbinic rulings.

As a result of these multiple forms of relationship between law and custom, one must come to understand that *the content of the law itself is always a product of the interaction between the dictates of those entrusted with interpreting and applying the law and the actual practices of those governed by it.* Law and custom, *din* and *minhag,* may pull in opposite directions, but they ultimately must take account of one another because neither automatically supersedes the other. As illustrated earlier, that is true even in American law, a fully functional and enforced legal system.

Because of this interaction, every legal system periodically has to catch up to the actual practices of the people it seeks to govern. Sometimes, as we have seen, the legal authorities will seek to uproot a custom that has emerged, and sometimes they will instead confirm it in law. Sometimes, they will do neither, letting varying customs in different regions determine what the practice will be. The United States is probably more sensitive than most nations to the need to allow local custom to govern, for the federalist system embodied in its constitution establishes the rights of states to determine many matters, ranging from education to welfare to zoning to criminal penalties.

252

CUSTOM: THE EXAMPLE OF WOMEN'S ROLES IN JEWISH LIFE

In what follows, I use the example of women's role in Jewish life to illustrate the interaction between custom and law. I am not claiming that all areas of the law interact with custom as this one does, but many do. Thus this is a good example of how customs work.

We err if we try to decide issues of women's status in Jewish law today on the basis of precedent because the texts and legal arguments were all post facto reflections of what was determined by custom in the first place. The historical context of Jewish law thus requires us, on the one hand, not to be too constrained by texts that limit the role of women because they were giving only retroactive justification for what common practice was at the time. On the other hand, we must not misuse texts to allow practices that they never intended.

As I shall show, it was not law but custom that determined the role of women in synagogue services, in witnessing, and in marriage and divorce. So to be true to historical precedent, we must give custom a much larger role in determining our own practices as well. We should be flexible, allowing some people to hold on to old and familiar customs, giving others time and support to adjust to new ones that have evolved over the last 50 years in many congregations, and simultaneously allowing those who are so inclined to shape new customs that enable women to function even more fully in Jewish life.

Lest I be misunderstood, I do *not* believe, à la Mordecai Kaplan, that custom should replace law in our time as a matter of general principle. In Chapter Six, I explained the advantages of law for any society. I am merely asserting that in the particular case of the role of women in Jewish life, the norms in our tradition are based on custom rather than law and this should affect how we treat them.

The Role of Custom in Determining Women's Status in Biblical and Talmudic Times

The biblical and talmudic sources on the role of women make clear that the legal status of women was not equal to that of men. Given

the role of women in other ancient cultures, this should not be surprising. At the same time, one also does not find a consistent picture
of women subservient to men. Instead, one finds a patchwork of
laws, in some of which women are equal to men, while in others
they are at a legal disadvantage.

Examples of this abound, but a few will suffice to make this clear.
None of the biblical stories or laws depicts a woman proposing marriage to a man or instituting a divorce, and, based on the Rabbis'
interpretation of Deuteronomy 24:1–4, later rabbinic law specifies
that only a man may institute those procedures.[5] This would argue
for women's subservience. On the other hand, women are specifically included in Deuteronomy's command that all Israelites are to
hear the Torah read every seven years (Deut. 31:12), and the Torah's
rules about accidental homicide, which specify that they apply to "a
man or a woman" (Num. 5:6), are used by the Rabbis to extend all of
the Torah's tort laws to women perpetrators and victims as well.[6]
Thus in some ways women had a lesser, and in some ways an equal,
status vis-à-vis men.

Moreover, there is a discrepancy between what the law says and
what we read in our sources' reports of our history. On the one hand,
when interpreting Deuteronomy's discussion of appointing a king
over the people (Deut. 17:15), the Rabbis limited eligibility for sov-
ereignty to men.[7] Deborah, however, had long before been the political and military leader of her people; and in times close to what was
probably the era of this rabbinic ruling, Shelomziyyon (Salome
Alexandra), the queen, ruled as well.[8] These examples indicate that
in ancient times, women could serve in these very public and important roles, contrary to what Jewish law later taught. Conversely, the
Talmud permits women to be among the seven who read the Torah
in the synagogue on the Sabbath. However, this was not their practice, for, as the Beraita itself explains, to have women read the Torah
would dishonor the men in the congregation.[9] We certainly do not
hear in later stories or rulings of many (any?) women who in fact
read the Torah in the synagogue, despite the legal permission
embedded in the sources for them to do so;[10] indeed, although men
and women sat together in the synagogues and even the Temple of
antiquity,[11] as Jewish worship developed during the Middle Ages,
women were sectioned off by a partition from men, who alone could
lead the services.

These kinds of disparities between what the legal texts say and what the stories report become especially striking in the extended discussion in the tractate Kiddushin about which commandments women are exempt from doing. The legal rationales for these exemptions are self-evidently weak, for the very verses that are quoted to exempt women from given commandments could just as easily be read to include them. Most depend on masculine forms of nouns or verbs, which, according to the rules of Hebrew grammar, can just as easily include women as exclude them—a fact that the Rabbis surely knew as well as we do. One must conclude, then, that the choice of whether to use the masculine noun or verb in question to designate men alone or both men and women was not at all determined by the grammar of the verses themselves but rather by the preexisting custom at the time.

The discussion in Kiddushin is based on the Mishnah's attempt to generalize over the commandments from which women are exempt. Its generalization, that women are exempt from positive, time-bound commandments, is quickly challenged in the Talmud, which adduces quite a few practices that do not fit this rule:

Is this a general principle? Unleavened bread [which it is a positive command to eat on the first night of Passover, in accordance with Exod. 12:18], rejoicing [on the festivals in accordance with Deut. 16:14], and assembling [on the Festival of Tabernacles in the seventh year, in accordance with Deut. 31:12] are all affirmative precepts limited to time, and yet incumbent on women. Furthermore, study of the Torah, procreation, and the redemption of the first-born son are affirmative precepts not limited to time, and yet women are exempt therefrom—Rabbi Johanan answered: We cannot learn from general principles, even when exceptions are stated.[12]

The Talmud's discussion and rulings, then, indicate quite clearly that neither a legal analysis of biblical verses nor even a rabbinic attempt to generalize over the practices of their time was the ground for determining what women may or may not do. That instead was decided on the basis of the multiple and inconsistent, but apparently well-established, customs of their community.

Medieval Texts vs. Practices Regarding Women

If custom ruled the day in governing the roles that women might have in society in biblical and rabbinic times, we should expect it to do so in medieval times as well, and it did. The clearest cases of this are in the laws governing the relationships between men and women. So, for example, while biblical, talmudic, and Muslim law all allow a man to marry more than one woman, Christian law does not, and so Ashkenazic Jewish men and women, who lived predominantly among Christians, were enjoined by Rabbenu Gershom from polygymy while Sephardic Jews, who continued to live among Muslims, were not restricted in that way.[13]

We do not, however, hear of women taking public roles in the synagogue, neither among Ashkenazim nor among Sephardim.[14] This is important to keep in mind when we read medieval texts that say, for example, that 10 are necessary for a prayer quorum (minyan) without specifying whether women may be counted toward that number.[15] It is certainly true that the authors of texts like that could have specified "10 men" if they meant to restrict those who count to males, but it is equally true that they could have specified "10 men or women" if they had meant that. It is a mistake, then, to read such texts as a justification for including women in the count; for that is reading the text totally divorced from the historical context from which it came and to which it undoubtedly referred. As a member of a Conservative synagogue that has been egalitarian since 1976, I, for one, am sorely tempted to read such texts in that way, but I must be honest in pointing out that that would be playing fast and loose with the plain meaning of the text when read, as it should be, in its historical context.

The same argument applies to solitary texts that seem to report that in some places women actually did what many of us now want to allow them to do. The medieval text that is used to indicate that even in those times women could be counted for a prayer quorum (minyan) is a good example of this. It is a comment of the Mordecai (13th-century), who, in turn, is reporting what he "found" in the writings of an earlier Rabbi Simhah, possibly the compiler of the Mahzor Vitri.[16] Even if such texts are to be credited, and even if they mean what we take them to mean, they represent exceptions to the rule that the overwhelming practice in the synagogues of our medieval and early modern ancestors was to count only men for the quorum and to permit only men to lead the services.

Conservative Movement Rulings and Customs on a Range of Issues Regarding Women

One identifying characteristic of the Conservative movement from its early history in North America is its evolving practices in regard to the role of women. Mixed seating in educational settings and in worship was established totally by the customs of the people affiliated with Conservative congregations; rabbis sought legally to justify this practice only after the fact.[17] Bat mitzvah ceremonies, initiated first by Mordecai M. Kaplan in 1922,[18] varied widely in degree of acceptance and in form through the 1960s, with girls doing for their bat mitzvah exactly what boys did for their bar mitzvah in some congregations and, at the other end of the spectrum, with girls' ceremonies restricted to Friday nights and to parts of the service not halakhically required. Here again custom ruled the day.

Because custom and law continually interact and affect each other, it should be no surprise that some steps in the evolution of the status of women were initiated by rabbis—or, at least, confirmed by them in very early stages of this increasing egalitarianism. Specifically, calling women to the Torah was officially permitted by the Committee on Jewish Law and Standards (CJLS) in 1954,[19] but it did not become widespread until the late 1970s or 1980s. Similarly, counting women for a minyan was approved as a majority decision of the committee in June 1973, but that too did not become widespread until the 1980s and 1990s.

In what was undoubtedly the most public forum for deciding an issue, in 1979 the Rabbinical Assembly asked the chancellor of the Jewish Theological Seminary to form a special commission to determine whether it was permissible to ordain women as rabbis. That commission voted in favor of women's ordination, leading to the first ordination of a woman by the seminary in 1985.[20] This decision was never officially confirmed by the CJLS, but now several members of that committee are themselves women rabbis, and so custom has ruled there as well. Because of the Rabbinical Assembly's rules regarding seniority and placement, it has taken some time for women rabbis to be eligible for appointment to large congregations on an equal footing with men; furthermore, women rabbis do not earn comparable salaries as their male colleagues in similar posts, and in some congregations there is still reticence to hire a woman rabbi altogether. The existence of women rabbis in the various settings and capacities in which they now serve, though, has created a whole panoply of new customs, not only in creative, new rituals but also in the ways in which rabbis and lay Jews understand and interact with each other.

Other customs regarding women have emerged, or are emerging, from the masses, just as one would expect for this genre of legal norms. So, for example, some women put on tefillin, others don only a tallit, and some wear neither of these in their worship. Some women wear head covering during worship and study (or always), and some do not. Some congregations insert the Matriarchs in the opening blessing of the *Amidah,* some do not, and some make it a prerogative of the one leading services to decide.

Women as Witnesses

Finally, we turn to what is perhaps the most difficult issue in this area to change legally—namely, to permit women to serve as witnesses on Jewish legal documents. In 1974, a minority of six members of the committee voted to permit women to serve as witnesses, but that vote was not substantiated by a responsum to justify the decision.[21] Still, only three votes were required under the committee's rules at that time to represent a valid option within the Conservative movement; the six votes in favor of permitting women to serve as witnesses would even satisfy the more stringent requirements enacted in 1985 for that status. Despite this show of support for the practice and despite the two responsa approved in October 2001 that thoroughly consider the sources and rule in favor of permitting women to be witnesses on Jewish legal documents,[22] women still do not serve as witnesses in any significant number.

I suggest that both the rule prohibiting women to serve as witnesses in classical Jewish law and the reticence of rabbis to permit them to do so even after the two responsa were approved both emanate from custom. First, as to the ban in classical Jewish law, the Sifrei, both Talmuds, and Maimonides all maintain that only men

JEWISH LAW AND CUSTOM

may serve as witnesses as a matter of biblical law.²³ This, however, is founded on reading the masculine plural for witnesses (*edim*) in either Deuteronomy 19:15 or Deuteronomy 17:6 as exclusively male in reference. Those verses, however, can just as easily be read to include women as to exclude them, and the Sifrei itself interprets the masculine plural for the litigants in these verses to include women. Thus here again the reason for restricting testimony to men was not based on the grammar of the Torah's verses. If historical records are to be believed, however, in the large majority of cases in antiquity it was indeed only men who served as witnesses.²⁴ The practice of restricting this to men, then, began in custom, which led to the Rabbis' interpretation of the Torah in conformity with this custom, which, in turn, extended the rule to Jewish communities over the centuries. This is Solomon Schechter's doctrine of "Catholic Israel" at its clearest and most compelling.

One important factor that undoubtedly led to this custom was that women were not educated. Now that they are, however, rabbis have sought ways to reverse this restriction. Rabbi Ben Zion Bergman, for example, suggested in a 1987 article that the traditional restriction of testimony to men was not based on a blanket devaluation of women, but rather on two specific factors that would undermine the accuracy of a woman's testimony: Women's lack of experience in the world at large would taint their understanding and memory of events, and women's financial dependence on their fathers or husbands would make them susceptible to undue influence by the men in their family in recalling or describing events. Rabbi Bergman then suggests that since these factors no longer apply to the women of contemporary times, the restriction on women's testimony should be reversed.²⁵ In the discussion that same year about ordaining women, Rabbis Joel Roth and Meir Rabinowitz argued in similar ways. Even these rabbis who advanced such arguments, though, differed on the extent to which we can rely on them to overturn longstanding practice, as the conclusions of Rabbis Bergman, Rabinowitz, and Roth demonstrate.²⁶

That is also true for the responsa that were ultimately presented to the CJLS on this issue in 2001. Rabbi Myron Geller argued to authorize women as witnesses on all documents. Rabbi Susan Grossman in principle accepts Rabbi Geller's conclusion that women are *legally* eligible to serve as witnesses in all ways that men are. but she worried that couples (and especially women) might suffer if their writ of divorce were signed by a woman and therefore not recognized as valid by Orthodox and some Conservative rabbis. She therefore delegates the question of using women as witnesses in divorce procedures to the Joint Bet Din as a matter of its internal *policy*. Rabbi Aaron Mackler, concerned with the same issue, instead invokes the medical model of informed consent, where patients must be competent to understand the possible outcomes of a medical procedure for their agreement to undergo it to be morally and legally valid. Even then, there are times when a physician must not acquiesce to a patient's informed wishes. For marriage (*ketubbot* and *kiddushin*) and conversion (*giyyur*), women should serve as witnesses only with the informed consent of the individual(s) directly affected and following a prudential judgment by the rabbi that the involvement of women witnesses would not impose undue risks in the particular case. Because of practical concerns for the well-being of individuals and of *klal Yisra'el* (the Jewish community), however, Rabbi Mackler ruled that women should not at the present time serve as witnesses for *gittin* (writs of divorce).[27]

Notice that in approving both Rabbi Geller's and Rabbi Grossman's responsa (but not Rabbi Mackler's), the CJLS indicated that these are valid differences in judgment and that local rabbis had to evaluate the arguments and their own particular situation in deciding which one to use. Thus here again the role of the local rabbi (*mara d'atra*) and the sensitivities and customs of his or her community are critical in determining the norms for the community. Moreover, the responsa themselves grew out of the customs and laws of Western countries authorizing women to be witnesses in civil law and the increasingly common customs of rabbis to allow women to serve as witnesses on Jewish documents (especially of marriage) as well. It is therefore important to note that, contrary to the claim that legal formalists might make, even before the responsa of Rabbis Geller and Grossman were formally approved by the CJLS, those rabbis who permitted women to serve as witnesses were *not* engaged in acts of civil disobedience or, worse, an abandonment of the law. It was, instead, a use of one of the sources of the law—namely, custom—to lead the way. This source may not have the advantages of law delineated earlier in the chapter, but it has reciprocal advantages, as also described earlier. Moreover, custom is an historically authentic source of law and, in this case, the very one that produced the law on witnesses in the first place. It thus seems to me to be absolutely fitting that the law that limited witnessing to males, a law generated originally by custom, should ultimately be changed legally as a result of the impetus of new customs.

Implications for Our Own Day

This sets the stage for my recommendations about how we should treat the status of women now. All in all, we find a veritable patchwork of practices in regard to women within traditional Jewish law and within current Jewish practice among both Conservative and Orthodox Jews. Some Conservative rabbis and laypeople advocate that we as a movement become egalitarian by fiat, enacting a *takkanah* to make women fully equal to men in all privileges and obligations of Jewish law. On the other end of the spectrum, others regret the extent to which Conservative decisions on these matters have already gone, claiming that Conservative Judaism has lost its claim to legitimacy as a halakhic movement by taking steps to enfranchise women without careful and closely reasoned rabbinic rulings justifying such action. Such people often feel downright attacked by any step to equalize women's status. In the meantime, some people have left the movement, most because we Conservative Jews have moved too slowly and too narrowly on these issues and some because we have moved too far and too fast.

I would suggest that we need new ways of speaking about these matters. We have sought warrant in the codes and responsa for equality for women. This has sometimes led to forced readings of texts and to conclusions that either ignore or distort what happened in Jewish communities historically and what motivates us today to act differently.

Some who have acknowledged this have advocated instituting a *takkanah,* once and for all making women equal to men in all matters of Jewish law. There is even some precedent for that in the *takkanah* enacted by the chief rabbinate of the Jewish community in Israel in 1943 that made daughters inherit equally with sons. Even without that specific ruling, Jewish legal history offers us the vehicle of *takkanah* to make significant changes that cannot be made through less disruptive techniques.[28]

Until recently, I too thought that we should enact a *takkanah* to equalize the status of women and men in Jewish law. However, I am faced with the fact that more than a few women object to wearing tefillin because it seems to them to be a man's garment. More broadly, I have come to recognize that we all must take more seriously the clear unwillingness of some of our most observant women to take on the responsibilities of Jewish law from which they are traditionally exempt. More broadly still, we dare not just brush aside as antiquarian or reactionary the feelings of those men and women within our movement who object to the changes that egalitarianism has brought.

Even that, though, may be much too intellectual a statement of the issue. Many of the problems in defining new liturgical and legal roles for women emerge from the differing levels of tolerance we individually have for trying out new customs while maintaining meaning and a sense of continuity from the ones that shaped our past. Objections to new egalitarian practices on the part of religiously committed Jews of both genders make even more sense when we remember that Jewish laws differentiating women from men are rooted in the customs of the times in which they were formulated in the first place; therefore, they are not open to change through rational, legal analysis alone but must rather be replaced, if at all, by new customs. These may seem strange at first but gradually become acceptable and eventually even cherished.

Consequently, we should certainly probe legal sources to discover what our ancestors actually did in these matters, and we should also apply legal methods to making women equal to men in Jewish law. At the same time, the real foundation for the laws that have come down to us on the roles of women is custom, and therefore, the generating force for changing those laws will also be custom. This would suggest a four-pronged approach:

1. Some customs have led to laws that indisputably harm women. These include legal institutions that chain a woman in Jewish law to a man to whom she has already been civilly divorced and the exclusion of women from Jewish education. These we must annul altogether—and the Conservative movement has already done so.[29] We should similarly declare both morally reprehensible and legally null and void the kind of extortion now going on in part of the Orthodox world in Israel, in which fathers marry off their minor daughters to men they refuse to identify as a ploy to force their wives either to stay with them in marriage or to give them money or custody rights

in divorce. In these and other cases in which the harm to women engendered by Jewish law is undisputed, we have already begun to do, and should continue to do, what we must to rid ourselves of such bad customs.

2. Most of the customs that have come down to us are appreciated by some and opposed by others. In such cases, I argue for tolerance on all sides. That is, we should allow a diversity of customs to take hold and develop as they may. This requires tolerance, but such diversity is in the very nature of custom. Thus, even though I myself am egalitarian in these matters, I would plead with my fellow egalitarians to respect the will of some synagogues to restrict some roles to men—and perhaps others to women. Conversely, those who wish to maintain the traditional role differentiation in services should recognize the foundation these matters have in custom, even those that ultimately found their way into codes or responsa. Consequently, in our own day, citing a text to justify exclusion of women from a given role will generally not suffice. We will instead need to confront the custom head-on, evaluating it in terms of its role in *our* community *now.*

This will not always be easy. In 1984, I wrote an article for the University of Judaism's University Papers series in which I suggested that the proper stance was "equal but distinct."[30] I wanted to recognize men and women as equal in their legal status and in their theological status as created in the divine image, but I also wanted to have our rituals express the fact that men and women differ from one another in important ways linked to their respective genders. Some of these differences, of course, are socially influenced (if not determined), and then one must ask whether such differentiations are justifiable or desirable. Increasingly, though, we have discovered that a number of the factors that differentiate men and women are biologically based, including the recent study based on functional magnetic resonance imaging (fMRI) of the brains of men and women as they respond to the same questions, an experiment that demonstrated that men and women think with different parts of their brains.[31] Indeed, as indicated by this and other studies carried out largely by women like Carol Gilligan, Deborah Tannen, and Nel Noddings,[32] men and women, as a result of both nature and nurture, are demonstrably different from each other in the way they think, talk, reason morally, and respond to life in general. Moreover, as it has become politically acceptable to acknowledge these distinctions,

263

men and women have dared to explore the meaning of their engendered states of being—as well as, and in no denigration of, their common humanity and, in our case, their common Jewish identity.

I, then, repeat the suggestion that I made at that time, but now with much more evidence. Jewish ritual life should incorporate many leadership roles that are open to both genders. On the other hand, there should be some elements of worship and rituals specific to women and others that are restricted to men. This would acknowledge in graphic, ritual terms that we are at once equal and different. If the slogan "separate but equal" had not gotten such bad press in American history because of its abuse in justifying situations that were definitely not equal, I might use that to summarize my position. Perhaps the phrase "equality with distinction"—or, as Rabbi Ben Zion Bergman suggested to me, "equal but *vive la différence!*—captures the position better while simultaneously avoiding negative associations.

My favorite example to justify this position is, appropriately, one that is based on custom. By law, both men and women are obligated to light Sabbath candles and to recite *Kiddush* on Friday nights.[33] When Jews of both genders are not present, people of only one gender are supposed to do both things. When Jews of both genders are in attendance, however, general custom has it that women light candles and men recite *Kiddush*. The distinction retains equality because family members pay roughly the same amount of attention to both.[34] When they do not, the factors that lead them to pay more attention to the one or the other vary according to the family custom, the age of the children, and so on. This can serve as a good example of how customs can emerge or even consciously be created to enable us to be equal but different in our religious lives as Jews.

Note that in this example, the choice of which would normally be done by men and which by women was not determined by anything inherently male in saying *Kiddush* in the home or anything inherently female in lighting candles there. The choice evolved as common practice; but, from a rational or even a symbolic point of view, it was largely arbitrary. That, too, is a factor to understand as we make our way into the new customs that are evolving. Although we should certainly seek to differentiate the roles of men and women in meaningful, symbolic ways if we can, that will not always be possible. In such circumstances, we may choose to let men and women

serve on an equal basis. In some cases, though, we may decide to differentiate their roles arbitrarily. So, for example, individual congregations might designate one Shabbat a month in which only women
serve as cantors, another Shabbat in which only men do, with the
remaining Sabbaths open to both genders. I would personally opt for
leaving this open to both genders at all times on a totally random
basis, but if designating specific Sabbaths each month were the practice in my synagogue, I would probably not only get used to it but
actually eventually prize it as a way of distinguishing men and
women without impugning their equality. Alternatively, a synagogue
might designate one Sabbath a month in which there would be, at
least as an option, separate minyanim for men and women to accomplish the same purpose.

3. Along with this toleration of varying degrees of adaptation of the
customs of our past, I hope that we develop new customs that
express both the equality and the distinctiveness of the genders. We
have already begun, whether intentionally or not, to do this. This is
especially evident in our emerging life-cycle rites.

Parents justifiably feel that their joy is no less for having a girl
than a boy, and the community's joy ought not be any less either.
Traditionally, the birth of a girl is marked by an aliyah for the father
(and now often the mother), accompanied by a blessing for the
mother's health and naming the newborn girl. Even if these ceremonies are done nicely and even if a festive *kiddush* is held in cele-
bration of the newborn afterward, modern couples have increasingly felt that these rites are not enough. They have consequently created new ceremonies that often take place at their home, just as a
boy's *brit milah* (ritual circumcision) usually does. Sometimes the
ceremony is called *brit banot,* "the covenant of the daughters," thereby emphasizing the parallelism between the new ceremonies for
girls with the traditional one for boys. Sometimes it is called *simhat
bat,* "the joy of a daughter," thereby indicating the differences
between this rite and the one for boys. Under either title, the ceremony itself may incorporate some of the same elements and language as the one for boys and may even be scheduled for the eighth
day after birth as a boy's circumcision would be, or it may veer
markedly from the ritual for boys. The point is that both the equal
significance and the distinctiveness of having a girl are being sym-
bolized by these new ceremonies.

Similar experimentation is happening with bat mitzvah ceremonies—again, some emphasizing the sameness of the event
marked by a bar mitzvah for boys and some stressing the differences.
Weddings are increasingly involving both bride and groom in more
active roles, both in planning the rite and in participating in it. So,
for example, if the groom is going to be called to the Torah in honor
of his forthcoming wedding in the synagogue in which he grew up
(his *aufruf*), the bride should be likewise called up for that honor in
her home synagogue, assuming that her synagogue calls women to
the Torah. In each case, if the person having the *aufruf* normally
gives a homily (*devar Torah*) as well, that should be true for both the
bride and the groom. Alternatively, at the wedding itself the groom
might give a word of Torah in advance of the ceremony (the *hassan's
tisch*, "the groom's table"), and the bride might do so as well (a *kallah's
tisch*, a "bride's table"). Similarly, if the bride follows the custom of
walking around the groom, the groom might then walk around his
bride (usually three times each)—and then, for the seventh circuit,
both together might walk around the wedding canopy that symbol-
izes their new home. My own children did all these things when they
were married.

Jewish rites of death and mourning are already quite egalitarian,
in that there is only one thing we do for men that we do not do for
women—namely, we traditionally bury a man's cut tallit (prayer
shawl) with him. Perhaps some ritual object connected with the
deceased woman could be buried with her, such as the head covering or the candlesticks she used for lighting Sabbath candles or her
tallit, if she wore one in life. That men prepare a man's body for bur-
ial and women prepare a woman's is not only important for reasons
of modesty but also to symbolize the embodied and engendered
nature of the deceased. The genders are equal but different even in
death. I would also encourage women to say *Kaddish* during the year
after a parent's death; a daughter's relationship with her parents may
be different from a son's, but it is no less close, and the law demands
honor of parents from daughters just as much as it does from sons.[35]

Although all of the ferment in our time about the changing definitions of male and female roles has clearly generated much anxiety
and even social upheaval, one distinctly positive result has been that
both men and women are thinking much more carefully about
Jewish law and practice. Rabbis working with families in prepar-
ing for a life cycle ceremony should take advantage of this new

consciousness. In addition to explaining the traditional rituals and their meanings, rabbis should point out that some families in our time are adding to those rituals or doing them in new ways. As Conservative Jews, we insist that those elements of the ceremonies that are now legally required be done, even if they were originally based in custom, but we should at least inform families of the possibility of using some of the new rituals that have been developed to accompany the traditional ones—and of creating new rituals of their own.[36] Some families may not want to take an active role in shaping the rituals of their life-cycle event, but others will, and all will minimally learn that these rituals are intended to express both what the Jewish tradition and what they themselves feel and hope for on this day. Some of the new rituals will, of course, succeed wonderfully, and some will fall flat; that is the nature of creativity. Ultimately, we will all be the richer as new customs emerge for us to use.

4. Finally, cognizant as I am of the continual interaction between law and custom, I would urge that we continue to probe our legal sources for legitimation of our new practices, but only where it is honest to the historical context of the sources as well as their language. I am, after all, deeply interested in the continuity, the authority, and the sense of roots that grounding our practices in legal sources can supply. Where history must be ignored, though, or even where the practice in question was only practiced by a small minority of Jews in the past, I would prefer that we candidly assert that we are creating new practices in response to our new egalitarian sensitivities. In doing so, we should call attention to the factors that differentiate our age from times past in these matters—especially the new Jewish and general educational opportunities open to women—to explain our deviation from previous practices. We should also point out, as I have maintained in this chapter, that many of the practices and laws of the past were themselves based on the customs of their times, that law and custom always influence each other, and that in our day as well the law must catch up to the new customs emerging in our communities.

At this time, though, we should *not* institute an amendment (*takkanah*) totally equalizing the status of the two genders. That should happen only in some future time, if ever, for it would be justified only if and when the customs of our community have totally, or at least overwhelmingly, become egalitarian. Delaying the institution of such an amendment will enable people of both genders to have some time to get used to women donning tefillin, for example, without prejudging the case from the outset to say that they must. We need to feel our way gradually into our new understandings of what it means to be a man or woman and how we are going to express those meanings in ritual and legal forms, and we must do this with mutual respect for both those of us who want to go slowly in this process and those of us who want to proceed more quickly.

Finally, it is important to note that the move toward more egalitarianism in modern customs is not just a function of the more egalitarian society in which we now live or even the increased economic resources that have allowed families to provide extended schooling for both their sons and their daughters. These developments in contemporary Jewish life emerge at least as much from the Jewish tradition itself. Although the customs and even some of the laws of the past clearly differentiated men from women, the core commitments of the Jewish tradition—"to do justice, to love kindness, and to walk modestly with your God" (Mic. 6:8)—make no such distinction.

When Israel stood at Sinai, the Rabbis tell us, the Israelites heard God's voice according to their individual sensitivities and abilities.[37] This did not preclude our tradition from having laws that governed everyone, but it did establish the theological basis for a diversity of practice among our ancestors, at least within certain bounds. These practices sometimes served as the source of the law, as they did in regard to most matters concerning the legal distinctions between men and women. In our own day, we must let custom evolve and determine these matters as it did in times past.[38]

ENDNOTES

1. For a more thorough discussion of the functioning of custom in Jewish law, see Dorff and Rosett, *A Living Tree,* pp. 421–434.
2. M. Bava Meẓia 7:1.
3. Uniform Commercial Code, §§1–205; reprinted in Dorff and Rosett, *A Living Tree,* p. 434.
4. B. Bava Meẓia 74a. I would like to thank Rabbi Ben Zion Bergman for pointing out this parallel to me.
5. See also M. Yevamot 14:1; B. Yevamot 112b; B. Gittin 49b; M.T. Laws of Divorce 1:1–2; S.A. Even ha-Ezer 120:1; cf. the commentary of Be'er Ha-golah there and 134:1–3.

6. See also Mekhilta, Nezikin 6 on Exod. 21:18; M. Bava Kamma 8:4; M.T. Laws of Injury and Damage 4:21; S.A. Hoshen Mishpat 424:9.

7. See also Sifrei Devarim, par. 157 (ed. Finkelstein), p. 208. Cf. B. Berakhot 49a; M.T. Laws of Kings 1:5.

8. On Deborah: Judg., 4–5. Shelomziyyon was the wife of Aristobulus I and Alexander Yanai, on whose death she alone ruled the Hasmonean kingdom during the years 76–67 B.C.E. See Gafni, "Salome Alexandra."

9. B. Megillah 23a. Cf. M.T. Laws of Prayer 12:17; Tur, S.A. Oraḥ Ḥayyim 282:3, which follow that version of the Beraita. Note that T. Megillah 3:5 does not mention the honor of the community but rather says two separate and, apparently, contradictory things: (1) "Anyone may ascend for the seven honors, even a minor, even a woman; (2) One may not appoint (literally, bring) a woman to read in public." Maimonides, as is his style, tries to iron out the inconsistency; he says: "A woman may not read in public because of the honor of the community. A minor who can read and knows to Whom prayer is addressed may ascend." Alfas (1013–1103), the Tur (Jacob ben Asher, died before 1340), and the Shulḥan Arukh (Yosef Karo, 1488–1575), however, retain the inconsistency in the original sources. Isserles, following the Ran and the Rivash, says, "They may be counted among the number of seven, but all of them may not be women or minors."

10. Even Rabbi Aaron Blumenthal, who in 1955 wrote a responsum to permit women to be called to the Torah, admits that "[t]here is no recorded instance of a woman called to the Torah either in the Talmud or in the Gaonic literature. However, there is a medieval decision which *seems* to be practical halachah" (emphasis added). He then cites a responsum of Rabbi Meir of Rothenburg (1220–1293), who says this: "In a city whose men are all Kohanim and there is not even one Israelite among them, it *seems* to me that one Kohen takes the first two *aliyot* and then women are to be called, for, 'All may ascend' " (emphasis added). This is hardly, though, a clear indication of an actual case or of accepted practice. Rabbi Meir's very words indicates that he is thinking through a logical conundrum in the law rather than recording what his community actually did (Blumenthal, "An Aliyah for Women," p. 275 [(in Siegel]).

11. Although the Talmud attests that in the Temple there was a separate section for women (B. Yoma 16a, 69b; B. Sukkah 51a–51b; B. Sotah 40b–41b; B. Zevaḥim 116b; B. Hagigah 16b), it is clear that both men and women were together there except for the Water-Drawing Festival on Sukkot, when a special balcony was constructed to separate the sexes because of the frivolity accompanying these ceremonies (M. Middot 2:5; T. Sukkah 4:1; B. Sukkah 51b–52a; J. Sukkah 5:2 [55b]). Furthermore, several sources indicate that women entered the sacred precincts outside the "women's section" whenever they brought sacrifices (M. Kritot 1:7; M. Qunim 1:4; M. Bikkurim 1:5; Sifra, Tazria 4 (ed. Weiss, p. 59b); T. Arakhin 2:1). The absence of any

mention of separating women in synagogue worship in talmudic literature and the fact that the majority of synagogues that have been excavated had only one prayer room both suggest that men and women sat together in ancient synagogues in both Israel and Babylonia. See Levine, *The Ancient Synagogue,* pp. 475–477. By the Middle Ages, however, the custom of separating men and women in services was clearly established.

12. B. Kiddushin 34a: The principle is stated in M. Kiddushin 1:7, and the talmudic discussion extends over several pages in B. Kiddushin 33b–36a. Rachel Biale suggests that the general rule that accurately characterizes the division between what women were required to do and what they were not is the home–community distinction—namely, that women were required to do everything that takes place in the home but not that which takes place in the community because the place of the woman was construed to be at home (Biale, *Women and Jewish Law,* p. 177).

13. In the Bible, Abraham, Jacob, and a number of kings have more than one wife. The Talmud permits a man to marry more than one wife, provided that he fulfills all of his obligations, including his sexual ones, to each wife: B. Yevamot 44a (where the recommended maximum is four!); B. Kiddushin 7a. Here again, though, there was apparently a discrepancy between what the law allowed and what custom dictated, for there is no case recorded in the Talmud of a rabbi or a plaintiff in a case who had more than one wife. See Biale, *Women and Jewish Law,* pp. 49–51.

14. See n. 10 regarding one such possible role—namely, being called to the Torah.

15. M. Megillah 4:3 and M.T. Laws of Prayer 8:4 both mention only a requirement for "10." See, however, S.A. Oraḥ Ḥayyim 55:1, 4, which specifies that males are required and that a woman may not count when there are fewer than 10 men.

16. Mordecai on B. Berakhot, n. 173. Rabbi Philip Sigal seems to put much weight on this text in justifying the counting of women for a prayer quorum, although he states other arguments as well (Sigal, "Women in a Prayer Quorum," esp. p. 287 and 292 n. 20 [in Siegel]).

17. Indeed, the few mentions of this in the archives of the Rabbinical Assembly specifically describe separate seating as a custom rather than a law and, therefore, leave it to the rabbi of each congregation to determine whether to maintain that traditional custom or whether to allow mixed seating: see Committee on Jewish Law and Standards, *Summary Index,* 13:27. The legal status of mixed seating was not discussed by the Committee on Jewish Law and Standards until the 1940s, after it had certainly become common practice in educational settings within the movement and even in worship in many synagogues. (There is some dispute about exactly how many. The committee report refers to "some," giving the impression that the vast majority did not have mixed seating at that time, but Rabbi Max Arzt,

in "Conservative Judaism as a Unifying Force," says, "In the course of a few decades such innovations as family pews and ceremonies of confirmation or Bas Mitzvah for girls have become the norm in most Conservative congregations and in many 'Orthodox' congregations" (p. 146 in Waxman). The influence of emerging attitudes toward women in general society is clear in the committee's report: "While the Committee realizes that the prevailing attitude about the place of woman in modern society is making it increasingly difficult to maintain the traditional policy of isolation towards women in the synagogue, nevertheless it feels lacking authority to repeal or even to declare obsolete this time-honored custom." Still, if the local rabbi felt the need to change the custom, he had authority to do so (B. Cohen, "Report of the Committee on Jewish Law," p. 1061). At that time, Rabbis Jacob Agus and David Aronson submitted responsa designed to permit mixed seating (Golinkin, *Proceedings of the Committee on Jewish Law and Standards of the Conservative Movement, 1927–1970*, pp. 1063–1079), but those responsa were not officially discussed by the committee.

18. Nadell, *Conservative Judaism in America*, p. 149.

19. The majority opinion by Rabbi Sanders Tofield ("Women's Place in the Rites of the Synagogue with Special Reference to the Aliyah") permitted women to have an aliyah only on special occasions, such as a Bat Mitzvah or on recovery from illness, and then only as additional *aliyot* to the usual number of the day (for example, after the seventh *aliyah* on Shabbat). The minority opinion by Rabbi David Blumenthal ("An Aliyah for Women"), however, permitted women to have *aliyot* on an equal basis with men, and by the rules of the CJLS at that time, individual rabbis were permitted to follow either the majority or minority opinion. The practice in many congregations since the 1980s has followed the minority decision at that time.

20. See Tucker, "Final Report of the Commission for the Study of the Ordination of Women as Rabbis."

21. There was a minority vote of the committee to allow women to be witnesses in 1974, but it was not rationalized by formal papers. See Committee on Jewish Law and Standards, *Summary Index*, p. 14:19. Rabbi Phillip Sigal, however, later wrote a paper to justify the ruling, a paper included in the records of the CJLS but not an official position of the CJLS. See Sigal, "Responsum on the Status of Women."

22. See the responsa by Rabbis Myron Geller and Susan Grossman on women as witnesses at www.rabbinicalassembly.org, under the link "Contemporary Halakhah." For a discussion of their varying approaches and that of Rabbi Mackler, see Dorff, *The Unfolding Tradition*, pp. 494–499.

23. See Chapter One, n. 40.

24. An important exception was the ability granted to a woman to testify to her divorce or to the death of her husband so that she could remarry; cf. M.T. Laws of Divorce 12:1,15–16.

25. Bergman, "A Conservative Approach to Halakhah," p. 52. In support of his thesis, he points out that Maimonides explains why we *do* accept the testimony of women when they claim that their husbands divorced them or died because ultimately we can determine whether she lied or not (M.T. Laws of Divorce 13:29; 13:24 in some editions). This suggests that the reason women were ineligible to testify in all other cases is not because they were suspected of being incorrigible liars but rather because, given the circumstances under which they lived, they could not be trusted to give *accurate* testimony.

26. Compare, for example, the opinions of Rabbis Mayer Rabinowitz and Joel Roth on this. Rabbi Roth clearly wants to permit women to be witnesses, and he suggests several ways to justify doing so; but he worries about the effects on the rest of the Jewish community of doing so. Rabbi Rabinowitz, on the other hand, says categorically that "we must reclassify the status of women vis-a-vis *edut* [testimony] based upon the realities of our era." See Rabinowitz, "On the Ordination of Women," pp. 117 and 119, and Joel Roth, "On the Ordination of Women as Rabbis," pp. 149 and 162.

27. See note 22 above.

28. For both a reference to that *takkanah* of the chief rabbinate and for a more general discussion of the role of *takkanot* in Jewish legal development, see Elon, "Takkanah," esp. p. 727, and "Takkanot Ha-Kahal."

29. Making girls and women eligible for the same educational opportunities with the same curriculum as boys and men has been the practice of the institutions within the Conservative movement from its very inception—with the notable exception, until 1983, of the rabbinical and cantorial schools. The Rabbinical Assembly's amendments of the *ketubbah,* its prenupial document of condition (*tenai be-kiddushin*), and, if all else fails, its willingness to annul a marriage retroactively (*hafka'at kiddushin*) have together freed many women from remaining chained to their former husbands. For a description of those measures, see Dorff and Rosett, *A Living Tree,* pp. 523–546.

30. Dorff, " 'Male and Female God Created Them.' "

31. See, for example, Gur et. al., "An fMRI Study of Sex Differences in Regional Activation to a Verbal and Special Task." In a 2004 meta-analysis of functional imaging studies, however, Sommer and her colleagues concluded that there was "no significant difference in language lateralization between men and women"; see I. Sommer, et al., "Do Women Really Have More Bilateral Language Representation than Men?" Responses to that study, however, indicate that whether there are differences between men and women in language acquisition and usage may well depend on the task: single-word-based tasks indicate no difference between the sexes, but listening to stories is handled differently by the two genders. See Kitazawa, "Sex Difference in Language Lateralization May Be Task-Dependent."

32. Gilligan, *In a Different Voice;* Noddings, *Caring;* and Tannen, *You Just Don't Understand.*

33. B. Berakhot 20b; B. Shabbat 31b; M.T. Laws of Idolatry 12:3; M.T. Laws of the Sabbath 5:3; S.A. Oraḥ Ḥayyim 263:2, 3; 271:2.

34. I recognize that, as the Rabbis interpreted them, *Kiddush* is a biblical requirement and lighting candles is rabbinic, but many people do not know that; and, in any case, people gathered at the table on Friday nights rarely feel this difference. Furthermore, the Rabbis themselves declare that the blessing over the candles should bless God "who has commanded us through His commandments and ordained that we should light the candle of Shabbat" because the Torah tells us to follow the rabbis' decrees (Deut. 17:10–11), thus rooting the lighting of candles in the Torah itself (B. Shabbat 23a; B. Sukkah 46a).

35. B. Kiddushin 30b (the Talmud's interpretation of M. Kiddushin 1:7) to require honor of parents by both sons and daughters. For more on filial and parental duties as delineated by Jewish law and tradition, see Dorff, *Love Your Neighbor and Yourself,* chap. 4.

36. *Lifecycles,* edited by Rabbi Debra Orenstein, presents a rich treasury of new ideas to express women's life passages and personal milestones in meaningful, but distinctly Jewish, ways. A similar book needs to be written for men!

37. Exodus Rabbah 5:9; 29:1; Pesikta de-Rav Kahana, Bahodesh ha-Shelishi on Exod. 20:2 (ed. Mandelbaum, p. 1:224).

PART IV

Explaining My Theory through Comparisons and Applications

CHAPTER EIGHT

Comparisons to the Right and the Left

Defining a term or concept involves describing what is included within the term in question as well as what is outside its limits. The Latin root of the word "define" literally means the setting of limits or boundaries (*finis*) around the thing being defined. (The same is true for the Hebrew word for "define," "*le-hagdir*," which literally means to put a fence [*geder*] around the thing being defined.) In this chapter, then, I shall briefly point out how my theory is similar to, but still differs from, other theories, especially those closely related to mine on both the right and the left. In the next chapter, I shall illustrate some of the practical implications of my theory of law, for that too helps explain its convictions and its import.

Before I explore the sample theories to my right and left, I would like to mention that my theory shares much in its basic convictions and/or its practical results with a number of theories written by others. Specifically, my theory, in whole or in part, has much in common with those of Solomon Schechter, Robert Gordis, Abraham Heschel, and Louis Jacobs. It is informed also by, but somewhat different from, the work of Mordecai Kaplan and Jacob Agus. Because I have discussed these theories at some length in my book *The Unfolding Tradition* and because the present book is, after all, about *my* theory and not theirs, I will not repeat that material here. Still, despite the similarities between my theory and those mentioned, I have written this book in the belief that my theory of Jewish law is distinct from others in its presentation, focus, depth on some topics and breadth on others, context, and/or practical implications. My discussion of the aspects of Jewish law that resemble a body (Chapter Two) is altogether lacking in theirs, and my description of the relationship of Jewish law to morality and custom (Chapters Six and Seven) is, in all modesty, both more extensive and deeper than theirs (except perhaps for that of Jacobs). If space allowed, I would explain and justify that claim further, but I will leave it to the reader to make those comparisons, perhaps with the help of the descriptions in *The Unfolding Tradition.*

A THEORY SLIGHTLY TO MY RIGHT: DAVID HARTMAN

Some 20 years ago I served as a respondent to Rabbi David Hartman when he was discussing his theory of law as presented in his book *A Living Covenant: The Innovative Spirit in Traditional Judaism.* I said then, and believe now, that his theory of Jewish law fits much better within Conservative Judaism than within Orthodoxy. He shrugged his shoulders, smiled, and called on the next questioner!

As the very title of Hartman's book announces, he puts great emphasis on the covenant theme as central to his understanding of Jewish law. As his subtitle indicates, he understands the covenant to be a living one, based on the ongoing relationship between God and the People Israel that is more like a marriage than the vassal treaties with kings on which the biblical covenant is historically based. This provides ample room for innovation by both parties in the content of its demands, including especially changes based on moral concerns. But the covenant does definitely demand many things of Jews, and so the language of commandment (mitzvah) is central to the relationship between God and the People Israel. Furthermore, he is not willing to limit the commandments to moral ones, as the early Reform movement did; the ritual commandments are important to "structure Judaic particularity and provide a vivid framework for expressing the community's particular passion for its God. . . . Through them the community builds familial solidarity grounded in a common memory and destiny. . . . They complement and absorb the ethical."[1] Although Jewish law is one good way to be ethical, Rabbi Hartman insists that it is not the only way and that Jews should not see Judaism as superior to other faiths or to secularists' morals. In all these ways, he and I are in agreement.

What, then, distinguishes us? In part, it is what he does not discuss but that I do. He says, "My book does not attempt to work out the way in which ethics can control halakhic development, nor does it try to establish the limits of tolerance and pluralism."[2] I explicitly try to do both of these things in Chapters Three, Six, and Seven herein. He also does not discuss the aspects of Jewish law that resemble a body, as I do in Chapter Two.

Beyond that, it is probably the case that he would not be prepared to hold some of the practical conclusions I have drawn in my rabbinic rulings on the basis of my theory. This, I think, is more a matter of our personal backgrounds and the communities in which we live than it is a dispute in theory.

Indeed, my suspicion is that since we share so much in our general approach to Jewish law, it is precisely elements of our personal biographies that lead us to different emphases and sometimes to different conclusions. This may disturb philosophers, for it indicates the limits of intellectual distinctions to describe all of reality, but it correctly exemplifies that people who hold theories are individuals, after all, and are influenced not only by their thoughts but also by their histories, emotions, and—perhaps especially—their associations.

A THEORY TO MY LEFT: EUGENE BOROWITZ

Some time after Rabbi Eugene Borowitz's book *Renewing the Covenant: A Theology for the Postmodern Jew* came out, I was asked to write a review for the journal *Conservative Judaism*.[3] In that article, I described the real innovation Rabbi Borowitz had made in Reform thought—namely, to say that for a Jew to exercise autonomy responsibly in choosing a form of Judaism, he or she must be a "Jewish self" and not just a "self." That is, Jews need to learn and experience their tradition and be aware of their ties to Jews of the past, present, and future as well as their individual instantiation of the Jewish covenant with God before they can appropriately and responsibly choose which parts of Jewish law to practice in their lives. At the same time, this emphasis on individual autonomy, I said, marked his theory as distinctly Reform and not Conservative. Rabbi Borowitz, a good friend and sparring partner, then wrote an open letter to me in the pages of a subsequent issue of *Conservative Judaism,* claiming that I had misunderstood his intentions, that he was not writing as a Reform spokesman but as an individual who had a particular theory of law, and that, moreover, his theory was very similar to my own![4] He pointed to some of the conclusions I had reached in my rabbinic rulings and my own theoretical commitment to the covenant between God and the People Israel.

I, in turn, responded to him; and we both regard the exchange as a wonderful example of how friends and colleagues can respectfully—and, we hope, insightfully—disagree.[5] In the end, I do not think that most individual Jews can possibly be expected to know enough to make the informed and honed decisions that Rabbi Borowitz demands of them; indeed, in his open letter to me, the individuals he mentions as carrying out these tasks were rabbinical students. Furthermore, I maintain that Jewish law, to be identifiably Jewish, must be framed not by individuals but rather by rabbis acting on the basis of their communal authority garnered through their ordination and their appointment to lead a community. To be sure, rabbis must interact with their communities and learn what will be acceptable and what not, for, as indicated in the chapters herein, the Talmud insists that "one must not decree a decree on a community that most cannot tolerate" and that "just as it is a commandment to speak about things that will be heard, so it is a commandment not to speak about things that will not be heard."[6] Still, ultimately, it must be rabbis who make these decisions and not individuals if we are ever to have anything identifiable as Jewish law. Finally, I believe that Jewish law is authoritative for all Jews for all the reasons I discuss in Chapter Four; Rabbi Borowitz encourages Jews to learn about Jewish law and to practice those parts of it that express their personal covenant with God and with the Jewish people, but whether to act according to Jewish law at all and, if so, how are ultimately the free choice of each individual Jew.

Although more can certainly be said in comparing the theories of Hartman and Borowitz to mine, I hope this is enough to illustrate some of the significant factors in both theory and social setting that distinguish our approaches to Jewish law. In addition, comparing my theory as I have just briefly done to two others nearby will further illustrate the convictions that ground my theory and the audience most likely to embrace it. I encourage the reader to compare my ideas to those further away, perhaps with the aid of what I have written in *The Unfolding Tradition* about a number of other theories, thus shedding yet more light on the fundamental underpinnings of my theory and on how it is unique.

ENDNOTES

1. Hartman, *A Living Covenant,* p. 96.
2. Ibid., p. 18.
3. Dorff, "Autonomy v. Community."
4. Borowitz, "The Reform Judaism of *Renewing the Covenant.*"
5. Dorff, "Matters of Degree and Kind."
6. On not to decree a decree that the majority cannot tolerate: B. Bava Batra 60b; B. Avodah Zarah 36a; B. Horayot 3b. On not to say something that will not be heard: B. Yevamot 65b; S.A. Oraḥ Ḥayyim 608:2, gloss. This latter principle is also in evidence in the oft-repeated rule that "It is better that the Children of Israel violate the law in error rather than purposely" (B. Shabbat 148b; B. Beẓah 30a; B. Bava Batra 60b; J. Eruvin 4a; M.T. Shevitat Asor 1:7; S.A. Yoreh De'ah 293:3, gloss), leading to the conclusion that rabbis should not protest a violation (even of the Torah) when their admonitions will not be heeded.

CHAPTER NINE

Applications of My Theory of Jewish Law to Specific Cases

The proof of the pudding is in the eating. Theories of law are not only intellectually interesting but also have practical import. As described in Chapter One, theories of law are based on specific views of human nature and human societies, the ideals toward which they should strive, and the role of law in the lives of individuals and communities. This broad picture affects how one understands the nature of the law (Chapters Two and Three) and the motivations to follow it (Chapter Four), continuity and change within the law (Chapter Five), and the roles of morality and custom in shaping its content (Chapters Six and Seven).

It is not surprising that one's underlying convictions on these matters also affect how one treats specific legal issues. In this chapter, I will illustrate how some of my own Jewish legal rulings grow out of my theory.

MY OWN EXPERIENCE IN MAKING JEWISH LEGAL DECISIONS

How do I get questions in the first place? Often they come from my students and then, like rabbis of congregations, I might answer them immediately or I might check some texts before answering. Sometimes I might consult with other rabbis who are known to have greater expertise than I do in the particular area of Jewish law in question, and sometimes other rabbis ask me about cases within the areas of Jewish law that I know well, both through text study and experience. (This is very much like American lawyers consulting with other lawyers who specialize in a given area of the law.) Historically, consultations happened through the mail, by which the questioner and respondent traded letters; this is the vast responsa literature, or, in Hebrew, *she'elot u'teshuvot* (questions and answers). Today, the same thing happens over the telephone or by e-mail. Because I work extensively in bioethics, rabbis contact me often about particular cases involving issues at the beginning and end of life; and because I have done research and published on other areas of ethics, I often receive calls and e-mail about other moral problems as well. Sometimes rabbis ask me questions about the dietary laws or the Sabbath, but I would imagine that other rabbis in the movement get called about those topics more than I do.

My job description as a faculty member at the University of Judaism (now the American Jewish University) since 1971 does not include making legal decisions for the university. In other cases, however, I have acted as a rabbi. For instance, in 1972, the president of the university appointed me as the rabbi in residence for Camp Ramah in California. In that capacity, I have made many decisions for the camp in many different areas of Jewish law from 1972 to 1991, and I still act as the consultant for the camp in Jewish legal matters. In 1994, the new president of the university appointed me as rector for the University of Judaism, defined as rabbi of the university, and so I now officially interpret Jewish law for that institution.

In addition, since December 1984, I have been a member of the Conservative movement's Committee on Jewish Law and Standards (CJLS). In that capacity, I have written close to 20 responsa. Most were written in response to rabbis asking that the CJLS address an issue for the entire Conservative movement. Some were generated by the committee members themselves in an effort to give guidance to the movement on important issues. In addition, I have written two rabbinic letters, one on intimate relations and one on poverty. These were not formal responsa written for the CJLS but were approved by the committee as educational materials about Jewish law on those topics. In what follows, then, I will summarize some of those materials as illustrations of how I have applied my own theory of Jewish law to specific cases.[1]

HOW MY THEORY AFFECTED SOME OF MY LEGAL DECISIONS

Practical Issues

In this section, I discuss these responsa: "Changing Realities and Relationships: The Use of All Wines"[2] and "The Use of Synagogues by Christian Groups."[3] In the very first responsum that I wrote for the CJLS, on the use of all wines, I confronted two aspects of the problem—namely, the materials with which the wine was made, and the rabbinic prohibition of wine made by gentiles. As for the first, a survey I conducted of some large and small California winemakers made it clear that practices vary greatly among them, and sometimes even the same winemaker changes the method from one crop to another. For the purposes of fulfilling the dietary laws (kashrut), it is important to note that some makers fine (that is, clarify) their wines with substances that are clearly kosher and pareve (that is, neither dairy nor meat—for example, bentonite, which is an aluminum silicate, or egg albumin); others use dairy products, especially for white wines (such as casein and its compounds); others use beef blood, which is clearly not kosher (in Europe only, because of a federal ban on using that in the United States); and others use materials (such as animal gelatin and isinglass made from sturgeon bladders) that are considered kosher and pareve by most but not kosher by some. Part of the process of writing a modern ruling, then, is to determine the facts of the case as they are now, which in wines as well as many other foods is often substantially different from the processes of the past.

Responsa must also take account of the history of a phenomenon to decide how to apply previous precedents to current realities. In this case, it turns out that fining wines is a relatively new process, beginning with the French kings of the 18th century, who clarified their wines as a mark of nobility; before then, people, including rulers, preferred full-bodied wines, including the pulp of the grape and even the skins. The winemaker interested in clarifying wines to appeal to new tastes intentionally introduced into the wine the fining agents used at that time (largely animal blood for red wines

285

and milk for white wines). Therefore, one could presumably *not* apply the principle in talmudic law that if something drops accidentally into something else (for example, a drop of milk into a meat soup), it is legally nullified if it is less than 1 in 60 parts. The inability to invoke that principle means that the kosher status of the wine would depend on the fining agent used.

Precisely at the time when fine wines were first being made, however, Rabbi Yehezkel Landau (the Noda Be'yehudah, 1713–1793) wrote a responsum declaring that even though winemakers intentionally introduce the fining agent into the wine to clarify it, they do not intend that it remain in the wine but rather that it precipitate through the wine as it carries the impurities to the bottom. Therefore, if any of the fining agent were left in the wine, it would be against their will and could be legally nullified if it were less than a 60th in volume of the wine, which it always is. This would then make the identity and kosher status of the fining agent irrelevant; even beef blood would be nullified, and the wine it clarified would be kosher and pareve.

Although Rabbi Moshe Feinstein in the 20th century accepted Rabbi Landau's ruling, most authorities do not. I, therefore, concluded that although one could rely on Rabbi Landau's ruling to establish the kosher status of wine for one's personal drinking, especially after the fact, one should not do so for sacramental purposes (for example for *Kiddush* on Sabbaths and festivals) nor should it be used for communal events, where some may not accept the lenient ruling. In light of the fact that most authorities did not accept Rabbi Landau's reasoning, I encouraged even individuals buying wine for their own consumption to check with the winemaker as to what fining agent was used to determine its kashrut status and whether it is dairy or pareve—especially if they like a particular wine and drink it often.

Still, the creativity that Rabbi Landau demonstrated in transforming the talmudic principle is the mark of a living legal system, in which old parts of the body of the law (in this case, the principle of nullification) are pressed into service to accommodate new circumstances. Furthermore, distinguishing the different contexts to which a ruling should apply (personal use vs. sacramental use vs. communal use) is also a critical mark of a living legal system, for what fits one context does not necessarily fit another, just as running is appropriate in some places but not in others.

The other concern in traditional Jewish law stems from a rabbinic decree during the Hadrianic persecutions after 135 C.E. prohibiting Jews from drinking wine made or even touched by gentiles. The stated purposes of that decree were two: To keep Jews from participating in the idolatrous practices of non-Jews, which often involved wine, and to discourage socializing among non-Jews to the point of ultimately marrying one of them. In taking modern circumstances into account, I concluded that "unless we have specific evidence to the contrary, we can assume that the Gentiles who produce and serve wine in the Western world are not 'idolaters' in the halakhic [Jewish legal] sense of that term. Moreover, since the prohibition against the use of wine made by Gentiles is no longer an effective means for preventing intermarriage, . . . we shall let the prohibition fall into disuse without protest." A living body of law sloughs off laws and gains new ones, just as the body sloughs off cells each day and gains new ones. Especially when the old laws embody assumptions about the world that are no longer true, it is right and proper to let the old laws fall into disuse.

The same revised understanding of Christians motivated my responsum on the use of synagogues by Christian groups. In it I discuss how to maintain the holiness of Jewish sacred spaces and avoid certain interactions with the Christian renters that would encourage intermarriage, while at the same time making synagogue space available to Christian groups seeking to establish themselves. Many Jewish groups, of course, do the reverse, using the social hall of a church for their worship and activities until they have enough members and money to build their own synagogue. Aside from the fairness and good neighborliness of reciprocating to Christian groups in like circumstances, the motivation for this responsum was frankly the much improved relations that Jews and Christians have in our time, due in large measure to *Nostra Aetate,* the Second Vatican Council's statement on the Jews in 1965, subsequent Vatican statements that expand on that base, and parallel statements in a number of Protestant denominations. Changed relationships and the imperative to sanctify God through our actions (*kiddush ha-Shem*) should have an impact on both our theology of the other and our laws.

Moral and Social Issues

In this section, I discuss these responsa that illustrate the import of changing moral sensitivities: family violence[4] and homosexual relations.[5] If old laws actually cause harm to people, then sometimes one should not wait until they fall into disuse but rather consciously amputate them from the body of the law. Sometimes this can be done by preferring one stream of legal thought within Jewish law to another. That was the case in regard to the permission granted in traditional Jewish law to parents to beat their children. In my responsum on family violence, I repudiated this precedent. The fact that the CJLS voted unanimously for my responsum indicates that sometimes the moral sensitivities of the age both should and do change the law dramatically.

In Chapter Six, I discussed the responsum on homosexuality that I wrote with Rabbis Daniel Nevins and Avram Reisner. Suffice it to say here that it grew out of both our new scientific knowledge about the etiology of sexual orientation and the inability of therapists to change it as well as the new moral sensitivity many of us have acquired toward gays and lesbians, largely because a much higher percentage of homosexuals than previously are now out of the closet. It is legally grounded in the Talmud's authorization to rescind rabbinic legislation to protect the dignity of human beings (kevod ha-briyyot). One particularly important facet of this value for this issue is the tradition's recognition that "it is not good for a person to live alone."[6] Although it permits lesbian sex and all forms of gay male sex other than anal intercourse, it also requires gays and lesbians to live by the other moral norms that affect heterosexuals, norms articulated in the Rabbinical Assembly's "Rabbinic Letter on Human Intimacy" such as modesty, fidelity, respect, health and safety, and holiness and include as well the duty to have and raise Jewish children.[7] The ruling, though, permits rabbis to perform commitment ceremonies and seminaries to ordain gays and lesbians.

The Jewish tradition is the rabbinic tradition—that is, it is based on how the Rabbis defined which books got into Holy Scriptures and the way that they interpreted the meaning of those Scriptures. Thus, it is certainly not standard practice for rabbis to ignore, let alone set aside, rabbinic precedent. We nevertheless did so in this case because of the new scientific evidence we now have about sexual orientation and, even more so, because of the Jewish value of honoring our fellow human beings that calls us to treat gays and lesbians with the dignity owed them as people created in the divine image.

Our ruling does not require either rabbis considering whether to perform a commitment ceremony or seminaries considering admission of a gay candidate to inquire as to whether the gay men involved intend to engage in anal sex, any more than rabbis or admissions committees normally inquire as to whether couples about to be married or married candidates for admission to rabbinical school abide by the restrictions against sexual relations during the woman's menstrual period (Lev. 15:19ff., 18:19, 20:18); in fact, our ruling specifically forbids asking about such matters as a violation of the privacy and the honor with which we must treat all human beings (kevod ha-briyyot). If either a heterosexual or a homosexual couple about to be joined asks about the Jewish norms that should govern their sexual lives, however, then the rabbi involved should explain them. Here we are invoking the talmudic principle that "Just as it is a commandment to speak to people about what they will hear, it is also a commandment not to speak to people about what they will not hear."[8]

The Jewish concepts and values mentioned here all combined to prompt the three of us to take this admittedly radical legal step of negating rabbinic legislation on this issue while still retaining biblical law. On the other hand, the reality is that the members of our movement do not agree about this issue, and, as the Rabbis of the Talmud asserted, "We may not execute a decree on the community unless most of its members can tolerate it."[9] Thus a ruling that would either simply reaffirm the bans of the past or wipe them away altogether, while certainly neater and cleaner, would not reflect the reality of where the movement actually stands at this moment in time. What happened instead—13 members of the committee voted for Rabbi Roth's ruling and 13 for ours—accurately reflects where the Conservative movement stands on this issue. (The rabbi who voted for both ours and Rabbi Roth's specified that he did so because he wanted to uphold the pluralism of the movement and thought that precisely equal votes for both rulings dramatically expressed this.)

Where does that leave the movement? As is always the case when multiple opinions are validated, individual rabbis will now decide which of the options to adopt in their own practice. Similarly, each of the five seminaries associated with the movement—two in North America, one in Buenos Aires, one in Jerusalem, and one in Budapest—will decide whether to open their doors to gay and lesbian candidates who are otherwise qualified. The Ziegler School of Rabbinic Studies at the University of Judaism (now the American Jewish University) in Los Angeles and the Jewish Theological Seminary of

America in New York have announced that they are open to receiving applications from gay and lesbian candidates for ordination; the Schechter Institute in Jerusalem and the Seminario Rabbinico Latin Americano in Buenos Aires have announced that they will not.

Some people will undoubtedly leave the movement over this issue, and others will now join a Conservative synagogue because it no longer is unanimously opposed to commitment ceremonies for gays and lesbians. As of this writing, a few synagogues that formerly refused to be part of the United Synagogue of Conservative Judaism because of its stance on homosexuals have already applied to join the organization; my guess is that a few synagogues might leave over this issue as well. Even with this movement of individuals and synagogues in and out of the movement due to our responsum, my own view is that all the talk about the movement disintegrating over this issue is very much exaggerated and that we will, as we did over the women's issues of the previous generation, display our usual capacity to live and let live.

Applying Jewish Law to New Technology

In this section, I discuss these responsa: " A Jewish Approach to End-Stage Medical Care"[10]; "Assisted Suicide"[11]; "Artificial Insemination, Egg Donation, and Adoption"[12]; "The Mitzvah Child" (with Rabbi Kassel Abelson)[13]; "Stem Cell Research;"[14] "Responsibilities for the Provision of Health Care" (with Rabbi Aaron Mackler)[15]; and "Privacy on the Internet" (with Rabbi Elie Spitz).[16] That modern medical technology has absolutely revolutionized medical care in our lifetime is, overwhelmingly, a good thing, but our new abilities to create and sustain life mean that we now face moral questions that our ancestors could never have even contemplated, let alone resolved. The same is true for the internet, which immensely expands our ability to communicate but which simultaneously poses new challenges to our privacy.

Each of my responsa on these issues in modern medical ethics seeks to address the new and often excruciatingly difficult moral issues that we face as a result of scientific breakthroughs. Is it always the case, for example, that we should seek to sustain life at all costs, even if this prolongs pain and suffering and gives the patient little hope of recovery? Where do we draw the line between compassionate medical care and battering patients to keep them alive? On the other hand, when are we alleviating pain and when is the dose of morphine that we are administering actually causing the person's death, thus making us nothing short of murderers? What about giving conscious patients more than enough pills to kill themselves? On the other end of life, which of the new techniques to become pregnant may an infertile couple use? Is there anything that they must not use? If they use anonymous donor sperm or eggs, what complications does that pose for the child's sense of his or her own identity? What challenges does the use of donor gametes pose for the social parents' sense of being the child's "real" parents? (These issues are exacerbated if the child is the biological child of one of the social parents but not the other, raising problems for the marriage as well.)

Sometimes, as in the case of embryonic stem cell research, the questions are completely new. It was only in 1997 that scientists could procure stem cells from embryos and work with them. This led to a host of questions about the status of the embryo, the mandate to heal, and the economic conditions that should govern the distribution of the products of embryonic stem cell research. Similarly, it has only been since the mid-1990s that not only military personnel, but civilians have had access to the Internet. In addition to making it possible for us to communicate instantaneously with people around the world, the Internet has made large quantities of information available to us at a keystroke. Most of the time these functions are a great boon, but these new abilities also unfortunately amplify the possibility of identity theft and of fraud. Rabbi Spitz and I therefore had to stretch the Jewish tradition's rules about privacy—guarding one's own as well as respecting others'—to make those Jewish values effective in our use of the Internet; no straightforward reading of any Jewish source would do that.

Although I have discussed these issues at length in the responsa and books indicated in the endnotes, let me give readers a brief taste of my rulings here so that they can get a sense of what this legal stretching looks like:

1. Life support. I ruled that in the case of people suffering from a terminal, irreversible illness, machines and medications may be used in an effort to extend their lives and improve their life's quality, but when those interventions are no longer accomplishing those aims, they may be removed. The same applies to artificial nutrition and hydration, which I see as medicine rather than normal food and liquids because they lack many of the characteristics of normal food and liquids and resemble medicine instead: they come into the body through tubes rather than by inserting into one's mouth and swallowing, and they lack the differences in temperature, texture, and taste that normal food and liquids have. The critical factor to be considered is not just the quantity of life, but the welfare of the patient (and not the welfare of the family, the doctor, the hospital, or the insurance company).

2. *Organ and tissue transplants.* Jews should make their organs available for transplant upon their death. They also may, but need not, donate organs (a kidney or a portion of their liver) during their life time. They should definitely register on the blood marrow registry and agree to donate their bone marrow if they are found to be a match for a cancer patient, and they should donate blood four or five times a year if they are eligible.

3. *Assisted suicide.* Those who support assisted suicide usually have the pure case in mind, where the person has uncontrollable pain and money is not an issue. In most cases, though, pain can be controlled, and money is very much an issue. Sometimes patients want to die rather than "squander" the funds they want to pass on to their heirs, and sometimes the heirs do not want Mom or Dad to "waste" that inheritance on futile health care. Furthermore, on a public policy level, permission to gain assistance in suicide is all too likely to become a requirement as insurance companies refuse to cover extensive, end-of-life care if patients may choose the much less expensive route of assisted suicide. For all these reasons and more, I ruled that even though I am very permissive with regard to removal of medical interventions and then palliative care to control pain, I would not allow assisted suicide.

4. *Assisted reproductive techniques.* Because age is the most important factor in infertility (although definitely not the only one), Jews should take steps to find a mate while in college and, if they find one, get married and begin to have children in graduate school rather than wait until their late twenties or thirties to do that. People who find themselves to be infertile no longer have any duty to procreate, and the Jewish community needs to avoid adding to their frustration

and instead support them as much as possible. Infertile Jews may, however, use any assisted reproductive techniques to have children of their own. They may also use donor eggs or sperm, even from anonymous donors, but that involves complications for all of the parties involved—donors, social parents, and children—that need to be addressed. Adoption is another alternative that is very much honored in the Jewish tradition.

5. *The Mitzvah Child.* In light of our small numbers (Jews constitute only 0.2% of the world's population, in comparison to Christians, who are 33%, and Muslims, who are 20%), and in light of our failure even to reproduce ourselves, those who can have children should seek to have at least two and then at least one more on behalf of the Jewish people. Obviously, to ensure the survival of our people and our tradition, we also need to take significant steps to improve Jewish education for Jews of all ages, and older and wealthier Jews need to provide the money for younger Jews to raise their children in Jewish settings (day care, schools, camps, youth groups). Here, the Talmudic precedent that grandparents are responsible for the Jewish education of their grandchildren (just as the parents are) should be taught. We also need to expand our efforts of bringing Jews by choice, as well as intermarried couples and their children, close to our community. But ultimately, procreation is a major issue for the Jewish community, and one cannot educate non-existent people.

6. *Stem Cell Research.* Jews have an obligation to heal the sick, and stem cell research may lead to cures for many diseases. The Torah and Talmud categorize embryos within a woman's uterus as less than full human beings. Modern science attests that the DNA of the infant is already there at conception, but it also indicates that even in couples not facing infertility problems, some 80% of fertilized eggs within a woman's womb will miscarry. We thus definitely do not have a human being at the moment of conception: we have a 20% chance of producing a human being. Embryos in a petri dish have absolutely no chance to become a person unless implanted into a woman's uterus, and so we are definitely not murdering a person in using such embryos for stem cell research. If it were not for the dangers involved in hyperovulating women, we might even use gametes donated for this purpose, but we certainly may and should use embryos that were created during the course of fertility treatments and that would otherwise be destroyed for this purpose.

7. *Privacy on the Internet.* Privacy–our own and that of others–is one of the ways we express our recognition of the image of God within us: just as God is only partially revealed to us, so we should be only partially revealed to others. Privacy is also an important element in human dignity. The classical tradition required that privacy be maintained in, for example, prohibiting Jews from opening other people's mail and in knocking before entering even one's own house. Rabbi Spitz and I extended this to the internet, demanding that we establish reasonable barriers to others invading our privacy (which we delineate in the responsum) and respect that of others.

GAINING MORAL GUIDANCE AND WISDOM IN COVENANT WITH GOD

When rabbis simply invoke a precedent, they are functioning as references–and, as such, may well be performing an important educational task–but not specifically as *poskim,* people charged with using judgment to decide cases. It is precisely when there are no clear precedents to govern a particular case, or when the precedents that exist are problematic for moral, social, economic, theological, or some other reason that a rabbi's legal mettle is tested. In such circumstances, rabbis must use not only their store of *knowledge* (and the textual and internet skills to learn what the traditional sources relevant to the case are), but also their skills of *judgment,* by which they weigh the relevance of the available precedents to their case and make their decision based on some rather than others. They must also have sensitivity to the particulars of the case at hand. That is why, through the history of Jewish law, it has been the local rabbi (the *mara d'atra*) who makes decisions for a given case rather than the head of the rabbinical academy (the *rosh yeshivah*). The latter might know more about the Jewish tradition, and the local rabbi might therefore consult him or her. Ultimately, though, the local rabbi must take responsibility for rendering a decision because only he or she can know the specifics of both the case and the people involved, and a good decision must take account of both.

Because many of these issues are new, at least in context and sometimes altogether, one cannot reasonably respond to them by simply looking up some precedent. In writing my rabbinic rulings on medical issues, I therefore sought to create a recognizably Jewish response to these issues by doing what some call "depth theology"-that is, by identifying the underlying perceptions of human beings, human society, the role of medicine in life, and the goals of both medicine and life as the Jewish tradition perceives all these things to arrive at rulings that reflect these values and perceptions. Similarly, in the ruling that Rabbi Elie Spitz and I wrote on maintaining privacy on the internet, we identified not only the tradition's rules about privacy, but also the underlying Jewish views of human individuals and communities and the values that prompt the tradition to insist on privacy in the first place and locate its limits. This is the way that my theory of law would direct us to proceed, applying the precedents of Jewish law (the DNA of the Jewish body of law, as it were) and the relationships and concepts entailed in the covenant with God and with Jews and other human beings to formulate a response that is sensitive to the new realities. Only with such a methodology can Jewish legal decisions actualize Judaism's views, values, and wisdom and be true to the Torah's promise that it will afford us both moral guidance and wisdom as we live in relationship with God:[17]

> See, I [Moses] have taught you laws and statutes, as the Lord my God has commanded me, for you to do accordingly in the land that you are about to enter and inherit. Observe and do them, for it is your wisdom and understanding in the eyes of the nations, who will hear all these laws and say, "Surely, that great nation is a wise and understanding people." For what great nation has gods close to it, as is the Lord our God whenever we call out to Him? And what great nation has righteous laws and statutes like this entire Teaching that I set before you this day? (Deut. 4:5–8)

ENDNOTES

1. Readers can find the sources of my legal claims in the responsa themselves, the sources of which are given in the following endnotes.
2. Available at www.rabbinicalassembly.org under the link "Contemporary Halakhah" and in Fine, ed., *Responsa 1980–1990 of the Committee on Jewish Law and Standards of the Conservative Movement,* pp. 295–318.
3. Available at www.rabbinicalassembly.org under the link "Contemporary Halakhah" and in Fine, ed., *Responsa 1980–1990 of the Committee on Jewish Law and Standards of the Conservative Movement,* pp. 165–184.
4. Available at www.rabbinicalassembly.org under the link "Contempor-

ary Halakhah" and in Abelson and Fine, eds., *Responsa 1991–2000 of the Committee on Jewish Law and Standards of the Conservative Movement*, pp. 773–816; and Dorff, *Love Your Neighbor and Yourself*, chap. 5.

5. My latest responsum on homosexual relations, written with Rabbis Daniel Nevins and Avram Reisner, can be found at www.rabbinicalassembly.org under the link "Contemporary Halakhah." My 1992 responsum on the topic can be found there as well; it is also in Abelson and Fine, eds., *Responsa 1991–2000 of the Committee on Jewish Law and Standards of the Conservative Movement*, pp. 691–711. I have also written about this subject in Dorff, *Matters of Life and Death*, pp. 139–151; "Learning about Homosexuality and Taking a New Stand"; and *Love Your Neighbor and Yourself*, pp. 120–126.

6. In regard to heterosexuals, this principle is enunciated toward the very beginning of the Torah (Gen. 2:19), and the Talmud uses it as the basis for deciding some issues in family law: see B. Yevamot 118b; B. Ketubbot 75a; B. Kiddushin 7a, 41a; B. Bava Kamma 111a.

7. See Dorff, *Love Your Neighbor and Yourself*, chap. 3.

8. B. Yevamot 65b.

9. B. Bava Batra 60b; B. Avodah Zarah 36a; B. Horayot 3b.

10. Available at www.rabbinicalasssembly.org, under the link "Contemporary Halakhah" and in Fine, ed., *Responsa 1980–1990 of the Committee on Jewish Law and Standards of the Conservative Movement*, pp. 519–580; Mackler, *Life and Death Responsibilities in Jewish Biomedical Ethics*, pp. 292–358; and Dorff, *Matters of Life and Death*, pp. 198–220.

11. Available at www.rabbinicalasssembly.org, under the link "Contemporary Halakhah" and in Abelson and Fine, eds., *Responsa 1991–2000 of the Committee on Jewish Law and Standards of the Conservative Movement*, pp. 379–399; Mackler, *Life and Death Responsibilities in Jewish Biomedical Ethics*, pp. 404–434; and Dorff, *Matters of Life and Death*, pp. 176–198.

12. Available at www.rabbinicalasssembly.org, under the link "Contemporary Halakhah" and in Abelson and Fine, eds., *Responsa 1991–2000 of the Committee on Jewish Law and Standards of the Conservative Movement*, pp. 461–509; Mackler, *Life and Death Responsibilities in Jewish Biomedical Ethics*, pp. 15–94; and Dorff, *Matters of Life and Death*, chaps. 3 and 4.

13. Available at www.rabbinicalassembly.org under the link "Contemporary Halakhah." See also Dorff *Love your Neighbor and Yourself*, (2003), pp. 100-104, 143-154.

14. Available at www.rabbinicalasssembly.org, under the link "Contemporary Halakhah" and in Dorff, "Stem Cell Research."

15. Available at www.rabbinicalassembly.org under the link "Contemporary Halakhah" and in print in Mackler, ed., *Life and Death Responsiblities in Jewish Biomedical Ethics* (2000), chap. 30, pp. 479-505. For a more exten-

sive discussion of this issue, see Dorff, *Matters of Life and Death*, (1998), chap. 12.

16. Available at www.rabbinicalassembly.org, under the link "Contemporary Halakhah" and, in a somewhat different form, in Dorff, *Love Your Neighbor and Yourself*, 2003), chap. 2.

17. The reader can read more about my methodology in Dorff, *Matters of Life and Death*, chaps. 1 and 2 and append.; Dorff, *To Do the Right and the Good*, chap. 1 and appends.; and Dorff, *Love Your Neighbor and Yourself*, chap. 1 and append.

Bibliography of Modern Sources

Abelson, Kassel, and David J. Fine, eds. *Responsa 1991–2000 of the Committee on Jewish Law and Standards of the Conservative Movement.* New York: Rabbinical Assembly, 2002.

Adler, Morris. *The World of the Talmud.* New York: Schocken, 1963.

Agus, Jacob. *Guideposts in Modern Judaism.* New York: Bloch, 1954.

_____. "Laws as Standards—The Way of Takkanot." In *Conservative Judaism* 6, no. 4 (summer 1950), pp. 8–26. Reprinted in his *Guideposts in Modern Judaism* (pp. 279–342). New York: Bloch, 1954; in *Conservative Judaism and Jewish Law* (pp. 28–45). Ed. Seymour Siegel. New York: Rabbinical Assembly, 1977; and in *The Unfolding Tradition.* (pp. 163–177). Ed. Elliot N. Dorff. New York: Aviv Press (Rabbinical Assembly), 2005.

Anonymous. Notes and Comments. *The New Yorker,* August 30, 1976, pp. 21–22. Reprinted in Dorff and Rosett, *A Living Tree,* pp. 489–492.

_____. "Mixed Pews in Jewish Tradition." In *Conservative Judaism* 11:1 (Fall, 1956), pp. 32–41; reprinted in Golinkin, *Proceedings of the Committee on Jewish Law and Standards of the Conservative Movement 1927–1970,* 3:1063–1072.

Anonymous. "CJF and Rabbinic Alumni Sponsor New York Premiere of Film and a Conversation on Rav Soloveitchik," In *Chevrusa,* 41, no. 3 (Spring, 2007), pp. 1, 16–17.

Aquinas, Thomas. *Basic Writings of St. Thomas Aquinas.* Ed. A. C. Pegis. New York: Random House, 1945.

Aronowicz, Annette. "Emanuel Levinas' Talmudic Commentaries: The Relation of the Jewish Tradition to the Non-Jewish World." In *Contem-porary Jewish Ethics and Morality: A Reader* (pp. 212–218). Eds. Elliot Dorff and Louis Newman. New York: Oxford, 1995.

Aronson, David. "On Mixed Seating and 'Orthodox' Traditions." In *Conservative Judaism* 11:1 (Fall, 1956), pp. 59–65. Reprinted in Golinkin, *Proceedings of the Committee on Jewish Law and Standards of the Conservative Movement*, 3:1073–1079.

Arzt, Max. "Conservative Judaism as a Unifying Force." In *Conservative Judaism* 5:4, (June 1949), pp. 10–20. Reprinted in *Tradition and Change: The Development of Conservative Judaism* (pp. 139–154). Ed. Mordecai M. Waxman, New York: Burning Bush Press (Rabbinical Assembly), 1958.

Bell, Robin. "ABC of Sexual Health: Homosexual Men and Women." *British Medical Journal* 318 (7181) (Feb. 13, 1999): 452–455.

Bergman, Ben Zion. "A Conservative Approach to Halakhah." In *Proceedings of the Rabbinical Assembly 1987* (pp. 47–54). Ed. Jules Harlow. New York: Rabbinical Assembly, 1988.

Berkovits, Eliezer. *Crisis and Faith.* New York: Sanhedrin Press, 1976.

_____. *Faith after the Holocaust.* New York: Ktav, 1973.

_____. *With God in Hell.* New York: Sanhedrin Press, 1979.

Biale, Rachel. *Women and Jewish Law.* New York: Schocken, 1984.

Blumenthal, Aaron. "An Aliyah for Women." In *Proceedings of the Rabbinical Assembly* 19 (1955), pp. 168–181. Reprinted in *Conservative Judaism and Jewish Law* (pp. 266–280). Ed. Seymour Siegel. New York: Rabbinical Assembly, 1977; and in *Proceedings of the Committee on Jewish Law and Standards of the Conservative Movement* (pp. 3: 1086–1099). Ed. David Golinkin. New York: Rabbinical Assembly, 1997.

Blumenthal, David R. *The Banality of Good and Evil: Moral Lessons from the Shoah and the Jewish Tradition.* Washington, D.C.: Georgetown University Press, 1999.

_____. 1993. *Facing the Abusing God: A Theology of Protest.* Louisville, Ky.: Westminster/John Knox.

Borowitz, Eugene. "The Reform Judaism of *Renewing the Covenant:* An Open Letter to Elliot Dorff." *Conservative Judaism* 50: 1 (Fall 1997), pp. 61–65. Reprinted in *The Unfolding Tradition: Jewish Law after Sinai* (pp. 469–474). Ed. Elliot Dorff. New York: Aviv Press (Rabbinical Assembly), 2005.

_____. *Reform Judaism Today.* New York: Behrman House, 1983.

_____. 1991. *Renewing the Covenant: A Theology for the Postmodern Jew.* Philadelphia: Jewish Publication Society.

Brockwell King, G. "The 'Negative' Golden Rule," In *Journal of Religion* 8:2 (April 1928), pp. 268–279.

Buber, Martin. *Israel and the World.* New York: Schocken Books, 1948.

_____. *On Judaism.* Trans. Eva Jospe. New York: Schocken Books, 1937; rpt. ed. 1967.

Cassuto, Umberto. *A Commentary on the Book of Exodus.* Jerusalem: Magnes Press [Hebrew University], 1967.

Cohen, A. *Everyman's Talmud.* New York: Dutton, 1949.

Cohen, Boaz. *Jewish and Roman Law: A Comparative Study.* 2 vols. New York: Jewish Theological Seminary of America, 1966.

_____. "Report of the Committee on Jewish Law." *Proceedings of the Rabbinical Assembly* 8 (1944), pp. 139–141. Reprinted in *Proceedings of the Committee on Jewish Law and Standards of the Conservative Movement, 1927–1970* (pp. 3: 1060–1062). Ed. David Golinkin. New York: Rabbinical Assembly, 1997.

Cohen, Gerson D. "The Song of Songs and the Jewish Religious Mentality." In *The Samuel Friedland Lectures 1960–1966* (pp. 1–21). No editor listed. New York: Jewish Theological Seminary of America, 1966.

Cohen, Hermann. *Religion and Hope: Selections from the Jewish Writings of Hermann Cohen.* Ed. and trans. Eva Jospe. New York: Norton, 1971.

_____. *Religion of Reason out of the Sources of Judaism.* Trans. Simon Kaplan. New York: Ungar, 1972.

Committee on Jewish Law and Standards. No editor listed. *Summary Index: The Committee on Jewish Law and Standards.* New York: Rabbinical Assembly, 1998.

Cover, Robert. "Nomos and Narrative." In *Harvard Law Review* 97: 4 (1983), pp. 4–65.

Davies, W. D. *Torah in the Messianic Age.* Philadelphia: Society of Biblical Literature, 1952.

Davis, Moshe. *The Emergence of Conservative Judaism.* Philadelphia: Jewish Publication Society, 1963.

Denise, Theodore C., Nicholas P. White, and Sheldon P. Peterfreund. *Great Traditions in Ethics.* 11th ed. Belmont, Calif.: Wadsworth/Thomson, 2005.

Dorff, Elliot N. "Autonomy v. Community." In *Conservative Judaism* 48, no. 2 (Winter 1996), pp. 64–68.

_____. *Conservative Judaism: Our Ancestors to Our Descendants.* New York: United Synagogue of Conservative Judaism, 1977. 2nd rev. ed., 1996.

_____. "The Covenant: How Jews Understand Themselves and Others." *Anglican Theological Review* 64, no. 4 (1982), pp. 481–501.

_____. "The Covenant: The Transcendent Thrust in Jewish Law." In *The Jewish Law Annual* 7 (1988), pp. 68–96. Reprinted in *Contemporary Jewish Ethics and Morality: A Reader* (pp. 59–78). Ed. Elliot Dorff and Louis Newman. New York: Oxford, 1995.

_____. "Custom Drives Jewish Law on Women." In *Conservative Judaism* 49: 3 (Spring 1997), pp. 3–21. Response to critics: *Conservative Judaism* 51:1 (Fall 1998), pp. 66–73. Reprinted in Walter Jacob and Moshe Zemer, eds. *Gender Issues in Jewish Law: Essays and Responsa* (pp. 82–106.). New York: Berghahn Books, 2001.

_____. "God and the Holocaust." *Judaism* 26:1 (Winter 1977), pp. 27–34.

_____. "The Interaction of Jewish Law with Morality." In *Judaism* 26:4 (Fall 1977), pp. 455–466.

_____. "Judaism as a Religious Legal System." *The Hastings Law Journal* 29 (1978), pp. 1331–1360.

_____. *Knowing God: Jewish Journeys to the Unknowable.* Northvale, N.J.: Aronson, 1992. Rpt. ed. Lanham, Md.: Rowman and Littlefield, 2004.

_____. "Learning about Homosexuality and Taking a New Stand." *The New Menorah Journal* 59 (Spring 2000), pp. 3–4.

_____. *Love Your Neighbor and Yourself: A Jewish Approach to Modern Personal Ethics.* Philadelphia: Jewish Publication Society, 2003.

_____. " 'Male and Female God Created Them': Equality with Distinction." In *University Papers.* Los Angeles: University of Judaism, March, 1984.

_____. "Matters of Degree and Kind: An Open Response to Eugene Borowitz's Open Letter to Me." *Conservative Judaism* 50:1 (Fall 1997), pp. 66–71.

_____. *Matters of Life and Death: A Jewish Approach to Modern Medical Ethics.* Philadelphia: Jewish Publication Society, 1998.

_____. "The Meaning of Covenant: A Contemporary Understanding." In *Issues in the Jewish-Christian Dialogue: Jewish Perspectives on Covenant, Mission, and Witness* (pp. 38–61). Eds. Helga Croner and Leon Klenicki. New York: Paulist Press, 1979.

_____. *Mitzvah Means Commandment.* New York: United Synagogue of America, 1989.

_____. "Revelation." In *Conservative Judaism* 31:1–2 (Fall–Winter 1976), pp. 58–69.

_____. "Stem Cell Research." In *Conservative Judaism* 55:3 (Spring 2003), pp. 3–29.

_____. "Study Leads to Action." In *Religious Education* 75:2 (March–April 1980), pp. 171–192.

_____. "Theological Reflections." In *My People's Prayer Book: Traditional Prayers, Modern Commentaries.* Vol. 4. *The Torah Service,* pp. 50, 54, 64, 66–68, 72, 75, 80, 82, 88, 95, 98–99, 104, 106–107, 126, 128–129, 134, 136–142, 146, 170, 173, 186, 191, 198, 208, 210. Ed. Lawrence Hoffman. Woodstock Vt.: Jewish Lights, 2000.

_____. "'This Is My Beloved, This Is My Friend' (Song of Songs 5:16): A Rabbinic Letter on Intimate Relations." New York: Rabbinical Assembly, 1996. Reprinted in *Love Your Neighbor and Yourself: A Jewish Approach to Modern Personal Ethics* (chap 3). Elliot Dorff. Philadelphia: Jewish Publication Society, 2003.

_____. *To Do the Right and the Good: A Jewish Approach to Modern Social Ethics.* Philadelphia: Jewish Publication Society, 2002.

_____. "Traditional Judaism." *Conservative Judaism* 34:2 (November–December 1980), pp. 34–38.

_____. "Two Ways to Approach God." In *Conservative Judaism* 30:2, (Winter 1976), pp. 58–67. Reprinted in *God in the Teachings of Conservative Judaism* (pp. 30–41). Eds. Seymour Siegel and Elliot Gertel. New York: Rabbinical Assembly, 1985.

_____. *The Unfolding Tradition: Jewish Law after Sinai.* New York: Aviv Press (Rabbinical Assembly), 2005.

_____. *The Way into Tikkun Olam (Fixing the World).* Woodstock, Vt.: Jewish Lights, 2005.

_____, and Louis Newman. *Contemporary Jewish Ethics and Morality: A Reader.* New York: Oxford University Press, 1995.

_____, and Arthur Rosett. *A Living Tree: The Roots and Growth of Jewish Law.* Albany: State University of New York Press, 1988.

Dworkin, Ronald. *Law's Empire.* Cambridge, Mass.: Harvard University Press, 1986.

Edwards, Paul. "Being-Itself and Irreducible Metaphors." In *Mind* 74 (1965), pp. 197–206.

Efrati, Jacob Eliyahu. *Tekufat ha-Saboraim v'Sifrutah* [Hebrew]. Petah Tikvah, Israel: Agudat Benai Asher (New York and Jerusalem: Philip Feldheim, distributor), 1973.

Ehrmann, Eliezer L., ed. *Readings in Modern Jewish History: From the American Revolution to the Present.* New York: Ktav, 1977.

Ekstrand, Maria L., Ron D. Stall, Jay P. Paul, Dennis H. Osmond, Thomas J. Coates. "Gay Men Report High Rates of Unprotected Anal Sex With Partners of Unknown or Discordant HIV Status." In *AIDS: Official Journal of the International AIDS Society* 13:12 (August 20, 1999):1525–1533.

Elon, Menachem. "Codification." *Encyclopaedia Judaica* 5:628–656.

_____. *Jewish Law: History, Sources, Principles.* Trans. Bernard Auerbach and Melvin J. Sykes. 4 vols. Philadelphia: Jewish Publication Society, 1994.

_____. "Takkanot." In *Encyclopaedia Judaica* 15:712–728.

_____. "Takkanot Ha-Kahal," In *Encyclopaedia Judaica* 15:728–737.

Fackenheim, Emil. *God's Presence in History.* New York: New York University Press, 1970. Rpt. ed., New York: Harper & Row, 1979.

_____. *The Jewish Return into History: Reflections in the Age of Auschwitz and the New Jerusalem.* New York: Schocken, 1978.

_____. *To Mend the World: Foundations of Post-Holocaust Thought.* New York: Schocken, 1989.

_____. *Quest for Past and Future.* Bloomington, Indiana University Press. 1968.

Feldman, David M. *Birth Control in Jewish Law.* New York: New York University Press, 1968. Rpt. ed. *Marital Relations, Abortion, and Birth Control in Jewish Law.* New York: Schocken, 1973.

Fine, David J., ed. *Responsa 1980–1990 of the Committee on Jewish Law and*

Standards of the Conservative Movement. New York: Rabbinical Assembly, 2005.

Fishbane, Michael. *Biblical Interpretation in Ancient Israel*. Oxford: Clarendon Press, 1985.

Fleischner, Eva, ed. *Auschwitz: Beginning of a New Era? Reflections on the Holocaust*. New York: Ktav, 1977.

Friedan, Betty. *The Feminine Mystique*. New York: W. W. Norton, 1963. Rpt. ed. 1997.

Friedman, Richard Elliott. *Who Wrote the Bible?* Englewood Cliffs, N.J.: Prentice-Hall, 1987. Rpt. ed. San Francisco: Harper SanFrancisco, 1997.

Fulghum, Robert. *All I Really Need to Know I Learned in Kindergarten: Uncommon Thoughts on Common Things*. New York: Villard Books, 1986.

Gafni, Isaiah, "Salome Alexandra," *Encyclopaedia Judaica* 14:691–693.

Garfiel, Evelyn. *The Service of the Heart: A Guide to the Jewish Prayer Book*. New York: Thomas Yoseloff, 1958.

Gellman, Yehudah (Jerome). "Conservative Judaism and Biblical Criticism." *Conservative Judaism*, 59:2 (Winter, 2007), pp. 50–67.

Gilligan, Carol. *In a Different Voice*. Cambridge, Mass.: Harvard, 1982.

Gillman, Neil. "A Conservative Theology for the Twenty-First Century." In *Proceedings of the Rabbinical Assembly* (pp. 9–22). Ed. Jules Harlow. New York: Rabbinical Assembly, 1993.

_____. *Sacred Fragments: Recovering Theology for the Modern Jew*. Philadelphia: Jewish Publication Society, 1990.

_____. "What Do American Jews Believe? A Symposium." *Commentary* 102, no. 2 (August 1996), pp. 39–40.

Glatzer, Nahum N. *Franz Rosenzweig: His Life and Thought*. New York: Schocken Books, 1953.

_____, ed. *On Jewish Learning*. New York: Schocken, 1965.

Golinkin, David, ed. *Proceedings of the Committee on Jewish Law and Standards of the Conservative Movement, 1927-1970*. 3 vols. New York: Rabbinical Assembly, 1997.

Gordis, Robert. *The Book of God and Man: A Study of Job*. London and Chicago: University of Chicago Press, 1965.

_____. *A Faith for Moderns*. New York: Bloch, 1960.

_____. "The Ordination of Women." In *The Ordination of Women as Rabbis: Studies and Responsa* (pp. 47–68). Ed. Simon Greenberg. New York: Jewish Theological Seminary of America, 1988.

_____. *The Song of Songs*. New York: Jewish Theological Seminary of America, 1961.

Graetz, Michael. "Reviving Takkanah in the Halakhic Process." In *Silence Is Deadly: Judaism Confronts Wifebeating* (pp. 197–202). Ed. Naomi Graetz. Northvale, NJ: Jason Aronson, 1998.

BIBLIOGRAPHY

Graff, Gil. *Separation of Church and State: Dina de-Malkhuta Dina in Jewish Law, 1750–1848.* Birmingham: University of Alabama Press, 1985.

Greenberg, Irving. 1977. "Cloud of Smoke, Pillar of Fire." In *Auschwitz: Beginning of a New Era? Reflections on the Holocaust* (pp. 7–55). Ed. Eva Fleischner. New York: Ktav, 1977. Reprinted in *Contemporary Jewish Ethics and Morality: A Reader* (pp. 396–416). Ed. Elliot Dorff and Louis Newman. New York: Oxford, 1995.

Greenberg, Simon. "On the Question of the Ordination of Women as Rabbis by the Jewish Theological Seminary of America." In *The Ordination of Women as Rabbis: Studies and Responsa* (pp. 69–92). Ed. Simon Greenberg. New York: Jewish Theological Seminary of America, 1988.

————. "A Revealed Law." *Conservative Judaism* 19:1 (Fall 1964), pp. 36–50. Reprinted in *Conservative Judaism and Jewish Law* (pp. 175–194). Ed. Seymour Siegel. New York: Rabbinical Assembly, 1977.

Greenwood, Gregory L., Michael V. Relf, Bu Huang, Lance M. Pollack, Jesse Canchola, and Joseph A. Catania. "Battering Victimization Among a Probability-Based Sample of Men Who Have Sex With Men." *American Journal of Public Health.* 92 (December, 2002): 1964–1969.

Grossman, Avraham. "Medieval Rabbinic Views on Wife-Beating, 800–1300." In *Jewish History* 5:1 (Spring 1991), pp. 53–62.

Gur, R. C., D. Alsop, D. Glahn, R. Petty, C. L. Swanson, J. A. Maldjian, B. I. Turetsky, J. A. Detre, J. Gee, R.E. Gur. "An fMRI Study of Sex Differences in Regional Activation to a Verbal and a Spatial Task." In *Brain and Language* 74:2 (September, 2000), pp. 157–170.

Ha-Am, Ahad. *Al Parshat Derakhim* [Hebrew]. Berlin: Yudisher Ferlag, 1930. Rpt. eds. Tel Aviv: D'vir, 1948, 1960.

Halevi, Judah. *The Kuzari: An Argument for the Faith of Israel.* Trans. Hartwig Hirschfeld. New York: Schocken, 1964. [Originally published 1905.]

Hartman, David. *A Living Covenant: The Innovative Spirit in Traditional Judaism.* New York: Free Press, 1985. Rpt. ed. Woodstock, Vt: Jewish Lights, 1997.

Hauptman, Judith. *Rereading the Rabbis: A Woman's Voice.* Boulder, Colo.: Westview Press, 1998.

Heschel, Abraham Joshua. *God in Search of Man: A Philosophy of Judaism.* New York: Harper & Row, 1955.

————. *Heavenly Torah As Refracted through the Generations (Torah min ha-shamyim b'aspakloriyah shel ha-dorot).* Ed. and trans. Gordon Tucker with Leonard Levin. New York: Continuum, 2005.

Hillers, Delbert R. *Covenant: The History of a Biblical Idea.* Baltimore: Johns Hopkins Press, 1969.

Hobbes, Thomas. *Leviathan.* Indianapolis, New York: Bobbs-Merrill, 1958. [Originally published 1651.]

Hoffman, Lawrence, ed. *My People's Prayer Book: Traditional Prayers, Modern Commentaries.* Vol. 4, *The Torah Service.* Woodstock Vt.: Jewish Lights, 2000.

Holmes, Oliver Wendell. "The Path of the Law." In *Harvard Law Review* 10 (1897), p. 457.

Hume, David. *Dialogues Concerning Natural Religion.* Indianapolis: Bobbs-Merrill, 1947. [Originally published in 1776].

Hyman, David A. "Rescue without Law: An Empirical Perspective on the Duty to Rescue," *Texas Law Review* 84:3 (February 2006), pp. 653–738.

Jacob, Walter, and Moshe Zemer, eds. *Gender Issues in Jewish Law: Essays and Responsa.* New York: Berghahn Books, 2001.

Jacobs, Louis. *Principles of the Jewish Faith.* Northvale, NJ: Jason Aronson, 1964. Rpt. ed. Lanham, Md,: Rowman and Littlefield, 1988.

Jospe, Alfred, ed. *Tradition and Contemporary Experience.* New York: Schocken/B'nai Brith Books, 1970.

Kadushin, Max. 1938. *Organic Thinking: A Study in Rabbinic Thought.* New York: Bloch.

_____. *Worship and Ethics.* Evanston, Ill. Northwestern University Press, 1964.

Kafka, Franz. 1998. *The Trial.* Breon Mitchell, trans. New York: Schocken (distributed by Pantheon Books). [Originally published in German in 1925.]

Kant, Immanel. *Fundamental Principles of the Metaphysic of Morals.* Trans. T. K. Abbot. London: Longmans, Green, 1898. [First published in German in 1785.]

Kaplan, Mordecai. *The Future of the American Jew.* New York: Reconstructionist Press, 1948, rpt. ed. 1967.

_____. *Judaism as a Civilization.* New York: Reconstructionist Press, 1934.

_____. *The Meaning of God in Modern Jewish Religion.* New York: Jewish Reconstructionist Foundation, 1947.

_____. *Questions Jews Ask: Reconstructionist Answers.* New York: Reconstruc-tionist Press, 1956.

_____. "Reply to Robert Gordis." In *The Reconstructionist* 8:15 (November 1942), pp. 15–21, 24. Reprinted in *Questions Jews Ask: Reconstructionist Answers* (pp. 264–276). Mordecai Kaplan, New York: Reconstructionist Press, 1956. Also reprinted in *The Unfolding Tradition* (pp. 121–129). Elliot Dorff, ed. 2005.

Katz, Steven T. *Post-Holocaust Dialogues: Critical Studies in Modern Jewish Thought.* New York: New York University Press, 1985.

Kelsen, Hans. *General Theory of Law and State.* Trans. Anders Wedberg. Cambridge, Mass.: Harvard University Press, 1945.

_____. *Pure Theory of Law.* Trans. May Knight. Berkeley and Los Angeles: University of California Press, 1967.

Kirschenbaum, Aaron. "The Good Samaritan in Jewish Law" [Hebrew]. *Dine Israel* 7 (1976), pp. 7–85. Summarized in English as "The Bystander's Duty to Rescue in Jewish Law." In *Journal of Religion and Ethics* 8 (1980), pp. 204–226.

Kitazawa, Shigeru, and Kenji Kansaku. "Sex Difference in Language Lateralization May Be Task-Dependent." In *Brain: A Journal of Neurology* 128:5 (2005), pp. E30ff.

Klausner, Joseph. *The Messianic Idea in Israel.* London: Allen & Unwin, 1956.

Kushner, Harold. *When Bad Things Happen to Good People.* New York: Schocken, 1981.

Lakoff, George, and Mark Johnson. *Metaphors We Live By.* Chicago: University of Chicago Press, 1980.

_____. *Philosophy in the Flesh: The Embodied Mind and Its Challenge to Western Thought.* New York: Basic Books, 1999.

Laumann, Edward O. *The Social Organization of Sexuality: Sexual Practices in the United States.* Chicago: University of Chicago Press, 1994.

Levinas, Emanuel. *Face to Face with Levinas.* Ed. Richard A. Cohen. Albany: State University of New York Press, 1986.

_____. *Nine Talmudic Readings by Emanuel Levinas.* Trans. Annette Aronowicz. Bloomington: Indiana University Press, 1990.

Levine, Lee I. *The Ancient Synagogue: The First Thousand Years.* New Haven, Conn.: Yale University Press, 2000.

Locke, John. *Two Treatises of Government.* New York: Cambridge University Press, 1960. [Originally published 1690.]

Lopes Cordozo, Nathan T. "On Bible Criticism and Its Counterarguments: A Short History." In his *Between Silence and Speech: Essays on Jewish Thought* (pp. 171–194). Northvale, NJ: Aronson, 1995.

Mackler, Aaron L., ed. *Life and Death Responsibilities in Jewish Biomedical Ethics.* New York: Jewish Theological Seminary of America (Finkelstein Institute), 2000.

Maritain, Jacques. *The Rights of Man and Natural Law.* New York: Scribners, 1949.

Mascall, Eric L. *Existence and Analogy.* London: Longmans, Green, 1949. Rpt. ed. Anchor Books, 1967.

Maybaum, Ignaz. *The Face of God after Auschwitz.* Amsterdam: Polak & Van Gennep, 1965.

McCarthy, D. J. *Old Testament Covenant: A Survey of Current Opinions.* Oxford: Basil Blackwell, 1973.

Moran, William. "Ancient Near Eastern Background of the Love of God in Deuteronomy." In *Catholic Biblical Quarterly* 25 (1963), pp. 77–87.

Morrow, Lance. "The Hazards of Homemade Vows." In *Time,* June 27, 1983, p. 78. Reprinted in *A Living Tree* (pp. 510–511).

Nadell, Pamela S. *Conservative Judaism in America: A Biographical Dictionary and Sourcebook*. New York: Greenwood, 1988.

Noddings, Nel. *Caring: A Feminine Approach to Ethics and Moral Education*. Berkeley: University of California Press, 1984.

Novak, David. *Covenantal Rights: A Study in Jewish Political Theory*. Princeton, N.J.: Princeton University Press, 2000.

_____. *The Image of the Non-Jew in Judaism: An Historical and Constructive Study of the Noahide Laws*. New York and Toronto: Mellen Press, 1983.

Obama, Barack. *The Audacity of Hope: Thoughts on Reclaiming the American Dream*. New York: Crown, 2006.

Orenstein, Debra, ed. *Lifecycles: Jewish Women on Life Passages and Personal Milestones*. Woodstock, Vt.: Jewish Lights, 1994.

_____, and Jane Rachel Litman, eds. *Lifecycles: Jewish Women on Biblical Themes in Contemporary Life*. Woodstock, Vt: Jewish Lights, 1997.

Patai, Raphael. *The Messiah Texts*. Detroit: Wayne State University Press, 1979.

Paul, Jay, Joseph Catania, Lance Pollack, Judith Moskowitz, Jesse Canchola, Thomas Mills, Diane Binson, and Ron Stall. "Suicide Attempts among Gay and Bisexual Men: Lifetime Prevalence and Antecedents." In *American Journal of Public Health* 92 (August, 2002): 1338–1345.

Penelhum, Terence. "Personal Identity." In *The Encyclopedia of Philosophy*, 6:95–107.

Petuchowski, Jakob J. *Ever since Sinai*. New York: Scribe, 1961.

_____. 1970. "Some Criteria for Modern Jewish Observance." In *Tradition and Contemporary Experience* (pp. 239–248). Ed. Alfred Jospe. New York: Schocken/B'nai Brith Books, 1970. Reprinted in *Contemporary Jewish Ethics and Morality: A Reader* (pp. 292–298). Ed. Elliot Dorff and Louis Newman. New York: Oxford, 1995.

_____. *Understanding Jewish Prayer*. New York: Ktav, 1972.

Pines, Shlomo, trans. 1963. *Guide of the Perplexed*. Chicago: University of Chicago Press.

Pritchard, James B., ed. *Ancient Near Eastern Texts Relating to the Old Testament*. Princeton, N.J.: Princeton University Press, 1950.

Quinn, Peter J. *The Molecular Biology of Cell Membranes*. Baltimore: University Park Press, 1976.

Rabinowitz, Mayer. "On the Ordination of Women: An Advocate's Halakhic Responses." In *The Ordination of Women as Rabbis: Studies and Responsa* (pp. 107–123). Ed. Simon Greenberg. New York: Jewish Theological Seminary of America, 1988.

Rosenzweig, Franz. 1965. "The Builders." In *On Jewish Learning* (pp. 72–92). Ed. Nahum N. Glatzer, New York: Schocken, 1965.

_____. *The Star of Redemption*. Trans. William W. Hallo. New York: Holt, Rinehart & Winston, 1970.

BIBLIOGRAPHY

Ross, Tamar. *Expanding the Palace of Torah: Orthodoxy and Feminism.* Waltham, Mass.: Brandeis University Press, 2004.

Roth, Joel. *The Halakhic Process: A Systemic Analysis.* New York: Jewish Theological Seminary of America, 1986.

————. "Homosexuality Revisited." Available at www.rabbinicalassembly .org, under the link, "Contemporary Halakhah," 2006.

————. "On the Ordination of Women as Rabbis." In *The Ordination of Women as Rabbis: Studies and Responsa* (pp. 127–185). Ed. Simon Greenberg. New York: Jewish Theological Seminary of America, 1988.

Rubenstein, Richard. *After Auschwitz: Radical Theology and Contemporary Judaism.* Indianapolis: Bobbs-Merrill, 1966. 2nd ed., Baltimore: Johns Hopkins, 1992.

Ruemafedi, Gary, Simone French, Mary Story, Michael D. Resnick, and Robert Blum. "The Relationship between Suicide Risk and Sexual Orientation: Results of a Population-Based Study." In *American Journal of Public Health* 88:1 (January, 1998), pp. 57–60.

Santoni, Ronald E. ed. *Religious Language and the Problem of Religious Knowledge.* Bloomington and London: Indiana University Press, 1968.

Schechter, Solomon. *Studies in Judaism.* 1st ser. Philadelphia: Jewish Publication Society, 1896.

Scholem, Gershom. *The Messianic Idea in Judaism.* New York: Schocken Books, 1971.

Schoville, Keith N. "Song of Songs." In *Encyclopaedia Judaica* 15:144–152.

Schulweis, Harold. *Evil and the Morality of God.* Cincinnati, Ohio: Hebrew Union College Press and New York: Ktav, 1984.

————. *For Those Who Can't Believe: Overcoming the Obstacles to Faith.* New York: HarperCollins, 1994.

Siegel, Seymour, ed. *Conservative Judaism and Jewish Law.* New York: Rabbinical Assembly, 1977.

————, and Elliot Gertel, eds. *God in the Teachings of Conservative Judaism.* New York: Rabbinical Assembly, 1985.

Sigal, Philip. "Responsum on the Status of Women: With Special Attention to the Questions of *Shaliah Tzibbur, Edut,* and *Gittin.*" In *Responsa 1980–1990 of the Committee on Jewish Law and Standards of the Conservative Movement* (pp. 11–39). Ed. Fine, David J. New York: Rabbinical Assembly, 2005.

————. 1974. "Women in a Prayer Quorum." *Judaism* 23:2 (1974), pp. 174–182. Reprinted in *Conservative Judaism and Jewish Law,* pp. 281–292. Ed. Seymour Siegel. New York: Rabbinical Assembly, 1977.

Smith, Allan L. ed. *Where We Stand.* New York: UAHC Press, 1997.

Sommer, Benjamin D. "Revelation at Sinai in the Hebrew Bible and in Jewish Theology." In *Journal of Religion* 79 (1999), pp. 422–451.

Sommer, Iris E. C., Andre Aleman, Anke Bouma, and Rene S. Kahn. "Do Women Really Have More Bilateral Language Representation than Men?

A Meta-Analysis of Functioning Imaging Studies." In *Brain: A Journal of Neurology* 127:8 (August, 2004), pp. 1845–1852.

Sperling, David. *Students of the Covenant: A History of Jewish Biblical Scholarship in North America.* Atlanta: Scholars Press, 1992.

Stall, Ron, G. L. Greenwood, M. Acree, J. Paul, and T. J. Coates. "Cigarette Smoking among Gay and Bisexual Men. In *American Journal of Public Health* 89 (Dec. 1999):1875–1878.

Stroll, Avrum. "Identity." In *The Encyclopedia of Philosophy* 4:121–124.

Tannen, Deborah. *You Just Don't Understand.* New York: Ballantine, 1990.

Tillich, Paul. *Dynamics of Faith.* New York: Harper & Row, 1957.

Tofield, Sanders. "Women's Place in the Rites of the Synagogue with Special Reference to the *Aliyah.*" In *Proceedings of the Rabbinical Assembly* 19 (1955), pp. 182–190. Reprinted in *Proceedings of the Committee on Jewish Law and Standards of the Conservative Movement, 1927–1970,* pp. 3:1100–1108. Ed. David Golinkin. New York: Rabbinical Assembly, 1997.

Trachtenberg, Joshua. *Jewish Magic and Superstition: A Study in Folk Religion.* New York: Behrman Jewish Book House, 1939.

Tucker, Gordon. "Final Report of the Commission for the Study of the Ordination of Women as Rabbbis." In *The Ordination of Women as Rabbis: Studies and Responsa* (pp. 5–30). Ed. Simon Greenberg. New York: Jewish Theological Seminary of America, 1988.

Washofsky, Mark. *Jewish Living: A Guide to Contemporary Reform Practice.* New York: UAHC Press, 2001.

Waxman, Mordecai M. *Tradition and Change: The Development of Conservative Judaism* New York: Burning Bush Press (Rabbinical Assembly), 1958.

Wyschograd, Michael. "Faith and the Holocaust." In *Judaism* 20:3 (Summer 1971), pp. 286–294.

Youngner, Stuart J., Renee C. Fox, and Laurence J. O'Connell, eds. *Organ Transplantation: Meanings and Realities.* Madison: University of Wisconsin Press, 1996.

Index

INDEX

Armed Forces, U.S., 131, 152. *see also* military
Ashkenazic Judaism, 49, 67, 256
association vs individualism. *see* individualism vs association
attitude of Jews toward law, 58, 108
Augustine, 213
authority. *See also* God, legislator, as; prophecy; rabbis, lawmakers, as
  conflicting decisions, 28–29, 181, 226–27, 237
  custom and, 73, 245–48, 251–52
  Divine, 29–30, 51–52, 99–101, 143–44, 190–91, 196, 199–200, 203–4
  human, 191–93, 196–200, 204–7, 208n3, 209n24
  legal theory and, 5, 13–16, 18–20
  morality provided to by law, 34–36, 138, 218
  ordination of rabbis as means of, 15, 197–98, 280
  Torah as legal, 14–15, 50–52, 54–55, 57, 112
autonomy, legal, 7, 12, 19, 78, 115, 168, 279

B

Bag, Ben Bag, 36
Balaam, 41–42n57
Bar Kokhba revolt, 13
baseball analogy for judgment, 20
beauty of life as motivation for law adherence, 179–80, 188n67, 206, 252
Bedan, 228
behavior, change in through custom, 247–48
Beraita, 254
Bergman, Rabbi Ben Zion, 259, 264
Berkovits, Eliezer, 51, 169
Biblical criticism, 29–37
Bill of Rights, the, 11, 201
birth and death of laws, 75–77
birth control, 53. *See also* abortion
Bleich, J. David, 51
Blumenthal, David, 169

body and soul of Jewish law, 45–46, 80n2, 87–96. *See also* organic aspects of Jewish law
Bolyai, Janos, 82n23
Borowitz, Eugene, 28, 115, 118, 279–80
Bowers v. Hardwick, 17
brit milah (ritual circumcision), 156, 178–79, 206, 265
Brother Daniel case, 7
Brown v. Board of Education (1954), 17, 248, 251
Buber, Martin, 118, 127n45
Buddhism, 65, 214
business law. *See also* commercial law
  custom, 247, 250
  motivations, 135, 141, 164
  systems, legal, 55, 58, 60, 62, 67, 73–74, 78
  theory, 13, 19

C

Camp Ramah, 47, 284
capital punishment, 6, 66–67, 74, 78, 182n4, 194, 203, 230, 237. *See also* death penalty, the
Cardozo, Justice Benjamin, 20–21, 58
Cassuto, Umberto, 55, 81n13
casuistic method, 49, 56, 215–16
Catholic Israel, 240, 246, 259
Catholicism, 211
cells
  growth of, 61, 68, 287
  stem, 60, 224, 290–91, 293
Central Conference of American Rabbis, 85n42
change
  behavior through custom, 247–48
  continuity, and, balancing, 189–207, 216–18, 226, 229–30, 233–34, 236
  covenant model, 107–8, 113–16
  legislative (*takkanot*), 57, 62–63, 107, 202, 261, 267
  metamorphic, 62–64, 68–69, 71–74
  morality, and, 212, 223
  organic aspect of, 61–64

INDEX